THE HEALTH PSYCHOLOGY
READER

THE HEALTH PSYCHOLOGY READER

EDITED BY
DAVID F. MARKS

SAGE Publications
London • Thousand Oaks • New Delhi

Preface, Introduction, introductions
   to Parts and editorial arrangement
   © David F. Marks 2002

First published 2002

SAGE Publications Ltd
6 Bonhill Street
London EC2A 4PU

SAGE Publications Inc.
2455 Teller Road
Thousand Oaks, California 91320

SAGE Publications India Pvt Ltd
32, M-Block Market
Greater Kailash -1
New Delhi 110 048

British Library Cataloguing in Publication data

A Catalogue record for this book is available from the British
Library

ISBN 0 7619 7270 6
ISBN 0 7619 7271 4 (pbk)

Library of Congress Control Number: 2001132916

Typeset by SIVA Math Setters, Chennai, India
Printed in Great Britain by The Cromwell Press,
Trowbridge, Wiltshire

CONTENTS

Acknowledgements   *viii*

Preface   *xi*

Introduction   1

**Part I: HEALTH PSYCHOLOGY'S DEVELOPMENT,
           DEFINITION AND CONTEXT**   9

1 Behavioral health's challenge to academic, scientific,
   and professional psychology   16
   Joseph D. Matarazzo

2 Redefining health psychology: Matarazzo revisited   40
   Mark McDermott

3 The need for a new medical model:
   a challenge for biomedicine   50
   George L. Engel

4 Theoretical tensions in biopsychosocial medicine   66
   David Armstrong

5 The rhetoric and reality of psychosocial theories of health:
   a challenge to biomedicine?   77
   Jane Ogden

Part II: THEORIES IN HEALTH PSYCHOLOGY   89

Introduction

6 Social foundations of thought and action: a social
   cognitive theory Englewood Cliffs, NJ: Prentice-Hall   94
   Albert Bandura

7 Emotion narratives: A radical new research approach   107
   Richard S. Lazarus

8   The role of theory in HIV prevention   120
    Martin Fishbein

9   Unraveling the mystery of health: How people
    manage stress and stay well   127
    Aaron Antonovsky

10 Some observations on health and socio-economic status   140
    Douglas Carroll, George Davey Smith and Paul Bennett

Part III: HEALTH BEHAVIOUR AND EXPERIENCE   163

Introduction

11 Context and coping: Toward a unifying
    conceptual framework   167
    Rudolf H. Moos

12 An 'ecological' approach to the obesity pandemic   186
    Garry Egger and Boyd Swinburn

13 Moving towards active living: Understanding
    the contextual nature of barriers to physical activity   195
    Susan Drew

14 Conditional versus unconditional risk estimates
    in models of AIDS-related risk behaviour   202
    *Frank W. van der Velde, Christa
    Hooykaas and Joop van der Pligt*

15 Health and romance: Understanding unprotected
    sex in relationships between gay men   218
    *Paul Flowers, Jonathan A. Smith,
    Paschal Sheeran, and Nigel Beail*

**Part IV: HEALTH BELIEFS, EXPLANATIONS, COMMUNICATIONS,
             EDUCATION AND PROMOTION   235**

Introduction

16 Cultural diversity in causal attributions
    for illness: the role of the supernatural   239
    Hope Landrine and Elizabeth A. Klonoff

17 Illness perceptions: a new paradigm for psychosomatics?   250
    John Weinman and Keith J. Petrie

18 Consumer/provider communication research: A personal
    plea to address issues of ecological validity,
    relational development, message diversity,
    and situational constraints   255
    Gary L. Kreps

19 From analysis to synthesis: Theories of health education   262
    Jeff French and Lee Adams

20 A new evidence framework for health promotion practice   271
    Gordon Macdonald

Part V: CRITICAL HEALTH PSYCHOLOGY   **281**

Introduction

21 Critical approaches to health psychology   286
    Wendy Stainton Rogers

22 Theorizing health and illness: Functionalism,
    subjectivity and reflexivity   304
    Henderikus J. Stam

23 A discourse-dynamic approach to the study
    of subjectivity in health psychology   319
    Carla Willig

24 Health psychology, embodiment and the question
    of vulnerability   341
    Alan Radley

25 Possible contributions of a psychology of liberation:
    Whither health and human rights?   352
    M. Brinton Lykes

Glossary   *373*

References   *378*

Index   *381*

ACKNOWLEDGEMENTS

The editor would like to thank the three co-authors of the textbook *Health Psychology: Theory, Research and Practice* Michael Murray, Carla Willig and Brian Evans, for their helpful advice on the content of the Reader. The editor would like to especially thank Michael Murray for convening the first international conference on Reconstructing Health Psychology in 1999 at which the authors of Chapters 22, 24 and 25 originally presented earlier versions of these chapters and which subsequently led to special issue of the *Journal of Health Psychology* edited by Murray (2000) where these three chapters originally appeared. The editor also thanks Catherine Marie Sykes, Jennifer McKinley and Tina Rochelle for their assistance while this Reader was being created.

The editor and the publishers also wish to thank the following for permission to use copyright material. Every effort has been made to trace all the copyright holders but if any have been inadvertently overlooked, the publishers will be pleased to make the necessary arrangements at the first opportunity.

Reading 1 American Psychological Association for Matarazzo, J.D. (1980). Behavioral health's challenge to academic, scientific, and professional psychology. *American Psychologist*, 37, 1–14.

Reading 2 British Psychological Society for McDermott, M. (2001). Redefining health psychology: Matarazzo revisited. *Health Psychology Update*, 10, 3–10.

Reading 3 American Association for the Advancement of Science for Engel, G.L. (1977). The need for a new medical model: a challenge for biomedicine. *Science*, 196, 129–36.

Reading 4 Elsevier Science Ltd for Amstrong, D. (1987). Theoretical tensions in biopsychosocial medicine. *Social Science and Medicine*, 25, 1213–18.

Reading 5 Sage Publications Ltd for extracts from Ogden, J. (1997). The rhetoric and reality of psychosocial theories, a challenge to biomedicine. *Journal of Health Psychology*, 2, 21–9.

Reading 6 Pentice Hall for Bandura, A. (1986). *Social foundations of thought and action*. Englewood Cliffs, NJ: Prentice-Hall.

Reading 7 Free Association Books for Lazarus, R.S. (1999). Emotion narratives: A radical new research approach. From R.S. Lazarus, *Stress and emotion*. Free Association Books, pp. 193–207.

Reading 8 Taylor & Francis Groups for Fishbein, M. (2000). The role of theory in HIV prevention. *AIDS Care*, 12, 273–8.

Reading 9 Estate of Aaron Antonovsky for extracts from Antonovsky, A. (1987). *Unravelling the mystery of health: How people manage stress and stay well*. San Francisco: Jossey Bass, pp. xi–xiv; 1–13.

Reading 10 Sage Publications Ltd for extracts form Carroll, D., Davey Smith, G. and Bennett, P. (1996). Some observations on health and socio-economic status. *Journal of Health Psychology*, 1, 23–39.

Reading 11 Kluwer Academic/Plenum Publishers for Moos, R.H. (1984). Context and coping: Toward a unifying conceptual; framework. *American Journal of Community Psychology*, 12, 5–25.

Reading 12 BMJ Publishing Group for Egger, G. and Swinburn, B. (1997). An ecological approach to the obesity pandemic. *British Medical Journal*, 315, 477–80.

Reading 13 British Psychological Society for Drew, S. (1996). Moving towards active living: Understanding the contextual nature of barriers to physical activity. *Health Psychology Update*, 23, 10–14.

Reading 14 Taylor and Francis Groups for van der Velde, F.W., van der Pligt, J. and Hoojkaas, C. (1996). Conditional versus unconditional risk estimates in models of aids-related risk behaviour. *Psychological and Health*, 12, 87–100.

Reading 15 British Journal of Health Psychology and The British Psychological Society for Flowers, P., Smith, J., Sheeran, P. and Beail, N. (1997). Health and romance: Understanding unprotected sex in relationships among gay men. *British Journal of Health Psychology*, 2, 73–86.

Reading 16 Kluwer Academic/Plenum Publishers for Landrine, H. and Klonoff, E.A. (1994). Cultural diversity in causal attributions for illness: the role of the supernatural. *Journal of Behavioral Medicine*, 17, 181–93.

Reading 17 Elsevier Science Ltd for Weinman, J. and Petrie, K.J. (1997). Illness perceptions: a new paradigm for psychosomatics? *Journal of Psychosomatic Medicine*, 42, 113–16.

Reading 18 Sage Publications Ltd for extracts from Kreps, G.L. (2001). Consumer/provider communication research: A personal plea to address issues of ecological validity, relational development, message diversity, and situational constraints. *Journal of Health Psychology*, (6) 5, 597–697.

Reading 19 Institute of Health Promotion and Education for French, J. and Adams, L. (1986). From analysis to synthesis. Theories of health education. *Health Education Journal* (45): 71–74.

Reading 20 Institute of Health Promotion and Education for Macdonald, G. (2000). A new evidence framework for health promotion. *Health Educaiton Journal*, 59, 3–11.

Reading 21 Sage Publications Ltd for extracts from Stainton-Rogers, W. (1996). Critical approaches to health psychology. *Journal of Health Psychology*, 1, 65–77.

Reading 22 Sage Publications Ltd for extracts from Stam, H.J. (2000). Theorizing health and illness: Functionalism, subjectivity and reflexivity. *Journal of Health Psychology*, 5, 273–84.

Reading 23 Sage Publications Ltd for extracts from Willig, C. (2000). A discourse-dynamic approach to the study of subjectivity in health psychology. *Theory and Psychology*, 10, 547–70.

Reading 24 Sage Publications Ltd for extracts from Radley, A. (2000). Health psychology, embodiment and the question of vulnerability. *Journal of Health Psychology*, 5, 298–304.

Reading 25 Sage Publications Ltd for extracts from Lykes, M.B. (2000). Possible contributions of a psychology of liberaztion: Whither health and human rights? *Journal of Health Psychology*, 5, 383–398.

PREFACE

The Health Psychology Reader provides a critical account of the state of health psychology at an early, formative stage of development. Primary sources of theory and research by some leading and up-and-coming figures have been compiled into a single volume. The Reader is designed to help make study of health psychology more thought-provoking and enjoyable. It is aimed at students of health psychology at all stages of study. The Reader will persuade one and all that there is still much to do. In fact, all of us are at the very beginning.

The Reader is a companion to the textbook *Health Psychology Theory, Research and Practice* (Marks, Murray, Evans and Willig, 2000). It can also be used as a stand alone resource for students using other health psychology texts. The editorial introductions pick out the highlights, questions and issues that spring from the text.

The selection of 25 chapters in five parts was chosen from a long list of about 50 items. *The Health Psychology Reader* is organised in five parts, each with five readings. Each part contains a brief introduction and a box with highlights, questions and issues. These sections guide the reader through some of the major areas of the field. The reader is encouraged to think critically about the issues that are discussed.

This material has been selected from literally thousands of possible entries. Many of the articles and books that make up this literature contain studies with large amounts of quantitative data. This data gathering is an important part of establishing the field. However, there is a need for more sophisticated theoretical approaches to provide better coherence and direction; open-ended, qualitative research that explores issues from perspectives other than the investigators'; and critical thinking about methods, concepts and assumptions. This Reader is a first attempt to give the field a push in these directions. My sincere thanks go to all of the authors of the works reproduced. Yours is the gift of opening eyes to the world of the possible.

INTRODUCTION

A Brief History of Health Psychology

In the era of the hunter-gatherer, cave paintings and other relics yield evidence of an early human fascination with an imagined world of spirits and magic. A key element in such icons is a desire for survival aided by communication between body and spirit with the mind as mediator. The idea of body–mind–spirit integration can be traced to the earliest period of history, circa 10,000 BC. Shamanistic healing practices of a spiritual nature survive to the present day. Contemporary concepts of healing, health and illness are founded on these ancient systems.

Early physicians, hypnotists and healers were intrigued by the mysterious ways in which the emotions affect bodily functioning. The hypnotists of the 18th and 19th centuries were aware of the power of imagination and suggestion over mental states, somatic perceptions and pain. The psychoanalysts developed theories about unconscious, emotional processes that apparently guide, not only dreams, but also behaviour and conscious experience. The field of psychosomatic medicine studies mind–body relationships in different conditions of mental and physical health. Health psychology applies psychological knowledge and techniques to health, illness and health care.

Like its parent discipline of psychology itself, health psychology has a short history but a long past. The term 'health psychology' entered the lexicon in the last quarter of the 20th century. After a gestation period in the 1970s, health psychology took its name in 1979 when the first book with the term 'health psychology' in the title was published (Stone et al., 1979). In the same year George Stone (1979), in 'Patient compliance and the role of the expert', argued that 'compliance' should be considered an attribute of the client–expert transaction rather than of the client alone.[1] Understanding the essentially social nature of client–professional transactions became a formative principle in the development of a new 'biopsychosocial' model as an alternative to the biomedical model.

The biopsychosocial model defines health and illness as: 'the product of a combination of factors including biological characteristics (e.g. genetic predisposition), behavioural factors (e.g. lifestyle, stress, health beliefs), and social conditions (e.g. cultural influences, family relationships, social support)' (American Psychological Association, 2001). This 'model'[2] is a foundation stone for the mainstream development of health psychology. The

Division of Health Psychology was founded within the American Psychological Association in 1980. The European Health Psychology Society was established in 1984 and the Health Psychology Section of the British Psychological Society in 1986.

The importance of psychological processes in the experience of health and illness is being increasingly recognised by professionals and lay people alike. Evidence for the role of behaviour in current trends of morbidity and mortality is accumulating apace. Epidemiological research shows that certain behaviours are strongly associated with morbidity and mortality (Marks, Murray, Evans and Willig, 2000). The 1980s and 1990s was a period of rapid growth for the field. Developments in clinical practice have also encompassed psychological knowledge and expertise, and health psychologists are in increasing demand in clinical and medical settings. In the USA, the single largest area of placement of psychologists in recent years has been in medical centres. Psychologists have become vital members of multidisciplinary clinical and research teams in rehabilitation, cardiology, paediatrics, oncology, anaesthesiology, family practice, dentistry, and other medical fields.

In reviewing the development of health psychology in the USA, Wallston (1993) stated:

> It is amazing to realise that formal recognition of the field of health psychology in the United States occurred less than 20 years ago. It is no longer correct to speak of health psychology as an 'emerging' speciality within American psychology; for the last dozen or so years, health psychology has flourished as one of the most vibrant specialties within the larger discipline of psychology. Not only is it recognised as a specialty in its own right, health psychology has had a profound impact upon clinical psychology, and has played a major (if not the major) role in developing and vitalising the interdisciplinary field called 'behavioural medicine'. (Wallston, 1993: 215)

The overlap with behavioural medicine in both theory and practice has been strong and, like behavioural medicine, health psychology is really an interdisciplinary field (Marks, 1996). Most of the leading causes of mortality have substantial behavioural components and these behavioural risk factors are the main focus of efforts in the area of health promotion and disease prevention, e.g. drug and alcohol use, unsafe sexual behaviour, smoking, diet, a sedentary lifestyle. Psychological methods and expertise are playing an increasing role in treatment and rehabilitation.

Contrasting Approaches to Health Psychology

Four parallel approaches to health psychology are evolving. The first is 'clinical health psychology' that is based on the biopsychosocial model and involves working within the health care system. It locates professional health psychology within hospitals and clinics and is similar in nature to (and partly overlapping with) clinical psychology. The environment for practice is the health care market place. Outside of the clinical domain, the second approach, 'public health psychology', includes psychological aspects of health education and health promotion. This has been discussed by health psychologists (Winett, King and Altman, 1989; Bennett and Murphy, 1997; Wardle, 2001) and health promotion specialists (see Reading 20, Macdonald, 2000; Nutbeam and Harris, 1999). Public health psychology sees individual health more as an outcome of social, economic and political determinants than a simple consequence of individual behaviour and lifestyle. Public health psychology is a multidisciplinary activity involving epidemiological studies, public health interventions and evaluation. The third approach is 'community health psychology' that is based on community research and social action. This is part of community psychology, working on health promotion and illness prevention among healthy people as members of communities and groups. The fourth evolving approach is that of 'critical health psychology' which aims to analyse how power, economics and macrosocial processes influence health, health care, health psychology, and to study the implications for health psychology theory and practice. A summary of the four approaches is presented in Table 1.

All four approaches are represented in this Reader. Many health psychologists use more than one of these approaches, and some use three or even all four. The four styles of working complement each other and, when they are integrated, will be a powerful set of tools for the improvement of the health care system. Clinical psychologists have been working within the health care system for several decades. The research, training and practice of clinical psychologists focus on mental health, mental illness and mental disabilities. Health psychologists' primary interest is the psychological aspects of physical health, physical illness and physical disabilities. The two sub-fields of clinical and health psychology complement each other and, ideally speaking, they should eventually merge. Bottlenecks at entry points into clinical psychology, and the rapid expansion of training in health psychology, mean that, in another decade or two, roughly equal numbers of professionals could populate the two sub-fields. National health services will be able to recruit psychologists specialising in either mental or physical health. Guidelines for professional training programmes and ethical codes of practice have been developed in the USA, Europe and elsewhere (Marks et al., 1998; Marks, Sykes and McKinley, in press). Training programmes at both masters and doctoral level are multiplying rapidly.

The success and future progress of health psychology depend upon the ability of practitioners to help to deliver genuine health improvements and more effective treatments. This is where the absolutely crucial importance of research comes into force. The research base of health psychology must be well founded and reflect the needs of the primary users. That's you, me, everyone who will, one day, end up in a clinic or a hospital or who wants to change things for the better. But health is not simply the business of the health care system but of society as a whole. Having good health across the population is a priority for any progressive society. If health for all is to be a

TABLE 1 The Characteristics of Clinical, Public, Community and Critical Health Psychology (Marks, 2002)

Characteristic	Clinical health psychology	Public health psychology	Community health psychology	Critical health psychology
Definition	'The aggregate of the specific educational, scientific, and professional contributions of the discipline of psychology to the promotion and maintenance of heath, the prevention and treatment of illness, the identification of etiologic and diagnostic correlates of health and illness and related dysfunctions, and the analysis and improvement of the health care system and health policy.' (Matarazzo, 1982)	The application of psychological theory, research and technologies Towards the improvement of the health of the population.	'Advancing theort, research and social action to promote positive well-being, increase empowerment, and prevent the development of problems of communities, groups and individuals.' (Society for Community Research and Action, 2001)	The analysis of how power, economics and macro-social processes influence health, health care and social issues, and the study of the implications for the theory and praxis of health work
Theory/ philosophy	Biopsychosocial model Health and illness are: 'the product of a combination of factors including biological characteristics (e.g. genetic predisposition), behavioural factors (e.g. lifestyle, stress, health beliefs), and social conditions (e.g. cultural influences, family relationships, social support)' (APA, 2001).	No single theory and philosophy; supportive role in public health promotion which uses legal and fiscal instruments combined with preventive measures to bring about health improvement. Working towards general theories, e.g. health literacy improves health.	Social and economic model: 'Change strategies are needed at both the individual and systems levels for effective competence promotion and problem prevention.' (Society for Community Research and Action, 2001). Acknowledges the interdependence of individuals and communities Shares some of the aims of public health psychology, e.g. improving health literacy	Critical psychology: Analysis of society and the values, assumptions and practices of psychologists, health care professionals, and of all those whom they aim to serve. Shares some of the aims of community health psychology, but with universal rather than local constituency
Values	Increasing or maintaining the autonomy of the individual through ethical intervention	Mapping accurately the health of the public as a basis for policy and health promotion, communication and interventions	Creating or increasing autonomy of disadvantaged and oppressed people through social action;	Understanding the political nature of all human existence, freedom of thought; compassion for others

(Continued)

TABLE 1 (Continued)

Characteristic	Clinical health psychology	Public health psychology	Community health psychology	Critical health psychology
Context	Patients in the health care system, i.e. hospitals, clinics, health centres	Schools, work sites, the media	Familes, communities and populations within their social, cultural and historical context	Social structures, economics, government, and commerce
Focus	Physical illness and dysfunction	Health promotion and disease prevention	Physical and mental health promotion	Power
Target groups	Patients with specific disorders	Population groups who are most vulnerable to health problems	Healthy but vulnerable or exploited persons and groups	Varies according to the context: from the entire global population to the health of an individual
Objective	To enhance the effectiveness of treatments	To improve the health of the entire population: reducing morbidity, disability, and avoidable mortality.	Empowerment and social change	Equality of opportunities and resources for health
Orientation	Health service delivery	Communication and intervention	Bottom-up, working with or alongside	Analysis, argument, critique
Skills	Assessment, therapy, consultancy and research	Statistical evaluation; knowledge of health policy; epidemiological methods	Participatory and facilitative; working with communities; community development	Theoretical analysis; critical thinking; social and political action; advocacy; leadership
Discourse and buzz words	'Evidence-based practice'; 'Effectiveness'; 'Outcomes'; 'Randomised controlled trials'	'Responsibility'; 'Behaviour change'; Risk'; 'Outcomes'; 'Randomised controlled trials'	'Freedom'; 'Empowering'; 'Giving voice to'; 'Diversity'; 'Community development'; 'Capacity building'; 'Social capital'; 'Sence of community'; 'Inequalities'; 'Coalitions'	'Power'; 'Rights'; 'Exploitation'; 'Oppression'; 'Neo-Liberalism'; 'Justice'; 'Dignity'; 'Respect'
Research methodology	Efficacy and effectiveness trials; Quantitative and quasi-experimental methods	Epidemiological methods; Large-scale trials; Multivariate statistics; Evaluation	Participant action research; coalitions between researchers, practitioners and communities; multiple methodologies	Critical analysis combined with any of the methods used in the other three approaches

real possibility, the inequities, which are so evident in our streets and in our statistics, must be significantly reduced. Current trends, however, show a widening of the gaps, so there is a lot of work to be done at the policy and economic levels. The psychological aspects of health and illness must be considered in the context of the economic and social environment of people's everyday lives.

Health Psychology is Still Developing

Health psychology is dynamic field that is still developing. It is not a fixed, well-established activity with well-tried practices and formulas. All who are in the health psychology field can influence its nature and progress. There is room for new ideas, debate and dialogue. Hot topics for discussion are: theories about the nature of health and its determinants; method; and embodiment – how the material and biological body can be the location for meaning, value and intention. Individual behaviour is both socially and biologically determined. The social context of experience and behaviour, and the social and economic determinants of health, are seen as fundamental to a full understanding of the field. Economic and political changes have considerable, long-lasting influence on human well-being. Warfare and terrorism remain intermittent threats to human security. The gap between the 'haves' and the 'have-nots' widens, the Western population is ageing, and the impacts of learned helplessness, poverty and social isolation are becoming increasingly salient features of society. The health and psychological impacts of global warming and energy addiction present many challenges for the 21st century. To quote Shelley Taylor: 'The only aspect of health psychology that is more exciting than its distinguished past and its impressive present, is its promising future' (Taylor, 1986: 17).[3]

As currently defined, health psychology is the application of psychological theory, methods and research to health, physical illness and health care. Human well-being is a complex product of genetic, developmental and environmental influences. In accordance with the World Health Organisation (WHO) definition, health is seen as well-being in its broadest sense, not simply the absence of illness. Expanding the WHO definition, well-being is the product of a complex interplay of biological, socio-cultural, psychological, economic and spiritual factors. The promotion and maintenance of health involves psychosocial processes at the interface between the individual, the health care system and society (Marks, Murray, Evans and Willig, 2000).

Health psychology is concerned with the psychological aspects of the promotion, improvement and maintenance of health. The *ecological context* of these psychological aspects of health includes the many influential social systems within which human beings exist: families, workplaces, organisations, communities, societies and cultures (Dahlgren and Whitehead, 1991; Marks, 1996; Marks, Murray, Evans and Willig, 2000). Any psychological activity, process, or intervention that enhances well-being is of interest to health psychology. Equally, any activity, process, or circumstance which has psychological components and which threatens well-being is of concern to health psychology. Interventions need to be designed in the light of the prevailing environmental conditions that contain the contextual cues for health-related behaviours.

The mission of health psychology is to promote and maintain well-being through the application of psychological theory, methods and research, taking into account the economic, political, social and cultural context. The vision of health psychology is to employ psychological knowledge, methods and skills towards the promotion and maintenance of well-being. The latter extends beyond hospitals and clinics – it includes health education and promotion among the healthy population as well as among those who are already sick.

The application of psychological knowledge, methods and skills in the promotion and maintenance of well-being is a multi-faceted activity; it is not possible to define the field narrowly. There are many different settings and situations in which psychologists may have a role in promoting and maintaining human health. The psychologist often will be working with lay people, many of whom are patients' relatives, acting as informal carers: 'People are not just consumers of health care, they are the true primary care providers in the health care system' (Sobell, 1995: 238). The psychologist will also work with communities, providing support and expertise to promote their agendas and goals and to help breakdown the barriers that are put up by more powerful factions to reduce their freedom and potential to flourish and grow.

Notes

1 For a brief biography of George Stone, see Marks (1997a).
2 In Parts I and V, we will have reasons to question the biopsychosocial model.
3 For a brief biography of Shelley Taylor, see Marks (1997b).

PART I

HEALTH PSYCHOLOGY'S DEVELOPMENT, DEFINITION AND CONTEXT

THE READINGS

1 Behavioral Health's Challenge to Academic, Scientific, and Professional Psychology
   Joseph D. Matarazzo
2 Redefining Health Psychology: Matarazzo Revisited
   Mark McDermott
3 The Need for a New Medical Model: A Challenge for Biomedicine
   George L. Engel
4 Theoretical Tensions in Biopsychosocial Medicine
   David Armstrong
5 The Rhetoric and Reality of Psychosocial Theories of Health: A Challenge to Biomedicine?
   Jane Ogden

The first question that must be addressed is: what *is* health psychology? In our textbook (HPTRP), we propose this definition:

> Health psychology is an interdisciplinary field concerned with the application of psychological knowledge and techniques to health, illness and health care. (Marks, Murray, Evans and Willig, 2000: 8)*

This definition is simple and succinct. It is also rather grand, some might say grandiose. Taking this definition at its face value, health psychology includes any application of psychology to any aspect of health, illness and health care. Wow — what an exciting (if daunting) challenge! Think of the implications. No limits are placed on the kinds of psychological knowledge and techniques, the kinds of health and illness, or the health care settings and systems to which psychological knowledge and techniques may be applied. In fact, it is a limitless set of tasks, both inside and outside of the health care system. Is health psychology sufficiently prepared in research, theory and practice to carry out this programme in an ethical and professional manner?

We are not the first psychologists to offer a grand vision of health psychology. That distinction belongs to Joseph Matarazzo (1980, 1982, see also Reading 1). Matarazzo's (1982) definition has become a litany for health psychologists across the globe. It states:

> Health psychology is the aggregate of the specific educational, scientific, and professional contributions of the discipline of psychology to the promotion and maintenance of health, the prevention and treatment of illness, and the identification of etiologic and diagnostic correlates of health, illness, and related dysfunction, *and to the analysis and improvement of the health care system and health policy formation.* (Matarazzo, 1982: p4, emphasis in original) (see Reading 1, pp. 22–3)

Matarazzo explains (Reading 1) that this definition was an expansion of an earlier one that he published in 1980. Matarazzo (1980, 1982) promoted this new field in the house journal of the American Psychological Association, the *American Psychologist*, giving the field its name, definition and *raison d'être*.[1] Matarazzo is considered one of the 'founding fathers' of health psychology, a polymath, a king of the health psychology castle.

Matarazzo has been especially interested in the role of *lifestyle* factors in health and illness, and the first reading reflects that interest. There has been increasing awareness over the last 50 years that the killer diseases of the affluent developed countries have behavioural determinants, especially smoking, drinking and diet. Another stimulus for the growth of health psychology referred to by Matarazzo has been the growing awareness of the social psychological context of health care delivery.

Matarazzo also quotes Knowles (1977) who asserted that *each individual has a moral obligation to preserve his/her own health.* The ideology of an individual

---

* The textbook *Health Psychology: Theory, Research and Practice* by Marks, Murray, Evans and Willig (2000) will be referred to hereafter as 'HPTRP' or as 'the textbook'.

moral responsibility to live healthily, and thus to be healthy, is a strong undercurrent within Western culture and it is a foundation stone of contemporary health psychology. Often, the ideology remains hidden, but it is there most of the time, not very far below the surface.

In making a case for the study of behavioural factors in health, illness, and health care in Reading 1, 'King Joe' Matarazzo goes much further than simply saying that psychologists are expert at analysing behaviour. He demarcates and defines two interrelated fields. He proposes that there are two interdisciplinary fields: **behavioural medicine**, concerned with health and illness or related dysfunction, and also **behavioural health**, a subspecialty within behavioural medicine, concerned with the maintenance of health and the prevention of illness. Matarazzo proposes that health psychology is a discipline-specific term describing psychology's role as a science and a profession in these two domains. For these reasons, Matarazzo's definitions deserve careful study.

Matarazzo's (1982) definition is the one that is cited repeatedly. It has become 'King Joe's mantra'. Many professional associations, students and scholars have unwittingly conflated his first and second definitions by citing Matarazzo's (1982) definition as 'Matarazzo (1980)'. This is not as trivial an error as it may appear because the difference in content is enormous. Matarazzo's (1982) definition ('Matarazzo 1') has a lot in its favour, because it excludes nothing that any psychologist, past, present or future, could possibly want to contribute to the health field. That is probably why health psychologists the world over have appropriated it without embarrassment.

Notice that Matarazzo's Reading 1 contains other definitions, including that of behavioural health, which states:

> *Behavioural health* is an interdisciplinary field dedicated to promoting a philosophy of health that stresses *individual responsibility* in the application of behavioural and biomedical science knowledge techniques to the *maintenance* of health and the *prevention* of illness and dysfunction by a variety of self-initiated individual or shared activities. (Matarazzo, 1982, p. 3) (see Reading 1, p. 20)

This definition (Matarazzo 2) is not a *scientific* definition but a *philosophical* and *moral* one. We saw this moral issue looming earlier when noting Matarazzo's approving quotation of Knowles (1977). This departure from a scientific definition towards the advocacy of a philosophical, ideological point of view is unusual in a scientific publication. Taken in its totality, this definition is difficult to accept for many reasons, none the least because it places the responsibility for health maintenance and illness prevention squarely on the shoulders of the individual. This is **individualism** in its purest form, a victim-blaming philosophy that is hard to reconcile with the idea that the health care system and civic society have a significant, caring role in health promotion and illness prevention and treatment for all of society's members. Should people who show signs of 'irresponsibility' in regards to 'the application of behavioural and biomedical science knowledge techniques' not be cared for? (e.g. smokers, heavy drinkers, or people who eat more than a threshold amount of fatty foods) It seems clear that in advocating a health care philosophy of individual responsibility

Matarazzo has stepped beyond scientific considerations and moved into politics and moral philosophy. This example illustrates the fact that science and psychology, while claiming to be value free, are embedded in a moral and political web of assumptions, values and ideology.

In Reading 2, Mark McDermott compares the pros and cons of the all-inclusive definition of Matarazzo 1 with a sanitised version of Matarazzo 2 as a working definition for health psychology. McDermott uses an extract of the original definition. He omits reference to the moral component, referring only to the scientific part of the definition. McDermott's removal of the moral component suggests a conscious rejection of it. However, this silent cut remains ambiguous. In inviting us to adopt this amputated version of Matarazzo 2, are we unwittingly accepting the hidden moral part as well? One of the strengths of the definition in HPTRP printed above is that it does not include any moral prescription about health being the responsibility of the individual.

I turn now to some of the theoretical foundations of health psychology. Ideology, preconceptions and imprecision remain as uninvited guests at the health psychology table. Cultural traditions and orthodoxy shadow-box with more radical-sounding revolutionaries while the majority of researchers and practitioners simply get on and do what they do best, rarely questioning the underlying assumptions. Health psychologists are generally kept fully occupied gathering those much sought after nuggets of scientific value and truth: their much-loved data! In HPTRP we write about frameworks, theories and models. Beyond these, there are, in the natural sciences, even grander levels of thinking which have been termed **paradigms** (Kuhn, 1970) or **programmes** (Lakatos, Worrall and Currie, 1980). These terms imply the bedrock of material that is at the most basic level of science, solid enough to build on and which does not readily crack or subside. This bedrock is so solid and incontestable that it never changes, no matter what new evidence or arguments come to light.

The field of psychology has not developed as a single paradigm that all psychologists feel comfortable signing up to in the manner of biology, physics or chemistry. However, this has not deterred psychologists from claiming a similar status to the natural sciences that have well-accepted paradigms in the Kuhnian sense. Biology has the theory of evolution, physics has quantum mechanics, and chemistry the periodic table. Psychology is a radically different kind of science from these other three because of the nature of its subject matter. Unlike the natural sciences, Psychology is concerned with the experience and behaviour of sentient beings who are conscious, intelligent, reflexive, subjective and social in nature, unlike purely material objects. However, by using experimental methods in laboratories, and following the **hypothetico-deductive method**, Psychology has successfully developed several major programmes of research, each with its own theories, methods and evidence base, namely, behaviourism, cognitivism, biopsychology and social psychology. In addition, to these branches of so-called 'pure psychology', applied psychologists are putting this knowledge into practice. Health is one sphere where this application of knowledge has a genuine potential to make improvements.

Health psychology is a branch of applied psychology. Having started in the 1970s, it is still at an early stage of development and in the process of establishing its identity in the world of health care. Its primary purpose has been to gather evidence that demonstrates relevance and added value to health, illness and health care. Having staked a claim in the world of health care, health psychology is devoting considerable resources to the justification of this claim. This justification has involved a considerable amount of data-gathering focused on theories of individual behaviour and experience.

The field has been associated with an idea known as the **biopsychosocial model** (BPSM). Although the BPSM is not really a model in the formal sense of the term,[2] it is a way of thinking about health and illness which has a useful heuristic function. The term 'model' is often used in psychology in a loose way to describe anything ranging from vague and imprecise ideas, to values or attitudes, to genuine models. The BPSM is more like an attitude than a model, an attitude that sees health and illness as products of a combination of circumstances including biological characteristics, behavioural factors and social conditions.

The BPSM is seen, by those who hold it, as a challenge to the **biomedical model** (BMM). Readings 3 to 5 are about these two models. George Engel (Reading 3) writes as a psychiatrist in the 1970s responding to what was perceived then as a 'crisis' for psychiatry with too many disparate theories and methods to be considered 'neat and tidy' like the rest of medicine. Engel discusses some problems with the BMM: its reductionistic, dualistic, pathogenic assumptions. Engel argues that:

> a medical model must also take into account the patient, the social context in which he lives, and the complementary system devised by society to deal with the disruptive effects of the illness, that is, the physician role and the health care system. This requires the biopsychosocial model (pp. 56–7).

Engel argues that 'the dichotomy between "disease" and "problems of living" is by no means a sharp one, either for patient or for doctor'. Engel discusses grief as an example of a typical borderline condition between a disease state and a condition of living by asking: 'When is grief a disease?' Engel argues for the more 'holistic' approach of general systems theory, after Von Bertalanffy (1968).

Engel's paper argues that medical practice should become a more caring, considerate and patient-orientated profession. It is hard to disagree with that. But his paper also leaves rather a lot unsaid. Engel advocates the BPSM without, somehow, ever defining it![3] This leaves open the possibility that different people will use the term in different ways making it a vague and woolly concept with health psychology, akin to the emperor, or empress, proudly showing off their invisible new clothes.

David Armstrong (Reading 4) points to some of the interesting tensions that Engel's 'model' engenders. Armstrong suggests that the social sciences should resist being coaxed into a revisionist form of biomedicine but continue to expose the inconsistencies within biomedicine rather than conspire to join it. Jane Ogden (Reading 5) finds that some rot has already set in. The rhetoric of the challenge by the BPSM to biomedicine has become reified. Yet Ogden exposes major discrepancies which are apparent between the professed aims and explanatory frameworks in both health psychology and medical sociology.

This discussion ends with the question of whether or not the so-called biopsychosocial model is really a model at all? Or is it simply a 'cuddly' label for a set of cosy beliefs about health, mind and behaviour, as unscientific as it is woolly and vague? If so, why has the idea of this new 'model' caught on so much in the social sciences? Is scientific opinion as easily swayed by the zeitgeist as the flim-flam of TV talkshows and glossy magazines? The history of science suggests that it can be.

The existence of health psychology does not rest solely upon the robustness of the BPSM as a scientific 'model'. It is not the BPSM's questionable status as a model that is really important. It is the set of values and assumptions that it represents, its symbolic value as a statement about health and healthcare that sees psychology, society and culture as important as DNA, cells and biology.

BOX 1: HIGHLIGHTS, QUESTIONS, ISSUES

1 What factors kindled the developing field of health psychology? Did it occur by accident purely by force of argument, empirical evidence, or ideology? Or was it a mixture of things?
2 How should health psychology be defined? By Matarazzo's first definition, or his second definition, or in some other way? Think about your reasons.
3 What is the biomedical model?
4 Is it really a 'model', or a way of thinking among medical doctors that nobody really believes anyway?
5 Why didn't Engel have much time for it?
6 How does the 'biopsychosocial' model attempt to improve upon it, and did it succeed in doing so?
7 Is the BPSM just rhetoric, as suggested in Reading 5?
8 Which of the five papers in this section do you personally like the best, and why?
9 Looking into your imaginary crystal ball, will health psychology still exist in another 50 years? If you think it will, what differences do you foresee in the health psychology of the future?
10 To what extent can health psychology be considered a profession as well as a new academic field? What reasons can you give to justify your answer?

Notes

1 For a brief biography of Joseph D. Matarazzo, see Marks (1997c).
2 See Chapter 1 of HPTRP.
3 A statement from Division 38 of the American Psychological Association concerning the BPSM is quoted in the Introduction. Stam also discusses the lack of a definition in Engel's formulation in Reading 22 of the Reader (p. 304).

1 BEHAVIORAL HEALTH'S CHALLENGE TO ACADEMIC, SCIENTIFIC, AND PROFESSIONAL PSYCHOLOGY

Joseph D. Matarazzo

In 1964 President Lyndon Johnson, first threatening and next fully using the power of the federal purse, informed this country's scientific and university professional manpower training communities that federal health-related funds should be used to support fewer basic and theoretical and more applied and practical research and training activities. The 1964 Congress and its successors, and Presidents Nixon, Ford, and Carter, all endorsed this demand that our scientific and teaching institutions refocus their priorities and begin to pay more attention to the human (and the ever-increasing financial) costs associated with the health of our citizens. Before proceeding to discuss these annually escalating financial and human costs and what might be done by psychologists and others to help reduce them, fairness requires that the many legitimate financial costs be excluded from the criticism that follows. Health care in the United States is expensive in part because our citizens, speaking, themselves or through third-party payers, have opted to pay for intensive care and renal dialysis units in hospitals, neonatal heart surgery, computerized axial tomography (CAT) scanners, and many other very costly diagnostic and critical-care life-support services. My criticism is not directed at such defensible costs but instead at the inordinate costs that are associated with preventable health conditions: those associated with smoking and other health risks associated with one's lifestyle. These latter unnecessary costs must be addressed by psychologists and representatives of the other disciplines interested in individual behavior.

It became obvious in the 1960s that health expenditures in the United States were growing at a faster rate than the gross national product. This imbalance became increasingly alarming, and it seemed that it might soon become insupportable. Table 1.1 – adapted from Gibson (1979) and Vischi, Jones, Shank, and Lima (1980) – presents some pertinent statistics. For example, in 1950 the $12.7 billion expenditure for health was only 4.5% of that year's gross national product of $284.8 billion, but by 1965 this percentage had increased to 6.2%, and by 1978 it had increased even further to 9.1%.

TABLE 1.1 **Total and Per Capita National Health Expenditures, by Source of Funds and Percentage Gross National Product (GNP)**

| | | Health expenditures | | | | | | |
| | | Total | | | Private | | Public | |
Year	GNP (billions)	Amount (billions)	Per capita	%GNP	Amount (billions)	%total	Amount (billions)	%total
1950	284.8	12.7	82	4.5	9.2	73	3.4	27
1955	398.0	17.7	105	4.4	13.2	74	4.6	26
1960	503.7	26.9	146	5.3	20.3	75	6.6	25
1965	688.1	43.0	217	6.2	32.3	75	10.7	25
1970	982.4	74.7	359	7.6	47.5	64	27.3	36
1975	1,528.8	131.5	605	8.6	75.8	58	55.7	42
1976	1,700.1	148.9	679	8.8	86.6	58	62.3	42
1977	1,887.2	170.0	769	9.0	100.7	59	69.3	41
1978[a]	2,107.6	192.4	863	9.1	114.3	59	78.1	41
1979[b]		212.9	968					

[a]Preliminary estimates. Adapted from Gibson, 1979, p. 22, and Vischi et al., 1980, p. 131.

[b]The *total* health expenditure costs for 1979 data are from the article, "United States Passes," 1980/1981.

As further revealed in Figure 1.1, a recent projection through the next decade by Rogers (1980), the president of the Robert Wood Johnson Foundation, indicates that by the year 1990 this figure will fall somewhere between 9.1% and 14% of the gross national product. Supporting his view, the most recent data (shown in the last row of Table 1.1) reveal that total health expenditures in the United States during 1979 reached $212.9 billion ("United States Passes," 1980/1981).

Table 1.1 shows that the per capita health expenditure was $863 in 1978 and $968 in 1979. We must ask whether our nation can afford to spend such a large sum on the health of its people every year. Few individuals in government or in the various segments of our health industry believe we are able to afford the present per capita expenditure, let alone sustain it or allow it to increase. The reduction of this financial burden is a national responsibility shared collectively by scores of constituencies, including consumers, providers of health services, legislators, the health industry generally, private philanthropy, the university and scientific communities, business and labor, and many others. Epidemiologists, physicians, health educators, medical sociologists, and individuals representing a number of these other constituencies are, in fact, actively attempting to cut down these health costs. This chapter highlights several specific areas of health expenditures that could be reduced by the efforts of another one of these constituencies – the science and profession of psychology. In particular, representatives of all areas of psychology who today increasingly identify themselves with *health psychology* can contribute to this. First, however, I must present an overview of several recent changes in the types of illnesses and dysfunctions that incapacitate 20th-century Americans. The reader wishing a more detailed review

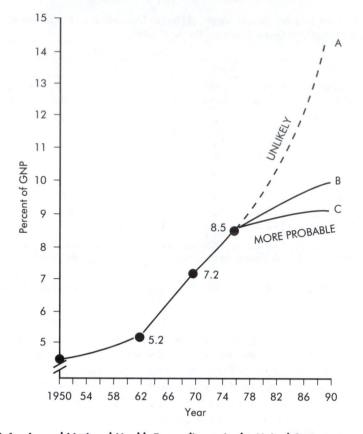

FIGURE 1.1   **Annual National Health Expenditures in the United States Expressed as a Percentage of Gross National Product (Adapted from Rogers, 1980: p. 5)**

of the literature on risk factors will find this in the recent reports of the U.S. Surgeons General and related official government publications (Califano, 1979a, 1979b, 1979c; Gibson, 1979; Harris, 1980, 1981; Vischi et al., 1980), as well as in any of the dozen or so handbooks of health psychology and behavioral medicine that have been published in the past three years.

Changing Patterns for Death and Disability

During the past 80 years developments in the basic and applied sciences and related disciplines associated with infectious disease, immunology, and epidemiology have markedly changed the illness patterns of Americans by reducing or eliminating such previously highly prevalent conditions as tuberculosis, influenza, measles, and poliomyelitis. Figures 1.2 and 1.3 from the 1979 *Surgeon General's Report on Health Promotion and Disease Prevention* by the then U.S. Secretary of Health, Education and Welfare

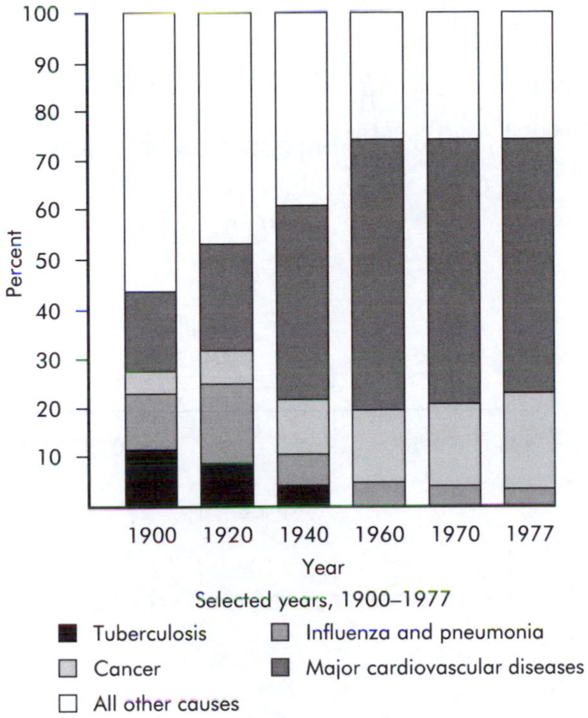

FIGURE 1.2   **United States Deaths from Selected Causes Expressed as a Percentage of all Deaths (Adapted from Califano, 1979b, p. 4, in the Public Domain)**

(Califano, 1979b, pp. 4; 94) present the evidence indicating that the human and financial toll from these four scourges has been reduced materially in our lifetimes.

Unfortunately, the reduction in these conditions has occurred along with an *increase* during the same years in such conditions as lung cancer, major cardiovascular disease, drug and alcohol abuse, and motorcycle and alcohol-related automobile accidents. The remaining data in Figure 1.2 and the additional data reported to the U.S. Congress by Califano (1979a, 1979b) shown in Figures 1.4, 1.5, and 1.6, reveal several of these increasing trends. There are, of course, many other conditions, illnesses, and disabilities that have not been mentioned. Those just named, however, represent the ones which in aggregate take an inordinate and unjustifiable human and financial toll.

Behavioral Health

In a previous article (Matarazzo, 1980), I traced the recent developments in federal funding of research and training as well as developments within

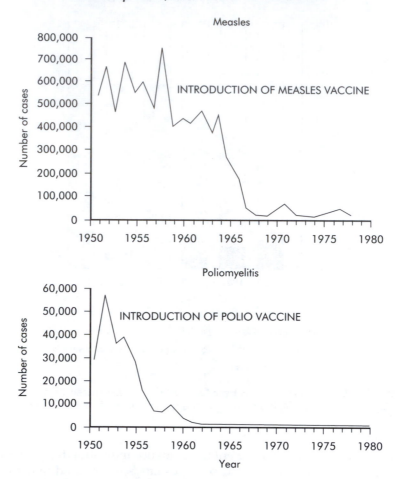

FIGURE 1.3   **Number of Cases of Measles and Poliomyelitis Reported in the United States (Adapted from Califano, 1979b, p. 94, in the Public Domain)**

some of the health disciplines themselves which were associated with a revival of interest in behavioral medicine and a new interest in behavioral health. I gave this latter field the following interim definition:

> *Behavioral health* is an interdisciplinary field dedicated to promoting a philosophy of health that stresses *individual responsibility* in the application of behavioral and biomedical science knowledge and techniques to the *maintenance* of health and the *prevention* of illness and dysfunction by a variety of self-initiated individual or shared activities. (Matarazzo, 1980, p. 813)

The decision to assign a formal name to this new interdisciplinary field was based on a number of factors. For example, the data in Figures 1.1 through 1.6 presented above support the charge by physician and social philosopher Knowles (1977) that:

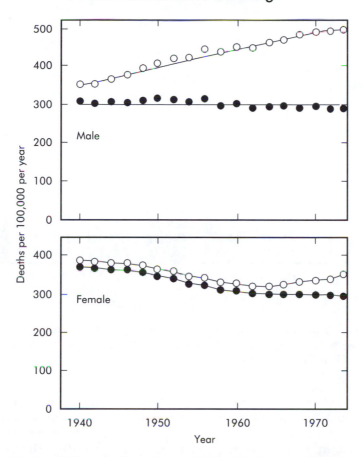

FIGURE 1.4 Annual Mortality from Cancers in the United States for White Adult Males and Females: Dark Circles Denote all Cancers, Light Circles Denote Lung Cancers (Adapted from Califano, 1979a, p. 162, in the Public Domain)

> Over 99 per cent of us are born healthy and made sick as a result of personal mis-behavior and environmental conditions. The solution to the problems of ill health in modern American society involves individual responsibility, in the first instance, and social responsibility through public legislature and private volunteer efforts in the second instance. (p. 58)

There is evidence that leaders in many health professions have taken Knowles' challenge seriously.

Health Psychology

Medicine (including its related disciplines of preventive medicine, cardiology, etc.) and the disciplines of medical sociology, health education, epidemiology, stress physiology, and others clearly are actively involved in

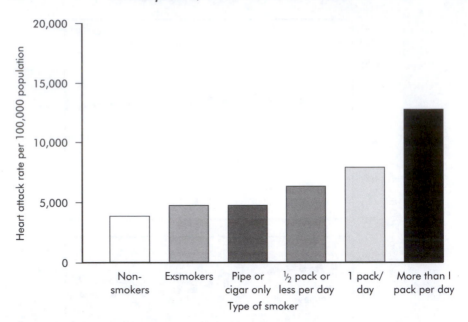

FIGURE 1.5   **Age-adjusted Rates of First Heart Attack for United States White Males Ages 30–59 Categorized by Smoking Status (Adapted from Califano, 1979b, p. 58, in the Public Domain)**

preventing illness and promoting good health. Articles documenting these contributions will be found in the journals of each of these disciplines. During the to 1980's past two decades psychology also has had its interest stimulated in this interdisciplinary field, and in 1978 the American Psychological Association established a division of health psychology in response to many concurrent developments in the field of health and illness. To add impetus to these developments within psychology, I recently offered the following as an initial description, subject to continuing modification by others, of this emerging field within psychology.

> *Health psychology* is the aggregate of the specific educational, scientific, and professional contributions of the discipline of psychology to the promotion and maintenance of health, the prevention and treatment of illness, and the identification of etiologic and diagnostic correlates of health, illness, and related dysfunction. (Matarazzo, 1980, p. 815)

The members of the Division of Health Psychology were recently polled by their officers, and by a small majority those voting preferred the following slightly modified interim definition for this emerging field.

> *Health psychology* is the aggregate of the specific educational, scientific, and professional contributions of the discipline of psychology to the promotion and maintenance of health, the prevention and treatment of illness, the identification of

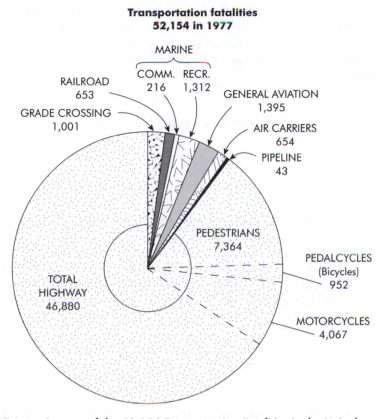

FIGURE 1.6   Sources of the 52,154 Transportation Fatalities in the United States During 1977 (Adapted from Califano, 1979a, p. 60, in the Public Domain)

etiologic and diagnostic correlates of health, illness, and related dysfunction, *and to the analysis and improvement of the health care system and health policy formation.* (added material italicized)

The casual reader of these interim definitions might misinterpret health psychology as pertaining *only* to the concerns of individual psychologists with an applied interest or focus (e.g. clinical psychologists), but nothing could be further from the truth. During the first century of the American Psychological Association three subject areas within psychology appear to me to have engaged the *common* interest of individual psychologists from such widely disparate subspecialties as experimental, clinical, physiological, social, industrial, child, educational, and related branches of psychology. These three subject areas with very wide appeal for all types of psychologists were: (a) individual differences, (b) a combination of learning theory and personality theory, and (c) individual psychopathology. Recent developments in medicine and psychology have given rise to the interdisciplinary field labeled *behavioral health,* and these developments have convinced me that health psychology (with its strong emphasis on the enhancement and promotion of health and the prevention of dysfunction in currently healthy children and adults) is a fourth area that can attract creative individual psychologists from seemingly disparate subfields of psychology.

Some Behavioral Health Challenges Awaiting Psychology

Study of Figures 1.1 through 1.6 shows that focusing some of this country's investigative, educational, and professional talent and resources on *changing the behavior of individual Americans* will reduce the human and financial costs associated with a number of preventable conditions. Today's indefensibly high health expenditures will therefore drop as well. National leaders of various persuasions agree that the costly toll from heart disease, cancer, and so on can be materially reduced. We can accomplish this if we can find ways to help our *currently healthy* citizens (1) refrain from smoking tobacco or abusing alcohol, drugs, and related deleterious substances; (2) reduce their salt and dietary cholesterol intake; (3) use dental floss; (4) fasten their seat belts; (5) exercise regularly; (6) establish proper sleep and rest habits; and (7) employ a few basic home, highway, and occupational health safety standards – to cite only a few examples. Therefore, in an effort to encourage psychologists from each of the subspecialties of our discipline to consider health psychology as a legitimate field in which to exercise their individual interests and employ their talents. I will discuss four of these seven areas that appear to me to be ones in which our science and profession can make a contribution with the knowledge currently extant in our discipline. Other psychologists could add to this list, which is meant merely to be illustrative.

Smoking

The data in Tables 1.2, 1.3, and 1.4 relate to smoking and highlight one of the more inviting challenges to psychology. Table 1.2 presents both a positive and a negative trend. Due to a massive national education program following the first Surgeon General's report to the nation on smoking (United States Public Health Service, 1964), and with considerable input from individual psychologists as well as representatives of a number of other disciplines (as revealed in the report forwarded to the U.S. Congress by Califano, 1979c), the percentage of male adult smokers of all ages in this country decreased from 52.6% to 39.3% from 1955 to 1975. This 1975 figure for men dropped to 36.1% in 1979 (Harris, 1981, p. 212). However, Table 1.2 also reveals that during the same period from 1955 to 1979 there was an *increase* in adult *female* smokers from 24.5% to 29.4%. Thus, although the massive national educational program that followed the first Surgeon General's report to the nation on smoking in 1964 helped reduce smoking

TABLE 1.2 **Percentage of Current and Former Male Female Adult Smokers in the United States in Different Age Groups**

Age	1955 Current smoker	1955 Former smoker	1964 Current smoker	1964 Former smoker	1966 Current smoker	1966 Former smoker	1970 Current smoker	1970 Former smoker	1975 Current smoker	1975 Former smoker	1979[a] Current smoker
Males											
21–24	51.4	3.6	67.0	9.5	61.9	7.2	49.8	20.0	41.3	16.0	
25–34	63.4	9.0	59.9	18.0	59.9	19.7	46.7	27.9	43.9	22.5	
35–44	62.1	11.1	59.9	22.9	59.0	21.9	48.6	31.4	47.1	25.8	
45–54	56.9	12.6	53.1	25.3	53.8	26.0	43.1	34.4	41.1	36.0	
55–64	43.6	15.7	50.9	24.5	47.7	31.0	37.4	41.4	33.7	38.8	
65+	22.3	13.6	29.9	27.0	27.8	29.5	22.8	43.8	24.2	36.2	
All ages	52.6	10.9	52.9	22.2	51.9	23.6	42.3	32.6	39.3	29.2	36.1
Females											
21–24	29.7	3.5	41.9	7.6	49.2	7.9	32.3	13.2	34.0	19.9	
25–34	35.8	5.8	40.6	9.3	45.1	12.0	40.3	18.9	35.4	16.5	
35–44	32.4	4.9	39.2	9.4	40.6	10.5	38.8	15.8	36.4	17.7	
45–54	22.8	3.9	36.4	6.8	42.0	9.6	36.1	15.5	32.8	15.5	
55–64	10.8	2.6	20.5	7.0	20.6	10.5	24.2	16.0	25.9	15.0	
65+	3.5	1.6	7.8	3.3	7.6	5.2	10.2	8.2	10.2	10.7	
All ages	24.5	3.9	31.5	7.4	33.7	9.4	30.5	14.8	28.9	14.5	29.4

[a]1979 data are from 1981 Report of the U.S. Surgeon General (Harris, 1981, pp. 212–213; see also Carrigan, Armstrong and Moehring, 1980).

TABLE 1.3   **Percentages of Regular Teenage Cigarette Smokers in the United States by Age Group**

Year	Ages 12–14 Male	Ages 12–14 Female	Ages 15–16 Male	Ages 15–16 Female	Ages 17–18 Male	Ages 17–18 Female	Ages 12–18 Male	Ages 12–18 Female
1968	2.9	.6	17.0	9.6	30.2	18.6	14.7	8.4
1970	5.7	3.0	19.5	14.4	37.3	22.8	18.5	11.9
1972	4.6	2.8	17.8	16.3	30.2	25.3	15.7	13.8
1974	4.2	4.9	18.1	20.2	31.0	25.9	15.8	15.3
1979[a]	3.2	4.4	13.5	11.8	19.3	26.3	10.7	12.7

[a]1979 data (ages 12–18) are from the American Cancer Society's five-year study entitled "Target Five" ("Fewer Smoking," 1981), and the 12–14- and 15–16-year-old data are from Harris (1980, p. 36).

among males by an impressive 16.5%, the same era witnessed a 4.9% increase in the percentage of female smokers. Many experts agree with the American Cancer Society that this increase for females is eloquent testimony to the power of the advertisements that were carefully crafted with the help of psychologists who are specialists in the field of subliminal motivational psychology. Examples of these skillfully crafted slogans are "You've come a long way, baby," with its strong but still subtle appeal to the women's liberation movement. The "Virginia Slims" brand name artfully takes advantage of the increasingly well-documented research finding that, for many female (and male) smokers, quitting the habit is associated with gaining weight (Blitzer, Rimm and Giefer, 1977).

The shift from males to females as the targets of these "educational" campaigns by the cigarette companies was not confined to adult females. As shown in the last column of Table 1.3, the percentage of smokers among teenage girls began to increase rapidly (from 8.4% to 15.3% among 12–18-year-old girls during 1968 to 1974). Table 1.3 also shows that by the year 1974 the percentage (20.2%) of smokers among 15–16-year-old girls had even exceeded the rate (18.1%) for similarly aged boys, whose increase during the same six-year period was only 1.1% above the 17.0% rate reached in 1968. The most recent figures show, however, a *decline* in smoking for *both* girls and boys. The current smoker figures for 1979 released by the American Cancer Society are 10.7% for teenage boys and 12.7% for teenage girls ("Fewer Smoking," 1981). Each of these facts constitutes robust evidence that smoking behavior is amenable to influence.

As an interesting datum for psychologists, the additional percentages shown in Table 1.4 make clear that, for both girls and boys, the time of greatest *susceptibility* to becoming a regular smoker is around age 12. The United States taxpayer has generously supported the post-World War II development of academic and professional psychology. Should not a greater portion of psychology's currently vast talents and resources be applied to stemming the health and financial costs associated with smoking by children and adults as just cited in the tables and figures? As the field which has the

TABLE 1.4 Distribution of U.S. 17-Year-Olds Who Had Ever Tried Smoking by Age at Which They First Tried Smoking, According to 1974 Current Smoker Status and Sex

Current smoker status	All ages	Age at which 17-year-olds first tried smoking (percent distribution)											Median age in years
		7 years and under	8 years	9 years	10 years	11 years	12 years	13 years	14 years	15 years	16 years	17 years	
Regular smoker													
Boys	100.0	8.2	4.9	6.6	8.7	4.7	15.8	11.5	14.8	14.3	7.6	2.9	12.6
Girls	100.0	3.2	3.6	–	6.8	3.5	12.1	10.6	23.0	15.0	18.5	3.7	13.9
Both	100.0	6.4	4.5	4.3	8.0	4.3	14.5	11.2	17.7	14.6	11.5	3.2	13.2
Tried smoking but not regular smoker													
Boys	100.0	6.8	6.0	8.0	10.7	6.0	15.6	10.1	11.7	11.8	10.3	3.7	13.3
Girls	100.0	5.9	1.1	4.3	5.8	2.7	10.4	11.9	10.7	19.3	22.1	5.8	15.2
Both	100.0	6.3	3.4	6.0	7.7	4.2	12.8	11.1	11.2	15.9	16.7	4.8	14.3
Total													
Boys	100.0	6.9	4.7	7.5	8.6	4.5	14.4	11.6	13.5	14.6	9.6	4.1	13.8
Girls	100.0	4.6	1.9	2.8	5.3	2.6	10.7	12.5	14.5	17.8	22.1	5.3	15.2
Both	100.0	5.9	3.4	5.4	7.1	3.6	12.8	12.0	13.9	16.0	15.2	4.6	14.5

longest history in the study of human behavior, and especially individual behavior, psychology has the scientific knowledge base, the practical applied experience, and the institutional supports for individuals within it to begin to make important contributions immediately in preventing smoking among our country's youth and in helping adults who wish to quit to do so successfully.

Fortunately some beginning initiatives have been taken. Experimental, social, clinical, and educational psychologists have applied aspects of the knowledge accumulated by each of these subspecialties to smoking behavior. Schachter and his colleagues have wed elements of general psychology with counterparts drawn from renal physiology and pharmacology in a novel set of interrelated experiments designed to demonstrate the relationship between physiological and psychological variables in making the smoking habit resistant 'to extinction (Schachter, 1977; Schachter, Kozlowski and Silverstein, 1977; Schachter, Silverstein, Kozlowski, Herman, and Liebling, 1977; Schachter, Silverstein, and Perlick, 1977). Hunt has written a series of papers (see Hunt and Matarazzo, 1982 in which he has drawn heavily on the literature of a number of older and current theories from experimental psychology in an attempt to provide a heuristically useful perspective of how the smoking habit is initiated, how it is maintained over time, and (for those individuals wishing to quit) how it is very resistant to cessation. He has drawn from the theoretical writings of psychology in such important areas as habit, motivation, reinforcement, associative learning, resistance to extinction, personality, and addiction. Hunt also has applied these theories in an effort to understand the special problem of relapse. In a similar vein, Leventhal has discussed similar problems associated with initiation, maintenance, and termination, but he has done so primarily by utilizing the data base and theoretical writings of social psychology (Leventhal and Cleary, 1980).

The special problem of preventing smoking in children also has attracted the interest of academic psychologists from a number of subspecialties, as well as colleagues from medicine and related professions. For example, Jessor and Jessor (1977) and Ajzen and Fishbein (1970, 1972) have proposed some heuristically highly useful theoretical models of why children begin to smoke, and social and other theoretically oriented psychologists should find this area a highly fruitful one within which to follow their own interests. Furthermore, Evans and his colleagues in Houston (Evans et al., 1978), Luepker and his colleagues in Minneapolis (Hurd et al., 1980), and Wynder and his colleagues in New York City (Botvin, Eng, and Williams, 1980; Williams, Carter, Arnold, and Wynder, 1979) each have shown that the numbers of new smokers among pre-teen sixth- and seventh-graders can be reduced by as much as 50% through the use of educational programs skillfully crafted from knowledge now available to social, educational, and clinical psychologists.

Additionally, one need not wait until the middle or end of the life cycle (as in the age groups for the health risks shown in Figures 1.2, 1.4, and 1.5)

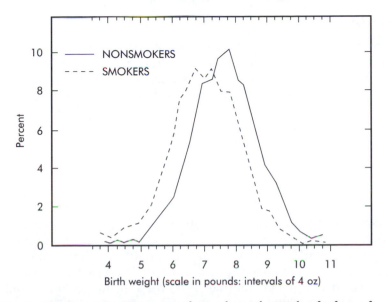

FIGURE 1.7 **Percentage Frequency Distribution by Birth Weight of Infants of Mothers Who Did Not Smoke During Pregnancy and of Those Who Smoked One Pack or more of Cigarettes per Day (Adapted from Califano, 1979c, ch. 8, p. 17, and Macmahon, Alpert and Salber, 1966)**

to see the later costs of beginning to smoke in one's teenage years. Smoking takes its toll long before that, and even on the fetus in its mother's womb. Figure 1.7 from Califano (1979c) shows a finding by Macmahon, Alpert, and Salber (1966) revealing that the birthweight of babies born to mothers who smoke is significantly lower than is that of newborns whose mothers do not smoke. Inasmuch as below-average birthweight is associated with impairment in intellectual abilities and a wide range of physical disabilities, each of which costs society billions of dollars per year, the contribution of psychology to finding ways to deter healthy mothers from smoking during pregnancy will go a long way toward cutting down the human and dollar costs now paid by our society in the lifetime health expenditure associated with the at-risk offspring of smoking mothers.

National polls have repeatedly shown that the majority of this country's regular smokers (27 million men, 25 million women, and 3 million teenagers in 1979) would like to quit smoking but have not been able to do so successfully. Nevertheless, since 1964 *some 30 million adult Americans have successfully stopped smoking.* The percentage of adult men (although not women) and teenage boys and girls who are current smokers is *decreasing* (Tables 1.2 and 1.3). Both of these statistics are robust evidence that the effort of psychologists and other workers in this health promotion field (preventing or ceasing smoking) has a good chance of meeting with success. Graduate education and research monies are available from several institutes to support such efforts.

Alcohol Use

Alcohol has been used by humans since time immemorial. Until the present generation, however, little was known of the probable costs to society of alcohol abuse. Some recent estimates of the costs associated with the marked abuse resulting in chronic alcoholism place these annually at $42 billion for the total economic cost and at $864 million for the costs related to the treatment of alcoholism (Vischi et al., 1980, p. 95). A recent literature review by Streissguth, Landesman-Dwyer, Martin, and Smith (1980) goes beyond the costs associated with *chronic* alcoholism and reveals an additional finding that the effect on the fetus of alcohol ingested by soon-to-be mothers who are merely *social drinkers* (2–3 drinks per day) may be even more devastating than the effect of tobacco on the fetus of such normal-appearing mothers. In the human fetus exposed to alcohol during gestation, the effect may be fetal alcohol syndrome (FAS), a condition characterized by mental retardation and a variety of related physiological abnormalities in some offspring. Based on their estimated prevalence for FAS of one such afflicted child per 750 births in the general population, Streissguth et al. (1980) conclude that these rates "make FAS one of the most common forms of mental retardation with a known etiology" (p. 356). However, the effects of alcohol on human health are far from clear cut. Specifically, the challenge for workers in the various health disciplines from these results by Streissguth et al., on social drinking is made even more compelling by recent reports that 2–3 drinks per day may, in fact, *prevent* the occurrence of other health risks, namely those associated with cardiovascular dysfunction, while also increasing some others (Kozararevic et al., 1980).

Furthermore, on the side of health impairment, additional recent reports by Galanter (1980) and by Parker, Birnbaum, Boyd, and Noble (1980) reveal that social drinking in young adults may produce marked loss of cognitive and neuropsychological capacities previously believed to be affected only by long-term chronic alcoholism. As cited in Califano (1979a) from a study by Donovan and Jessor (1978) and reproduced in Figure 1.8, problem drinking is present even among teenage youth, so the long-term human costs of both social and problem drinking present another challenge to psychologists interested in health psychology. Abuse of alcohol has been implicated as a major etiologic factor in a large number of the chronic medical conditions associated with today's high cost of hospital care in general hospitals as well as with mortality and disability associated with tragedies on our highways and streets. As the writings of the National Institute on Alcohol Abuse and Alcoholism during the past decade have made clear, alcohol abuse is a problem for both sexes, all ages, and all socioeducational groups. Psychologists can contribute a great deal toward helping currently healthy, nonalcoholic Americans who wish to drink socially learn to do so with less cost to themselves, to their families, their employers, and to society.

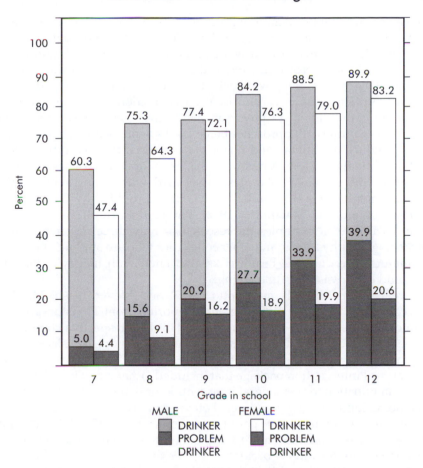

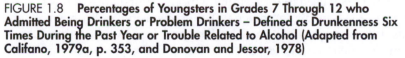

FIGURE 1.8   **Percentages of Youngsters in Grades 7 Through 12 who Admitted Being Drinkers or Problem Drinkers – Defined as Drunkenness Six Times During the Past Year or Trouble Related to Alcohol (Adapted from Califano, 1979a, p. 353, and Donovan and Jessor, 1978)**

Evidence for the deleterious effect of tobacco and alcohol on the health of our youth and older citizens continues to accumulate with each passing year. It is my hope that interested psychologists from each of our specialty areas, as members of a discipline with a long history of ethically based experience in the study of persuasion and behavior change, will join with scientists, educators, and applied workers in other disciplines to help those citizens who wish to do so take individual action to reduce this national cost in human mortality and morbidity and billions of dollars annually.

Healthier Diets and Related Risk Reduction

There is a consensus among leaders in cardiology that the use of too much salt in daily meals (as well as smoking and abuse of alcohol) is related to the increasing numbers of Americans suffering from high blood pressure and from related cardiovascular dysfunctions. Furthermore, although not unanimous in this opinion, many cardiologists believe that too much saturated fat and plasma cholesterol characterize the average American diet and that these dietary factors, along with lack of exercise, result in increased morbidity and mortality due to cardiovascular dysfunction. A number of groups (made up of psychologists, physicians, and other colleagues) recently have provided examples of approaches behavioral scientists now are developing to help reduce the human and financial costs associated with these dietary and multiple risk factors. A review of the behavioral approaches being used to reduce the cardiovascular risks associated with eating foods high in plasma cholesterol and saturated fat has been provided by Carmody, Fey, Pierce, Connor, and Matarazzo (1982). Rather than duplicate that review here, I will cite as examples the research of only three research teams of psychologists, physicians, and other colleagues who are applying behavioral techniques to reduce the health risks associated with life-style (including diet) and cardiovascular functioning.

Foreyt, Scott, Mitchell, and Gotto (1979) and Mever, Nash, McAlister, Maccoby, and Farquhar (1980) recently reported from Houston and from Stanford, respectively, a striking reduction in their respective communities in the number of individuals at risk for heart disease due to risks associated with poor diet, smoking, and not enough exercise. Through the use of an educational intervention package that included either a diet booklet, or education in nutrition, or behavioral intervention utilizing group discussion, or a combination of these procedures, Foreyt et al., showed that the levels of cholesterol in their target population could be reduced significantly. However, as is shown in Figure 1.9, the maintenance of these initial losses beyond six months did *not* occur.

Meyer et al. (1980) used (with seemingly more maintenance of this success at follow up) a mass media campaign utilizing television, radio, newspapers, billboards, bus posters, direct mail leaflets, and face-to-face techniques as components of their community intervention and also produced significant *decreases* in some of the risk factors associated with cardiovascular disease among their target samples. Problems with this research program have been identified by Kasl (1980) and by Leventhal, Safer, Cleary, and Gutmann (1980), and rebutted in turn by Meyer, Maccoby, and Farquhar (1980). Comparable criticisms no doubt could be raised about the community research program in Houston by Foreyt et al., and about the even larger-scale community program being carried out by Puska (McAlister, Puska, Koskela, Pallonen, and Maccoby, 1980) and his colleagues in Finland with the help of some of these Stanford University psychologist-colleagues from the United States. In this Finnish study, called the North Karelia Project, a mass television educational campaign has resulted in dietary and other risk-factor changes that already appear to have reduced mortality and morbidity associated with cardiovascular dysfunction. The impacts of the dietary changes are confounded in this multiple-risk intervention study with the

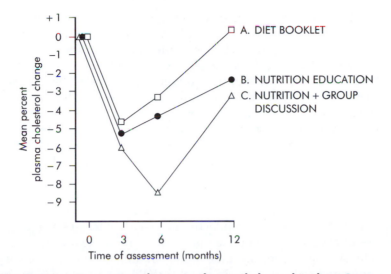

FIGURE 1.9   Mean Percentage Change in Plasma Cholesterol in Three Groups Receiving Different Interventions (Adapted from Foreyt, Scott, Mitchell and Gotto, 1979, p. 449)

smoking intervention and thus are not easily partialled out. However, as to reduction in smoking per se, in the most recent publication (McAlister et al., 1980) this cross-cultural group of psychologists and physicians reported that 10,000 of 40,000 adult Finnish smokers had quit the habit as a result of the educational intervention and were still not smoking at the six-month follow-up.

Although the literature on multiple risk-factor intervention briefly cited in this section represents but a small fraction of the voluminous literature on the behavioral treatment of dietary risks associated with cardiovascular dysfunction, it may suffice as preliminary evidence that psychologists and colleagues from other disciplines are making headway in applying psychological knowledge in the reduction or prevention of a number of *behavioral* risks associated with an increased probability of cardiovascular disease. Reducing the costs associated with cardiovascular diseases has been given a high priority both by the Congress of the United States and the National Heart, Lung, and Blood Institute, and therefore a relatively large source of monies for research and research training also awaits psychology departments and individual psychologists with an interest in this challenging field (Matarazzo, 1980).

Automobile and Motorcycle Accidents

Both the levels of mortality (shown earlier in Figure 1.6) and the morbidity resulting from automobile and motorcycle accidents extract human and health expenditure costs that could be reduced substantially (Califano, 1979b, pp. 59–63). Califano reports that approximately 1 death in 40 in the

United States is related to a motor vehicle and that deaths involving motor vehicle occupants constitute the largest group of fatal injuries for all ages between birth and old age. Psychology quite likely can do little about some of the causes of these vehicular deaths (e.g. maintenance and other road characteristics, amount of highway travel versus travel by air, and the cost–benefit ratios employed by manufacturers to make their automobiles more crashworthy). There are, however, above and beyond the role of alcohol, two major areas associated with motor vehicle crashes to which the knowledge base of general psychology seems to me readily applicable. These are *speed* at which we drive and our use and nonuse of *seat belts* as a form of safety restraint.

It is obvious to anyone who watches television and reads our newspapers that our vast auto industry (in common with cigarette, deodorant and soap makers, and other product manufacturers) makes extensive use of general principles of psychology to market its product. Yet this same auto industry appears to have spent precious little money in utilizing comparable psychological principles to help our citizens (especially our youthful new drivers) learn to drive at and maintain speeds that will better insure the safety of life and limb. Our nation's governors, and our President Reagan, did in fact recently utilize this country's gas and oil crisis to persuade Americans to reduce their highway driving speed to 55mph. The immediate result was an estimated saving of 5,000 lives annually (Califano, 1979a, p. 61).

I hope that this recent experience will encourage interested individual psychologists to approach federal funding agencies as well as their elected municipal, state, and federal officials and offer their talents in a search for innovative approaches that will help our citizens voluntarily elect to continue to drive at these safer speeds. Norway and other countries have cut down the increasing numbers of deaths of their citizens by legally forbidding the driving of any motor vehicle following the use of alcohol in any amount. Americans as a nation have opted for the moment not to resort to similar stiff prison sentences (or execution, as in one Middle Eastern country) as a means of reducing the mortality and morbidity associated with automobile accidents.

Yet, Americans are conscious of the risk of vehicular collisions, as evidenced by the popularity early in the 1970s of automobiles equipped with seat belts. In Australia, vehicle occupant deaths decreased by some 25% after seat belts were required by law. Furthermore, reasoned opinion suggests that if Americans wore a combined lap and shoulder belt the likelihood of death and serious injury would be reduced by about 60% of that shown in Figure 1.6 (Califano, 1979b, p. 61). Sadly, research to date has revealed that the mass education campaigns designed to motivate drivers to *voluntarily* use seat belts have been singularly unsuccessful (Kelley, 1979; Robertson, 1976, 1978). Clearly, the reasons for this lack of success are numerous and quite likely complex. However, in common with pediatric psychologist Christophersen (1977), I believe this seat belt problem constitutes a salient and challenging real-life laboratory for research by interested psychologists and their graduate students.

The bases for my faith lie in the history of our field's contributions in human factors research during the period from the beginning of the Second World War in 1939 to the spectacular triumph of our nation's aerospace industry in 1969, when this country successfully wed man and machine and placed two men on the moon. I thus find it inconceivable that the talent of psychology cannot design a motivationally salient system involving a seat belt or similar restraining safety system that Americans will use voluntarily and as comfortably as today they use the brakes on their automobiles. Both during the Second World War and in more recent space programs, psychology added its talent to that of specialists from other disciplines and helped design and engineer highly sophisticated and relatively safe man–machine systems in which the person's human factor capacities and motivations were first studied and then fully utilized in the design of a safe man–machine system. My reading of the zeitgeist is that the U.S. Department of Transportation as well as a number of NIH institutes would welcome research applications in this area from psychologists. Psychologists with ideas for curricular and related educational programs in safe driving for our youth also quite likely will be accorded considerable interest.

Behavioral Health's Challenge to Psychology

I sense strongly that a consensus has emerged from many quarters: To successfully grapple with one of the more important challenges of the last two decades of the 20th century, we must aggressively investigate and deal effectively with the role of the individual's behavior and life-style in health and dysfunction. Furthermore, representatives from many segments of our society are increasingly looking to the science and profession of psychology for help with this problem. Although it has been a leader in the field of *mental* health since the Second World War, in my opinion psychology as a discipline has been curiously slow to recognize the opportunities offered it by these national developments as they relate to the *physical* health of our nation. Yet, during the past several years, the National Institutes of Health, the National Science Foundation, and other federal funding agencies, responding to pressures from our citizens and their elected officials, almost monthly have asked graduate departments of psychology to submit proposals for basic and applied research in areas relating to physical health and behavior (Matarazzo, 1980). Some of these requests for proposals invite applications in the field of *behavioral medicine* and focus on needs of actual patients – those who are ill and disabled and who are being treated by physicians in hospitals and in private offices. This population of patients continues to provide excellent opportunities for *licensed* medical and clinical psychologists whose interests in health psychology are directed toward actual clinical application and research, as well as for physiological and other qualified psychologists whose interests are in basic research. However, the field of *behavioral health* offers academic, research, and applied psychologists from every specialty comparable opportunities for research, teaching, and practice (as health educators), but with currently healthy people. There is much more that could be done at the interfaces of *normal* physical health and behavior. Four such areas where medicine and psychology interact include basic and applied research in physiological, experimental, biological, and social psychology with normal individuals. Each of these has a long history of research and teaching in our universities.

Furthermore, as many of us in teaching are aware, undergraduate and graduate students of psychology have, for over a decade, pleaded with their teachers that academic and research psychology deploy some of its resources into human areas that are "more relevant." Many psychologists are coming to agree with their students and with our elected officials that the challenge of enhancing and promoting the health of our currently healthy American children and adults offers every specialty of psychology a wide range of laboratories for "pure" as well as "applied" research. This challenge also offers a perspective within which to teach the subject matter that will help produce as well-founded an academic education in psychology as is currently afforded by our animal laboratories or by the content of our present courses and textbooks.

I therefore have concluded that the ball is now in psychology's court. It is up to those among us who are interested in behavioral health to take the initiatives that will allow us to participate in a new research and teaching enterprise which is professionally stimulating and to also contribute a needed public service while we are doing so. I am aware that there are many additional areas for research and education in behavioral health which I did not deal with here but which also require (and will challenge) the talent and imagination of psychologists and their colleagues in the biomedical and the behavioral sciences. Psychologists wishing a fuller introduction to the large number of areas which need help from our discipline should peruse the US government's explicit invitation in this area, *Healthy People: The Surgeon General's Report on Health Promotion and Disease Prevention,* which the then-Secretary of HEW (Califano, 1979a, 1979b) recently forwarded to the United States Congress.

References

Ajzen, I., and Fishbein, M. The prediction of behavior from attitudinal and normative variables. *Journal of Experimental and Social Psychology*, 1970, *6*, 466–487.

Ajzen, I., and Fishbein, M. Attitudes and normative beliefs as factors influencing behavioral intentions. *Journal of Personality and Social Psychology*, 1972, *21*, 1–9.

Blitzer, P. H., Rimm, A. A., and Giefer, E. E. The effect of cessation of smoking on body weight in 57,032 women: Cross-sectional and longitudinal analyses. *Journal of Chronic Diseases*, 1977, *30*, 415–429.

Botvin, G. J., Eng, A., and Williams, C. L. Preventing the onset of cigarette smoking through lifeskills training. *Preventive Medicine*, 1980, *9*, 135–143.

Califano, J. A., Jr. *Healthy people: Background papers*. Washington, D.C.: U.S. Government Printing Office, 1979. (a)

Califano, J. A., Jr. *Healthy people: The Surgeon General's Report on Health Promotion and Disease Prevention*. Washington, D.C.: U.S. Government Printing Office, 1979. (b)

Califano, J. A., Jr. *Smoking and health: A report of the Surgeon General*. Washington, D.C.: U.S. Government Printing Office, 1979. (c)

Carmody, T. P., Fey, S. G., Pierce, D. K., Connor, W. E., and Matarazzo, J. D. Behavioral treatment of hyperlipedemia: Techniques, results and future directions. *Journal of Behavioral Medicine* 1982, *5*, 91–116.

Carrigan, W. T., Armstrong, A. B., Moehring, J. T. (eds), *Basic data relating to the National Institutes of Health*. Washington, D.C.: U.S. Government Printing Office, 1980.

Christophersen, E. R. Children's behavior during automobile rides: Do car seats make a difference? *Pediatrics*, 1977, *60*, 69–74.

Donovan, J. E., and Jessor, R. Adolescent problem drinking: Psychosocial correlates in a national sample study. *Journal of Studies in Alcohol*, 1978, *39*, 1506–1524.

Evans, R., Rozelle, R. M., Mittelmark, M. B., Hansen, W. B., Bane, A. L. and Havis, J. Deterring the onset of smoking in children: Knowledge of immediate physiological effects and coping with peer pressure, media pressure, and parent modeling. *Journal of Applied Social Psychology*, 1978, *8*, 126–135.

Fewer smoking: More concede hazard. *Sunday Oregonian*, January 25, 1981, p. 5.

Foreyt, J. P., Scott, L. W., Mitchell, R. E., and Gotto, A. M. Plasma lipid changes in the normal population following behavioral treatment. *Journal of Consulting and Clinical Psychology*, 1979, *47*, 440–452.

Galanter, M. Young adult social drinkers: Another group at risk? *Alcoholism: Clinical and Experimental Research*, 1980, *4*, 241–242.

Gibson, R. M. National health expenditures, 1978. *Health Care Financing Review*, 1979 (Summer).

Harris, P. R. *The health consequences of smoking for women: A report of the Surgeon General*. Washington, D.C.: U.S. Government Printing Office, 1980.

Harris, P. R. *The health consequences of smoking (the changing cigarette): A report of the Surgeon General*. Washington, D.C.: U.S. Government Printing Office, 1981.

Hunt, W. A., and Matarazzo, J. D. Smoking behavior. In R. J. Gatchell, A. Baum, and J. E. Singer (eds), *Behavioral medicine and psychology: Overlapping disciplines*. Hillsdale, N.J.: Erlbaum, 1982.

Hurd, P. D. et al. Prevention of cigarette smoking in seventh grade children. *Journal of Behavioral Medicine*, 1980, *3*, 15–28.

Jessor, R., and Jessor, S. L. *Problem behavior and psychosocial development: A longitudinal study of youth*. New York: Academic Press, 1977.

Kasl, S. V. Cardiovascular risk reduction in a community setting: Some comments. *Journal of Consulting and Clinical Psychology*, 1980, *48*, 143–149.

Kelley, A. B. A media role for public health compliance? In R. B. Haynes, D. W. Taylor, and D. L. Sackett (eds), *Compliance in health care*. Baltimore, Md.: Johns Hopkins University Press, 1979.

Knowles, J. H. The responsibility of the individual. In J. H. Knowles (ed), *Doing better and feeling worse: Health in the United States*. New York: Norton, 1977.

Kozararevic, D. J., McGee, D., Vojvodic, N., Racic, Z., Dawber, T., Gordon, T. and Zuzel, W. Frequency of alcohol consumption and morbidity and mortality: The Yugoslavia Cardiovascular Disease Study. *The Lancet*, 1980, *1*, 613–616.

Leventhal, H., and Cleary, P. D. The smoking problem: A review of the research and theory in behavioral risk modification. *Psychological Bulletin*, 1980, *88*, 370–405.

Leventhal, H., Safer, M. A., Cleary, P. D., and Gutmann, M. Cardiovascular risk modification by community-based programs for life-style change: Comments on the Stanford study. *Journal of Consulting and Clinical Psychology*, 1980, *48*, 150–158.

Macmahon, B., Alpert, M., and Salber, E. J. Infant weight and parental smoking habits. *American Journal of Epidemiology*, 1966, *82*, 247–261.

Matarazzo, J. D. Behavioral health and behavioral medicine: Frontiers for a new health psychology. *American Psychologist*, 1980, *35*, 807–817.

McAlister, A., Puska, P., Koskela, K., Pallonen, U., and Maccoby, N. Mass communication and community organization for public health education. *American Psychologist*, 1980, *35*, 375–379.

Meyer, A. J., Maccoby, N., and Farquhar, J. W. Reply to Kasl and Leventhal et al. *Journal of Consulting and Clinical Psychology*, 1980, *48*, 159–163.

Meyer, A. J., Nash, J. D., McAlister, A. L., Maccoby, N., and Farquhar, J. W. Skills training in a cardiovascular health education campaign. *Journal of Consulting and Clinical Psychology*, 1980, *48*, 129–142.

Parker, E. S., Birnbaum, I. M., Boyd, R. A., and Noble, E. P. Neuropsychologic decrements as a function of alcohol intake in male students. *Alcoholism: Clinical and Experimental Research*, 1980, *4*, 330–334.

Robertson, L. S. Estimates of motor vehicle seat belf effectiveness and use: Implications for occupant crash protection. *American Journal of Public Health*, 1976, *I*, 859–864.

Robertson, L. S. The seat belt use law in Ontario, Canada: Effects of actual use. *Canadian Journal of Public Health*, 1978, *69*, 154–157.

Rogers, D. E. Adjusting to a no-growth future: Imperative for academic medicine in the 1980's. *Cornell University Medical College Alumni Quarterly*, 1980, *43* (May), 3–9.

Schachter, S. Nicotine regulation in heavy and light smokers. *Journal of Experimental Psychology: General*, 1977, *106*, 5–12.

Schachter, S., Kozlowski, L. T., and Silverstein, B. Effects of urinary pH on cigarette smoking. *Journal of Experimental Psychology: General*, 1977, *106*, 13–19.

Schachter, S., Silverstein, B., Kozlowski, L. T., Herman, C. P., and Liebling, B. Effects of stress on cigarette smoking and urinary pH. *Journal of Experimental Psychology: General*, 1977, *106*, 24–30.

Schachter, S., Silverstein, B., and Perlick, D. Psychological and pharmacological explanations of smoking under stress. *Journal of Experimental Psychology: General*, 1977, *106*, 31–40.

Streissguth, A. P., Landesman-Dwyer, S., Martin, J. C., and Smith, D. W. Teratogenic effects if alcohol in humans and laboratory animals. *Science*, 1980, *209*, 353–361.

United States passes annual physical. *American Medical News*, December 26, 1980–January 2, 1981, p. 9.

United States Public Health Service. *Smoking and health*. Washington, D.C.: United States Department of Health, Education, and Welfare, 1964.

Vischi, T. R., Jones, K. R., Shank, E. L. and Lima, L. H. *The alcohol, drug abuse, and mental health national data book*. Washington, D.C: U.S. Government Printing Office, 1980.

Williams, C. L., Carter, B. J., Arnold, C. B. and Wynder, E. L. Chronic disease risk factors among children. The know your body study. *Journal of Chronic Diseases*, 1979, 32, 505–513.

2 REDEFINING HEALTH PSYCHOLOGY:
Matarazzo Revisited

Mark McDermott

The Definitional Problem

The much-cited definition of health psychology published by Matarazzo (1980) has been appropriated extensively by this new and still emerging sub-discipline. His definition of health psychology is:

> ... the aggregate of the specific educational, scientific and professional contributions of the discipline of psychology to the promotion and maintenance of health, the prevention and treatment of illness, the identification of etiologic and diagnostic correlates of health and illness and related dysfunctions, and the analysis and improvement of the health care system and health policy (p. 815).

Almost every health psychology textbook and introductory chapter on health psychology quotes this definition verbatim, giving it pride of place at the beginning, and by implication valorising its content. This includes, for example, the fourth edition (and the three previous editions) of the influential text *Health Psychology* as authored by Taylor (1999[1994]; pp. 3–4). Other authors do likewise. For example, in the UK, Ogden's (1996) health psychology text includes this definition on the fourth page of her book, whilst Maes and van Elderen (1998) include it on the second page (p. 591) of their health psychology chapter in Eysenck's introductory psychology textbook *Psychology, An Integrated Approach*. And so the pattern continues with Edelman (2000) featuring it on page 16 of *Psychosocial Aspects of the Health Care Process*. Indeed, this quotation from Matarazzo (1980) is used verbatim by The British Psychological Society's (BPS) Division of Health Psychology (DHP) as its working definition (see p. 1 of the DHP, 1998 'Application pack' pamphlet). Yet despite ubiquitous citing of the definition, criticism of it has been sparse and ongoing discussion of its implications for the developing field of health psychology has been negligible. Thus, this definition has achieved a dominance and status with which psychologists unwittingly have colluded for the last 20 years.

The question arises, then, as to why this is so, or as Szasz (1997) expressed it: 'qui bono?' … 'who benefits?'. The answer lies in the realisation that health psychology since its inception in the mid-to-late 1970s has been a developing sub-discipline and like all new sub-disciplines that initially have to map out their territory, it has sought to keep as many alternative route-ways for future development open and to enlist as many supporters as possible to ensure its survival and growth. Matarazzo's definition serves this function well as it is a very broad and inclusive one. It is in no sense excluding or exclusive. So, who benefits from this broad, inclusive definition? The answer is: any psychologist whose work has anything either directly or indirectly to do with 'health', with all the benefits (in terms of prestige, access to potential study participants and research funds) that such an association may bring.

Matarazzo's definition of health psychology, I maintain, is over-inclusive, encompassing as it does any topic connected with 'health'. This inclusivity no longer serves health psychology (or indeed psychology in general) well, as the imperialist aspirations of this definition have spawned an empire which is unsustainable as a single unit and thereby health psychology is in danger of fragmentation and collapse. Specifically, Matarazzo's definition has allowed health psychology to inhabit all of the domains of health care delivery, whether it be primary, secondary or tertiary care. Yet secondary interventions and those aimed at rehabilitation have been dispensed for many years by clinical psychologists, who involve themselves in behavioural medicine, as well as with the remediation of mental health difficulties. Further, if we understand the role of psychologists in 'primary care' in terms of the delivery of psychological services at the point of first contact, i.e. in GP practices and surgeries, then we find clinical psychology also fully in evidence there. Thus, with clinical psychology so well established in most of the levels of intervention that are delivered within the UK National Health Service, if follows that there is little territory left for health psychology to inhabit and make its own and that therefore it must appropriate some of clinical psychology's traditional areas of work in order to survive. Matarazzo's definition of health psychology allows much room for such a possibility to be realised. Arguably then, UK clinical psychology has experienced the growth of health psychology as a potential invader of its professional territory and role (along with the rise of counselling psychology). Indeed, it appears that in order to fend off the threat from health psychology, some clinical psychology departments in the UK have reinvented and re-branded themselves as Departments of 'Clinical Health Psychology'. Health psychology in the UK, then, is in imminent danger of being subsumed through osmosis by clinical psychology. Some psychology practitioners in the UK now are calling themselves 'clinical health psychologists', with some health psychologists on occasion colluding with such confusion, perhaps enjoying the status associated with the mistaken identity of their occupational relatives. What evidence is there, then, of such professional reinvention and conflation of terms?

Evidence of Conflation, Confusion and Osmosis

Looking through the pages of The British Psychological Society's monthly *Appointments Memorandum,* it can be seen that there is recurrent evidence in the form of job advertisements of this attempt by clinical psychology (whether deliberate or not) to reinvent itself and appropriate the banner of 'health psychology'. During the 11-month period from May 1999 through to March 2000 there were seven advertisements in the monthly *Memorandum* which were notable for their conflation of the terms 'clinical' and 'health' psychology.

In the May 1999 *Memorandum,* one advertisement by a local health service in the north of England asked for a 'consultant clinical psychologist', underneath which were written the words 'Adult Health Specialty', duties centering on coronary care and pain management. In the same issue a university department asked for a 'Research Assistant in Health/Clinical Psychology', with applicants being invited to work on a study of smoking cessation intervention, candidates being asked to have an MSc in Health Psychology. In the June 1999 edition, a large Community Health Services NHS Trust advertised for a 'Grade B Clinical Psychologist' to work in a 'Clinical Health Psychology Service', it being stipulated that there were 'close links with the Sub-Department of Clinical Health Psychology and the Health Behavioural Unit within the University'. Similarly, the same *Memorandum* carried an advertisement for a 'Clinical neuropsychologist – Grade A' to work within a 'Health Psychology Department' in an NHS Trust, the job specification involving assessment and intervention with acquired brain injury patients and people with other neurological problems. Likewise, in August 1999 an advertisement by an NHS Trust for a 'Clinical Psychologist (Health Psychology/Primary Care)' specified that '... we are looking for a Clinical Psychologist' to work in 'Acute Hospital Settings', service provision including: 'pain management, haematology, burns and plastic surgery, HIV/AIDS, neuropsychology' and 'primary care...'. In the March 2000 edition, the 'Health Psychology/Academic Department of Research' in a General Hospital advertised for a 'Health Psychologist' to research 'self management in chronic illness'. Enquiries were stipulated, however, as having to be made to a 'Consultant Clinical Psychologist'. Finally, in March 2000, the Psychology and Counselling Service of another large Community Health Services NHS Trust placed an advertisement for a 'Clinical Psychologist' to apply for the post of 'Head of the clinical health psychology specialty team', the remit of the job being to work in both acute and community settings, including services to people with 'HIV & AIDS, ... sexual health and physical health'. All seven advertisements were placed by different health trusts.

Thus, over the space of 11 months, seven advertisements were placed which conflated and confused 'clinical psychology' with 'health psychology'. This is perhaps not many. However, my search was not exhaustive during these months and was carried out on an *ad hoc* basis. Others like these may well have been missed. Whatever the exact number of these kinds of advertisements, they do provide evidence which suggests that some clinical psychologists may be attempting to subsume health psychology before health psychology has a chance to subsume any of clinical psychology's traditional domains of activity. It is interesting to note, for example, that from the text of one of these advertisements, a highly prestigious university has created within its five-star research rated psychology department a sub-department of what it calls 'clinical health psychology'. Within this sub-department is based a clinical psychology training course with a large annual intake but in which no health psychology MSc course is taught, that being delivered within another department in the university, namely in its Academic Department of Psychiatry.

Would we as a profession accept, then, a university department of educational psychology reinventing itself as a 'sub-department of clinical educational psychology', if it were thought that commonalities existed between educational psychology and clinical psychology? It is doubtful that this would be accepted without much public debate amongst the membership of the BPS (as is ongoing, for example, regarding the viability of providing generic training components across applied postgraduate psychology courses). There may well be good reasons for such a coalescing of the two domains. For example, emotional disturbance in children quite often may be related to specific learning difficulties in the classroom. The 'educationalist-as-therapist' is an appealing notion in such a circumstance. However, it is doubtful whether psychologists in education or psychologists in the UK National Health Service would countenance such a unification of roles without extended deliberation. Yet in the UK over the last decade there has been a gradual conjoining of 'clinical' and 'health' psychology, without any major consultation process having been undertaken by the collective members of the profession as a whole.

Yet the hybrid of clinical health psychology is now upon us, emerging from an almost subliminal osmotic process. At the 2000 Division of Health Psychology annual conference in Canterbury, a symposium (convened on behalf of the Division of Clinical Psychology Special Interest Group in Physical Health and Disability), sought to discuss 'The interface between health psychology and clinical health psychology'. Allusion to such an interface in the title perhaps implies the two components are distinguishable in some meaningful and substantive way. Yet it is not clear how they are so. Likewise, this year has seen for the first time the publication of an *Introduction to Clinical Health Psychology* (Bennett, 2000). The content of this book covers core aspects of health psychology but also explores 'hospital issues' and application of psychological principles in facilitating individual behavioural and emotional change. So, now we have 'health psychologists', 'clinical psychologists' and 'clinical health psychologists'. Cooper (1986) also proposed the emergence of 'clinical occupational psychologists'. Perhaps we should have a job description for 'occupational health psychologists' as well? Would such diversity be functional, though, in multi-disciplinary teams in which each of these different types of psychologists might find themselves present? Non-psychology colleagues in such teams would surely be confused, bemused and even amused, as no doubt would some psychology colleagues.

So what is to be made of all this? One interpretation of these developments is that they represent clinical psychology's genuine attempt to initiate collaborative work with health psychology, rather than a defensive manoeuvre on its part. It is apparent, nevertheless, that the rise of health psychology over the last two decades has engendered a reaction of some sort from clinical psychology, whether non-defensive or otherwise in kind, which is not necessarily to the formers' advantage.

Perhaps such conflation of the two sub-disciplines is unlikely to be a problem in the future, with the Society's 'Division of Health Psychology' stipulating strict criteria for health psychology training, membership of the division and designation thereafter of appropriately qualified individuals as health psychologists. However, such criteria do not prevent researchers and students from routinely describing their research as that of 'health psychology'. Should a colleague, for example, who conducts research about the beneficial effects of orienting around virtual reality environments on the spatial abilities of elderly people with mild dementia describe his or her research as that of 'health psychology'? Certainly there are implications for health and well-being but is such work truly that of 'health psychology', it falling within the remit of rehabilitation and the treatment of illness rather than the maintenance of health?

It is unquestioning use of Matarazzo's all-inclusive definition which has led to the problems so far described and to the discipline's relative inability to delineate a discrete frame of reference in which to work. This over-inclusivity is likely to prove detrimental to the long-term well-being of health psychology since such a broad definition does not allow for the subject area to distinguish itself clearly from other sub-disciplines, in particular from clinical psychology and behavioural medicine.

Indeed, it is this lack of a distinct self-identity that has led to confusion amongst non-health psychologists as to what health psychology is and is not. Clinical psychology's response to the lack of clarity has been to re-label areas of clinical practice that used to fall under the heading of 'behavioural medicine' as now 'health psychology' or 'clinical health psychology'. We have seen this in the content of the seven advertisements previously considered wherein health psychology is equated by clinical psychologists with topics such as pain management, HIV/AIDS, sexual health and managing chronic illness. Yet still further evidence of this is provided by Kennedy (1992) who reviewed the content of health psychology modules on UK post-graduate clinical psychology training courses. Under the guise of health psychology, 13 clinical psychology courses taught 'pain and pain management', 11 'cardiovascular diseases', 10 'psychology and medicine', six 'doctor–patient communication', 'HIV', 'preparation for surgery', and 'psychosomatic medicine', five taught about 'diabetes', 'gynaecology and obstetrics', 'psychological aspects of cancer', and 'substance abuse', four taught on 'coping with physical illness', and on 'terminal care', three taught about 'bereavement', 'eating disorders', 'health attitudes', 'physical disability', and 'stress', two included 'health promotion', and 'smoking' and one course taught about either 'ageing', 'burns', 'hypnosis', 'placebo effects', 'psychoneuroimmunology' (PNI), 'skin disorders', 'suicide' or 'risk behaviours'. What is notable about this survey are those topics which occurred frequently, for instance the behavioural medicine stalwart of pain management, and those which occurred relatively seldom, in particular health attitudes, stress, health promotion, psychoneuroimmunology, and risk behaviours. Ironically, the latter topics lie at the very heart of contemporary health psychology courses, such as the model post-graduate course proposed by Abraham (1998) at Sussex University. It is evident from Kennedy's (1992) list that for many clinical psychologists 'health psychology' merely has been a synonym for 'behavioural medicine'. But topics found in a health psychology curriculum are quite different from the emphasis found within the traditional domains of behavioural medicine. These are not simply interchangeable. So, what else might health psychology be, if not merely clinical psychology's re-branding of behavioural medicine, or indeed if not merely its compliant servant?

A Definitional Focus and Solution

It is to Matarazzo's (1980) article to which again we must turn for a more satisfactory answer to the question 'what is health psychology?' and for an answer which, if adopted, does not lead to a conflict of interest between clinical psychology and health psychology and which would resolve the conflation of terms that at present we are witnessing in the UK. A relatively much under-cited definition of what Matarazzo called 'behavioural health' appeared in the same 1980 article and constitutes a compelling alternative to the all-inclusive definition of health psychology as considered so far. 'Behavioural health' Matarazzo defined as a:

> ... new interdisciplinary subspecialty ... specifically concerned with the maintenance of health and the prevention of illness and dysfunction in currently healthy persons. (p. 807)

What is being suggested here then, is that health psychology reformulates itself in terms of this definition of 'behavioural health'. The emphasis is indeed upon health, upon the psychology of health promotion, and the maintenance of health, upon psychological processes involved in risk reduction and the primary prevention of illness, rather than upon the treatment of or recovery from illness. In this way, secondary and tertiary care remain the sole domains of clinical psychology, whilst health psychology truly becomes a psychology of health, rather than a psychology of illness, albeit the latter dichotomy being difficult to delineate in absolute terms. Such a focus would still hold out the opportunity to work in multidisciplinary settings with other psychologists but without confusion of roles and occupational identities. The presiding framework of a biopsychosocial approach to understanding those processes that underpin health and well-being would continue to be a hall-mark of this more focused and invigorated health psychology. Such propositions are consistent with those of Marks (1996) who likewise is critical of the 'clinical' and 'illness' foci of health psychology.

By defining its territory more precisely in this way, health psychology will have an improved chance of enduring as a discrete sub-discipline than it does currently. Over the last three years there have been movements within psychology which resonate very well with such a refocusing, specifically the recent emergence of so-called 'positive psychology' as espoused by Seligman (1997). For his American Psychological Association (APA) presidential year (1998), Seligman announced an initiative to re-focus psychology, saying that: '... we have done a lot of good repairing damage. The problem is, we've forgotten about one of our missions: making normal people's lives more fulfilling and productive' (1997, p. 35). This re-focusing on the conditions which support health and well-being is not just a passing fashion. 'Positive psychology' looks set to stay. Indeed, at the BPS 2000 annual conference there was a day-long symposium entitled 'Positive psychology: A new approach for the Millennium', organised by the Society's student members. This is the first time such a symposium has occurred in a psychology conference in Britain. Likewise, January 2000 saw the publication by the APA of a special issue of the *American Psychologist*, introduced by Seligman and Csikszentmihalyi, on 'happiness, excellence and optimal human functioning'. The issue features various evidence-based articles: one by Diener on subjective well-being, on optimism by Peterson, on socio-economic status, close relationships and happiness by Myers, on positive illusions by Taylor, and one on emotional states and physical health by Salovey and colleagues, amongst others.

So, the form and content of positive psychology is already in place. Much of that form and content is enshrined within Matarazzo's (1980) definition of behavioural health. If health psychology were to adopt such a definition, doubtless it would be met with a chorus of approval from 'positive psychology'. As positive psychology perhaps suggests, health psychology would do well to define its legitimate and singular domain of activity, both in terms of research and practice, as one focusing on the psychology of illness prevention and health promotion in already 'healthy' individuals – that is to say upon primary interventions, rather than on secondary, remedial or rehabilitative ones, the latter being addressed sufficiently already by clinical psychology colleagues. Such a move would clarify the scope and identity of health psychology and would secure its future. Indeed, there needs to be a separate psychology of 'health' and 'wellness' since health and quality of life are not just defined by the absence of illness. Further, it is not safe to assume that by studying those psychological processes which are implicated in the aetiology of illness and disease, that by default is being studied the opposite 'side' of those processes which are involved in the production of health and well-being. The psychology of health and the psychology of illness often involve quite different underlying processes. For example, a psychology of happiness cannot be built and extrapolated solely from an understanding of how daily hassles and aversive loss events are involved as precursors of low mood states – the simple absence of these phenomena is not a sufficient condition for the experience of high subjective well-being. Other factors must be considered for the origins of mental health to be understood.

Apart from the rise of positive psychology, there are other encouraging signs that a health psychology as described here is a viable proposition. For example, despite the predominance of generic introductory health psychology textbooks which espouse the virtues of Matarazzo's longer, overly-inclusive definition, there are two texts by UK authors which explore the relationship between psychology and preventive health, those by Bennett and Murphy (1997) and Pitts (1996). These texts provide us with exemplars and the beginnings of what a more focused and positive health psychology could be. Fortunately they are not lone voices calling for psychologists to involve themselves more frequently in primary prevention through the promotion of health behaviours. Kaplan (2000), for example, has written critically of an over-emphasis upon early diagnosis and treatment as a means of preventing illness progression and of insufficient attention being paid to the promotion of healthy life-styles. Further impetus for such a change in emphasis in health psychology is provided by ongoing government public health initiatives, as to be found for example in the UK Department of Health's (1999) policy document *Saving Lives: Our Healthier Nation*. Therein, the wish is expressed to '... improve the health of everyone' (p. 1), and the importance of '... health improvement as a key role for the NHS' (p. 2) is stressed. An allied document (Department of Health, 2000) also describes the setting up of so-called 'healthy living centres' which seek '... to promote health in its broadest sense' (p.1). This is an opportune time, then, for health psychology to develop and clarify its focus in the way that has been outlined here.

The apposite defining of health psychology is an important issue, for numerous reasons described in this chapter. The identity of health psychology is not a static and already decided issue. This is evidenced, for example, by the convening of the 'First International Conference on Critical and Qualitative Approaches to Health Psychology', held at St. John's University, Newfoundland, Canada in July 1999, the conference entitled 'Reconstructing Health Psychology'. It seems many health psychologists besides myself, then, think health psychology is in need of some reconstruction. Doubtless the goal of keeping separate the psychological domains of health and clinical psychology will be difficult to achieve, given predictable opposition and the inter-connected and over-lapping nature of the phenomena of which they are constituted. The success of such an endeavour, however, is necessary if health psychology is to thrive and endure as a discrete sub-discipline within psychology as a whole.

Note

This article is based on a paper presented at The British Psychological Society Annual Conference, Winchester, England, 13–16 April, 2000.

References

Abraham, C. (1998) Proposed MSc in health psychology. Brighton: University of Sussex.

Bennett, P. (2000) *Introduction to Clinical Health Psychology*. Buckingham: Open University Press.

Bennett, P. and Murphy, S. (1997) *Psychology and Health Promotion*. Buckingham: Open University Press.

British Psychological Society (1998) Division of Health Psychology, application pack. Leicester: British Psychological Society.

Cooper, C. (1986) Job distress: Recent research and the emerging role of the clinical occupational psychologist. *The Psychologist: Bulletin of the British Psychological Society, 39*, 325–331.

Department of Health (1999) Saving lives: *Our Healthier Nation*. (www.doh.gov.uk/ohn) London: UK Department of Health.

Department of Health (2000) *Healthy Living Centres*. (www.doh.gov.uk/hlc). London: UK Department of Health.

Edelman, R.J. (2000) *Psychosocial Aspects of the Health Care Process*. Harlow: Prentice Hall.

Kaplan, R.M. (2000) Two pathways to prevention. *American Psychologist, 55*, 4, 382–396.

Kennedy, P. (1992) Health psychology input to clinical psychology training courses. *Clinical Psychology Forum, 46*, 7–9.

Maes, S. and van Elderen, T. (1998) Health psychology and stress. In M. Eysenck (ed) *Psychology, An Integrated Approach*. Harlow: Addison Wesley Longman.

Marks, D. (1996) Health psychology in context. *Journal of Health Psychology, 1*, 1, 7–21.

Matarazzo, J. (1980) Behavioral health and behavioral medicine: Frontiers for a new health psychology. *American Psychologist, 35*, 807–817.

Ogden, J. (1996) *Health Psychology, A Textbook*. Buckingham: Open University Press.

Pitts, M. (1996) *The Psychology of Preventive Health*. London: Routledge.

Seligman, M. (1997) In R.A. Clay, 'Prevention is theme of the '98 presidential year'. *The Monitor*, December, p. 35. Washington DC: The American Psychological Association.

Seligman, M. and Csikszentmihalyi, M. (2000) Positive psychology: Special issue on happiness, excellence and optimal functioning. *American Psychologist, 55,* 1, 5–183.

Szasz, T. (1997) Address to the Critical Psychiatry Group, The Institute of Psychiatry, Denmark Hill, London, (13 November).

Taylor, S. (1999[1994]) *Health Psychology* (4th edn). New York: McGraw-Hill.

3 THE NEED FOR A NEW MEDICAL MODEL:
A Challenge for Biomedicine

George L. Engel

[...]

The Biomedical Model

The dominant model of disease today is biomedical, with molecular biology its basic scientific discipline. It assumes disease to be fully accounted for by deviations from the norm of measurable biological (somatic) variables. It leaves no room within its framework for the social, psychological, and behavioral dimensions of illness. The biomedical model not only requires that disease be dealt with as an entity independent of social behavior, it also demands that behavioral aberrations be explained on the basis of disordered somatic (biochemical or neurophysiological) processes. Thus the biomedical model embraces both reductionism, the philosophic view that complex phenomena are ultimately derived from a single primary principle, and mind–body dualism, the doctrine that separates the mental from the somatic. Here the reductionistic primary principle is physicalistic; that is, it assumes that the language of chemistry and physics will ultimately suffice to explain biological phenomena. From the reductionist viewpoint, the only conceptual tools available to characterize and experimental tools to study biological systems are physical in nature (4).

The biomedical model was devised by medical scientists for the study of disease As such it was a scientific model; that is, it involved a shared set of assumptions and rules of conduct based on the scientific method and constituted a blueprint for research. Not all models are scientific. Indeed, broadly defined, a model is nothing more than a belief system utilized to explain natural phenomena, to make sense out of what is puzzling or disturbing. The more socially disruptive or individually upsetting the phenomena, the more pressing the need of humans to devise explanatory systems. Such efforts at explanation constitute devices for social adaptation.

Disease *par excellence* exemplifies a category of natural phenomena urgently demanding explanation (5). As Fabrega has pointed out, "disease" in its generic sense is a linguistic term used to refer to a certain class of phenomena that members of all social groups, at all times in the history of man, have been exposed to. "When people of various intellectual and cultural persuasions use terms analogous to 'disease,' they have in mind, among other things, that the phenomena in question involve a person-centered, harmful, and undesirable deviation or discontinuity ... associated with impairment or discomfort" (5). Since the condition is not desired it gives rise to a need for corrective actions. The latter involve beliefs and explanations about disease as well as rules of conduct to rationalize treatment actions. These constitute socially adaptive devices to resolve, for the individual as well as for the society in which the sick person lives, the crises and uncertainties surrounding disease (6).

Such culturally derived belief systems about disease also constitute models, but they are not scientific models. These may be referred to as popular or folk models. As efforts at social adaptation, they contrast with scientific models, which are primarily designed to promote scientific investigation. The historical fact we have to face is that in modern Western society biomedicine not only has provided a basis for the scientific study of disease, it has also become our own culturally specific perspective about disease, that is, our folk model. Indeed the biomedical model is now the dominant folk model of disease in the Western world (5, 6).

In our culture the attitudes and belief systems of physicians are molded by this model long before they embark on their professional education, which in turn reinforces it without necessarily clarifying how its use for social adaptation contrasts with its use for scientific research. The biomedical model has thus become a cultural imperative, its limitations easily overlooked. In brief, it has now acquired the status of *dogma*. In science, a model is revised or abandoned when it fails to account adequately for all the data. A dogma, on the other hand, requires that discrepant data be forced to fit the model or be excluded. Biomedical dogma requires that all disease, including "mental" disease, be conceptualized in terms of derangement of underlying physical mechanisms. This permits only two alternatives whereby behaviour and disease can be reconciled: the *reductionist*, which says that all behavioral phenomena of disease must be conceptualized in terms of physico- chemical principles; and the *exclusionist*, which says that whatever is not capable of being so explained must be excluded from the category of disease. The reductionists concede that some disturbances in behavior belong in the spectrum of disease. They categorize these as mental diseases and designate psychiatry as the relevant medical discipline. The exclusionists regard mental illness as a myth and would eliminate psychiatry from medicine. Among physicians and psychiatrists today the reductionists are the true believers, the exclusionists are the apostates, while both condemn as heretics those who dare to question the ultimate truth of the biomedical model and advocate a more useful model.

Historical Origins of the Reductionistic Biomedical Model

In considering the requirements for a more inclusive scientific medical model for the study of disease, an ethnomedical perspective is helpful (6). In all societies, ancient and modern, preliterate and literate, the major criteria for identification of disease have always been behavioral, psychological, and social in nature. Classically, the onset of disease is marked by changes in physical appearance that frighten, puzzle, or awe, and by alterations in functioning, in feelings, in performance, in behavior, or in relationships that are experienced or perceived as threatening, harmful, unpleasant, deviant, undesirable, or unwanted. Reported verbally or demonstrated by the sufferer or by a witness, these constitute the primary data upon which are based first-order judgments as to whether or not a person is sick (7). To such disturbing behavior and reports all societies typically respond by designating individuals and evolving social institutions whose primary function is to evaluate, interpret, and provide corrective measures (5, 6). Medicine as an institution and as a discipline, and physicians as professionals, evolved as one form of response to such social needs. In the course of history, medicine became scientific as physicians and other scientists developed a taxonomy and applied scientific methods to the understanding, treatment, and prevention of disturbances which the public first had designated as "disease" or "sickness."

Why did the reductionistic, dualistic biomedical model evolve in the West? Rasmussen identifies one source in the concession of established Christian orthodoxy to permit dissection of the human body some five centuries ago (8). Such a concession was in keeping with the Christian view of the body as a weak and imperfect vessel for the transfer of the soul from this world to the next. Not surprisingly, the Church's permission to study the human body included in tacit interdiction against corresponding scientific investigation of man's mind and behavior. For in the eyes of the Church these had more to do with religion and the soul and hence properly remained its domain. This compact may be considered largely responsible for the anatomical and structural base upon which scientific Western medicine eventually was to be built. For at the same time, the basic principle of the science of the day, as enunciated by Galileo, Newton, and Descartes, was analytical, meaning that entities to be investigated be resolved into isolable causal chains or units, from which it was assumed that the whole could be understood, both materially and conceptually, by reconstituting the parts. With mind–body dualism firmly established under the imprimatur of the Church, classical science readily fostered the notion of the body as a machine, of disease as the consequence of breakdown of the machine, and of the doctor's task as repair of the machine. Thus, the scientific approach to disease began by focusing in a fractional-analytic way on biological (somatic) processes and ignoring the behavioral and psycho-social. This was so even though in practice many physicians, at least until the beginning of the 20th century, regarded emotions as important for the development and course of disease. Actually, such arbitrary exclusion is an acceptable strategy in scientific research, especially when concepts and methods appropriate for the excluded areas are not yet available. But it becomes counterproductive when such strategy becomes policy and the area originally put aside for practical reasons is permanently excluded, if not forgotten altogether. The greater the success of the narrow approach the more likely is this to happen. The biomedical approach to disease has been successful beyond all expectations, but at a cost. For in serving as guideline and justification for medical care policy, biomedicine has also contributed to a host of problems, which I shall consider later.

Limitations of the Biomedical Model

We are now faced with the necessity and the challenge to broaden the approach to disease to include the psychosocial without sacrificing the enormous advantages of the biomedical approach. On the importance of the latter all agree, the reductionist, the exclusionist, and the heretic. In a recent critique of the exclusionist position, Kety put the contrast between the two in such a way as to help define the issues (9).

> According to the medical model, a human illness does not become a specific disease all at once and is not equivalent to it. The medical model of an illness is a process that moves from the recognition and palliation of symptoms to the characterization of a specific disease in which the etiology and pathogenesis are known and treatment is rational and specific.

Thus taxonomy progresses from symptoms, to clusters of symptoms, to syndromes, and finally to diseases with specific pathogenesis and pathology. This sequence accurately describes the successful application of the scientific method to the elucidation and the classification into discrete entities of disease in its generic sense (5, 6). The merit of such an approach needs no argument. What do require scrutiny are the distortions introduced by the reductionistic tendency to regard the specific disease as adequately, if not best, characterized in terms of the smallest isolable component having causal implications, for example, the biomedical; or even more critical, is the contention that the designation "disease" does not apply in the absence of perturbations at the biochemical level.

Kety approaches this problem by comparing diabetes mellitus and schizophrenia as paradigms of somatic and mental diseases, pointing out the appropriateness of the medical model for both.

> Both are symptom clusters or syndromes, on described by somatic and biochemical abnormalities, the other by psychological. Each may have many etiologies and shows a range of intensity from severe and debilitating to latent or borderline. There is also evidence that genetic and environmental influences operate in the development of both.

In this description, at least in reductionistic terms, the scientific characterization of diabetes is the more advanced in that it has progressed from the behavioral framework of symptoms to that of biochemical abnormalities. Ultimately, the reductionists assume schizophrenia will achieve a similar degree of resolution. In developing his position, Kety makes clear that he does not regard the genetic factors and biological processes in schizophrenia as are now known to exist (or may be discovered in the future) as the only important influences in its etiology. He insists that equally important is elucidation of "how experiential factors and their interactions with biological vulnerability make possible or prevent the development of schizophrenia." But whether such a caveat will suffice to counteract basic reductionism is far from certain.

The Requirements of a New Medical Model

To explore the requirements of a medical model that would account for the reality of diabetes and schizophrenia as human experiences as well as disease abstractions, let us expand Kety's analogy by making the assumption that a specific biochemical abnormality capable of being influenced pharmacologically exists in schizophrenia as well as in diabetes, certainly a plausible possibility. By obliging ourselves to think of patients with diabetes, a "somatic disease," and with schizophrenia, a "mental disease," in exactly the same terms, we will see more clearly how inclusion of somatic and psychosocial factors is indispensable for both: or more pointedly, how concentration on the biomedical and exclusion of the psychosocial distorts perspectives and even interferes with patient care.

In the biomedical model, demonstration of the specific biochemical deviation is generally regarded as a specific diagnostic criterion for the disease. Yet in terms of the human experience of illness, laboratory documentation may only indicate disease potential, not the actuality of the disease at the time. The abnormality may be present, yet the patient not be ill. Thus the presence of the biochemical defect of diabetes or schizophrenia at best defines a necessary but not a sufficient condition for the occurrence of the human experience of the disease, the illness. More accurately, the biochemical defect constitutes but one factor among many, the complex interaction of which ultimately may culminate in active disease or manifest illness (10). Nor can the biochemical defect be made to account for all of the illness, for full understanding requires additional concepts and frames of reference. Thus, while the diagnosis of diabetes is first suggested by certain core clinical manifestations, for example, polyuria, polydipsia, polyphagia, and weight loss, and is then confirmed by laboratory documentation of relative insulin deficiency, how these are experienced and how they are reported by any one individual, and how they affect him, all require consideration of psychological, social, and cultural factors, not to mention other concurrent or complicating biological factors. Variability in the clinical expression of diabetes as well as of schizophrenia, and in the individual experience and expression of these illnesses, reflects as much these other elements as it does quantitative variations in the specific biochemical defect.

Establishing a relationship between particular biochemical processes and the clinical data of illness requires a scientifically rational approach to behavioral and psychosocial data, for these are the terms in which most clinical phenomena are reported by patients. Without such, the reliability of observations and the validity of correlations will be flawed. It serves little to be able to specify a biochemical defect in schizophrenia if one does not know how to relate this to particular psychological and behavioral expressions of the disorder. The biomedical model gives insufficient heed to this requirement. Instead it encourages bypassing the patient's verbal account by placing greater reliance on technical procedures and laboratory measurements. In actuality the task is appreciably more complex than the biomedical model encourages one to believe. An examination of the correlations between clinical and laboratory data requires not only reliable methods of clinical data collection, specifically high-level interviewing skills, but also basic understanding of the psychological, social, and cultural determinants of how patients communicate symptoms of disease. For example, many verbal expressions derive from bodily experiences early in life, resulting in a significant degree of ambiguity in the language patients use to report symptoms. Hence the same words may serve to express primary psychological as well as bodily disturbances, both of which may coexist and overlap in complex ways. Thus, virtually each of the symptoms classically associated with diabetes may also be expressions of or reactions to psychological distress, just as ketoacidosis and hypoglycemia may induce psychiatric manifestations, including some considered characteristics of schizophrenia. The most essential skills of the physician involve the ability to elicit accurately and then analyse correctly the patient's verbal account of his illness experience. The biomedical model ignores both the rigor required to achieve reliability in the interview process and the necessity to analyse the meaning of the patients' report in psychological, social, and cultural as well as in anatomical, physiological, or biochemical terms (7).

Diabetes and schizophrenia have in common the fact that conditions of life and living constitute significant variables influencing the time of reported onset of the manifest disease as well as of variations in its course. In both conditions this results from the fact that psychophysiologic responses to life change may interact with existing somatic factors to alter susceptibility and thereby influence the time of onset, the severity, and the course of a disease. Experimental studies in animals amply document the role of early, previous, and current life experience in altering susceptibility to a wide variety of diseases even in the presence of a genetic predisposition (11). Cassel's demonstration of higher rates of ill health among populations exposed to incongruity between the demands of the social system in which they are living and working and the culture they bring with them provides another illustration among humans of the role of psychosocial variables in disease causation (*12*).

Psychological and social factors are also crucial in determining whether and when patients with the biochemical abnormality of diabetes or of schizophrenia come to view themselves or be viewed by others as sick. Still other factors of a similar nature influence whether or not and when any individual enters a health care system and becomes a patient. Thus, the biochemical defect may determine certain characteristics of the disease, but not necessarily the point in time when the person falls ill or accepts the sick role or the status of a patient.

"Rational treatment" (Kety's term) directed only at the biochemical abnormality does not necessarily restore the patient to health even in the face of documented correction or major alleviation of the abnormality. This is no less true for diabetes than it will be for schizophrenia when a biochemical defect is established. Other factors may combine to sustain patienthood even in the face of biochemical recovery. Conspicuously responsible for such discrepancies between correction of biological abnormalities and treatment outcome are psychological and social variables.

Even with the application of rational therapies, the behavior of the physician and the relationship between patient and physician powerfully influence therapeutic outcome for better or for worse. These constitute psychological effects which may directly modify the illness experience or indirectly affect underlying biochemical processes, the latter by virtue of interactions between psychophysiological reactions and biochemical processes implicated in the disease (*11*). Thus, insulin requirements of a diabetic patient may fluctuate significantly depending on how the patient perceives his relationship with his doctor. Furthermore, the successful application of rational therapies is limited by the physician's ability to influence and modify the patient's behavior in directions concordant with health needs. Contrary to what the exclusionists would have us believe, the physician's role is, and always has been, very much that of educator and psychotherapist. To know how to induce peace of mind in the patient and enhance his faith in the healing powers of his physician requires psychological knowledge and skills, not merely charisma. These too are outside the biomedical framework.

The Advantages of a Biopsychosocial Model

This list surely is not complete but it should suffice to document that diabetes mellitus and schizophrenia as paradigms of "somatic" and "mental" disorders are entirely analogous and, as Kety argues, are appropriately conceptualized within the framework of a medical model of disease. But the existing biomedical model does not suffice. To provide a basis for understanding the determinants of disease and arriving at rational treatments and patterns of health care, a medical model must also take into account the patient, the social context in which he lives, and the complementary system devised by society to deal with the disruptive effects of illness, that is, the physician role and the health care system. This requires a biopsychosocial model. Its scope is determined by the historic function of the physician to establish whether the person soliciting help is "sick" or "well"; and if sick, why sick and in which ways sick; and then to develop a rational program to treat the illness and restore and maintain health.

The boundaries between health and disease, between well and sick, are far from clear and never will be clear, for they are diffused by cultural, social, and psychological considerations. The traditional biomedical view, that biological indices are the ultimate criteria defining disease, leads to the present paradox that some people with positive laboratory findings are told that they are in need of treatment when in fact they are feeling quite well, while others feeling sick are assured that they are well, that is, they have no "disease" (5, 6). A biopsychosocial model which includes the patient as well as the illness would encompass both circumstances. The doctor's task is to account for the dysphoria and the dysfunction which lead individuals to seek medical help, adopt the sick role, and accept the status of patienthood. He must weigh the relative contributions of social and psychological as well as of biological factors implicated in the patient's dysphoria and dysfunction as well as in his decision to accept or not accept patienthood and with it the responsibility to cooperate in his own health care.

By evaluating all the factors contributing to both illness and patienthood, rather than giving primacy to biological factors alone, a biopsychosocial model would make it possible to explain why some individuals experience as "illness" conditions which others regard merely as "problems of living," be they emotional reactions to life circumstances or somatic symptoms. For from the individual's point of view his decision between whether he has a "problem of living" or is "sick" has basically to do with whether or not he accepts the sick role and seeks entry into the health care system, not with what, in fact, is responsible for his distress. Indeed, some people deny the unwelcome reality of illness by dismissing as "a problem of living" symptoms which may in actuality be indicative of a serious organic process. It is the doctor's, not the patient's, responsibility to establish the nature of the problem and to decide whether or not it is best handled in a medical framework. Clearly the dichotomy between "disease" and "problems of living" is by no means a sharp one, either for patient or for doctor.

When is Grief a Disease?

To enhance our understanding of how it is that "problems of living" are experienced as illness by some and not by others, it might be helpful to consider grief as a paradigm of such a borderline condition. For while grief has never been considered in a medical framework, a significant number of grieving people do consult doctors because of disturbing symptoms, which they do not necessarily relate to grief. Fifteen years ago I addressed this question in a paper entitled "Is grief a disease? A challenge for medical research" (*13*). Its aim too was to raise questions about the adequacy of the biomedical model. A better title might have been, "When is grief a disease?," just as one might ask when schizophrenia or when diabetes is a disease. For while there are some obvious analogies between grief and disease, there are also some important differences. But these very contradictions help to clarify the psychosocial dimensions of the biopsychosocial model.

Grief clearly exemplifies a situation in which psychological factors are primary; no preexisting chemical or physiological defects or agents need be invoked. Yet as with classic diseases, ordinary grief constitutes a discrete syndrome with a relatively predictable symptomatology which includes, incidentally, both bodily and psychological disturbances. It displays the autonomy typical of disease; that is, it runs its course despite the sufferer's efforts or wish to bring it to a close. A consistent etiologic factor can be identified, namely, a significant loss. On the other hand, neither the sufferer nor society has ever dealt with ordinary grief as an illness even though such expressions as "sick with grief" would indicate some connection in people's minds. And while every culture makes provisions for the mourner, these have generally been regarded more as the responsibility of religion than of medicine.

On the face of it, the arguments against including grief in a medical model would seem to be the more persuasive. In the 1961 paper I countered these by comparing grief to a wound. Both are natural responses to environmental trauma, one psychological, the other physical. But even at the time I felt a vague uneasiness that this analogy did not quite make the case. Now 15 years later a better grasp of the cultural origins of disease concepts and medical care systems clarifies the apparent inconsistency. The critical factor underlying man's need to develop folk models of disease, and to develop social adaptations to deal with the individual and group disruptions brought about by disease, has always been the victim's ignorance of what is responsible for his dysphoric or disturbing experience (*5, 6*). Neither grief nor a wound fits fully into that category. In both, the reasons for the pain, suffering, and disability are only too clear. Wounds or fractures incurred in battle or by accident by and large were self-treated or ministered to with folk remedies or by individuals who had acquired certain technical skills in such matters. Surgery developed out of the need for treatment of wounds and injuries and has different historical roots than medicine, which was always closer in origin to magic and religion. Only later in Western history did surgery and medicine merge as healing arts. But even from earliest times there were people who behaved as though grief-stricken, yet seemed not to have suffered any loss; and others who developed what for all the world looked like wounds or fractures, yet had not been subjected to any known trauma. And there were people who suffered losses whose grief deviated in one way or another from what the culture had come to accept as the normal course; and others whose wounds failed to heal or festered or who became ill even though the wound had apparently healed. Then, as now, two elements were crucial in defining the role of patient and physician and hence in determining what should be regarded as disease. For the patient it has been his not knowing why he felt or functioned badly or what to do about it, coupled with the belief or knowledge that the healer or physician did know and could provide relief. For the physician in turn it has been his commitment to his professional role as healer. From these have evolved sets of expectations which are reinforced by the culture, though these are not necessarily the same for patient as for physician.

A biopsychosocial model would take all of these factors into account. It would acknowledge the fundamental fact that the patient comes to the physician because either he does not know what is wrong or, if he does, he feels incapable of helping himself. The psychobiological unity of man requires that the physician accept the responsibility to evaluate whatever problems the patient presents and recommend a course of action, including referral to other helping professions. Hence the physician's basic professional knowledge and skills must span the social, psychological, and biological, for his decisions and actions on the patient's behalf involve all three. Is the patient suffering normal grief or melancholia? Are the fatigue and weakness of the woman who recently lost her husband conversion symptoms, psychophysiological reactions, manifestations of a somatic disorder, or a combination of these? The patient soliciting the aid of a physician must have confidence that the M.D. degree has indeed rendered that physician competent to make such differentiations.

A Challenge for Both Medicine and Psychiatry

The development of a biopsychosocial medical model is posed as a challenge for both medicine and psychiatry. For despite the enormous gains which have accrued from biomedical research, there is a growing uneasiness among the public as well as among physicians, and especially among the younger generation, that health needs are not being met and that biomedical research is not having a sufficient impact in human terms. This is usually ascribed to the all too obvious inadequacies of existing health care delivery systems. But this certainly is not a complete explanation, for many who do have adequate access to health care also complain that physicians are lacking in interest and understanding, are preoccupied with procedures, and are insensitive to the personal problems of patients and their families. Medical institutions are seen as cold and impersonal; the more prestigious they are as centers for biomedical research, the more common such complaints (14). Medicine's unrest derives from a growing awareness among many physicians of the contradiction between the excellence of their biomedical background on the one hand and the weakness of their qualifications in certain attributes essential for good patient care on the other (7).

Many recognize that these cannot be improved by working within the biomedical model alone.

The present upsurge of interest in primary care and family medicine clearly reflects disenchantment among some physicians with an approach to disease that neglects the patient. They are now more ready for a medical model which would take psychosocial issues into account. Even from within academic circles are coming some sharp challenges to biomedical dogmatism (*8, 15*). Thus Holman ascribes directly to biomedical reductionism and to the professional dominance of its adherents over the health care system such undesirable practices as unnecessary hospitalization, overuse of drugs, excessive surgery, and inappropriate Utilization of diagnostic tests. He writes, "While reductionism is a powerful tool for understanding, it also creates profound misunderstanding, when unwisely applied. Reductionism is particularly harmful when it neglects the impact of nonbiological circumstances upon biologic processes." And, "Some medical outcomes are inadequate not because appropriate technical interventions are lacking but because our conceptual thinking is inadequate" (*15*). How ironic it would be were psychiatry to insist on subscribing to a medical model which some leaders in medicine already are beginning to question.

Psychiatrists, unconsciously committed to the biomedical model and split into the warring camps of reductionists and exclusionists, are today so preoccupied with their own professional identity and status in relation to medicine that many are failing to appreciate that psychiatry now is the only clinical discipline within medicine concerned primarily with the study of man and the human condition. While the behavioral sciences have made some limited incursions into medical school teaching programs, it is mainly upon psychiatrists, and to a lesser extent clinical psychologists, that the responsibility falls to develop approaches to the understanding of health and disease and patient care not readily accomplished within the more narrow framework and with the specialized techniques of traditional biomedicine. Indeed, the fact is that the major formulations of more integrated and holistic concepts of health and disease proposed in the past 30 years have come not from within the biomedical establishment but from physicians who have drawn upon concepts and methods which originated within psychiatry, notably the psychodynamic approach of Sigmund Freud and psychoanalysis and the reaction-to-life-stress approach of Adolf Meyer and psychobiology (*16*). Actually, one of the more lasting contributions of both Freud and Meyer has been to provide frames of reference whereby psychological processes could be included in a concept of disease. Psychosomatic medicine – the term itself a vestige of dualism – became the medium whereby the gap between the two parallel but independent ideologies of medicine, the biological and the psychosocial, was to be bridged. Its progress has been slow and halting, not only because of the extreme complexities intrinsic to the field itself, but also because of unremitting pressures, from within as well as from without, to conform to scientific methodologies basically mechanistic and reductionistic in conception and inappropriate for many of the problems under study. Nonetheless, by now a sizable body knowledge, based on clinical and experimental studies of man and animals has accumulated. Most, however, remains unknown to the general medical public and to the biomedical community and is largely ignored in the education of physicians. The recent solemn pronouncement by an eminent biomedical leader (2) that "the emotional content of organic medicine [has been] exaggerated" and "psychosomatic medicine is on the way out" can only be ascribed to the blinding effects of dogmatism.

The fact is that medical school have constituted unreceptive if not hostile environments for those interested in psychosomatic research and teaching, and medical journals have all too often followed a double standard in accepting papers dealing with psychosomatic relationships (*17*). Further, much of the work documenting experimentally in animals the significance of life circumstances or change in altering susceptibility to disease has been done by experimental psychologists and appears in psychology journals rarely read by physicians or basic biomedical scientists (*11*).

General Systems Theory Perspective

The struggle to reconcile the psychosocial and the biological in medicine has had its parallel in biology, also dominated by the reductionistic approach of molecular biology. Among biologists too have emerged advocates of the need to develop holistic as well as reductionistic explanations of life processes, to answer the "why?" and the "what for?" as well as the "how?" (*18, 19*). Von Bertalanffy, arguing the need for a more fundamental reorientation in scientific perspectives in order to open the way to holistic approaches more amenable to scientific inquiry and conceptualization, developed general systems theory (*20*). This approach, by treating sets of related events collectively as systems manifesting functions and properties on the specific level of the whole, has made possible recognition of isomorphies across different levels of organization, as molecules, cells, organs, the organism, the person, the family, the society, or the biosphere. From such isomorphies can be developed fundamental laws and principles that operate commonly at all levels of organization, as compared to those which are unique for each. Since systems theory holds that all levels of organization are linked to each other in a hierarchical relationship so that change in one affects change in the others, its adoption as a scientific approach should do much to mitigate the holist-reductionist dichotomy and improve communication across scientific disciplines. For medicine, systems theory provides a conceptual approach suitable not only for the proposed biopsychosocial concept of disease but also for studying disease and medical care as interrelated processes (*10, 21*). If and when a general-systems approach becomes part of the basic scientific and philosophic education of future physicians and medical scientists, a greater readiness to encompass a biopsychosocial perspective of disease may be anticipated.

Biomedicine as Science and as Dogma

In the meantime, what is being and can be done to neutralize the dogmatism of biomedicine and all the undesirable social and scientific consequences that flow therefrom? How can a proper balance be established between the fractional-analytic and the natural history approaches, both so integral for the work of the physician and the medical scientist (22)? How can the clinician be helped to understand the extent to which his scientific approach to patients represents a distinctly "human science," one in which "reliance is on the integrative powers of the observer of a complex non-replicable event and on the experiments that are provided by history and by animals living in particular ecological settings," as Margaret Mead puts it (23)? The history of the rise and fall of scientific dogmas throughout history may give some clues. Certainly mere emergence of new findings and theories rarely suffices to overthrow well-entrenched dogmas. The power of vested interests, social, political, and economic, are formidable deterrents to any effective assault on biomedical dogmatism. The delivery of health care is a major industry, considering that more than 8 percent of our national economic product is devoted to health (2). The enormous existing and planned investment in diagnostic and therapeutic technology alone strongly favors approaches to clinical study and care of patients that emphasize the impersonal and the mechanical (24). For example, from 1967 to 1972 there was an increase of 33 percent in the number of laboratory tests conducted per hospital admission (25). Planning for systems of medical care and their financing is excessively influenced by the availability and promise of technology, the application and effectiveness of which are often used as the criteria by which decisions are made as to what constitutes illness and who qualifies for medical care. Thus frustration of those who find what they believe to be their legitimate health needs inadequately met by too technologically oriented physicians is generally misinterpreted by the biomedical establishment as indicating "unrealistic expectations" on the part of the public rather than being recognized as reflecting a genuine discrepancy between illness as actually experienced by the patient and as it is conceptualized in the biomedical model (26). The professionalization of biomedicine constitutes still another formidable barrier (8, 15). Professionalization has engendered a caste system among health care personnel and a peck order concerning what constitute appropriate areas for medical concern and care, with the most esoteric disorders at the top of the list. Professional dominance "has perpetuated prevailing practices, deflected criticisms, and insulated the profession from alternate views and social relations that would illuminate and improve health care" (15, p. 21). Holman argues, not unconvincingly, that "the Medical establishment is not primarily engaged in the disinterested pursuit of knowledge and the translation of that knowledge into medical practice; rather in significant part it is engaged in special interest advocacy, pursuing and preserving social power" (15, p. 11).

Under such conditions it is difficult to see how reforms can be brought about. Certainly contributing another critical essay is hardly likely to bring about any major changes in attitude. The problem is hardly new, for the first efforts to introduce a more holistic approach into the undergraduate medical curriculum actually date back to Adolph Meyer's program at Johns Hopkins, which was initiated before 1920 (27). At Rochester, a program directed to medical students and to physicians during and after their residency training, and designed to inculcate psychosocial knowledge and skills appropriate for their future work as clinicians or teachers, has been in existence for 30 years (28). While difficult to measure outcome objectively, its impact, as indicated by a questionnaire on how students and graduates view the issues involved in illness and patient, care, appears to have been appreciable (29). In other schools, especially in the immediate post-World War II period, similar efforts were launched, and while some flourished briefly, most soon faded away under the competition of more glamorous and acceptable biomedical careers. Today, within many medical schools there is again a revival of interest among some faculty, but they are few in number and lack the influence, prestige, power, and access to funding from peer review groups that goes with conformity to the prevailing biomedical structure.

Yet today, interest among students and young physicians is high, and where learning opportunities exist they quickly overwhelm the available meager resources. It would appear that given the opportunity, the younger generation is very ready to accept the importance of learning more about the psychosocial dimensions of illness and health care and the need for such education to be soundly based on scientific principles. Once exposed to such an approach, most recognize how ephemeral and insubstantial are appeals to humanism and compassion when not based on rational principles. They reject as simplistic the notion that in past generations doctors understood their patients better, a myth that has persisted for centuries (30). Clearly, the gap to be closed is between teachers ready to teach and students eager to learn. But nothing will change unless or until those who control resources have the wisdom to venture off the beaten path of exclusive reliance on biomedicine as the only approach to health care. The proposed biopsychosocial model provides a blueprint for research, a framework for teaching, and a design for action in the real world of health care. Whether it is useful or not remains to be seen. But the answer will not be forthcoming if conditions are not provided to do so. In a free society, outcome will depend upon those who have the courage to try new paths and the wisdom to provide the necessary support.

Summary

The dominant model of disease today is biomedical, and it leaves no room within its framework for the social, psychological, and behavioral dimensions of illness. A biopsychosocial model is proposed that provides a blueprint for research, a framework for teaching, and a design for action in the real world of health care.

References and Notes

1   [...]
2   *RF Illustrated*, 3, 5 (1976).
3   [..]
4   R. Rosen, in *The Relevance of General Systems Theory*, E. Laszlo, Ed. (Braziller, New York, 1972), p. 45.
5   H. Fabrega, *Arch. Gen Psychiatry* **32**, 1501 (1972).
6   H. Fabrega, *Science*, **189**, 969 (1975).
7   G. L. Engel, *Ann. Intern. Med.* **78**, 587 (1973).
8   H. Rasmussen, *Pharos* **38**, 53 (1975).
9   S. Kety, *Am. J. Psychiatry* **131**, 957 (1974).
10 G. L. Engel, *Perspect. Biol. Med.* **3**, 459 (1960).
11 R. Ader, in *Ethology and Development*, S. A. Barnett, Ed. (Heinemann, London, 1973), p. 37; G. L. Engel, *Gastroenterology* **67**, 1085 (1974).
12 J. Cassel, *Am. J. Public Health* **54**, 1482 (1964).
13 G. L. Engel, *Psychosom. Med.* **23**, 18 (1961).
14 R. S. Duff and A. B. Hollingshead, *Sickness and Society* (Harper & Row, New York, 1968).
15 H. R. Holman, *Hosp. Pract.* **11**, 11 (1976).
16 K. Menninger, *Ann. Intern. Med.* **29**, 318 (1948); J. Romano, *J. Am. Med. Assoc.* **143**, 409 (1950); G. L. Engel, *Midcentury Psychiatry*, R. Grinker, Ed. (Thomas, Springfield, Ill., 1933), p. 33; H. G. Wolff, Ed, *An Outline of Man's Knowledge* (Doubleday, New York, 1960), p. 41; G. L. Engle, *Psychological Development in Health and Disease* (Saunders, Philadelphia, 1962).
17 G. L. Engel and L. Salzman, *N. Engl. J. Med.* **288**, 44 (1973).
18 R. Dubos, *Mirage of Health* (Harper & Row, New York, 1959); *Reason Awake* (Columbia Univ. Press, New York, 1970); E. Mayr, in *Behavior and Evolution*, A. Roe and G. G. Simpson, Eds (Yale Univ. Press, New Haven, Conn., 1958), p. 341; *Science* 134, 1501 (1961); *Am. Sci.* 62, 650 (1974); J. T. Bonner, *On Development. The Biology of Form* (Harvard Univ. Press, Cambridge, Mass., 1974); G. G. Simpson, *Science* **139**, 81 (1963).
19 R. Dubos, *Man Adapting* (Yale Univ. Press, New Haven, Conn., 1965).
20 L. von Bertalanffy, *Problems of Life* (Wiley, New York, 1952); *General Systems Theory* (Braziller, New York, 1968). See also E. Laszlo, *The Relevance of General Systems Theory* (Braziller, New York, 1972); *The Systems View of the World* (Braziller, New York, 1972); Dubos (*19*).
21 K. Menninger, *The Vital Balance* (Viking, New York, 1963); A. Sheldon, in *Systems and Medical Care*, A. Sheldon, F. Baker, C. P. McLaughlin, Eds (MIT Press, Cambridge, Mass., 1970), p. 84; H. Brody, *Perspect. Biol. Med.* **16**, 71 (1973).
22 G. L. Engel, in *Physiology, Emotion, and Psychosomatic Illness*, R. Porter and J. Knight, Eds (Elsevier-Excerpta Medica, Amsterdam, 1972), p. 384.
23 M. Mad, *Science* **191**, 903 (1976).
24 G. L. Engel, *J. Am. Med. Assoc.* **236**, 861 (1976).
25 J. M. McGinnis, *J. Med. Educ.* **51**, 602 (1976).

26 H. Fabrega and P. R. Manning, *Psychosom. Med.* **35**, 223 (1973).

27 A. Meyer, *J. Am. Med. Assoc.* **69**, 861 (1917).

28 A. H. Schmale, W. A. Greene, F. Reichsman, M. Kehoe G. L. Engel, *Adv. Psychosom. Med.* 4, 4 (1964); G. L. Engel, *J. Psychosom. Res.* **11**, 77 (1967); L. Young, *Ann. Intern. Med.* **83**, 728 (1975).

29 G. L. Engel, *J. Nerv. Ment. Dis.* **154**, 159 (1972); *Univ. Rochester Med. Rev.* (winter 1971–1972), p. 10.

30 G. L. Engel, *Pharos* **39**, 127 (1976).

4 THEORETICAL TENSIONS IN BIOPSYCHOSOCIAL MEDICINE

David Armstrong

The concept of biopsychosocial medicine was advanced by Engel [1] in 1977 and has since achieved wide currency. As developed by Engel it was intended to save psychiatrists, who were then (and largely still are) torn between pursuing a biological reductionist model of mental illness, and hence becoming manqué neurologists, and a more psychosocial approach which lost psychiatry its historic, if tenuous, relationship with medicine by endorsing mental illness as categories of 'problems of living'. By and large the rest of the world has wisely declined to get involved with the identity problems of psychiatry but in this instance the concept of biopsychosocial medicine seems to have been taken up with alacrity by many outside the troubled waters of psychiatry and equated with a more general notion of humanist medicine. The Science Citation Index alone records over 250 papers since 1977 referencing the original Engel article. Does this mean that we have discovered, in Engel's words, 'a new medical model'? Does it mean, as later commentators have argued, that biopsychosocial medicine is the new concept to underpin a truly unified medicine of man? This chapter argues, alas, that these optimistic claims are ill-founded; specifically, Engel's original formulation is found to be grossly medicocentric and sociologically naive. Finally a case is advanced, not for seeing biopsychosocial medicine as an opportunity for social science to merge with medicine, but for social science to treat the advent of biopsychosocial medicine seriously as a topic warranting study and explanation in its own right.

Engel's Model

The corner-stone of Engel's model is systems theory which he borrows from biology to provide the framework to integrate the biological, psychological and social domains. Thus, each apparently separate discipline is seen to operate at one level of a more general hierarchy of inter-related levels. Recognition of this hierarchy enables identification of related events in different levels and so the development of 'fundamental laws and principles that operate commonly at all levels of organisation, as compared to those which are unique for each' (p. 134). Within such a schema the reductionist and holistic components of medicine could therefore, he claimed, be integrated, and biomedicine broadened from its traditional narrow purview 'to include the psychosocial without sacrificing the enormous advantages of the biomedical approach' (p. 131).

Why should biomedicine need broadening? It had in Engel's view been 'successful beyond all expectations', but there had been a cost in terms of a 'host of problems' which included 'such undesirable practices as unnecessary hospitalisation, overuse of drugs, excessive surgery, and inappropriate use of diagnostic tests' (p. 134). Besides, psychiatry needed rescuing.

In addition Engel identified some 'consumer' concerns. He wrote of 'a growing uneasiness among the public … that health needs are not being met and that biomedical research is not having a sufficient impact in human terms'. Physicians lacked 'interest and understanding, are preoccupied with procedures, and are insensitive to the personal problems of patients and their families. Medical institutions are seen as cold and impersonal' (p. 134).

Whereas 'internal' problems within biomedicine are no doubt containable, consumer dissatisfaction is a more serious worry. If consumers want a more psychosocial approach then they might (and indeed in many instances have already done so) turn to 'alternative' practitioners who may be more sympathetic to a psychosocial perspective. There are two ways for medicine to handle such a challenge. One is to 'marginalise' the alternative: historically this is the usual strategy employed to deal with 'unorthodox' systems of medicine, and indeed in more recent years has formed a large part of the approach to the behavioural sciences as any medicine school curriculum will illustrate. The other way is to 'incorporate' the potential threat, and in systems theory we surely see a clear example of this strategy. Medicine is under fire for failing to address the psychosocial domain; if medicine continues treating the psychosocial at arms length it therefore risks its historical ascendancy in health care provision; the solution then is biopsychosocial medicine which at once both encompasses and neutralises any threat, all in the name of a progressive model of illness. In effect, far from systems theory creating a 'new model' based on an integrated hierarchy, it would seem to offer both a strengthening of traditional biological, reductionist medicine and, at the same time, ensure the continued subsidiary status of the social sciences.

Systems theory works well for this purpose because it maintains the dominance of the biological over the social; as Day puts it, 'the biopsychosocial approach is the study of biological paradigms within social parameters' [2]. But in addition to placing the biological at the head of the disciplinary table, systems theory neutralises any potential challenge from an unruly social science at the bottom by removing conflict from the agenda. Disciplines at different levels of the systems hierarchy might have different and conflicting explanations of the same phenomenon but rather than one explanation being in a position to challenge another they are reduced to simply different levels of analysis. Thus, for example, labelling, life event, psychoanalytic and organic theories of mental illness become not alternatives but different, though compatible, 'levels' of explanation. No wonder that Engel sees bio-psychosocial medicine as resolving the endemic conflicts in psychiatry – but at what price?

Since the demise of structural-functionalism the social sciences have seemed reasonably content with conflict, above all perhaps because conflict reveals the workings of power. Attempts to foist a theoretical framework on the field of health and illness which apparently dissipates conflict is there-fore surely an expression of power. The direct beneficiaries – aside from Engel's wandering psychiatrists – would seem to be proponents of the bio-medical paradigm. Not unexpectedly then biopsychosocial medicine has had support from psychiatrists, 'liberal' physicians, and social scientists based in medical schools desperate for a way of reconciling their craft with the dominant ideology of biomedicine. But what does biopsychosocial medicine offer social science?

The Psychosocial Chorus

The core tenet of biomedicine is the reduction of illness of the 'lesion'. The lesion is that skin-encapsulated malfunction in the workings of the body, diagnosed and diagnosable by medicine thereby giving biomedicine its status and legitimacy in modern society. Is there any challenge to these central assumptions in the 'new medical model'?

It is clear that within the biopsychosocial perspective medicine's hege-mony is not negotiable in so far as the patient is concerned. The fact that ill-ness is localised to the lesion inside the body has always ensured medical dominance in biomedicine because only the physician can have access to this truth [3]. Under the new regime the patient would remain, as under the old one, subservient to medicine. The fact, as Engel expressed it, that patients remained 'incapable of helping themselves' (p. 133) would mean that what-ever the claims of the new model there would always be a central role for the hidden lesion which only medicine was competent to identify. Engel was in no doubt about it: 'It is the doctor's, not the patient's, responsibility to estab-lish the nature of the problem and to decide whether, or not it is best handled in a medical framework' (p. 133).

But what of the supposed 'liberating' effect of the psychosocial perspec-tive? Engel offered six, somewhat overlapping, ways in which the psycho-social should be allied to the biological to constitute his 'new model'. First, because the lesion itself did not create sufficient conditions for the patient's experience of disease, it was important to know how the 'variabil-ity in the clinical expression' of disease could affect patient perceptions. Thus patients with the same underlying disease/lesion, such as diabetes or schizophrenia (to use Engel's examples), respond according to both the 'quantitative variations in the specific defect' (p. 132) and on individual psychosocial differences.

A second and related point was that because diagnosis depends on inference from the clinical manifestations of the lesion to the lesion itself, the process required 'not only reliable methods of clinical data collection ... but also basic understanding of the psychological, social and cultural determinants of how patients communicate symptoms of disease' (p. 132). In other words the psychosocial domain was an important factor in the identification of the biological 'real' basis of illness.

The third way in which the psychosocial might link with the pathological was through its effects on 'the time of onset, the severity, and the course of a disease'. The core of disease was still the lesion but its precursors could be psychosocial, though not exclusively. 'Life changes' could interact with somatic factors to bring about the disease. Equally it was psychosocial factors which were clearly important in showing the ill person that they were truly sick; and the corollary was that the patient might not be returned to full health even in the face of correction or major alleviation of the underlying biochemical abnormality because of the patient's insistence on holding onto patient status. Finally, even though treatment would be addressed to the underlying lesion, psychosocial factors could intrude, through the effects of the physician–patient relationship on the outcome.

In each of these instances the role of psychosocial factors is clearly circumscribed. At no point do they challenge the dominance of the medical practitioner nor undermine or threaten the supremacy of the reductionist doctrine of the lesion contained in the biomedical model. Indeed, on the contrary, they strengthen biomedicine by ensuring that the patient – so often an awkward and unpredictable factor in the smooth operation of clinical work – is successfully 'managed'. The patient would no longer be an impediment to diagnosis or treatment, no longer a malingerer or a recidivist when it came to compliance, but a helpful assistant to the clinician's application of a regime of biomedicine.

Critical Sociology

Engel's vision was of a social science subservient to the biomedical enterprise because he could not see that the 'lesion' or biological abnormality was anything but the very truth of illness. However, he seemed unaware of sociological arguments which challenged this version of illness.

First, the whole context of Engel's discussion of biomedicine is the belief in 'science'. Models are held to be 'scientific', or not scientific, the former being based on the (unspecified) 'scientific method'. Indeed the history of medicine – in the finest Whiggish tradition – is the emancipation of scientific enlightenment as biomedicine 'evolved' with the retreat of retrograde practices such as the Church's proscription of human dissection. Today he sees biomedicine beset by 'dogmatism' which prevents it from reforming.

The solution is education in the psychosocial dimensions of illness and health care 'soundly based on scientific principles' (p. 135).

The self-congratulatory history which Engel draws upon is the norm in those hagiographic accounts of the past which physicians both write and repeat, but it completely ignores more critical work over the last 20 years or so which sharply test the credibility of these 'progressive' histories. Engel seems unaware of the Kuhnian revolution in the philosophy of science which has transformed the supposed distinction between science and non-science – though arguably even according to more conventional Popperian accounts Engel's distinction is hardly sustainable. Engel also seems unaware of work in the sociology of the professions which would equate the rise of the modern medical profession and the consequent triumph of biomedicine as the result of political manoeuvring and monopoly practices [4, 5]. In this scenario 'science' is simply the legitimating agent: thus when biomedicine extended its power in the past it was, for Engel, the triumph of science. Now, when it does not do what Engel thinks it should be doing then it becomes the vested interests of dogmatism, which in their turn have to be fought with yet more science.

Second, and following on from his sanitised history, is Engel's fervent belief that biomedicine has finally identified the core of illness in the form of the biological lesion. Certainly biomedicine has until now ignored the psychosocial causes, reactions to and consequences of illness but these, in the new model, can simply be tacked on to a more fundamental truth, the biological basis of disease. This is sociologically naive because Engel fails to realise that the very concept of disease, in being evaluative, is a reflection not of biological norms but of social ones.

Engel writes of the disease lesion being an 'abnormality' in the body. But how does biomedicine – or indeed any medicine – know what is abnormal? Of course it is taught, it is recognised, it is in the textbooks. But how did it receive that recognition?

The problem is the meaning of 'normal'. Biomedicine tends to assume that 'normal' is used in the statistical sense as referring to the usual or common. This might fit with many diseases which are, in frequency, relatively rare, but it fails to explain those 'disease' processes such as atherosclerosis which are endemic in Western societies, nor, more seriously, which biological parameters can be legitimately assessed for how common or rare they are. In other words, looking at the body as a multiplicity of biological structures and processes, there must be hundreds if not thousands of criteria by which any individual is in the 'abnormal' group – after all everyone is supposedly biologically unique – whether it is the number of cells in their left adrenal gland or the shape of their nose. But clearly not all these 'abnormalities' represent diseases, far from it, only those which are said to interfere with proper functioning. So how is 'proper' functioning determined? Either one has a direct line to heaven or one must rely on *social* assessment of what is expected from individuals in our society. In short, the notion of abnormality embedded in disease is not the statistical but the social or ideal. Thus, for example, whether certain biological changes are to be labelled as pathological/disease or involution/ageing simply depends on whether they are socially expected and accepted as inevitable or whether they are believed inappropriate by our current standards [6]. Perhaps Sedgewick's example is the best illustration that the disease category is underpinned by social purposes and evaluations: fungus is a disease of wheat but if we wished to eat the fungus rather than the wheat then its disease status would disappear [7].

There is of course nothing new in this form of analysis. Indeed it goes back to at least Freidson's 1970 observation that disease may or may not have a basis in biological reality, but it always has a basis in social reality [8]. This insight has since been developed in medical sociology [9], and even second year medical students are taught it [10], but Engel would appear to be too rooted in his biomedical paradigm to see that the social could be anything but a bit-player on the stage of medicine.

The argument that disease categories are fundamentally social in basis applies of course to any system of medicine, not only biomedicine. In essence all cultures will make (social) evaluations of health/illness processes to identify 'diseases' or their equivalents. Then these diseases have to be 'explained' [11]. To judge from historical and cross-cultural evidence there are various forms this explanation can take. Biomedicine, and the primacy of the internal lesion, therefore provide another set of sociological puzzles: how is it that for the last 200 years we have opted for reductionist biomedicine as the explanatory framework of illness, and what are the effects of this strategy?

The Clinico-pathological Correlation

In his account of the emergence of biomedicine at the close of the 18th century Foucault identified the 'discovery' of the clinico-pathological correlation as the central feature of the new medicine [12]. This correlation was based on the supposed link between the biological lesion in the body's tissues and its manifestation in the 'clinical' realm. Thus inflammation in the intestines produced pain and tenderness which could be identified 'outside' the body through, on the one hand, the patient's self-reported experiences, and on the other, the doctor's skills at reading the indications of hidden disease. The end of the 18th century therefore saw the emergence of two core concepts of biomedicine, the symptom/history and the sign/examination. By identifying the symptom (say, pain) through taking the history, and by eliciting the sign (say, tenderness) through the techniques of clinical examination, the doctor was able to infer the presence of the lesion (in this case inflammation) because of the supposed correlation between inflammation and pain/tenderness.

The lesion, whose presence was required to complete the correlation, was usually inside the body. Rarely it could be directly visualised lying on the skin, sometimes it could be seen via one of the body's orifices by means of one of the 'scopes' which were rapidly invented during the 19th century for just this purpose. However, the major source of knowledge about the lesion came from opening the body up. In part this fell to the surgeons who were frequently able to visualise the pathology which they had only been able to infer from the outside. But in the main it was in the post-mortem room that the truth of illness was established. The post-mortem was the crucial component in the new clinico-pathological correlation. Evidence for the correctness of the clinical inference could only be found after death. Thus the post-mortem room with its principal actors of clinician and pathologist was the fulcrum of knowledge production, both in the early 19th century and within biomedicine today.

There are in fact grounds, as suggested below, for arguing that the 'correlation' between the pathological and the clinical is not as clear-cut as medicine might imagine. In part, whether there is or is not a relationship between the Pathological and the clinical is an empirical issue; but it is also a question about the social practices which govern the production of the correlation. Invited to a 'straight-forward' post-mortem as a part of his research into suicide, Atkinson observed the pathologist examining the heart of the deceased very closely [13]. 'I didn't realise you were looking for anything in particular,' he said, 'what are you expecting to find?' 'The cause of death, I've got to have a cause of death', replied the coroner's officer. At this moment the pathologist looked up from his examination of the heart: 'Well, I'd like to give you (medical) "shock" … because the shock of the operation is what really stopped his heart beating, but the coroner doesn't like "shock" does he?' The coroner's officer confirmed that this was true, to which the pathologist responded 'I could give you "heart failure" then – how would that be?' 'That'll do me fine', was the reply (p. 98). In fact this process of fabricating disease entities was precisely what Atkinson's namesake observed in the wards of Edinburgh medical school where the immutability of the clinico-pathological correlation was displayed in a masterly exhibition of theatre [14]. Disease is a blur in the experience of medicine but is made concrete, tangible and exact by its social practices.

It is this process of creating and maintaining an interrelationship between the clinical and the pathological which is of sociological interest. On the one hand there is experience, subjective, casual, unreliable, imprecise; on the other hand its supposed pathological correlate, objective, ordered, real, analysable, separate. In this sense the pathological/biological is no more than the matrix on which and into which clinical experience is organised. The 'lesion' acts as a template on which to rationalise the myriad and confusing phenomena of the social state we call illness. The clinico-pathological correlation which sustains that reality is itself an artefact of social life which both links and prioritises levels of experience. The medical textbook therefore is a remarkable document: it has managed to inscribe the ephemeral social into the apparently timeless biological.

Psychosocial Analyses

What then should be the role of social science in relation to biomedicine and its young offspring, biopsychosocial medicine? First, surely it should not become hopelessly embroiled with one historically specific model of illness, particularly one which places the biological lesion at the core of illness. Indeed, as this chapter might suggest, there are probably many 'political' assumptions in biomedicine and biopsychosocial medicine which merit further investigation. Second, if social science is to get involved in questions about the status of illness it would seem more promising to explore those anomalies of the biomedical paradigm when the clinico-pathological correlation fails to explain illness.

In evaluating screening programmes epidemiologists use a two-by-two table to show their results and calculate the test's sensitivity and specificity. The cells of this table are constructed around the results of the screening test under study and the reference test against which it will be evaluated (Figure 4.1).

The four cells of the table contain true and false positives and true and false negatives. Now exactly the same table can be used to show the clinico-pathological correlation, using the presence or absence of pathology as the reference test and the presence or absence of clinical indicators as the screening test. Constructing such a table for a specific disease such as ischaemic heart disease produces a picture like this (Figure 4.2).

Each of these cells can be used to show a different role for social science in relation to medicine. First, there are the 'true positive', those 'classical' cases in which both clinical and pathological phenomena are reported to occur concurrently: this is the stuff of biomedicine, and where biopsychosocial medicine might ameliorate some of the excesses of biomedicine. But in terms of numbers, taking either deaths or illnesses, it is probably the smallest cell.

The next group, the 'false negatives' are those who, despite having the supposed biological lesion, show no 'clinical' manifestations of it. It has been reported that at least a quarter of all heart attacks are of the 'silent' type [15]: the real figure is probably much larger given the difficulty of identifying them, especially the mild ones. How should social science treat this category? It might be the basis of a direct challenge to the integrity of biomedicine. Is the supposed clinico-pathological correlation simply an artefact? In which case how is it constructed and maintained in ongoing clinical practice? What is the relationship between 'internal states' and experience? Certainly there is increasing evidence that the experience of 'symptoms' is not anything like as highly correlated with internal biochemical state as once believed [16]. Exploration of the clinico-pathological correlation in this way may lead to new ways of seeing illness, while at the same time undermining the credibility of the clinico-pathological correlation.

The other group who do not fit the classical clinico-pathological correlation are the 'false negatives', those patients who experience signs and symptoms of, say, ischaemic heart disease but in whom there is no

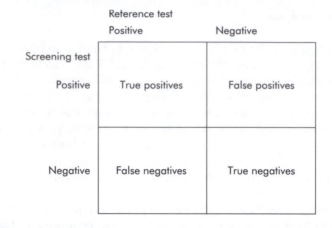

FIGURE 4.1

Clinicot picture

	Positive	Negative
Present	True positives: real ischaemic heart disease	False positives: pseudo – disease
Negative	False negatives: silent coronaries	True negatives: healthy

FIGURE 4.2

apparent pathological lesion. In many cases of angina, often in young men, cardiography fails to reveal a heart lesion [17]. These people are often quite debilitated by their symptoms and can thus fairly be said to be 'sick'; however biomedicine can offer them very little ('at least it is not real disease'). This phenomenon, of symptoms without a lesion, would seem to be quite common across a range of so-called diseases. In part, understanding these illnesses, as with 'silent' disease, requires investigation of the nature of bodily experiences and their psychological and social concomitants, but again it would need a critical or at least sceptical view of the clinico-pathological correlation.

Finally there is a large group which medicine does at least recognise: the 'healthy', those 'true negatives' with neither the clinical nor pathological characteristics of disease. In recent years this group has been the target of an unprecedented barrage of propaganda from biomedicine about their health, and the risks of moving into the 'true positive' category. If the biomedical model is either flawed or limited, as discussed above, then these health promotion strategies must be similarly constrained. Indeed there is the possibility that medical strategies directed at people in the 'true' cells is itself generating in some way the cases in the 'false' cells. After all, the table and its four cells is an artefact of biomedicine itself and as such requires its own integral analysis.

Conclusion

Engel clearly is firmly fixed into biomedicine and its root biological context. His 'new model' is therefore nothing of the kind. It is simply the old one with a gloss. However, this is not to cast the new model aside without some admiration for its audacity. Biopsychosocial medicine might rescue psychiatry; it also may rescue biomedicine, at least from some of its severest critics; and finally it offers the opportunity of putting social science firmly in its place: an emasculated, uncritical appendage of a reinvigorated biomedicine.

Social science and medicine are linked together, but the precise nature of that relationship is surely more negotiable than Engel might imply. Engel offers a rather one-sided alliance in the form of biopsychosocial medicine, an attempt to integrate biomedicine with psychosocial perspectives. The alternative strategy is multifaceted. The biopsychosocial approach might be used in those circumstances in which it really is the only way for biomedicine to shift its perspective, but nothing in it supports its endorsement as the panacea or the 'new model' which reconstructs the world of illness. More constructively, social science can pursue two other courses. First, a critical examination of biomedicine and its assumptions; second, an analysis of new ways of conceptualising the nature of illness. These two currents might well at times come together if it is realised that the experience of our own bodies as itself bound up with a biomedical view of the world.

References

1 Engel G. L. The need for a new medical model: a challenge for biomedicine. *Science* **196**, 129, 1977.
2 Day S. B. The advance to biopsychosocial medicine. *Soc. Sci. Med.* **21**, 1335, 1985.
3 Jewson N. D. The disappearance of the sickman from medical cosmologies, 1770–1870. *Sociology* **10**, 225, 1976.
4 Johnson T. *Professions and Power*. Macmillan, New York, 1972.
5 Berlant J. L. *Professions and Monopoly*. University of California Press, 1975.
6 Armstrong D. Pathological life and death: medical spatialisation and geriatrics. *Soc. Sci. Med.* **15**, 253, 1981.

7   Sedgewick P. Mental illness *is* illness. *Salmagundi* **20**, 196, 1973.
8   Freidson E. *Profession of Medicine*. Dodds & Mead, New York, 1970.
9   Wright P. and Treacher A. *The Problem of Medical Knowledge*. Edinburgh University Press, 1982.
10 Armstrong D. *An Outline of Sociology as Applied to Medicine*. Wright, Cambridge, Mass., 1983.
11 Young A. Some implications of medical beliefs and practices for social anthropology. *Am. Anthrop.* **78**, 5, 1976.
12 Foucault M. *The Birth of the Clinic*. Tavistock, London, 1973.
13 Atkinson J. M. *Discovering Suicide: Studies in Social Organisation of Sudden Death*. Macmillan, New York, 1978.
14 Atkinson P. *The Clinical Experience*. Gower, New York, 1981.
15 Kannel W. B. and Abbott R. D. Incidence and prognosis of unrecognised myocardial infarction. *New Engl. J. Med.* **311**, 1144, 1984.
16 Pennebaker J. W. Accuracy of symptom perception. In *Handbook of Psychology and Health* (Edited by Baum A. *et al.*), Vol. IV. Erlbaum, New Jersey, 1984.
17 Bass C. Gardner W. N. and Jackson G. et al. Unexplained breathlessness and psychiatric morbidity in patients with normal and abnormal coronary arteries. *Lancet* **1**, 605, 1983.

5 THE RHETORIC AND REALITY OF PSYCHOSOCIAL THEORIES OF HEALTH:

A Challenge to Biomedicine?

Jane Ogden

A discipline's textbook reflects the contemporary state of that discipline. Textbooks can be neither revisionist nor revolutionary as they both describe and construct the breadth and limitations of the field. Therefore, an examination of textbooks can provide insights into the consensual nature and aims of the discipline. Accordingly, texts in health psychology and medical sociology can be used to reveal the implicit aims and assumptions of the respective disciplines.

Introduction: The Rhetorics of Health Psychology and Medical Sociology

Introductory chapters in health psychology textbooks state: 'The biomedical model is facing a serious challenge' (Sheridan and Radmacher, 1992, p. 4); 'An alternative to the medical model is clearly needed' (Kaplan, Salliss and Patterson, 1993, p. 8), and 'Does the biomedical model need improvement? Yes, Let's see why' (Sarafino, 1990, p. 10). Such proclamations suggest that the discipline of health psychology aims to challenge the biomedical model of health and illness. In parallel, statements from medical sociology textbooks indicate a similar adversarial alignment between the discipline and biomedicine. For example, Stacey (1988) describes a range of 'challenge [that] have been presented to biomedicine from within and without' (p. 174) and more specifically, Nettleton (1995) states 'The sociology of health and illness has sought to offer alternative ways of interpreting medicine ... through criticism of the biomedical model' (p. 4) which is followed by a section called 'Challenges to biomedicine' (p. 5). Similarly, Armstrong, in the introduction to his textbook (1994) states that 'The arguments in the rest of the book, which attempt to identify some deficiencies of the biomedical model ... is an attempt to redress the balance' (p. 2). In short, the stated aims of both health psychology and medical sociology indicate that these disciplines present themselves in conflict with biomedicine. This chapter examines which aspects of biomedicine they purport to challenge and to what extent they succeed. The chapter then analyses the discrepancy between this 'rhetoric' of the textbooks and the 'reality' of the disciplines both in terms of the potential functions of the 'rhetoric' and the reflections of this discrepancy in the changing configuration of the boundaries of the human body.[1]

Psychosocial Causes of Health and Illness

Biomedical theory and research examine etiology in terms of factors such as viruses, bacteria, lesions and carcinogens. Both health psychology and medical sociology question this perspective, with the former arguing that psychological factors contribute to the causes of illness, and the latter emphasizing the role of social factors: 'Health status is clearly the consequence of factors other than biological ... related to social structures and vary according to gender, social class, "race" and age' (Nettleton, 1995, p. 6). For example, research in health psychology has examined the role of stressors in illness, and theoretical perspectives such as the transactional model of stress have suggested that appraising a potential stressor as stressful may contribute to a deterioration in health (Lazarus and Folkman, 1987). It has been argued that the subsequent stress may result in changes in health related behaviours such as smoking, alcohol intake, diet and exercise (e.g. Krantz, Glass, Contrada and Miller, 1981). Similarly, medical sociologists have emphasized the role of life events in illness, and research has suggested that life events that are appraised as stressful may contribute to psychological problems such as depression, chronic illnesses such as coronary heart disease and acute problems such as appendicitis (e.g. Brown and Harris, 1978, 1989). The work of McKeown (1979) also illustrates a similar emphasis on psychosocial causality with health psychologists highlighting McKeown's argument that illnesses in the 20th century are predominantly caused by behaviour and medical sociologists focusing on McKeown's emphasis on the role of social environment in the elimination of past illnesses.

A parallel argument can be seen with the recent emphasis on the role of social support in protecting or facilitating illness. In particular, the frequently cited longitudinal study by Berkman and Syme (1979) outlining the role of social support in mortality plays a central role of social support in mortality plays a central role in the theoretical development of both health psychology and medical sociology, with the former tending to emphasize social support as a perception and the latter locating the support in the environment. Such theoretical developments are encapsulated in Engel's biopsychosocial model which proposes that health and illness are the result of a complex interplay of the multitude of psychosocial factors (1977) and are further operationalized within other additional disciplinary perspectives such as behavioural medicine and behavioural health. Within this framework, the discipline of health psychology emphasizes the 'bio/psycho' components, and medical sociology focuses on 'bio/social' factors. These theoretical frameworks and the corresponding emphasis on beliefs, behaviours and environmental factors aim to develop an alternative way of thinking about the biomedical models' approach to understanding the causes of illness.

An Integrated Individual

With its separation of disease of the mind and diseases of the body and its corresponding speciality divisions, biomedicine describes an individual who is dualistic. Health psychology, however, argues for an integration of the mind and the body, sometimes referred to as an holistic, or whole person, approach and challenges Cartesian dualism: 'We learn in health psychology that the mind and the body are thoroughly intertwined' (Sarafino, 1990). Central to this perspective is the analysis of pain as a perception and an asserted progression from a biomedical division between organic ('real') and psychogenic ('all in the mind') pain. The Gate Control Theory (Melzack and Wall, 1965, 1982) argued that pain should be conceptualized as a perception involving an interpretation and appraisal of physical stimuli. Within this perspective, proponents of the theory argue for an integration of mind and body and a departure from earlier models which described the individual as divided. A similar integration is suggested within contemporary models of stress. For example, the transactional theory (e.g. Lazarus, 1975; Lazarus and Folkman, 1987) proposed that stress was the result of the interpretations appraisal and adaptation to physical stressors – the mind and body are integrated to create the experience of stress. Models of illness onset, emphasizing behaviours such as smoking, exercise and screening, similarly advance a disintegration of the mind/body boundary.

In parallel, research in medical sociology also emphasizes the increasing permeability of boundaries. Medical sociology argues that the individual is located in a social world that determines his or her illness profiles. For example, studies have illustrated the role of social class in predicting coronary heart disease and diet (Marmot and Theorell, 1988) and changes in health and illness during economic recession (Brenner, 1977; Eyer, 1977). Factors such as gender and ethnicity have also been examined in terms of differences in illness threshold (Nathanson, 1977) and their relationship to the allocation of resources and material factors (e.g. Arber, Gilbert and Dale, 1985; Donovan, 1984). Such research emphasizes the location of the individual within a social context and attempts to bridge the social/body divide of biomedicine. In summary, research within both health psychology and medical sociology presents itself as a challenge to the biomedical models' conceptualization of a divided self and asserts a model of an integrated individual.

Non-medical Outcomes

The final challenge to biomedicine is that of medical outcomes. Whereas biomedicine defines outcomes in terms of medically derived factors such as longevity, disease-free intervals and death, health psychology emphasize the role of behaviour (e.g. Kaplan, 1990) and medical sociology describes a need to focus on the patient's own personal assessments of health status. For example, subjective health measures were developed in the 1970s as an attempt to depart from traditional 'objective' assessments of outcome. Early measures examined the effect of illness on functioning and were often called activities of daily living scales (ADL) and were limited to specific activities. However, self-report questionnaires such as the Nottingham Health Profile (NHP) (Hunt, McEwen and McKenna, 1986) and the SF–36 (Ware et al., 1986) were developed to evaluate an individual's own assessment of their broader health status. For example, the NHP consists of items relating to pain, physical mobility, sleep, energy, social isolation and emotional reactions. The SF–36 asks similar questions and includes additional items on factors such as social functioning and general health. In addition, quality of life measures have also been developed which measure subjective health in terms of an integration of ADL and psychological well-being (e.g. Fallowfield, 1990). Such measures are used within both health psychology and medical sociology and emphasize outcome in terms of the individual's own self-assessment and represent a departure from traditional medical outcomes such as longevity and disease-free intervals. Similarly, research has increasingly examined the consequences of health-related interventions in terms of patient satisfaction and compliance (e.g. Ley, 1988) and behaviour change (e.g. Kaplan, 1990). Health psychology, in particular has focused on the latter. For example, Kaplan, in his article 'Behavior as the central outcome in health care' (1990) argues that we should challenge the biomedically defined outcomes such as morbidity and mortality and replace them with a focus on behavior. He suggests that 'Recognizing that health outcomes are behavioral directs intervention towards whatever method produces the most health benefit at the lowest cost' (p. 1211).

In summary, health psychology and medical sociology emphasize their adversarial alignment with the biomedical model in terms of the causes of illness, an integrated individual and the definition of outcomes. Theoretical developments within these disciplines support this challenge and promote an emphasis on psychosocial etiology, a disintegration of self-boundaries and subjective patient-defined outcomes. However, are these developments really a challenge? Are these psychosocial approaches really different from biomedicine?

A Failure to Challenge?

Factors such as behaviours, beliefs and stressors are not presented as alternatives but as facilitating existing medical causes, the real precipitants. Smoking as a behaviour does not cause lung cancer, it simply provides a medium for exposing the individual to carcinogens Correspondingly, stress as an experience results in fatty deposits, and beliefs about safe sex may contribute to the probability of exposure to the HIV virus. A psychological approach to etiology is not a substitute for medical causes of health and illness. Therefore, although the rhetoric of health psychology indicates a challenge to biomedical causes of illness, examination of the explanatory frameworks suggests an implicit acceptance of this perspective. For example, on considering cross-cultural differences in lay beliefs about the causes of health and illness, Sarafino, in his textbook (1990), clearly disparages non-medical explanatory frameworks: 'Recall our discussion of the widespread beliefs in the middle ages about the causes of illness. Today educated people in technological societies generally reject such ideas. But less sophisticated people do not.' He then continues to describe an account of one such person who states 'I've heard of people with snakes in their body, how they got there I don't know' …. 'Sarafino analysed this account by arguing 'Although this account was given by a disadvantaged person in the United States it is typical of the level of knowledge generally found in people in under-developed countries' (p. 25).

Likewise the discipline's analysis of treatment and intervention rejects non-medical explanations of the mechanisms involved. In the context of a cross-cultural analysis of pain management, Gatchel, Baum, and Krantz (1989) focused on acupuncture and explain that it 'originated in ancient China some two thousand years ago' and that the Chinese explain its effect as a result of 'Chi'i [which] flowed through these meridians' (p. 256). This alternative explanation is juxtaposed to the 'correct' explanation: it 'probably achieves its effects by causing the release of endogenous opiate-like substances' (p. 257). As a discipline, health psychology aims to prioritize psychological causes and to acknowledge the role of individual beliefs. However, it implicitly accepts biomedicine's fundamental predicate – the model of etiology.

A parallel pattern can be seen within medical sociology, although with more subtlety than within health psychology. Class, gender and ethnicity do not cause illness but create a proximity between the individual and medical causal factors. Social factors are no substitutes for the real culprits. For example, when considering cross-cultural models of health, Fitzpatrick (1982) argues that 'When a Zande becomes ill or has an accident he may ascribe his misfortune to witch craft…. These sound strange ways of explaining illness, but the fact is that for the Azande they work…. Thus the logic is explained and in any specific episode always "makes sense"' (p. 12). Such an analysis is careful to respect non-medical explanatory frameworks but implicitly rejects them as incorrect. Psychosocial theories of etiology are implicitly biomedical.

The challenge to biomedical dualisms shows a similar pattern. For example, the Gate Control Theory of pain only points towards an interaction of mind and body, not an integration of these components of the individual. Likewise, the transactional theory of stress examines how perceptions may impact on the body, but the mind and body are defined as separate entities which interact: they are not one. The mind/body boundary remains intact. In its call for a disintegration of this boundary, health psychology contextualizes its analysis of a need for an holistic individual alongside philosophers such as Plato and Descartes who are seen as the enemy to be challenged and Aquinas and St Paul who are cited to reflect the golden age of holistic medicine (Hippocrates appears to have an ambiguous relationship with the mind/body problem as he is frequently cited as belonging to both camps). This retrospective construction of a time of both dualism and holism provides health psychology theorists both with an object to be challenged and a faith that this challenge is possible. In addition, this construction creates a separation between the discipline of health psychology and the problem of mind/body dualism. However, perhaps the mind/body divide is not a reflection of a biomedical perspective to be challenged by health psychology but a problem created by the very existence of these two disciplinary frameworks. Foucault (1973) argues that modern medicine was developed at the beginning of the 19th century and constructed a physical body which was analysed, examined and described. Prior to this time, accounts of the body would have been unrecognizable to the modern biomedical eye. Accordingly, modern medicine described its new object as supplanting previous and different models of the body. The end of the 19th century saw the emergence of the discipline of psychology. In parallel with the previous studies of the body, psychological discourses analysed, examined and described the mind. However, the mind was not developed in order to supersede the body but was described to supplement it. Therefore, the discipline of psychology described its object, the mind, as separate and distinct from the object of medicine, the body. In effect, psychology itself developed the mind/body divide – the problem it is aiming to solve; the existence of psychology as a discipline constructs the very mind/body boundary that it is ostensibly aiming to disintegrate: the juxtaposition of psychology and biomedicine maintains the interaction and non-integration of the mind and the body.

A similar pattern can be seen for the social/body divide. Medical sociology argues that 'The main determinants of inequalities in health are, however, generally viewed as lying in the material circumstances, lifestyles and behaviours of social classes which produce differences in exposure and resistance to disease' (Morgan, Calnan and Manning, 1985, p. 217). The social and the body may interact but remain separated. In parallel to health psychology, sociology, which first emerged at the end of the 19th century, located its individual within the social world and medical sociology located its individual within the medical world. Accordingly, the discipline of medical sociology constructs and maintains the social/body boundary it purports to challenge. Therefore, both the disciplines of health psychology and medical sociology can be seen as implicitly biomedical as they construct their object of study as divided according to biomedical dualisms.

And, finally, are the psychosocial outcomes of dysfunction, quality of life and subjective status different from medically defined morbidity? Are patient compliance and satisfaction a departure from a focus on the value on medical information and medical authority? And are behaviour changes such as smoking cessation and dietary improvements distinct from medical mediators of longevity?

Privileging Biomedical Discourses

The inadequate departure from biomedicine's definitions of causality, the implicit construction of biomedical boundaries and the acceptance of medical outcomes, not only, however, represents a failure to challenge biomedicine by constructing an implicit role for physical causes and a physical and separate body but illustrates a privileging of biomedical discourses. In discussions of cross-cultural models of health and illness, there is a privileging of a medical perspective – Western medicine is correct, other models are interesting but misinformed. In parallel, models of causality prioritize the role of physical input, psychological and social factors contribute but are simply facilitative and secondary to medical causes. Likewise, the mind and the social world interact and mediate the body, but the body provides the fundamental object to be mediated. An illustration of this privileging process can be found by an examination of the opening chapter headings to most health psychology textbooks, with titles such as 'Physiological bases of behaviour and health' (Gatchel et al., 1989); 'The body's physical systems' (Sarafino, 1990): 'The psychobiological mechanisms of health and disease' (Sheridan and Radmacher, 1992) illustrated throughout with diagrams of the respiratory, digestive, cardiovascular and nervous systems. Similarly, medical sociology texts show a comparable pattern. Stacey (1988) argues 'it is important to acknowledge the biological base … [which] is common to all human beings' (pp. 2, 3) and that there are 'varied interpretations of the biological base' (p. 3) suggesting the biological phenomena exist to be made sense of. Further, in a series of books examining the experience of illness ('experience' focusing on individual meaning, and 'illness' differentiating itself from the underlying disease), each book commences with chapters termed 'Understanding multiple sclerosis' (Robinson, 1988); 'Diabetes mellitus, its nature and prevalence' (Kelleher, 1988); and 'Medical aspects' (Humphrey, 1989), which describe the physical processes for each problem. The physical body is presented as the essential hardware to be moderated by the optional psychosocial software.

Health psychology and medical sociology confront biomedicine in terms of causality, but themselves are an implicit endorsement of medical causes. Further, they challenge a dualistic individual, but are intrinsic to the mechanisms creating the divides. Their challenge to medical outcomes indicates a similar pattern; although terms such as patient satisfaction, compliance and functioning may illustrate an attempted departure from medical outcomes in the same way that 'psychology' and 'sociology' constitute a divided individual by defining their object as non-medical, 'health' and 'medical' can only define their outcome as being biomedical. In addition, they not only fail to challenge the dominance of the biomedical model, they privilege the physical body – the backbone of biomedicine.

For the challenge to be a success, psychosocial theories need to be different from biomedicine. But are they? Psychosocial theories appear to be implicitly biomedical in their analyses of etiology, the individual and outcomes. With general practice increasingly emphasizing the psychological and social well-being of its patients (Balint, 1964; Department of Health, 1989; Freeling, 1983; Pill and Stott, 1982), is biomedicine biomedical or implicitly psychosocial? The rhetoric of health psychology and medical sociology describes a challenge to the biomedical model. An analysis of the reality suggests that this challenge is unsuccessful. Why is there this discrepancy? If these psychosocial theories fail to challenge biomedicine, why the rhetoric to the contrary?

The Reality is Right: so why the Rhetoric?

Latour (1987) describes rhetoric as a 'fascinating albeit despised discipline' which has 'studied how people are made to believe and behave and [has] taught people how to persuade others' (p. 30). Further, he describes the role of 'implicit' and 'explicit' interests of the scientists using the rhetoric; rhetoric may serve to benefit interested parties (Latour, 1987). Accordingly, the rhetoric of psychosocial textbooks may serve the interests of the authors and publishers, who by suggesting that their approach is original and different, grab their readers' attention: controversy may contribute to book sales and personal reputations (Woolgar, 1981). In contrast, the rhetoric may serve the interests of the respective disciplines. Central to medical sociology is the study of the 'dominant' medical profession, a questioning of 'how a profession succeeded in claiming the right to an exclusive monopoly of health care in the advanced industrial societies' and 'in pulling the wool over everybody's eyes including their own' (Hart, 1985, p. 18). Perhaps, the rhetoric of 'taking on' the influential medical model enables the psychosocial disciplines to accrue scientific credibility, to gain access to the medical world of employment and funding and to define a role for themselves in the development of health-care policy. Alternatively, the rhetoric may serve the interests of biomedicine. Far from confronting their adversary, psychosocial theories of etiology, the individual and outcomes, may maintain the perpetuate it. In addition, this failure to challenge may support and promote it. Kuhn (1962) argues that shifts between paradigms occur when the weight of unexplained anomalies – outliers to the dominant theoretical perspective – becomes too great for the paradigm to bear. Health psychology and medical sociology provide biomedicine with a theoretical explanation of cause, individuality and outcome for its anomalies, so preventing a paradigm shift. Furthermore, by offering alternatives to 'causality', 'individuality' and 'outcomes', psychosocial approaches to health endorse these fundamental parameters of biomedicine. Accordingly, the psychosocial rhetoric of a challenge serves the needs of the biomedical model and the professionals working within it (Armstrong, 1987).

The stated aims of health psychology and medical sociology are not reflected in their explanatory frameworks; a discrepancy between rhetoric and reality exists; if this account of the reality is right, the disciplines fail and the rhetoric serves the needs of interested parties. Within this analysis, rhetoric has its conventional meaning of overblown claims which reflect a battle for power both within and between disciplines. However, such an analysis describes an unproblematic relationship between rhetoric and reality. Is rhetoric simply functional? Can rhetoric fail? Can such a discrepancy exist? Why privilege the reality? Perhaps the rhetoric is right?

The Rhetoric is Right

Latour (1987) describes a 'black box' as a theory, or 'fact' which is accepted and that 'no matter how controversial their history, how complex their inner workings, how large the commercial or academic networks that hold them in place, only their input and output count' (p. 3). A black box is a given truth. He argues that black boxes are closed by gathering support in terms of 'the number of associations necessary to drive readers out and force them into accepting a claim as a fact' (p. 62). He further argues that these associations can be accrued by the use of rhetoric which increases in intensity along with the controversy and that a similar process is necessary if a black box is ever opened. In line with this, the rhetorical statements of psychosocial texts can be seen as a threat to the black box of biomedicine; they illustrate an assault on the box by the attackers and a closure by the defense. However, such an analysis again regards rhetoric as simply functional. Latour argues that 'we must eventually come to call scientific and rhetoric' (p. 62). Accordingly, the rhetoric not only serves to close and open the black box, the rhetoric is the black box. The rhetoric is all there is. The rhetoric is the reality. So what is this reality?

The Construction and Dissolution of Boundaries

If rhetoric is seen not as the linguistic representation of an underlying reality but rather as the means by which that reality is fabricated, then health psychology, medical sociology and biomedicine may be seen as mutually dependent. Each fabricates the boundaries of itself in relation to others. However, these boundaries do not reflect a separation between discrete but cooperative entities. As the rhetoric of health psychology and medical sociology suggests an adversarial alignment between these disciplines and biomedicine, the constructed boundaries delineate areas of conflict. Therefore, biomedicine may not have been superseded, as proposed by the stated aims of the disciplines, but the rhetoric to challenge is reflected in the adversarial nature of the boundaries. However, although the rhetoric of health psychology and medical sociology is adversarial, the disciplines are cooperative to the extent that their existence depends on their difference from each other.

Further, these disciplinary boundaries are also reflected in both the existence and nature of the boundaries of the body. Accordingly, in the same way that health psychology and medical sociology challenge the dominance of biomedicine, contemporary models of the individual indicate a parallel adversarial alignment of the mind, the social and the body; again, the rhetoric finds expression. But such adversarial boundaries are not static or unchanging but dynamic, and as the boundaries between the disciplines begin to blur and dissolve (biomedicine is implicitly psychosocial?: psychosocial theories are implicitly biomedical?) so do the boundaries of the body (the body is the mind? the mind is the body? the body is the social world?). And as they dissolve, the disciplinary boundaries become visible for study (health/psychology, medical/sociology) and the boundaries of the body likewise emerge as areas of enquiry (the problem of dualisms).

The rhetoric to challenge the dominance of biomedicine is not reflected in the reality of these psychosocial disciplines. Accordingly, the rhetoric serves the needs of interested parties – the authors, the publishers, the respective disciplines? Perhaps, the rhetoric, however, is the reality. The rhetoric is all there is. The rhetoric of a challenge, therefore, is reflected in the existence and nature of the disciplinary boundaries. Further, it is reflected in the contemporary challenge to the dominance of the physical body. The rhetoric to challenge and overturn biomedicine belies the reality of psychosocial theory, but the rhetoric of a challenge is the reality.

Note

1 Central to my analysis of the role of 'rhetoric' and 'reality' and the investigation of the discrepancy between the two is a recognition and exploration of the changing meanings of these words. Such meaning is located within a variety of theoretical contexts and is therefore problematic and not absolute. Accordingly these terms could be used in quotation marks; however, this punctuation is not used throughout the article as it would be obtrusive.

References

Arber, S., Gilbert, G. N., and Dale, A. (1985). Paid employment and women's health: A benefit or a source of role strain? *Sociology of Health and Illness*, 7, 375–400.

Armstrong, D. (1987). Theoretical tensions in biopsychosocial medicine. *Social Science and Medicine, 25*, 1213–1218.

Armstrong, D. (1994). *Outline of sociology as applied to medicine*. Oxford: Butterworth Heinemann.

Balint, M. (1964). *The doctor, his patient and the illness*. London: Pitman.

Berkman, L. F., and Syme, S. L. (1979). Social networks, host resistance and mortality: A nine-year follow-up study of Alameda County residents. *American Journal of Epidemiology, 109*, 186–204

Brenner, M. H. (1977). Health costs and benefits of economic policy. *International Journal of Health Services, 7*, 581–623.

Brown, G. W., and Harris, T. O. (1978). *Social origins of depression*. New York: Free Press.

Brown, G. W., and Harris, T. O. (eds) (1989). *Life events and illness*. New York: Guilford.

Department of Health (1989). *Working for patients*. London: HMSO.

Donovan, J. (1984). Ethnicity and health: A research review. *Social Science and Medicine, 19*, 663–670.

Engel, G. L. (1977). The need for a new medical model: A challenge for biomedicine. *Science, 196*, 129–135.

Eyer, J. (1977). Does unemployment cause the death rate peak in each business cycle? A multifactorial model of death rate change. *International Journal of Health Services, 7*, 625–662.

Fallowfield, L. (1990). *The quality of life: The missing measurement in health care*. London: Souvenir.

Fitzpatrick, R. M. (1982). Social concepts of disease and illness. In D. L. Patrick, and G. Scambler, (eds), *Sociology as applied to medicine* (pp. 3–17). London: Baillière Tindall.

Foucault, M. (1973). *The birth of the clinic: An archeology of medical perception*. London: Tavistock.

Freeling, P. (1983). *A workbook for trainees in General Practice*. Bristol: Wright.

Gatchel, R. J., Baum, A., and Krantz, D. S. (1989). *An introduction to health psychology*. New York: McGraw-Hill.

Hart, N. (1985). *The sociology of health and medicine*. Ormskirk: Causeway Press.

Humphrey, M. (1989). *Back pain*. London: Routledge.

Hunt, S., McEwen, J., and McKenna, S. P. (1986). *Measuring health status*. London: Croom Helm.

Kaplan, R. M. (1990). Behavior as the central outcome in health care. *American Psychologist, 45*, 1211–1220.

Kaplan, R. M., Sallis, J. F., and Patterson, T. L. (1993). *Health and human behaviour*. New York: McGraw-Hill.

Kelleher, D. (1988). *Diabetes*. London: Routledge.

Krantz, D. S., Glasss, D. C., Contrada, R., and Miller, N. E. (1981). *Behavior and health. National science foundations second five-year outlook on science and technology*. Washington, DC: US Government Printing Office.

Kuhn, T. (1962). *The structure of scientific revolutions*. Chicago, IL: University of Chicago Press.

Latour, B. (1987). *Science in action*, Cambridge, MA: Harvard University Press.

Lazarus, R. S. (1975). A cognitively oriented psychologist looks at biofeedback. *American Psychologist, 30*, 553–561.

Lazarus, R. S., and Folkman, S. (1987). Transactional theory and research on emotions and coping. *European Journal of Personality, I,* 141–170.

Ley, P. (1988). *Communicating with patients.* London: Croom Helm.

Marmot, M. G., and Theorell, T. (1988). Social class and cardiovascular disease: The contribution of work. *International Journal of Health Services, 18,* 659–674.

McKeown, T. (1979). *The role of medicine.* Oxford: Blackwell.

Melzack, R., and Wall, P. D. (1965). Pain mechanisms: A new theory. *Science, 150,* 971–979.

Melzack, R., and Wall, P. D. (1982). *The challenge of pain.* New York: Basic Books.

Morgan, M., Calnan, M., and Manning, N. (1985). *Sociological approaches to health and medicine.* London: Routledge.

Nathanson, C. A. (1977). Sex, illness and medical care: A review of data, theory and method. *Social Science and Medicine, 11,* 13–25.

Nettleton, S. (1995). *The sociology of health and illness.* Cambridge: Polity.

Pill, P., and Stott, N. C. H. (1982). Concepts of illness causation and responsibility: Some preliminary data from a sample of working class mothers. *Social Science and Medicine, 16,* 315–322.

Robinson, I. (1988). *Multiple sclerosis:* London: Routledge.

Sarafino, E. P. (1990). *Health psychology: Biopsychosocial interactions.* New York: Wiley.

Sheridan, C. L., and Radmacher, S. A. (1992). *Health psychology: Challenging the biomedical model.* New York: Wiley.

Stacey, M. (1988). *The sociology of health and healing: A textbook.* London: Unwin Hyman.

Ware, J. E., Brook, R. H., and Rogers, W. H. (1986). Comparison of health outcomes at a health maintenance organisation with those of fee for service care. *Lancet, 1,* 1017–1022.

Woolgar, S. (1981). Interests and explanations in the study of social science. *Social Studies of Science, 11,* 365–397.

PART II

THEORIES IN HEALTH PSYCHOLOGY

THE READINGS

6 Social Foundations of Thought and Action: A Social Cognitive Theory. Englewood Cliffs. NJ: Prentice Hall.
   Albert Bandura

7 Emotion narratives: A Radical New Research Approach
   Richard S. Lazarus

8 The Role of Theory in HIV Prevention
   Martin Fishbein

9 Unraveling the Mystery of Health: How People Manage Stress and Stay Well
   Aaron Antonovsky

10 Some Observations on Health and Socio-economic Status
   Douglas Carroll, George Davey Smith and Paul Bennett

Part II introduces some key theoretical concepts that have been influential within health psychology. Theory in health psychology is founded on three core assumptions:

individualism: this is an ideological position that privileges the individual person as a self-contained, autonomous agent, 'the ties between individuals are loose: everyone is expected to look after himself of herself and his or her immediate family' (Hofstede, 1997, p. 51). Individualism is a characteristic of cultures in developed countries, the top-ranked individualistic countries being the USA, Australia, the UK, Canada and the Netherlands (Hofstede, 1997, p. 53).[1] Of central importance to individualism is the construct of:

the **self**: refers to the personality or ego seen as an agent, conscious of his or her own continuing identity, said to be the core, identifying characteristics of each person (cf. Drever, 1952). The construct is also commonly applied as a prefix to refer to an individual's perceptions, beliefs and expectations about herself or himself, e.g. 'self-image', 'self-control', 'self-concept', 'self-perception', 'self-esteem', 'self-efficacy', etc. These self-related cognitions are an essential part of the processes of:

social cognition: referring to how an individual person's thoughts and actions follow goal-directed rules acquired by observation and participation in social events. Social cognitive theory is concerned with how people exercise control over their behaviour and environment. The assumption that people are individualistic agencies concerned primarily with self-preservation is pervasive within the discourse, theory and research of health psychology. A key person responsible for the development and empirical testing of social cognitive theory has been Albert Bandura.

Albert Bandura's concept of '**self-efficacy**', the perceived ability to manage or cope with specific tasks and situations, is the subject of the first reading in this part (Reading 6). People's perceptions of their capabilities are a key factor in determining what each person is able to achieve. Self-efficacy is a jargon term for the concept of the **self-image** applied in a more technical fashion to a person's perceived competence to successfully carry out a specific task or skill. The self-image was popularised in the 1960s in self-help books such as Maxwell Maltz's (1960) *Psycho-Cybernetics*. It can be traced back to Epictetus and the stoical philosophers. Through his version of social cognitive theory, Bandura has successfully given the scientific legitimacy to an age-old philosophical concept that has become a foundation stone for psychology of behaviour change and performance. Self-efficacy is today a basic construct in any theory of behaviour change. It is an individualistic concept focused on the individual's agency, mastery and sense of control. It is also a very useful and powerful construct because it is a strong predictor of behaviour change.

Richard Lazarus, in Reading 7, reviews his and Susan Folkman's (1984) **theory of stress and coping** in the light of more recent ideas concerning systems theory and emotion. The theory of Folkman and Lazarus is a 'classic' in the field of stress and coping and Lazarus' review of 1999 is of great interest because it shows how the theory has been developed after 15 years of further thinking and research. Lazarus is critical of the box-and-arrows approach to theorising which he and Folkman had used in their earlier book on stress and coping. This reading continues with an interesting discussion of what Lazarus terms the 'objective versus subjective'. Lazarus declares that he believes that it is the person-environment relationship, *as construed by the person*, which is the best strategy for gaining an understanding of stress, emotion and adaptation. Lazarus' reading concludes with a brief discussion of the perspectives offered in emotion **narratives** of self-other-environmental events.

Martin Fishbein (Reading 8) reviews another 'classic' model, that of Ajzen and Fishbein (1980). The context for Fishbein's discussion is the fight to curtail the spread of HIV/AIDS. With 36 million people living with **HIV/AIDS** (United Nations General Assembly on HIV/AIDS, 2001) and with no vaccine and no cure, this is a disease of major proportions. The high cost of anti-retroviral drugs ($1,000 per person per year) as compared to the average amount spent on health care in Africa ($10 per person per year) has led to a heated debate on the best use of global funds to fight the disease, prevention or treatment. Brazil and South Africa have already won battles against the pharmaceutical industry to produce their own cheaper, locally produced generic drugs. It seems clear that efforts must be made both to prevent the spread of AIDS and to develop a vaccine.

Fishbein presents an **integrative model** that he believes is applicable in both Western and non-Western cultures. Fishbein is convinced that the integrative model is complete and states that we do not need any new theories of behaviour change *'because we already know how to do this'* (p. 125). However, Fishbein admits that we do need new theories about how to 'mobilize communities and get increased participation' (p. 125). The psychological context includes emotion and motivation as well as cognition and cognition is not always rational or factually based. Some men in South African communities believe that sex with a virgin will cure them of AIDS, thus spreading the disease among girls.

Next are two extracts of Aaron Antonovsky's salutogenetic theory from his book *Unraveling the Mystery of Health: How People Manage Stress and Stay Well* (Reading 9). A sociologist, who emigrated from New York to Israel in 1960, Antonovsky was strongly opposed to social injustice, discrimination and intolerance. Antonovsky argues for research directed towards the psychological understanding of wellness, a true psychology of health. Of key importance has been Antonovsky's concept of **sense of coherence**.[2]

Douglas Carroll, George Davey Smith and Paul Bennett (Reading 10) shift our focus from the study of individuals to that of populations that are structured by **socio-economic status**. Epidemiological studies reveal patterns of health (as measured by mortality) and illness (or morbidity) that are exceedingly robust across space and time. The authors draw attention to the need for concepts and theories that address the links between individual health and socio-economic status. Once these links have been understood, the real challenge will be to implement successful change. This may not be 'mission impossible', but it is certainly a massive challenge.

We have turned full circle. Antonovsky was writing about social class, life expectancy and mortality 30 years earlier than Douglas Carroll, Davey Smith and Bennett (e.g. see Antonovsky, 1967). Whether the current experience of the **widening health and wealth gaps** in Western societies can be reversed in another 30 years is anybody's guess. However, it does seem unlikely. Social differences are mirrored geographically by differences in the environment and housing which have remained almost constant in London for 100 years (Dorling et al., 2000). The historical, cultural and economical determinants of individual behaviour are extremely robust and resistant to change. When we take a population perspective, these contextual pressures control peoples' life chances to a greater degree than individual plans and choices. This does not mean that individuals cannot improve their lots by dint of their education, hard work and/or entrepreneurial skills. It is simply that when we look across the whole population the 'yuppies'[3] are by far out-numbered by people who are dispossessed, unemployed, or on low incomes. This is why we argue in HPTRP that health psychology must consider the potential for individual behaviour change in its full political, economic, social, cultural, and spiritual context.

HIGHLIGHTS, QUESTIONS, ISSUES

1 Can Bandura's concept of self-efficacy be translated into ordinary English? Is Bandura's self-efficacy theory saying anything new?
2 How does Lazarus's (1999 – Reading 7) position compare with that of Lazarus and Folkman (1984)?
3 Do you agree with Fishbein's conclusion that his model of behaviour change is applicable across all cultures?
4 What is meant by the concept of 'salutogenesis'?
5 Does Antonovsky's construct of sense of coherence make sense to you?
6 Think of ways of applying the SOC concept to a health care setting you are familiar with. How could the concept be applied in this setting?
7 Health psychology in the 20th century was based on the ideology of individualism. What are the limitations of this position?
8 What would a more collectivist or communitarian health psychology be like?
9 What are the possible psychosocial mediators of the link between poverty and ill health?
10 Think of psychological theories that may cast some light on this issue.

Notes

1 It is an interesting fact that these five countries are where health psychology has been the most energetically developed.
2 For a brief biography of Antonovsky, see Marks (1997d).
3 Yuppies: young upwardly-mobile people.

6 SOCIAL FOUNDATIONS OF THOUGHT AND ACTION

Albert Bandura

[…]

Competent functioning requires both skills and self-beliefs of efficacy to use them effectively. Operative efficacy calls for continuously improvising multiple subskills to manage ever changing circumstances, most of which contain ambiguous, unpredictable, and often stressful elements. Even routinized activities are rarely performed in exactly the same way. Initiation and regulation of transactions with the environment are, therefore, partly governed by judgments of operative capabilities – what people think they can do under given circumstances. Perceived self-efficacy is defined as people's judgments of their capabilities to organize and execute courses of action required to attain designated types of performances. It is concerned not with the skills one has but with judgments of what one can do with whatever skills one possesses.

Judgments of personal efficacy are distinguished from response-outcome expectations. Perceived self-efficacy is a judgment of one's capability to accomplish a certain level of performance, whereas an outcome expectation is a judgment of the likely consequence such behavior will produce. For example, the belief that one can high jump six feet is an efficacy judgment; the anticipated social recognition, applause, trophies, and self-satisfactions for such a performance constitute the outcome expectations.

An outcome is the consequence of an act, not the act itself. Serious confusions arise when an act is misconstrued as an outcome of itself, as when jumping six feet is viewed as a consequent. An act must be defined by the criteria that state what it is, for example, a leap upward of a designated height. To regard a six-foot high jump as an outcome would be to misinterpret the specification criteria of an act as the consequences that flow from it. If an act is defined as a six-foot leap, then a six-foot leap is the realization of the act, not a consequent of it. Failure to complete a designated act (e.g. knocking off a crossbar by failing to jump six feet) cannot be the outcome of that act because it was never fully executed. The failed jump is an incomplete act that produces its own divergent collection of outcomes, be they social, physical, or self-evaluative.

Outcome expectations are also sometimes misconstrued as the effectiveness of a technique (Maddux, Sherer, and Rogers, 1982; Manning and Wright, 1983). Means are not results. An efficacious technique is a means for producing outcomes, but it is not itself an outcome expectation. For example, an effective cognitive skill for solving problems can be put to diverse uses to gain all kinds of outcomes. Useful means serve as the vehicles for exercising personal efficacy.

Efficacy and outcome judgments are differentiated because individuals can believe that a particular course of action will produce certain outcomes, but they do not act on that outcome belief because they question whether they can actually execute the necessary activities. Thus, expectations that high grades gain students entry to medical school and that medical practice yields high incomes will not steer undergraduates into premedical programs who have serious self-doubts that they can master the science requirements.

Dependence of Expected Outcomes on Performance Efficacy Judgments

In transactions with the environment, outcomes do not occur as events disconnected from actions. Rather, most outcomes flow from actions. Hence, how one behaves largely determines the outcomes one experiences. Similarly, in thought, the types of outcomes people anticipate depend largely on their judgments of how well they will be able to perform in given situations. Drivers who judge themselves inefficacious in navigating winding mountain roads will conjure up outcomes of wreckage and bodily injury, whereas those who are fully confident of their driving capabilities will anticipate sweeping vistas rather than tangled wreckage. The social reactions people anticipate for asserting themselves depend on their judgments of how adroitly they can do it. Tactless assertiveness will produce negative counterreactions, whereas adept assertiveness can elicit accommodating reactions. In social, intellectual, and physical pursuits, those who judge themselves highly efficacious will expect favorable outcomes, self-doubters will expect mediocre performances of themselves and thus negative outcomes.

As the above examples illustrate, one cannot sever expected outcomes from the very performance judgments upon which they are conditional. One must distinguish between the source of outcome expectations and their role in regulating behavior. Because outcomes emanate from actions in no way detracts from the regulatory influences of those envisioned outcomes. It is because people see outcomes as contingent on the adequacy of their performances, and care about those outcomes, that they rely on self-judged efficacy in deciding which courses of action to pursue. Physical and psychological well-being is better served by action based on self-appraisal of efficacy than by mindless leaps into action without regard to one's capabilities.

For activities in which outcomes are either inherent to the actions or tightly linked by social codes, outcome expectancies cannot be disjoined from the self-judged performances from which they flow. Physical injury from a poorly executed gymnastic routine typifies inherent linkage; money gained as the prize for winning an athletic contest typifies prescribed social linkage. It is because expected outcomes are highly dependent on self-efficacy judgments that expected outcomes may not add much on their own to the prediction of behavior. If you control for how well people judge they can perform, you account for much of the variance in the kinds of outcomes they expect. Hence, in analyses that statistically control for the effects of the various factors, perceived self-efficacy predicts performance much better than expected outcomes in such diverse activities as phobias, assertiveness, smoking cessation, athletic feats, sales performances, and pain tolerance (Barling and Abel, 1983; Barling and Beattie, 1983; Godding and Glasgow, 1985; Lee, 1984a, 1984b; Manning and Wright, 1983; Williams and Watson, 1985).

Outcome expectations can be dissociated from self-efficacy judgments when either no action can produce a selected effect or extrinsic outcomes are loosely linked to level or quality of performance. Such structural arrangements permit social biases to come into play, so that the same performance attainments may produce variable and often inequitable outcomes. In prejudicially structured systems, variations in performance, however skillfully executed, may have little or no effect on some desired outcomes. Thus, for example, when athletes were rigidly segregated by race, black athletes could not gain entry to major league baseball no matter how well they pitched or batted.

Expected outcomes are also partially separable from self-efficacy judgments when extrinsic outcomes are fixed to a minimum level of performance, as when a designated level of productivity produces a fixed pay but better performance brings no additional monetary benefits. When effects are socially linked to some minimal standard, performance exerts only partial control over outcomes. However, in most everyday activities, variations in performance produce concurrent changes in outcomes. Indeed, even small variations in performance can produce markedly different effects, as when a slight swerve of an automobile on a crowded freeway can cause an instant collision.

[…]

Perceived Self-efficacy in the Self-regulation of Pain

Self-management of pain is a markedly different area of functioning that illustrates further the generality of the self-efficacy mechanism across modes of influence. Pain is a complex psychobiologic phenomenon, influenced by psychosocial factors, rather than simply a sensory experience arising directly from stimulation of pain receptors. The subjective experience of pain depends not only on sensory stimulation but also on what one attends to, how the experience is cognitively appraised, and on self-activation of physiological systems by means of various coping techniques. The same intensity of pain stimulation can thus give rise to varying subjective experiences of pain.

That psychosocial factors can significantly influence pain is revealed in analgesic placebo responses. Placebo pills can bring pain relief to many people. The analgesic potency of placebos closely mimics the pharmacologic properties of drugs, producing additive effects, dose-level effects, and greater pain relief from a placebo injection than from a placebo pill (Evans, 1974). Misbeliefs about the substance being taken can counteract the usual pharmacologic action of drugs, as well as invest inert substances with analgesic potency (Wolf, 1950). For example, nausea is eliminated by an emetic that ordinarily induces nausea and vomiting if it is presented to patients as a drug that alleviates stomach upset. In the latter instances, beliefs override physiological reactions activated by the pharmacologic action of drugs. Psychological coping techniques enable people to reduce even more effectively the amount of pain they experience and the amount of analgesic medication they require (Neufeld and Thomas, 1977; Turk, Meichenbaum, and Genest, 1981).

Research has clarified some aspects of the physiological mechanisms mediating pain reduction. The brain possesses an endogenous system that produces endorphins and enkephalins that play an important role in the regulation of pain. These are morphine-like substances the body uses to relieve pain. Studies by Levine and his associates indicate that the endorphinergic systems can be activated by psychological means (Levine, Gordon, and Fields, 1978; Levine, Gordon, Jones, and Fields, 1978). Patients experiencing postoperative dental pain are administered either morphine or a placebo intravenously. About one third of the patients achieve pain relief from the placebo. Naloxone is an opiate antagonist that attaches to opiate receptors and impedes endorphins from blocking the transmission of pain impulses. Administration of naloxone produces a sudden rise in pain in patients who achieved relief from the placebo but does not affect the placebo nonresponders. Such findings indicate that placebo analgesia is mediated by endorphin release. The pain relief achieved by psychological means is thus just as real and explainable in terms of opioid activation as is the pain relief gained through pharmacologic analgesics.

There are several ways in which perceived self-efficacy can bring belief from pain. People who believe they can alleviate pain are likely to mobilize whatever ameliorative skills they have learned and to persevere in their attempts. If pain mounts, the self-inefficacious are likely to give up quickly, whereas those who believe they can exercise some control over their pain will be more tenacious in their efforts. A sense of coping efficacy also cuts down on distressing anticipations that create aversive physiological arousal and bodily tension which only exacerbate sensory pain and discomfort. Dwelling on pain sensations makes them more noticeable and thus more difficult to bear. Perceived self-efficacy can moderate pain by diverting attention from pain sensation to ameliorative activities. The more attentionally demanding the coping activities, the less attention pain sensations can command. To the extent that pain sensations are supplanted in consciousness they are felt less.

That perceived self-efficacy may mediate the potency of different psychological analgesics was put to test by Reese (1983). People received one of three modes of treatment for alleviating cold pressor pain produced by placing one's hand in ice water. In the cognitive mode, they were taught cognitive techniques, including attention diversion, pleasant imagery, coping self-instruction, and dissociation; in the motoric mode they used muscular self-relaxation to cope with pain; in the ministration drawing on the placebo modality, they were administered a placebo described as a medicinal analgesic. Each of these treatments increased perceived self-efficacy to cope with and ameliorate pain. The more self-efficacious the persons judged themselves to be, the less pain they experienced in later cold pressor tests, and the higher was their pain threshold and pain tolerance.

Coping by cognitive means proved more effective than muscular relaxation in controlling pain which, in turn, was better than placebos. Research by Neufeld and Thomas (1977) reveals that the benefits of relaxation stem more from boosts in perceived coping efficacy than from the muscular exercises themselves. Mere belief, created by the false feedback that one is a skilled relaxer for controlling pain, increased pain tolerance in the absence of any differences in actual muscular relaxation. In the study by Reese (1983), it was the participants for whom placebo medication raised perceived self-efficacy that the placebo was an effective analgesic. Perceived self-efficacy in controlling pain predicted not only positive placebo responders but negative placebo responders as well. Participants who continued to distrust their pain controlling efficacy after receiving the placebo medication became even less tolerant of pain.

That perceived self-efficacy makes pain easier to manage is corroborated by studies of acute and chronic clinical pain. Women who had been taught relaxation and breathing exercises to reduce pain during their first childbirth differed in how much control they believed they could exercise over pain while giving birth (Manning and Wright, 1983). Their perceived self-efficacy predicted how well they managed pain during labor and delivery. The higher their perceived self-efficacy, the longer they tolerated labor pain before requesting medication and the less pain medication they used. Shoor and Holman (1984) document the influential role of perceived self-efficacy in managing the chronic pain of arthritis. When patients are equated for degree of physical debility and other relevant factors, those who believe they can exercise some influence over their pain and how much their arthritic condition affects them lead more active lives and experience less pain.

The evidence discussed above testifies to the effectiveness of psychological means of pain control. Their analgesic potency depends, in part, on the extent to which they provide people with pain coping skills and strengthen their perceived self-efficacy in exercising some control over their pain. The analysis needs to be pursued further to identify the mechanisms by which self-percepts of efficacy enhance pain tolerance. There is some reason to believe that psychological techniques may produce analgesic effects mainly through nonopioid mechanisms. Stress can activate endogenous opioids that block pain transmission (Bolles and Fanselow, 1982). It is not the physically painful stimulation, *per se*, but the psychological stress over its uncontrollability that seems to be the important factor in opioid activation (Hyson, Ashcraft, Drugan, Grau, and Maier, 1982).

Pain sensations can be blocked at the level of physiological transmission or psychological awareness. Because a high sense of coping efficacy makes aversive situations less stressful, it may reduce stress-activated opioids. While there may be less opioid blockage of pain, a high efficaciousness that occupies consciousness with engrossing matters can block awareness of pain sensations by a nonopioid cognitive mechanism. The attentional resources available at any given moment are severely limited. Therefore, it is hard for people to attend to more than one thing at a time. Effective diversion of attention to absorbing matters could attenuate perception of pain sensations without implicating endorphins.

Analgesic reactions may be mediated primarily by a nonopioid mechanism when people have effective means of coping with painful conditions, but by an opioid mechanism when they lack coping techniques for attenuating pain or for blocking it from awareness. Most likely both mechanisms operate in the regulation of pain, but their relative contribution to pain sensitivity and tolerance may vary with degree of controlling efficacy and stages of coping. A strong sense of efficacy increases pursuit of pain-producing activities, as in arthritis, or willingness to bear mounting pain stimulation (Reese, 1983; Shoor and Holman, 1984). The exercise of self-efficaciousness may heighten pain stimulation to the point where psychological analgesics no longer work effectively, thus activating opioid mechanisms in later stages of coping.

[...]

Perceived Self-regulatory Efficacy

The exercise of influence over one's own behavior is not achieved by a feat of willpower. Self-regulatory capabilities require tools of personal agency and the self-assurance to use them effectively (Bandura, 1982a). People who are skeptical of their ability to exercise adequate control over their motivation and behavior tend to undermine their efforts in situations that tax capabilities. Relapses in the self-regulation of refractory behavior provide a familiar example.

Marlatt and Gordon (1980) have postulated a common relapse process for heroin addiction, alcoholism, and smoking in which perceived self-regulatory efficacy operates as a contributing factor. The common precipitants of breakdowns in self-control typically include inability to cope with negative emotions, social pressures to use the substance, and interpersonal conflict. Such experiences undermine perceived efficacy to resist use of the substances (Barrios and Niehaus, 1985). People who have the skills and assurance in their coping efficacy mobilize the effort needed to succeed in high-risk situations. Mastery of problem situations further strengthens self-regulatory efficacy. In contrast, when coping skills are underdeveloped and poorly used because of disbelief in one's efficacy, a relapse will occur. Selective recall of the pleasures, but not the adverse effects, of the substance creates further strains on efforts at self-regulation. Faultless self-control is not easy to come by even for pliable habits, let alone for dependence on addictive substances. The self-diagnostic significance given to occasional slips can bolster or undermine self-regulatory inefficacy. Having labeled themselves as powerless, people abandon further coping efforts, resulting in a total breakdown in self-control.

Studies of behavior that is amenable to change but where the changes are difficult to sustain over a long time indicate that perceived self-inefficacy increases vulnerability to relapse. In this research investigators measure the self-judged efficacy of cigarette smokers to resist smoking under various social and stressful inducements after they had quit smoking through various means (DiClemente, 1981; Colletti, Supnick, and Payne, 1985; McIntyre, Lichtenstein, and Mermelstein, 1983; Walker and Franzini, 1983). Although all participants stop smoking, they do not exhibit the same level of self-efficacy that they can resist craving for cigarettes. Compared to abstainers, relapsers express lower self-efficacy at the end of treatment about their ability to resist cigarettes in situations that commonly prompt smoking. The higher the perceived self-regulatory efficacy, the more success there is in checking smoking during the follow-up period. The predictiveness of perceived self-efficacy is confirmed with biochemical measures of tobacco use (Colletti, Supnick, and Payne, 1985; Godding and Glasgow, 1985; Killen, Maccoby, and Taylor, 1984). Neither demographic factors, history of smoking behavior, nor degree of physical dependence on nicotine differentiates relapsers from abstainers. Evidence that past successes and failures in breaking the smoking habit are unrelated to perceived self-efficacy after treatment (Reynolds, Creer, Holroyd, and Tobin, 1982) indicates that self-percepts of efficacy are not simply reflections of past coping experiences.

In a microanalysis of the relation between self-percepts of efficacy and smoking behavior, Condiotte and Lichtenstein (1981) assessed, at the completion of treatment, people's perceived capability to resist the urge to smoke in a variety of situations. Perceived self-regulatory efficacy predicted, months later, which participants would relapse, how soon they would relapse, and even the specific situations in which they would experience their first slip. Moreover, perceived self-efficacy at the end of treatment predicts how participants are likely to respond to a subsequent relapse, should it occur. Highly self-efficacious persons are inclined to regard a slip as a temporary setback and reinstate control; the less self-efficacious peers display a marked decrease in perceived self-efficacy and relapse completely. Measures of perceived self-efficacy can be used to gauge progress and guide optimal timing of new challenges and mastery tests. By identifying areas of vulnerability, people can be taught how to deal effectively with risky situations that get them into trouble and tax their self-regulatory capabilities.

Coping skills and belief in one's self-regulatory ability are built, in large part, through mastery experiences. Substance abuse poses special challenges in this regard. Triumphs over slips can strengthen perceived coping efficacy, but, in so doing, they may foster periodic lapses into old habits through assurance that one can always reinstate control. In studying the effects of controlled relapse, Cooney, Kopel, and McKeon (1982) had participants in a smoking-cessation program smoke a cigarette and then resume control, while others were told to avoid the cigarette because control is unachievable after relapse. Controlled relapse strengthened, and abstinence admonitions lowered, perceived self-efficacy in copying with slips. But the participants who practiced reinstating control resumed smoking sooner. It is also note-worthy that, whereas perceived self-efficacy for resisting inducements is a consistently good predictor of enduring abstinence, perceived self-efficacy for overcoming slips is not.

Programs aimed at abstinence build self-efficacy to resist inducements to use the substance and try to strengthen resistance by lowering perceived self-efficacy to handle the substance – one drink leads to a drunk, as the warning goes. This strategy poses its own risks. Should a slip occur, which is not uncommon among former substance abusers, the instilled diminished self-efficacy for recovery encourages total abandonment of self-regulatory efforts. The challenge is how to strengthen both resistive and recovery self-efficacy so that self-belief in each of these capabilities serves the purpose of abstinence. This may require instilling strong resistive self-efficacy and only moderate recovery self-efficacy, sufficient to counteract judgment of com-plete self-inefficacy should a slip occur, but not so strong as to embolden trial of the substance.

Interactive Perceived Efficacy and Health Behavior

Social environments may place constraints on what people do or may aid them to behave optimally. Whether their endeavors are socially impeded or supported will depend, in part, on how efficacious others perceive them to be. The impetus for interpersonal judgments of efficacy is strongest in close relationships involving interdependent consequences. This is because actions of a partner based on faulty self-percepts of efficacy can produce detrimental consequences for all concerned. Since risky actions are also the means of securing valued benefits, veridical mutual judgments of efficacy provide a reliable basis to promote advantageous endeavors and to dissuade foolhardy ones. Full understanding of how perceptions of efficacy affect courses of action in close social interdependencies requires analysis of interactive efficacy determinants.

Recovery from a heart attack offers an important problem in which to study both the impact of interactive efficacy and the contribution of self-percepts of efficacy to health-promoting habits. In recovering from a heart attack the restoration of perceived physical efficacy is an essential ingredient in the process. The heart heals rapidly. But psychological recovery is slow for patients with uncomplicated myocardial infarction who believe their cardiac capability is too impaired to resume their customary activities. They avoid physical exertion and recreational activities they previously enjoyed, they are slow to resume vocational and social life on the belief they will over-burden their debilitated cardiac capacity, and they fear that sexual activities will do them in. The rehabilitative task is to restore a sense of cardiac efficacy so that postcoronary patients can lead full, productive lives.

Physicians typically use one or more of the four principal sources of efficacy information in efforts to convince postcoronary patients of their cardiac robustness. Enactive efficacy information is compellingly conveyed by strenuous treadmill exercises. Vicarious efficacy information is provided by enlisting the aid of former patients who exemplify active lives. Persuasive efficacy information is furnished by informing patients about what they are capable of doing. The meaning of physiological efficacy information is explained to ensure that patients do not misread their physiology, for example, by misinterpreting cardiac acceleration as portending a reinfarction or misattributing common bodily disturbances to an impaired heart. Patients who regard themselves as physically efficacious perform heavier workloads on the treadmill, and treadmill exercises and explanatory consultation, in turn, augment perceived physical efficacy (Ewart, Taylor, Reese, and DeBusk, 1983). Perceived physical capability is a better predictor of resumption of an active life than cardiovascular capacity as reflected in peak heart rate on the treadmill.

Psychological recovery from a heart attack is a social rather than individual matter. Wives' notions about their husbands' cardiac and physical capabilities can aid or retard the recovery. In a study exploring this process (Taylor, Bandura, Ewart, Miller, and DeBusk, 1985), several weeks after patients had experienced a myocardial infarction their self-percepts of physical efficacy were measured for physical exertion, cardiac capability, emotional stress, and sexual activities before and after treadmill exercises. Judgments of cardiac efficacy are especially interesting because postinfarction patients are likely to base their level of activity on how robust they perceive their heart to be. Spouses' judgments of their husbands' physical efficacy were also measured with three levels of involvement in the treadmill activity – when she was uninvolved in the treadmill exercises; when she was present to observe the husband's stamina as he performed treadmill with increasing workloads; or when she herself performed strenuous treadmill exercises to experience personally the physical demands of the task, after having observed her husband do the same. In the informative consultation with the medical staff, which followed the treadmill activity, couples received information about the patient's cardiac functioning and its relation to physical, vocational, and sexual activity. Their stamina on the treadmill is presented to patients as a generic indicant of their cardiovascular robustness; that is, the workloads they performed far exceed the strain that everyday activities might place on their cardiovascular system.

Treadmill activities increased patients' perceptions of their physical and cardiac efficacy. Wives who were either uninvolved in, or merely observers of, the treadmill activity continued to perceive their husbands' cardiovascular capabilities as impaired, even after receiving medical counseling to the contrary. In contrast, wives who personally experienced the strenuousness of the treadmill activity raised their perceptions of their husbands' physical and cardiac efficacy after they observed their husband's treadmill attainments and received medical counseling. The joint beliefs of patients and wives in the patients' cardiac capabilities was a consistently good predictor of cardiovascular functioning on treadmill tests conducted months later. Perceived cardiac efficacy predicted future level of cardiovascular functioning with initial treadmill performance partialled out, whereas initial treadmill performance did not with perceived efficacy partialled out. Wives who judge that their husbands have a robust heart are much more likely to encourage them to resume an active life than those who believe the heart is impaired and vulnerable to further damage. Pursuit of an active life improves patients' ability to manage energetic activities without over-taxing the cardiovascular system.

There is a good deal of research to indicate that perceived self-efficacy mediates health behavior. Unless people believe they can master and adhere to health-promoting habits, they are unlikely to devote the effort necessary to succeed. Thus, those who consider themselves incapable of kicking the smoking habit do not even try, despite grim health warnings, whereas the more self-efficacious override their cravings and break their smoking habit (DiClemente, Prochaska, and Gilbertini, 1985). The improvements patients with pulmonary disease derive from various behavioral and cognitive treatments partly depend on the degree to which their beliefs about their physical efficacy have been raised (Kaplan, Atkins and Reinsch, 1984). The more efficacious they judge themselves to be, the more physically active they become, and the greater the respiratory volumes and capacities they achieve. That health behavior is mediated through changes in perceived self-efficacy is further documented in the studies reviewed earlier on control of tension headaches and self-management of pain.

The diverse ways in which the exercise of perceived self-efficacy improves physiological functioning can combine to contribute significantly to psychological and physical well-being. A field experiment designed to retard or reverse deteriorative functioning in the elderly provides testimony for the health benefits of controllability (Langer and Rodin, 1976; Rodin and Langer, 1977). Elderly residents in a nursing home who were given personal control over their daily activities were happier, more actively interested and sociable, and physically healthier than those for whom the staff structured their activities.

Persuasive communications are widely used to get people to adopt health practices designed to prevent illness. In such health messages, appeals to fear depicting the ravages of disease are used as motivators, and recommended preventive practices are provided as guides for action. The early emphasis on fear arousal proved counterproductive in that it fostered avoidance of the grisly messages and undermined people's perceived ability to control health threats (Beck and Frankel, 1981; Leventhal, 1970). People need knowledge of potential dangers to warrant action, but they do not have to be frightened to act, anymore than students have to be scared out of their wits to study or homeowners to insure their households.

What people need is knowledge about how to regulate their behavior and firm belief in their personal efficacy to turn concerns about future maladies into effective preventive actions. Beck and Lund (1981) studied the persuasiveness of health communications in which the seriousness of periodontal disease and susceptibility to it were varied. Patients' perceived efficacy that they could stick to the required hygienic routine was a good predictor of whether they adopted it, whereas fear arousal predicted neither intention nor behavior. The perceived inefficacy barrier to preventive health is all too familiar in peoples' resignation concerning different health risks over which they can exercise control. For instance, obsese persons who judge themselves incapable of shedding their excess pounds permanently are disinclined to mount the effort needed to do so, however perturbed they might be about the health and personal costs of obesity. The self-inefficacious not only forego preventive practices, but if they judge themselves incapable of managing pain, they are prone to avoid corrective treatment as well (Klepac, Dowling and Hauge, 1982). To be most effective, health communications should instill in people the belief that they have the capability to alter their health habits. Communications that explicitly do so increase people's determination to modify habits detrimental to health (Maddux and Rogers, 1983). To strengthen the staying power of instilled self-beliefs, the communications should emphasize that success requires perseverant effort so that people's sense of personal efficacy is not undermined by a few setbacks.

References

Bandura, A. (1982a). Self-efficacy mechanism in human agency. *American Psychologist, 37,* 122–147.

Barling, J. and Abel, M. (1983). Self-efficacy beliefs and tennis performance. *Cognitive Therapy and Research, 7,* 265–272.

Barling, J. and Beattie, R. (1983). Self-efficacy beliefs and sales performance. *Journal of Organizational and Behavior Management, 5,* 41–51.

Beck, K. H. and Frankel, A. (1981). A conceptualization of threat communications and protective health behavior. *Social Psychology Quarterly, 44,* 204–217.

Beck, K. H. and Lund, A. K. (1981). The effects of health threat seriousness and personal efficacy upon intentions and behavior. *Journal of Applied Social Psychology, 11,* 401–415.

Bolles, R. C. and Fanselow, M. S. (1982). Endorphins and behavior. *Annual Reviews of Psychology, 33,* 87–101.

Colletti, G., Supnick, J. A. and Payne, T. J. (1985). The smoking self-efficacy questionnaire (SSEQ): Preliminary scale development and validation. *Behavioral Assessment, 7,* 249–260.

Condiotte, M. M. and Lichtenstein, E. (1981). Self-efficacy and relapse in smoking cessation programs. *Journal of Consulting and Clinical Psychology, 49,* 648–658.

Cooney, N. L., Kopel, S. A. and McKeon, P. (1982). *Controlled relapse training and self-efficacy in ex-smokers.* Paper presented at the annual meeting of the American Psychological Association, Washington, D.C.

DiClemente, C. C. (1981). Self-efficacy and smoking cessation maintenance: A preliminary report. *Cognitive Therapy and Research, 5,* 175–187.

DiClemente, C. C., Prochaska, J. O. and Gilbertini, M. (1985). Self-efficacy and the stages of self-change of smoking. *Cognitive Therapy and Research.*

Evans, F. J. (1974). The placebo response in pain reduction. In J. J. Bonica (ed.), *Advances in neurology* (Vol. 4, pp. 289–296). New York: Raven.

Ewart, C. K., Taylor, C. B., Reese, L. B. and DeBusk, R. F. (1983). Effects of early post-myocardial infarction exercise testing on self-perception and subsequent physical activity. *American Journal of Cardiology, 51,* 1076–1080.

Godding, P. R. and Glasgow, R. E. (1985). Self-efficacy and outcome expectancy as predictors of controlled smoking status. *Cognitive Therapy and Research. 9,* 123–31.

Hyson, R. L., Ashcraft, L. J., Drugan, R. C., Grau, J. W. and Maier, S. F. (1982). Extent and control of shock affects naltrexone sensitivity of stress-induced analgesia and reactivity to morphine. *Pharmacology Biochemistry & Behavior, 17,* 1019–1025.

Kaplan, R. M., Atkins, C. J. and Reinsch, S. (1984). Specific efficacy expectations mediate exercise compliance in patients with COPD. *Health Psychology, 3,* 233–242.

Killen, J. D., Maccoby, N. and Taylor, C. B. (1984). Nicotine gum and self-regulation training in smoking relapse prevention. *Behavior Therapy, 15,* 234–248.

Klepac, R. K., Dowling, J. and Hauge, C. (1982). Characteristics of clients seeking therapy for the reduction of dental avoidance: Reactions to pain. *Journal of Behaviour Therapy and Experimental Psychiatry, 13,* 293–300.

Langer, E. J. and Rodin, J. (1976). The effects of choice and enhanced personality responsibility for the aged: A field experiment in an institutional setting. *Journal of Personality and Social Psychology, 34,* 191–198.

Lee, C. (1984a). Accuracy of efficacy and outcome expectations in predicting performance in a simulated assertiveness task. *Cognitive Therapy and Research, 8,* 37–48.

Lee, C. (1984b). Efficacy expectations and outcome expectations as predictors of performance in a snake-handling task. *Cognitive Therapy and Research, 8,* 509–516.

Leventhal, H. (1970). Findings and theory in the study of fear communications. In L. Berkowitz (ed.), *Advances in experimental social psychology* (Vol. 5, pp. 119–186). New York: Academic Press.

Levine, J. D., Gordon, N. C. and Fields, H. L. (1978). The mechanism of placebo analgesia. *The Lancet,* September 23 pp. 654–657.

Levine, J. D., Gordon, N. C., Jones, R. T. and Fields, H. L. (1978). The narcotic antagonist naloxone enhances clinical pain. *Nature, 272,* 826–827.

Maddux, J. E. and Rogers, R. W. (1983). Protection motivation and self-efficacy: A revised theory of fear appeals and attitude change. *Journal of Experimental Social Psychology, 19,* 469–479.

Maddux, J. E., Sherer, M. and Rogers, R. W. (1982). Self-efficacy expectancy and outcome expectancy: Their relationships and their effects. *Cognitive Therapy and Research, 6,* 207–212.

McIntyre, K. O., Lichtenstein, E. and Mermelstein, R. J. (1983). Self-efficacy and relapse in smoking cessation: A replication and extension. *Journal of Consulting and Clinical Psychology, 51*, 632–633.

Manning, M. M. and Wright, T. L. (1983). Self-efficacy expectancies, outcome expectancies and the persistence of pain control in childbirth. *Journal of Personality and Social Psychology, 45*, 421–431.

Marlatt, G. A. and Gordon, J. R. (1980). Determinants of relapse: Implications for the maintenance of behavior change. In P. O. Davidson and S. M. Davidson (eds), *Behavioral Medicine: Changing health lifestyles* pp. 410–452. New York: Brunner/Mazel.

Neufeld, R. W. J. and Thomas, P. (1977). Effects of perceived efficacy of a prophylactic controlling mechanism on self-control under pain stimulation. *Canadian Journal of Behavioural Science, 9*, 224–232.

Reese, L. (1983). *Coping with pain: The role of perceived self-efficacy.* Unpublished doctoral dissertation, Stanford University, Stanford, CA.

Reynolds, R., Creer, T. L., Holroyd, K. A. and Tobin, D. L. (1982). *Assessment in the treatment of cigarette smoking: The development of the smokers' self-efficacy scale.* Paper presented at the meeting of the Association of Behavior Therapy, Los Angeles.

Rodin, J. and Langer, E. J. (1977). Long-term effects of a control-relevant intervention with the institutionalized aged. *Journal of Personality and Social Psychology, 35*, 897–902.

Shoor, S. M. and Holman, H. R. (1984). Development of an instrument to explore psychological mediators of outcome of chronic arthritis. *Transactions of the Association of American Physicians, 97*, 325–331.

Turk, D., Meichenbaum, D. and Genest, M. (1981). *Cognitive therapy of pain.* New York: Guilford.

Walker, W. B. and Franzini, L. R. (1983). *Self-efficacy and low risk aversive group treatments for smoking cessation.* Paper presented at the annual convention of the western Psychological Association, San Francisco.

Williams, S. L. and Watson, N. (1985). Perceived danger and perceived self-efficacy as cognitive mediators of acrophobic behavior. *Behavior therapy, 16*, 136–146.

Wolf, S. (1950). Effects of suggestion and conditioning on the action of chemical agents in human subjects-the pharmacology of placebos. *Journal of Clinical Investigation, 29*, 100–109.

7 EMOTION NARRATIVES:
A Radical New Research Approach

Richard S. Lazarus

In Lazarus and Folkman (1984), we dealt mainly with psychological stress, with only a single chapter devoted to emotion from a cognitive-motivational-relational perspective. When I started the present book [Stress and emotion. A new synthesis] I was convinced that psychological stress and emotion should be portrayed categorically rather than dimensionally and studied as a system of interrelated variables that includes not only harm, threat, and challenge – that is, the stress emotions – but would also include emotions that are usually referred to as positively toned.

However, partly as a result of a recent experience I had as a commentator on an interesting and challenging article by Somerfield and commentators (1997), who presented a systems theory model of stress and coping for applied research, I have developed a new viewpoint about the best research strategy for the emotions. Somerfield's presentation was a target article that attracted comments by fourteen active research scholars, many of them well known. He summarizes his basic thesis in the abstract for his article:

> Contemporary conceptual models of stress and coping are intricate systems for-mulations that depict adaptation as a dynamic, interactional process. The inherent complexity of these models presents conceptual and methodological challenges that make testing a complete model difficult. This article makes a case for a more microanalytic strategy for applied coping research that, by centering attention and available resources on selected high-frequency, high-stress problems, permits more conceptually sophisticated and clinically informative analyses. (p. 133)

My own comments were largely supportive of Somerfield's view that stress and coping must be approached in a holistic way as a system of many variables and processes. I did, however, have some reservations about his main recommendation – namely, that research be concentrated on a single, well-defined stressor, such as cancer. Other commentators addressed the same point, while indicating substantial support for the basic systems research premise.

Confusion is created by trying to compare coping in people who are struggling with many different kinds of stress, which makes it sensible to suggest that coping comparisons be restricted to the same kind of stress. There is also much data showing that coping varies when its must deal with diverse harms/losses, threats, and challenges. Each type of stress creates distinctive demands, constraints, and opportunities and, therefore, cannot be approached effectively by a common coping strategy. It is sound to say, as Somerfield does, that concentrating on a single stressful event or set of transactions would reduce the confusion resulting from this dependence of coping on the kind of stress being faced.

However, this solution is probably impractical because major and complex medical illnesses, and even the various cancers, have distinctly different psychological ramifications. Many of the demands, constraints, and resources involved in each particular illness, or even each type of cancer, are distinctive and call for different coping processes. This makes it important to compare appraisal and coping processes across illness, whether in the same study or as several overlapping research projects.

Thus, having as we do a separate National Institute of Health for each major illness, such as heart disease, cancer, and so on, makes it difficult to learn in what ways the psychological impact of one illness overlaps and differs from that of other illnesses. Not only does Somerfield's proposal of selecting a single disease fail to solve the problem of enabling us to compare coping within common sources of psychological stress, but it adds a further problem of narrowing too much the scope of the inquiry. Over the course of writing for publication my comments on Somerfield's proposal, and as a result of later ruminations, I began to have increasing doubts about a systems research approach as a solution to psychology's current doldrums.

My second reservation concerns the viability of a systems theory research approach, regardless of how it is organized. Although I view systems research as an idealized way of thinking about and doing research from a traditional scientific standpoint, and I believe it has much to offer, I do not think it is a practical strategy for adding to our knowledge and understanding of so complex a system as stress and emotion. The high costs of longitudinal systems research, which is what would be needed to fulfill Somerfield's programme, and established institutional patterns with their well-entrenched professional reward systems, would inhibit researchers and supporting agencies from following his recommendations.

There are also too many antecedent, mediating, and outcome variables to deal with for an adequate test of this strategy. I believe the good idea of doing research within a systems theory framework is likely to fail. And restricting one's research to a modest number of variables to make it more practical reduces the value of systems thinking and research.

Still another reservation, which goes to the heart of my concerns about psychological science itself, is that systems theory research is dependent entirely on a traditional analytic science cause-and-effect framework, which in itself is incomplete as an approach to gaining knowledge (Lazarus, 1998).

I have been at pains to show that we should view what we are studying when looking for causal variables as part-whole relationships or as limited systems operating within larger systems. After we have broken a phenomenon down in a reductive, analytic search for causal components – that is, part processes – the whole phenomenon must still be resynthesized to what it is in nature. Traditional science does not, as a rule, put them back together again, and often treats the parts as if they were the whole.

As a result of my growing reservations about these issues, I became interested in a different approach to the emotions – one that adopts a narrative perspective. In Lazarus and Lazarus (1994) my wife and I came close to proposing such an approach, but we did not because that book was intended for nonprofessionals. I present such an approach in this chapter.

But before embarking on the narrative methodology for the study of the emotions, I want to be fair to the systems view, which I had previously espoused (see Lazarus, 1990), and whose logical virtues I can still appreciate. I also want to verbalize more fully and clearly some other reservations about systems research on stress and emotion. Allow me, therefore, to backtrack to a systems view of stress, coping, and the emotions, and to consider some of its problems in more detail, after which I try to formulate a narrative approach that could guide programmatic research.

A Systems Theory Approach

In Lazarus and Folkman (1984), we presented several charts identifying the variables of a psychological stress and coping system as then conceptualized. One (p. 305) was a theoretical schematization of stress, coping, and adaptation. A second (p. 307) looked more closely at the portion of the first chart that dealt microanalaytically with mediating processes over time and across diverse types of encounters. A third chart (p. 308) distinguished among types of variables and processes, including causal antecedents, mediating processes, and immediate effects, which were presented at three levels of analysis, the social, psychological, and physiological.

These charts portrayed what we believed then to be the most important variables of a systems approach to stress and coping, which interact to produce the state of mind and adaptational patterns that characterize a stressful transaction. The basic chart is reproduced again below in Figure 7.1a.

I have also added to and modified Figure 7.1a slightly to make it more complete in the light of afterthoughts during the intervening years. The revision is shown in Figure 7.1b. A few more causal antecedents have been added in keeping with my present intention to integrate stress and emotion within the same analytic system. I have also added a new mediating appraisal construct – namely, benefit – which underlies positively toned emotions, the idea of core relational themes, and an outcome variable that consists of immediate and long-term emotions.

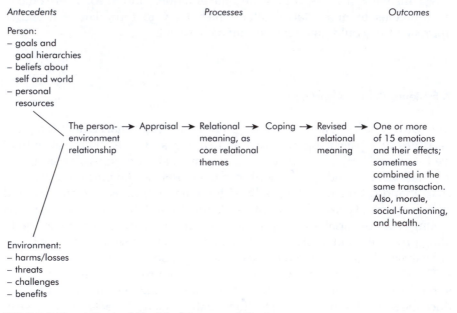

Causal Antecedents	Mediating Processes Time 1 … T2 … T3 … Tn Encounter 1 … 2 … 3 … n	Immediate Effects	Long-term Effects
Person variables Values-commitments Beliefs: Existential sense of control	Primary appraisal Secondary appraisal Reappraisal	Physiological changes Positive or negative feelings Quality of encounter outcome	Somatic health/illness Morale (well-being) Social functioning
Environment Situational demands, constraints Resources (e.g. social network) Ambiguity of harm Imminence of harm	Coping Problem focused Emotion focused Seeking, obtaining, and using social support		

Resolutions of each stressful encounter

FIGURE 7.1a **A Theoretical Schematization of Stress, Coping, and Adaptation. From Lazarus and Folkman, 1984, p. 305**

Antecedents	Processes	Outcomes
Person: – goals and goal hierarchies – beliefs about self and world – personal resources	The person-environment relationship → Appraisal → Relational meaning, as core relational themes → Coping → Revised relational meaning →	One or more of 15 emotions and their effects; sometimes combined in the same transaction. Also, morale, social-functioning, and health.
Environment: – harms/losses – threats – challenges – benefits		

FIGURE 7.1b **A Revised Model of Stress and Coping**

The original figures for the second and third charts in the 1984 book have again been reproduced in Figures 7.2 and 7.3.

To make the psychodynamics of Figure 7.1a fully comprehensible, one would need to set up separate figures representing different temporal moments and conditions for each process variable in the system – namely, appraisal, coping, and the relational theme for each emotion. I struggled for

Mediating processes

Time 1	Time 2	Time 3	... Time N
Encounter 1	Encounter 2	Encounter 3	... Encounter N

Appraisal-reappraisal

Coping
  Problem-focused
  Emotion-focused

Social support
  Emotional
  Tangible
  Informational

FIGURE 7.2   **A Transactional Model: Ipsative-normative Arrangement. From Lazarus and Folkman (1984), p. 307**

a long time to no avail to think of ways of putting the theory together in a single figure, or even a figure for each emotion, but this strategy became too complex and cumbersome.

If we are to do justice to all the important variables and their sites of influence, in addition to the multiplication of figures the system would need to have more than a two-dimensional space. All that one can do with most figures is to list the variables for each epistemic category – that is, antecedents, mediating processes, immediate, and long-term consequences – and to suggest, somewhat vaguely, the process relationships with arrows.

Although I have used figures sparingly in previous writing, I have always been wary of them and the arrows employed to show the directional influences of the variables and their feedback loops. Figures like these, and those with boxes connected with multiple arrows, suggest much more knowledge and detailed conceptualizations than are available at present. They leave out crucial processes and relationships, and they often obscure what one wants to communicate because the arrows are, at best, suggestive, and do not identify the diverse contexts so important to what happens in nature. I fear that what they do is to grossly oversimplify the system, and create only the illusion of understanding.

For example, appraising and coping processes influence just about everything in the system, but the specifics of this influence are not communicated by a generalized arrow or double arrow – the forms of influence are too complex and conditional to be adequately portrayed in such on oversimplified, schematic way. Similarly, there are so many different kinds of coping processes, and their influences are so complex and conditional, that a few arrows tell us little. In effect, for a broad theory the "right medicine" must lie in the details, and psychological scientists who present only simplifying principles, believing that they can be diagrammed neatly, may be fooling themselves and managing to undercut the richness and complexity inherent in the principles being portrayed.

	Causal Antecedents	Mediating Processes	Immediate Effects	Long-term Effects
SOCIAL	Socioeconomic status Cultural templates Institutional systems Group structures (e.g. role patterns) Social networks	Social supports as proffered Available social/institutional means of ameliorating problems	Social disturbances Government responses Sociopolitical pressures Group alienation	Social failure Revolution Social change Structural changes
PSYCHOLOGICAL	Person variables Values-commitments Beliefs-assumptions (e.g. personal control) Cognitive coping styles Environmental (Situational) variables Situational demands Imminence Timing Ambiguity Social and material resources	Vulnerabilities Appraisal-reappraisal Coping Problem focused Emotion focused Cultivating, seeking, and using social support Perceived social support Emotional Tangible Informational	Positive or negative feelings Quality of outcome of stressful encounters	Morale Functioning in the world
PHYSIOLOGICAL	Genetic or constitutional factors Physiological conditioning— Individual response Stereotype (e.g. Lacey) Illness risk factors (e.g. smoking)	Immune resources Species vulnerability Temporary vulnerability Acquired defects	Somatic changes (precursors of illness) Acute illness	Chronic illness Impaired physiological functioning Recovery from illness Longevity

FIGURE 7.3 **Three Levels of Analysis. From Lazarus and Folkman, 1984, p. 308**

Besides, the essence of an adaptational transaction is that the whole system changes from moment to moment and from one emotional context to another, sometimes as a result of a seemingly minor statement, action, or expressive gesture. This change, which may be profound, as when there is a complete transformation of the emotional content, can be the result of a single antecedent variable, mediating process, or outcome, yet lead to major reappraisals that profoundly change the relational meanings of the transaction for those engaged in it.

In Figure 7.2 in Lazarus and Folkman (1984), we tried to suggest temporal and condition-induced changes by representing them as mediating processes. In one row, we used the designations "$T1$, $T2$, $T3$, Tn" to represent time; a second row employed the designations 'Encounter 1, 2, 3, n' to represent conditions. As I said, there seems to be no handy way to portray the multiple contents of these processual changes, except in a set of schematizing snapshots, like the separate frames of a film. So we must not go overboard about the value of a few simplifying diagrams. They obscure as much as they clarify.

My reservations about systems theories, which provide merely general guidelines for research variables worthy of study, were strengthened by failure to find a workable diagrammatic formula nearly 15 years after the Lazarus-Folkman book appeared. The unsuccessful struggle to find one helped fuel my growing interest in narrative strategies. The main issues, however, are not diagrammatic, but lie in the assumptions we must make, which are addressed below.

One of the commentators on Somerfield's article, David Spiegel (1997), mentioned narrative analysis in his comments, which I found apt and instructive and compatible with my own outlook. I quote some of what he wrote below (p. 170), though I have broken up some of his longer statements into several paragraphs to increase clarity and sharpen the emphasis:

> Professor Somerfield asks us in his interesting article to re-examine the archetypal epistemological problem. We must to some extent impose our perceptions upon the world in order to perceive, organize and understand it, and yet we always do so at a price.
>
> Modern psychological science has been biased towards quantitative analysis of data, a rather Aristotelian viewpoint, but also toward the goal of platonic simplicity of theory. We are often caught in the dilemma that *our theories are either too elegant to be meaningful or too full of meaning to be elegant.*
>
> Coping is an important construct and yet it has become clear that it has a short life span – that we must ask the question 'Coping by whom? At what time in response to what stressor? And in what context?'
>
> It is a healthy development in research that rigorous investigations are starting to utilize techniques that a decade ago would have been considered hopelessly messy, such as narrative analysis. Thus, researchers are beginning to address the common complaint of clinicians, that they fail to adequately take into account the existential reality of individuals in life threatening situations. Developments in cognitive psychology have been similarly helpful.

> We have moved from an era of arid behaviorism in which the very brain that distinguishes human experiences from that of all other animals was slighted as a black box and largely ignored, to one in which the perceptual, emotional and cognitive processing of information has become an interesting and important problem to be examined. (italics added)

When he says in the statement I have italicized that 'our theories are either too elegant to be meaningful or too full of meaning to be elegant,' Spiegel's phraseology is epigrammatically pure and absolutely delightful. I was so pleased by it that I wrote it down for later use, and trotted it out here in developing this argument.

In thinking about the contents of this quotation, by the way, the reader should remember that in my version of a systems analysis the antecedents consist of objective variables of the person and the environment, but it is the person's construal of these that counts – that is, what I have been calling appraisal and relational meaning. As Somerfield acknowledges in his author's response to the commentators, research can be variable centred or person centred, and which is chosen makes a vital difference in how one looks at the emotion process (see also Magnussor and Bergman, 1997).

Now, however, we must revisit the distinctions between objective and subjective and think them through more carefully. They are especially relevant to the variable-versus person-centred distinction, which seems not to have been as carefully drawn as it should be for maximal clarity.

Revisiting Objective Versus Subjective

This distinction really depends on whose perspective is being used to refer to the person and the environment in the person-environment relationship. When, for example, personality psychologists attempt to measure or describe the personality of an individual, or many individuals, their perspective is usually variable centred and objective. It does not matter what are the sources of data, personality tests, or clinical inferences. It is the professional or research observer who is making the assessment, and with the intention of describing persons as they really are, not as they think they are.

The same would apply it one attempted to describe the self or the environment on the basis of a consensus of observers. Even if one considers the perspective of a single individual, a person-centred approach can remain objective in that it is the observer who defines what the person is like and how that person views self and world. This contrasts with a person-centred perspective that is entirely subjective – that is, when the view of self and world is from an individual person's own perspective.

The tricky part of these two distinctions, person versus variable centred, and objective versus subjective, is that we tend to think of variable centred as objective and person centred as subjective. However, this association is not always an accurate rendition of the research possibilities and even less of the research realities. We must think of the permutations and combinations as a fourfold table, one with four cells – namely, variable centred and objective, variable centred and subjective, person centred and objective, and person centred and subjective, though they are not equally probable in all four cells.

Regardless of our biased impression, however, there is no reason variable and person centred could not be considered from *both* the objective and subjective frame of reference, though to do so may seem like a stretch and a bit awkward. It becomes evident that the objective versus subjective, and variable-versus person-centred distinctions can involve all sorts of permutations and combinations.

This reasoning must still be applied to the narrative approach in the study of the emotions. In doing so, it might be useful to draw on an analogy between biography and autobiography. In biography, it is someone else who is telling the life story. Biographers may use a mixture of objective and subjective sources of data, but the presumption is usually made that the biographer is searching for objective truth, not merely the truth as viewed by the subject of the biography. Autobiographers, conversely, are telling their own life story as conceived by the storyteller. It is usually written from a subjective frame of reference, even if the author maintains the illusion that this life is being described objectively.

It behoves us to keep this analogy in mind when we examine the narrative approach to the emotions. Although a narrative is usually viewed from a subjective frame of reference, if the preceding reasoning viewed from a subjective frame of reference, if the preceding reasoning is sound, it could be made to reflect either an objective or a subjective frame of reference. This would depend, of course, on who is doing the assessment of self and world. Remember too that my own bias is that it is the person-environment relationship, as construed by the person, which is the best strategy for obtaining an adequate understanding of stress, emotion, and adaptation.

A different but related comment on Somerfield's thesis, which was made by Hannalore Weber (1997), emphasizes personal goals as the main organizing principle wherein meaning is achieved. Although she focuses on a person-centred perspective, her statement of this is not necessarily limited to the principle of methodological subjectivity. Personal goals as personality dispositions can be measured subjectively by asking the person about goals and goal hierarchies, or independently of the person's appraisal. This would highlight the difference between subjective and objective approaches, assuming that they are not highly correlated.

In so saying, allow me also to remind you that my kind of subjectivism presumes that a person always negotiates between the desire to know the truth and the desire to view the truth in the most positive light possible to preserve hope and sanguinity. In other words, because wish and reality both contribute to what is appraised, mine is a modified subjectivism; therefore, it must remain on friendly terms with objective, variable-centred research.

Returning now to the problems of systems theory research on stress and emotion, objective variables operate at a different level of analysis than relational meanings, which are strongly subjective, and often partly private until we try to make them public. I am somewhat uncertain about the wisdom of putting these levels of analysis together in the same schematization; doing so might conflate their role and significance.

One good reason for putting them together, however, is for the unique purpose of testing whether the individual's subjective perspective conforms to the objective evidence, base on the judgments of observers. In doing this, we must be wary about presuming that if the two sources of knowledge disagree, the discrepancy implies psychopathology. Inevitably there is the question of which to base our inferences on, the subjective or the objective. My own guess is, more often than not, that the subjective is closer to the truth, but others may take a different view.

Although it would be useful to compare the objective and subjective frames of reference, putting them together routinely in the same correlational matrix in ordinary systems research on the variables that might account for stress, emotion, and adaptation carries a major analytic danger. It mixes apples and oranges, so to speak, especially if the relationship between them is weak or modest, which is an empirical question. Perhaps a transformation is needed, such as Block's (1961) Q-sort methodology for mixed types of data.

Given the preceding reasoning, I now offer what I believe is a viable commonsense alternative – namely, a narrative or storied approach to each emotion, whose time may have come. If my concerns about levels of analysis could be assuaged, then this approach might make it possible to combine variable- and person-centred, subjective and objective, and normative and individualistic perspectives within the same research designs without losing the special values of each.

If we want to study emotion narratives as science, we must combine the narratives of many individuals to see in what ways the stories are shared and reflect the collective experience of people in each of the emotions, and in what ways they diverge. It will be necessary to do this to determine the prototypical narrative for each emotion, and to consider subvarieties that deserve being treated as special categories – but more of this shortly.

Emotion Narratives

A narrative approach to persons and their lives is not new to psychology. It has gained considerable favour in recent years. The list of those who have drawn on it or made it central to their thinking is growing. A modest sampling, however, would include Bruner (1990), Cohler (1982), Coles (1989), Gergen and Gergen (1986), Josselson and Lieblich (1993), McAdams (1996, 1997), Polkinghorne (1988), Sarbin (1986), and from a psychoanalytic perspective, Schafer (1981) and Spence (1982).

It is notable that work of this kind thrived mostly in the 1980s and 1990s, the period during which interest in the emotions also burgeoned. The cognitivizing of psychology since the 1970s, which meant a firm rejection of radical behaviourism and the wider acceptance of a cognitive-mediational perspective, probably had much to do with this.

There has not been, as far as I know, a systematic portrayal of a narrative approach to the emotions, one that would also provide for programmatic research to fit a narrative conceptualization. Although appraisal theory often sounds like a narrative (e.g. Shaver, et al., 1987), and makes use of a similar perspective, no one at present seems to know exactly how to go about developing a narrative approach, so much of what is written below may seem to have a radical flavour.

What is an emotion narrative, and what is its structure? To use the imagery of Lazarus and Lazarus (1994), it is a dramatic plot or story that describes the provocation of the emotion and its background, which helps define what made some action, or lack of action when it was desired, provocative, and how it progressed and turned out. The drama begins with the provoking action and proceeds through the continuing transaction – usually interpersonal. The provocation is best viewed as the figure in a *figure-ground* relationship.

Generally, to understand the emotional reaction to a provocation requires more than an examination of the initial action. We need to know its *background*, which takes the form of a history of the relationship and the relevant personality variables (dispositions) that shape the emotional reactions of the persons who play a role in the ongoing transaction.

The important personality variables consist of goals and goal hierarchies (in layperson's terms, what is important and unimportant to the person), beliefs about self and world, and personal resources. Goals and beliefs, and the mutual actions and reactions that occur, furl *situational intentions* that are present either before or during the transaction. Beliefs include what the parties have learned to expect from each other, and in what ways they are motivationally important to each other.

These person-centred and environmental variables (most often what another person does) set the stage for appraisals by both parties – these might be similar or quite different – of the relational meaning of what is happening, which in turn, shapes the emotions aroused and how they change over the course of the encounter. Appraisals and reappraisals generate coping processes, which are adaptationally relevant responses to complex demands, constraints, and opportunities, and are a key part of the emotion process. These cognitive-motivational-relational processes influence and change the *relational meanings* constructed from the chain of events that characterizes the emotional drama.

Unless we want to use only a snapshot of a single moment rather than a continuing picture, the narrative does not end with the emotional reaction of one or both participants. Emotional encounters proceed continuously over time, as in a drama or film, and when they end – if they ever do – it may be only temporarily, as the parties separate, resolve their conflict, or terminate the transaction or business.

We could, for example, define an ending as the close of a particular kind of business that is being transacted and the beginning of another, based on each person's goals and situational intentions. Depending on personal characteristics, and the depth and continuity of the relationship, the emotional transaction may not really end, however, until the departure or death of one or both of the participants; it may still continue to fester in the mind of a survivor.

Like the fiction writer of a dramatic story, the film director who decides when to shut off the camera for dramatic effect, or because the conflict has been resolved, it is often arbitrary when we say the transaction has ended. In most relationships, each new transaction tends to repeat previous ones, though the details are likely to differ and new issues may emerge. Relationships do not usually remain static, but change over time, without old features necessarily being discarded.

As I said, the emotion process can be seen in figure-ground terms, the background in the form of a relational history. This background has as much to do with why what occurred was an emotional provocation, as does the figural act itself. Thus, Klos and Singer (1981) report that the arousal of anger in parent–child relationships they studies was influenced by the history of interpersonal stress even more than the provocative action itself, which is what most observers would be inclined to blame.

What occurred leads to several alternative short-term outcomes – for example, an impasse, partial resolution, full resolution, continuing emotional distress, deepening resentment, a parting of the ways, violence, and so forth, none of which is readily predictable without a full grasp of the figure and background of these event and what is in the minds of the two participants. What happens in this flow influences the emotional states and actions of the provocateur, as well as the recipient, and this recurrent feedback constitutes a kind of social dialogue in which the roles of provocateur and recipient can be reversed any number of times.

References

Block, J. (1961). *The Q-sort method is personality assessment and psychiatric research.* Springfield, IL: Charles. C. Thomas.

Bruner, J. S. (1990). *Acts of meaning.* Cambridge, MA: Harvard University Press.

Cohler, B. J. (1982). Personal narrative and the life course. In P. B. Baltes and O. G. Brim Jr. (eds), *Life span development and behavior* Vol. 4, pp. 205–241. New York: Academic Press.

Coles, R. (1989). *The call to stories.* Boston: Houghton Mifflin.

Gergen, K. J. and Gergen, M. M. (1986). Narrative form and the construction of psychological science. In T. R. Sarbin (ed.), *Narrative psychology: the storied nature of human conduct* pp. 22–44. New York: Praeger.

Josselson, R. and Lieblich, A. (eds) (1993). *The narrative study of lives*. Newbury Park, CA: Sage.

Klos, D. S. and Singer, J. L. (1981). Determinants of the adolescent's ongoing thought following simulated parental confrontations. *Journal of Personality and Social Psychology, 41,* 975–987.

Lazarus, R. S. and Commentators. (1990). Theory-based stress measurement. *Psychological Inquiry, 1,* 3–51.

Lazarus, R. S. (1998a). *Fifty years of research and theory by R. S. Lazarus: Perennial historical issues*. Mahwah, NJ: Erlbaum.

Lazarus, R. S. (1998b). Coping with aging: Individuality as a key to understanding. In I. H. Nordhus, G. VandenBos, S. Berg, and P. Fromholt (eds), *Clinical Geropsychology* pp. 109–127. Washington, DC: American Psychological Association.

Lazarus, R. S. and Folkman, S. (1984). *Stress, appraisal and coping*. New York: Springer.

McAdams, D. P. (1996). Personality, modernity, and the stored self: A contemporary framework for studying persons. *Psychological Inquiry, 7,* 295–321.

McAdams, D. P. (1997). *The stories we live by: Personal myths and the making of the self*. New York: Guilford.

Magnusson, D. and Bergman, L. R. (1997). Individual development and adaptation: The IDA Program. *Reports from the Department of Psychology*. Stockholm, Sweden: Stockholm University.

Polkinghorne, D. (1988). *Narrative knowing and the human sciences*. Albany: State University of New York Press.

Sarbin, T. (ed.) (1986). *Narrative psychology: The storied nature of human conduct*. New York: Praeger.

Schafer, R. (1981). Narration in psychoanalytic dialogue. In W. J. J. Mitchell (ed.), *On narrative* pp. 25–49. Chicago: University of Chicago Press.

Shaver, P., Schwartz, J., Kirson, D., and O'Connor, C. (1987). Emotion knowledge: Further exploration of a prototype approach. *Journal of Personality and Social Psychology, 52,* 1061–1086.

Somerfield, M. R., and Commentators. (1997). The utility of systems models of stress and coping for applied research: The case of cancer adaptation. *Journal of Health Psychology, 2,* 133–172.

Spence, D. (1982). *Narrative truth and historical truth*. New York: Norton.

Spiegel, D. (1997). Understanding risk assessment by cancer patients: A commentary on Somerfield. *Journal of Health psychology, 2,* 170–171.

Weber, H. (1997). Sometimes more complex, sometimes more simple: A commentary on Somerfield. *Journal of Health Psychology, 2,* 171–172.

8 THE ROLE OF THEORY IN HIV PREVENTION

Martin Fishbein

We are now [in 2002] at the end of the second decade of the AIDS epidemic. Unfortunately, although we've made enormous progress in prolonging and improving the quality of life of those infected with HIV, we still have neither a cure for, nor a vaccine to prevent, this disease. Perhaps more important, it has become increasingly clear that preventing the transmission and the acquisition of HIV must focus upon behaviour and behaviour change. AIDS is first and foremost a consequence of behaviour. It is not who one is, but what one does, that determines whether he or she will expose themselves or others to HIV. As Kelly et al. (1993) pointed out, the task confronting the behavioural sciences is to develop theory-based intervention programmes to reduce 'risky' and increase 'healthy' behaviours. And I think it's safe to say that we have come a very long way in doing so.

In the past five years, there has been a growing recognition that behavioural science theory and research can play an important role in protecting and maintaining the public health (see, for example, Fishbein et al., 1996b). For example, in February of 1997, the National Institute of Health's (NIH) Office of Medical Applications Research conducted a Consensus Development Conference to evaluate the effectiveness of behavioural intervention methods to reduce the risk of HIV infection. A 12-member, non-federal, expert panel concluded that, 'Behavioral interventions to reduce risk for HIV/AIDS are effective and should be disseminated widely' (NIH, 1997).

Clearly, however, not all interventions are equally effective. What behavioural science theory and research can do is to provide guidelines for developing effective behaviour change programmes. For example, we have learned that the most effective interventions will be those directed at changing specific behaviours (e.g. walk for 20 minutes, three times a week) rather than behavioural categories (e.g. exercise) or goals (e.g. lose weight) (Fishbein et al., 1992). With respect to STDs/HIV, it's important to recognize that while the use of a male condom may be a behaviour for men, it is a goal for women. In addition, condom use is not a single behaviour but a behavioural category – condoms are used for different sexual activities with different types of partner, and always using a condom for vaginal sex with one's spouse or main partner is a very different behaviour to always using a condom for vaginal sex with a commercial sex worker, or always using a condom for anal sex with one's spouse.

Generally speaking, the definition of any given behaviour includes at least four elements: the action (e.g. using), the target (e.g. a condom), the context (e.g. anal sex with one's regular partner) and the time period in which the behaviour is observed or expected (e.g. always). Changes in any one element also change the behaviour one is observing. Thus for example, as indicated above, 'always using a condom for anal sex with my regular partner' is a different behaviour to 'always using a condom for anal sex with my occasional partners'. Similarly, 'always using a condom for anal sex in Location A' is a different behaviour to 'always using a condom for anal sex in Location B'.

So to be effective, interventions should focus upon specific behaviours and, perhaps not surprisingly, the most effective interventions will be those directed at a single behaviour rather than at multiple behaviours. This is because each behaviour is substantively unique, and the substantive factors influencing one behaviour are often very different to those influencing another behaviour. Despite this substantive uniqueness, there appear to be only a limited number of theoretical variables underlying any given behaviour.

Figure 8.1 provides an integration of several different leading theories of behavioural prediction and behaviour change (Ajzen and Fishbein, 1980; Bandura, 1986; 1994; Becker, 1974; Fishbein et al., 1991; 1992; Rosenstock et al., 1994). Before describing this model, however, there is one important point that needs to be made. I have often heard people argue that theoretical models such as the one presented in Figure 8.1 are 'Western' or 'US' models that don't apply to other cultures or countries or that these types of model are not culturally specific. In marked contrast, I would argue that when properly applied these models are culturally specific. For example, the relative importance of each of the variables in the model is expected to vary as a function of both the behaviour and the population under consideration. As I will try to demonstrate, when properly applied, these types of models require one to understand the behaviour from the perspective of the population being considered. In addition, I would argue that each of the variables in the model can be found in almost any culture or population. Indeed, the theoretical variables contained in the model described in Figure 8.1 have been tested in over 50 countries in both the developed and the developing world. So as I go through the elements of the model, I would ask you to consider whether there is anything in the model that is not relevant to the culture or population you wish to study.

Looking at Figure 8.1, it can be seen that any given behaviour is most likely to occur if one has a strong intention to perform the behaviour, if one has the necessary skills and abilities required to perform the behaviour, and if there are no environmental constraints preventing behavioural performance. Indeed, if one has made a strong commitment (or formed a strong intention) to perform a given behaviour, and if one has the necessary skills

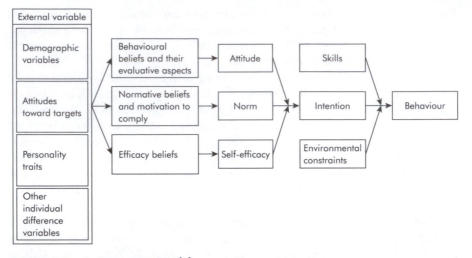

FIGURE 8.1   **An Integrative Model**

and the ability to perform the behaviour, and if there are no environmental constraints to prevent the performance of that behaviour, the probability is close to one that the behaviour will be performed (Fishbein et al., 1992).

Clearly, very different types of intervention will be necessary if one has formed an intention but is unable to act upon it, than if one has little or no intention to perform the behaviour in question. Thus, in some populations or cultures, the behaviour may not be performed because people have not yet formed intentions to perform the behaviour; while in others, the problem may be a lack of skills and/or the presence of environmental constraints. In still other cultures, more than one of these factors may be relevant. For example, von Haeften et al. (1999) present intention and behaviour data from, among other groups, commercial sex workers (CSWs) in Seattle, Washington. Perhaps not surprisingly, over 95% of female CSWs intend to use condoms for vaginal sex with their clients and almost 75% report carrying out these intentions. In contrast, only 30% intend to use condoms for vaginal sex with their main partners, and of those, only 40% are able to act on their intentions. Clearly if people have formed the desired intention but are not acting on it, a successful intervention will be directed either at skills building or will involve social engineering to remove (or to help people overcome) environmental constraints.

On the other hand, if strong intentions to perform the behaviour in question have not been formed, the model suggests that there are three primary determinants of intention: the attitude toward performing the behaviour (i.e. the person's overall feelings of favourableness or unfavourableness toward performing the behaviour), perceived norms concerning performance of the behaviour (including both perceptions of what others think one should do as well as perceptions of what others are doing), and one's self-efficacy with respect to performing the behaviour (i.e. one's belief that one can perform the behaviour even under a number of difficult circumstances). As indicated above, it is important to recognize that the relative importance of these three psychosocial variables as determinants of intention will depend upon both the behaviour and the population being considered. Thus, for example, one behaviour may be primarily determined by attitudinal considerations, while another may be primarily influenced by feelings of self-efficacy. Similarly, a behaviour that is attitudinally driven in one population or culture may be normatively driven in another. Thus, before developing interventions to change intentions, it is important to first determine the degree to which that intention is under attitudinal, normative or self-efficacy control in the population in question. Once again, it should be clear that very different interventions are needed for attitudinally controlled behaviours than for behaviours that are under normative influence or are strongly related to feelings of self-efficacy. Clearly, one size does not fit all and interventions that are successful in one culture or population may be a complete failure in another.

The model in Figure 8.1 also recognizes that attitudes, perceived norms and self-efficacy are all, themselves, functions of underlying beliefs – about the outcomes of performing the behaviour in question, about the normative proscriptions and/or behaviours of specific referents and about specific barriers to behavioural performance. Thus, for example, the more one believes that performing the behaviour in question will lead to 'good' outcomes and prevent 'bad' outcomes, the more favourable one's attitude toward performing the behaviour. Similarly, the more one believes that specific others think one should (or should not) perform the behaviour in question, and the more one is motivated to comply with those specific others, the more social pressure one will feel (or the stronger the subjective norm) with respect to performing (or not performing) the behaviour. Finally, the more one perceives that one can (i.e. has the necessary skills and abilities to) perform the behaviour, even in the face of specific barriers or obstacles, the stronger will be one's self-efficacy with respect to performing the behaviour.

It is at this level that the substantive uniqueness of each behaviour comes into play. For example, the barriers to using and/or the outcomes (or consequences) of using a condom for vaginal sex with one's spouse or main partner may be very different from those associated with using a condom for vaginal sex with a commercial sex worker or an occasional partner. Yet it is these specific beliefs that must be addressed in an intervention if one wishes to change intentions and behaviour. And although an investigator can sit in her or his office and develop measures of attitudes, perceived norms and self-efficacy, she or he cannot tell you what a given population (or a given person) believes about performing a given behaviour. Thus one must go to members of that population to identify salient outcome, normative and efficacy beliefs. One must understand the behaviour from the perspective of the population one is considering.

Finally, Figure 8.1 also shows the role played by more traditional demographic, personality, attitudinal and other individual difference variables (such as perceived risk). According to the model, these types of variable play primarily an indirect role in influencing behaviour. For example, while men and women may hold different beliefs about performing some behaviours, they may hold very similar beliefs with respect to others. Similarly rich and poor, old and young, those from developing and developed countries, those who do and do not perceive they are at risk for a given illness, those with favourable and unfavourable attitudes toward family planning, etc. may hold different attitudinal, normative or self-efficacy beliefs with respect to one behaviour but may hold similar beliefs with respect to another. Thus, there is no necessary relation between these 'external' or 'background' variables and any given behaviour. Nevertheless, external variables such as cultural differences and differences in a wide range of values should be reflected in the underlying belief structure.

This model represented by Figure 8.1 has now served as the theoretical underpinning for two large multi-site studies supported by the US Centers for Disease Control and Prevention (CDC). The first, known as the AIDS Community Demonstration Projects (CDC, 1996; CDC AIDS Community Demonstration Projects Research Group, 1999; Fishbein et al., 1996a; Higgins et al., 1997), attempted to reach members of populations at risk for STDs/HIV that were unlikely to come into contact with the health department. The second, known as Project RESPECT, was a multi-site randomized controlled trial designed to evaluate the effectiveness of STDs/HIV counselling and testing (Kamb et al., 1996, 1998). Project RESPECT asked whether prevention counselling or enhanced prevention counselling were more effective in increasing condom use and reducing incident STDs than standard education.

Although based on the same theoretical model, these two interventions were logistically very different. In one, the intervention was delivered 'in the street' by volunteer networks recruited from the community. In the other, the intervention was delivered one-on-one by trained counsellors in an STD clinic. Thus one involved community participation and mobilization while the other involved working within established public health settings. In addition, one was evaluated using the community as the unit of analysis while the other looked for behaviour change at the individual level.

Despite these logistic differences, both interventions produced highly significant behavioural change. In addition, in the clinic setting (where it was feasible to obtain biologic outcome measures), the intervention also produced a significant reduction in incident STDs. I would argue that the success of these two interventions is largely due to their reliance on established behavioural principles. More importantly, it appears that theory-based approaches that are tailored to specific populations and behaviours can be effective in different cultures and communities.

And at this point I would like to suggest that community participation and community mobilization are not 'theories of behavioural change', but instead are best viewed as strategies for change – while we do need theories to help us understand how to mobilize communities and get increased participation, these types of theory are very different to theories of behavioural prediction and behaviour change. More specifically, these types of theory do not help us identify the determinants of behaviour or behaviour change. Indeed, I think it's now safe to say that by helping us identify the determinants of specific behaviours, our current theories of behaviour and behaviour change have given us the tools we need to change behaviour. I believe that we really do know how to change behaviour, and I would argue that we really don't need 'new' theories of behaviour and behaviour change. What we do need, however, is for investigators and interventionists to better understand and correctly utilize existing, empirically supported behavioural theories in developing and evaluating behaviour change interventions.

References

Ajzen, I. and Fishbein, M. (1980). *Understanding attitudes and predicting social behaviour.* Englewood Cliffs, NJ: Prentice Hall.

Bandura, A. (1986). *Social foundations of thought and action: a social cognitive theory.* Englewood Cliffs, NJ: Prentice Hall.

Bandura, A. (1994). Social cognitive theory and exercise of control over HIV infection. In: R.J. Diclemente and J.L. Peterson (eds), *Preventing AIDS: theories and methods of behavioural interventions* (pp. 25–60). New York: Plenum Press.

Becker, M. (1974). The health belief model and personal health behavior. *Health Education Monographs, 2,* 324–473.

CDC (1996). Community-level prevention of human immunodeficiency virus infection among high-risk populations; the AIDS Community Demonstration Projects. *Morbidity and Mortality Weekly Report – Recommendations and Reports, 45*(RR-6).

CDC AIDS Community Demonstration Projects Research Group (1999). Community-level HIV intervention in 5 cities: final outcome data from the CDC AIDS Community Demonstration Projects. *American Journal of Public Health, 89*(3), 1–10.

Fishbein, M., Bandura, A., Triandis, H.C., Kanfer, F.H., Becker, M.H. and Middlestadt, S.E. (1992). Factors influencing behavior and behavior change: final report – theorist's workshop. Rockville, ML: National Institute of Mental Health.

Fishbein, M., Guenther-Grey, C., Johnson, W.D., Wolitski, R.J., McAlister, A., Rietmeijer, C.A., O'Reilly, K. and The AIDS Community Demonstration Projects (1996a). Using a theory-based community intervention to reduce AIDS risk behaviours: the CDC's AIDS Community Demonstration Projects. In: S. Oskamp and S.C. Thompson (eds), *Understanding and preventing HIV risk behavior: safer sex and drug use* (pp. 177–206). Thousand Oaks, CA: Sage.

Fishbein, M., Guinan, M., Holtgrave, D.R. and Leviton, L.C. (1996b). Behavioral science in HIV prevention. Special Issue, *Public Health Reports, 111.* (Suppl. 1).

Fishbein, M., Middlestadt, S.E. and Hitchcock, P.J. (1991). Using information to change sexually transmitted disease-related behaviors: an analysis based on the theory of reasoned action. In: J.N. Wasserheit, S.O. Aral and K.K. Holmes (eds) *Research issues in human behavior and sexually transmitted diseases in the AIDS era.* Washington, DC: American Society for Microbiology, 243–257.

Higgins, D.L., Galavotti, C., O'Reilly, K., Sheridan, J. and The AIDS Community Demonstration Projects (1997). Evolution and development of the AIDS Community Demonstration Projects. In: N.H. Corby and R.J. Wolitski (eds), *Community HIV prevention: the long Beach AIDS Community Demonstration Project* (pp. 5–20). California State University, CA: The University Press.

Kamb, M.L., Dillon, B., Fishbein, M., Willis, K.L. and The Project RESPECT Study Group (1996). Quality assurance of HIV prevention counseling in a multi-center randomized controlled trial. *Public Health Reports, 111* (Suppl. 1), 99–107.

Kamb, M.L., Fishbein, M., Douglas, J.M., Rhodes, F., Rogers, J., Bolan, G., Zenilman, J., Hoxworth, T., Mallotte, C.K., Iatesta, M., Kent, C., Lentz, A., Graziano, S., Byers, R.H., Peterman, T.A. and The Project RESPECT Study Group (1998). HIV/STD prevention counselling for high-risk behaviors; results from a multi-center, randomized controlled trial. *Journal of the American Medical Association, 280*(13), 1161–1167.

Kelly, J.A., Murphy, D.A., Sikkema, K.J. and Kalichman, S.C. (1993). Psychological interventions to prevent HIV infection are urgently needed: new priorities for behavioural research in the second decade of AIDS. *American Psychologist, 48*(10), 1023–1034.

National Institutes of Health (1997). Interventions to prevent HIV risk behavior. Bethesda, MA: Consensus Development Conference Statement, 14 May.

Rosenstock, I.M., Strecher, V.J. and Becker, M.J. (1994). The health belief model and HIV risk behaviour change. In: R.J. Diclemente and J.L. Peterson (eds), *Preventing AIDS: theories and methods of behavioural interventions* (pp. 5–24) New York: Plenum Press.

Von Haeften, I., Fishbein, M., Kasprzyk, D. and Montano, D. (1999). Acting on one's intention: variations in condom use intentions and behavior as a function of type of partner, gender, ethnicity and risk. Paper presented at the 4th AIDS Impact Conference, Ottawa, Canada.

9 UNRAVELING THE MYSTERY OF HEALTH:

How People Manage Stress and Stay Well

Aaron Antonovsky

In 1970 a very concrete experience occurred which led to a fundamental turning point in my work as a medical sociologist. I was in the midst of analysis of the data in a study of adaptation to climacterium of women in different ethnic groups in Israel. One of these groups consisted of women born in central Europe between 1914 and 1923, who were, therefore, aged 16 to 25 in 1939. We had, for a reason I never quite remembered, asked a simple yes-no question about having been in a concentration camp. Imagine a table comparing emotional health ratings of a group of concentration camp survivors to those of a control group. The plausible stressor hypothesis is confirmed beyond the .001 level. Looking at the percentages of unimpaired women, we find that 51 percent of the control group women, compared to 29 percent of the survivors, were in quite good overall emotional health. Focus not on the fact that 51 is far greater than 29, but consider what it means that 29 percent of a group of concentration camp survivors were judged to be in reasonable mental health. (The physical health data tell the same story.) To have gone through the most unimaginable horror of the camp, followed by years of being a displaced person, and then to have reestablished one's life in a country which witnessed three wars ... and still be in reasonable health. This, for me, was the dramatic experience which consciously set me on the road to formulating what I cam to call the salutogenic model, formally published in 1979 in *Health, Stress, and Coping*.

Some readers will surely be familiar with the book. For those who are not, let me recapitulate the argument. My point of departure was grounded in the data which indicate that at any one time, at least one third and quite possibly a majority of the population of any modern industrial society is characterized by some morbid, pathological condition, by any reasonable definition of the term. Illness, then, is not a relatively rare deviance. A pathological orientation seeks to explain why people get sick, why they enter a given disease category.

A salutogenic orientation (which focuses on the origins of health) poses a radically different question: why are people located toward the positive end of the health ease/dis-ease continuum, or why do they move toward this end, whatever their location at any given time?

The first answer I considered, as suggested in a voluminous literature, was that their life stressor experiences – stressors ranging from the microbiological to the societal-cultural levels – were low. But, I argued, this hypothesis is untenable. In the very nature of human existence, stressors are omnipresent. Yet many people, though far from most, even with a high stressor load, survive and even do well. Barring stressors that directly destroy the organism, people's health outcomes are unpredictable. *This is the mystery the salutogenic orientation seeks to unravel.* Confronting a stressor, I proposed, results in a state of tension, with which one must deal. Whether the outcome will be pathological, neutral, salutary depends on the adequacy of tension management. The study of factors determining tension management, then, becomes the key question of the health sciences.

Since I was not concerned with the study of diseases (as significant a question as this is), my tentative answer to the question was expressed in the concept of *generalized resistance resources* (GRRs) – money, ego strength, cultural stability, social supports, and the like – that is, any phenomenon that is effective in combating a wide variety of stressors. Reviewing the literature, I discussed a very wide range of GRRs, ranging from immunopotentiators to magic. But what was lacking was a culling rule by which one could identify a phenomenon as a GRR without having to wait and see whether it worked, or, better still, to understand how a phenomenon served as a GRR.

The answer to the salutogenic question that I developed was the *sense of coherence concept* (SOC). What is common to all GRRs, I proposed, was that they facilitated making sense out of the countless stressors with which we are constantly bombarded. In providing one repeatedly with such experiences, they generate, over time, a strong sense of coherence. This central concept of the book was defined as *a global orientation that expresses the extent to which one has a pervasive, enduring though dynamic, feeling of confidence that one's internal and external environments are predictable and that there is a high probability that things will work out as well as can reasonably be expected.*

Most of the rest of *Health, Stress, and Coping* was devoted to reviewing the empirical evidence which suggested that the SOC-health hypothesis was plausible. There were studies whose findings linked given variables to health without offering explanations. Other studies proposed ad hoc explanations of such linkages. In both cases, I suggested that the SOC construct would more adequately help us to understand the data. Of even greater import, the model suggested the possibility of integrating a considerable body of seemingly disparate findings and ideas.

This, in brief, is the salutogenic model. The book seemed to have appeared at the right time. Disenchantment with the increasingly expensive technology of the medical care system, concern with the ever less humane overtones of the focus on the organic pathology of diseases, the beginning of a movement toward self-care, a growing awareness of the role of social factors in shaping well-being – all these set the stage for a serious consideration of the origins of health. *Salutogenesis* has a long way to go before it becomes a household word like *alienation*; and the sense of coherence is still, to my discomfort, all too often called the sense of control or the sense of cohesion. But the concepts have begun to take hold; the mode of thought has become more familiar.

Health, Stress, and Coping was written as a culmination, a pulling together of the variety of research problems with which I had wrestled for well over a decade. I had no clear audience in mind. What the book did, I believe, was propose a model and set an agenda. The present volume takes up the items on this agenda. The intellectually curious reader interested in the historical development of the salutogenic model would do well to go through the first book, but such preparation is hardly essential for an understanding of this one.

This new book's intended audience is quite varied, since I am concerned with a problem rather than with a discipline. First and foremost, perhaps, it is addressed to those in the new and rapidly expanding field which is most often called behavioral medicine (Matarazzo and others, 1984; Gentry, 1984): social, developmental, and clinical psychologists and social workers who, as researchers, teachers, and therapists, are directly confronted with human struggles in a stressful world. I should also like to think that the book will be meaningful for those who make up my own primary reference group, medical sociologists. I find it somewhat distressing that we have largely left the issues of stressors and coping, so clearly rooted in macro-structural and cultural contexts, in the hands of the psychologists, who ask relevant but different questions. Social epidemiologists (or at least those who do not simply define themselves, as the quip has it, as broken down by age and sex) and others in the realm of public health will, I believe, find my work most germane to their concerns. In writing, I have also had another group in mind: nurses, going through the fascinating throes of formulating a new professional identity, are perhaps more open to my ideas and ways of thinking than almost anyone else. For the same structural reason, graduate students, who read voraciously and have not yet attained paradigmatic closure, concerned with health and illness, whatever their fields, will respond to the book. And finally, I continue to hope (sometimes against hope) that at least some physicians will see more than the disease. I should like to think that doctors, particularly those specializing in primary care (but also those in fields like rehabilitation medicine and geriatrics), will give them powerful tools for understanding, and perhaps even for action.

[...]

Toward a New View of Health and Illness

Scarcely a week passes in which I do not encounter a paper to which my response is "My God, if only the author had thought salutogenically!" A recent example, possibly piquant: Laudenslager and others (1983) were concerned with the immunosuppressive consequences of shock treatment administered to rats under different psychosocial conditions. Their data support the hypothesis that the rats given inescapable shock would show the lowest level of lymphocyte proliferation – that is, the most immunosuppression – compared with the other three groups: escapable shock, restrained controls, and home-cage controls. This finding constitutes the total focus of the authors' discussion. But in presenting the data, they note in passing that in one of the two measures of lymphocyte proliferation there was no significant difference among the three control groups, while on the second the escapable shock group showed the highest level, significantly different not only from the inescapable shock group but also from the restrained controls. "Thus the ability to exert control over the stressor completely prevented immunosuppression," the authors duly write (p. 569). The discussion disregards what seems to me this most exciting finding. Evidently a shock stressor can have salutary consequences for an organism, provided it is escapable. But when one thinks only of the pathogenic consequences, one misses the vista that such a finding opens up.[1]

The contention that the salutogenic orientation is not just the other side of the coin from the pathogenic orientation but, rather, is radically different and at least of equal significance must meet several tests. First, does it provide a powerful impetus for looking at data in a different way, a way in which the pathogenically oriented researcher would not ordinarily analyze the data? Second, does it lead to the formulation of different significant questions and hypotheses? And third, perhaps the most stringent test of all, does it provide the basis for hypotheses that conflict with those derived from a pathogenic orientation, allowing the testing of the two approaches? These tests are formulated in terms of research. Analogous questions are applicable to the work of the practitioner.

Let me be quite unequivocal about the two sources of the salutogenic orientation. The first is the fundamental assumption of heterostasis, disorder, and pressure toward increasing entropy as *the* prototypical characteristic of the living organism. This assumption, in stark contrast to that of the pathogenic orientation, which assumes that now and then "normally self-regulatory, homeostatic processes become disregulated" (Schwartz, 1979, p. 565), led me to explore the epidemiological data on health and illness, which brought me to the inescapable conclusion that disease, however defined, is very far from an unusual occurrence.[2]

It may well be that the pessimistic cast of my nature and philosophical outlook – the second source – shaped this very fundamental assumption and the way I read the data. But personal motivations are irrelevant to the contention, if it indeed meets the tests proposed.

In Chapter 2 of *Health, Stress, and Coping* (Antonovsky, 1979, pp. 36–37) I briefly considered the "other side of the coin" question. Let me now turn to a considerably more elaborate set of arguments that have fortified my commitment to the salutogenic orientation. I would point to six aspects of the issue.

Continuum of Dichotomy?

The first aspect may well lead to the alienation of some who have responded most enthusiastically to *Health, Stress, and Coping*, because they read into it what they wished to and did not see what I intended to say. Surely in part the fault is mine, for here and there as I reread what I wrote, and occasionally listen to what I say in talking about the book, I find references to putting the salutogenic question as "How come anyone ever 'makes it'?" or "How can we explain health rather than disease?" Given the (in my view, most welcome) development of the holistic health movement and the increased emphasis on health maintenance and promotion, my putting the question in this way has led to my being perceived as part of that camp. Flattering as this may be, it is unmerited, for it derives from a misinterpretation.

By and large, the health-oriented emphasis, no less than the traditional medical disease-oriented position, is based on the perception of a fundamental dichotomy between healthy and sick people. Those who adopt the former position would allocate attention and resources to keeping people healthy, preventing them from becoming sick. Those who take the latter stance focus on treating those who are sick, seeking to prevent death and chronicity and to restore health if possible. The former argue that it is much more efficient to invest resources in health maintenance; the latter respond – to the extent that there is any dialogue – that no humane society can disregard the present suffering of those who are sick.

What both disregard is that the shared underlying dichotomous premise is a less powerful way of looking at matters than what I have called the health ease/dis-ease continuum. We are all terminal cases. And we all are, so long as there is a breath of life in us, in some measure healthy. The salutogenic orientation proposes that we study the location of each person, at any time, on this continuum. Epidemiological study would focus on the distribution of groups on the continuum. The clinician would seek to contribute to movement of individual persons for whom he or she is responsible toward the health pole.

Coser's (1963) study of two hospital wards exemplifies the implications of adopting one or the other approach. In both cases the patients were extremely ill, quite close to the sick pole of the continuum. But in one ward, staff labeled the patients as terminal cases, concentrating on neatness, cleanliness, order, and comfort (in that order). In the other, the unit was formally defined as a rehabilitation center. As one of sociology's classic dictums has it, "If men define situations as real, they are real in their consequences." Since the study focused on the problem of staff alienation, its major finding was that the "terminal ward" nurses were far more alienated. We are not provided with any information about the consequences for the health status of the patients. I would, however, be surprised if differences in use of pain medication, death rates, and perhaps even "recovery" were not apparent.

The Story or the Disease?

Adoption of the dichotomous mode of thinking tends to lead inexorably to a narrow focus on "the coronary in 504," in the familiar language of house staff. The focus is narrow in two senses. First, attention is given to the pathology, not to the human being who has a particular medical problem. Conceivably this approach is justified and powerful in acute medical emergencies, so beloved of TV dramas. But in most cases, to be blind to the sickness of the person, to his total life situation, to his suffering, is not only inhumane; it leads to a failure to understand the etiology of the person's state of health. Second, the pathogenicist becomes a narrow specialist in one particular disease, rather than gaining an understanding of dis-ease, not to speak of health ease. He may live, eat, breathe, and dream of that disease; he learns nothing, reads nothing, and talks of nothing but the disease. There is neither personal nor structured communication between the cancer expert and the coronary disease expert. The both deal with phenomena that have a common name – *disease* – and therefore must have something in common in disregarded.

I would make it clear that my concern here is not with the question of humane sensitivity. The pathogenically oriented clinician is as likely to be compassionate as is the salutogenically oriented one. The former, however, is bound to miss data of great etiological significance that become available to the latter, who investigates the "story" of the person. In the same way, the researcher, looking for the specific germ that causes the disease, is prevented from learning from advances in other fields. And once again, those who focus on prevention of specific diseases are subject to the same blinders.

The concept of the story is taken from Cassell's (1979) profound analysis of the medical concept of causality. In it he tells of the elderly patient hospitalized for a serious, advanced problem of the knee. Symptom identification, diagnostic hypothesis, confirmation, and institution of appropriate therapy followed in short order, leading to discharge – and ensuring rehospitalization in short order. For what was learned only by accident by a medical student was that this elderly gentleman had been been widowed a year before, had moved to this strange city where he had no friends or relatives, had only a small income, and lived in a fourth-floor walk-up. The knee was very real and very serious. This was what had led to hospitalization this time; the next time, it could have been malnutrition, pneumonia, or depression and suicide attempt. The salutogenic approach does not guarantee problem solution of the complex circularities of people's lives, but at the very least it leads to a more profound understanding and knowledge, a prerequisite for moving toward the healthy end of the continuum.

Salutary Factors and Risk Factors

The pathogenic orientation is committed to the proposition that diseases are caused by bugs – microbiological, psychosocial, chemical, or what have you – singly, as in the germ theory, or multifactorially, as the more sophisticated have it. The Type A behavior pattern contributes to coronary heart disease, learned helplessness to depression, or internalization of hostility to cancer, to take some examples now current. Hypotheses are formulated not only with respect to specific diseases, as noted above, but overwhelmingly in terms of risk factors. The risk factor, or the stressor, has captured the imagination. Consider, for example, the overwhelming investment in the Holmes-Rahe (1967) life events scale in the field of stress research.

The salutogenic orientation, in contrast, leads one to think in terms of factors promoting movement toward the healthy end of the continuum. The point is that these are often *different* factors. One moves toward it not only by being low on risk factor A, B, and C. In the field of stress research, the idea is best understood if one contrasts the focus on stressors to the concern with coping mechanisms. But even in this field, the question most often asked is how one copes with a given stressor, rather than what factors not only act as buffers but contribute directly to health. In the field of industrial sociology, it has long been known that there are some factors that contribute to work satisfaction and others – different ones – that contribute to dissatisfaction. The question one asks – about movement toward pathology or movement toward health – determines the hypotheses.

Let me give a few examples. Dirks, Schraa, and Robinson (1982) formulated hypotheses predicting which of 587 discharged severe, chronic asthma patients would be rehospitalized within six months. The data confirm their idea that panic/fear responses on the MMPI and symptom mislabeling are good predictors. This concern, then, is with the maladaptive, pathological outcome. But 6 percent of the patients were not rehospitalized. Had the researchers been salutogenically oriented, they might have sought hypotheses about strengths, predicting *non*-rehospitalization among this severely ill population.

Similarly, Zimmerman and Hartley (1982) identified the 14 percent of women employed in four companies who had high blood pressure. They obtained data on 40 variables, almost all of which express hypotheses predicting to hypertension. Almost accidentally we learn that only 6 percent of the workers in the two unionized plants were hypertensive, compared with 25 percent in the nonunionized plants. We have, of course, no way of knowing whether the former "compensated" by being depressive instead of hypertensive. This could only be learned from a study that dealt with overall health. We cannot ask the authors to forget their interest in hypertension. But we can suggest to them that if they had formulated hypotheses predicting to normotension, they might have learned a great deal.

During the past few years, when I have urged the salutogenic approach to colleagues, I have been amazed and delighted at the fruitfulness of the hypotheses generated when one asks, "What predicts to a *good* outcome?" True, I am doubly pleased when the sense of coherence (SOC) is seen as relevant to the question. But even when it is not, consideration of salutary factors has inevitably led to promising directions. My experience has largely been with research colleagues; my hunch is that the approach would be no less fruitful in the hands of clinicians.

The Stressor: Pathogenic, Neutral, or Salutogenic?

Implicit in the above is that the pathogenic orientation invariably sees stressors as pathogenic, as risk factors, which at best can be reduced, inoculated against, or buffered. True, some stressors – for example, the ax descending on one's head – are very predictably destructive of health, irrespective of one's coping resources. But the assumption that "stressors are inherently bad" is tenuous.

After discussing the ubiquity of stressors at length (1979, pp. 93–96), I made clear why I thought that this assumption was misleading. I called attention to Selye's suggestion about eustressors and the concept of potentiation, in the context of my distinction between tension and stress. The point, then, need not be elaborated here, although I would note that, judging from responses to the book, relatively few people, to my regret, have paid attention to what I regard as an important and fruitful distinction. The issue is raised in the present context – the arguments for the importance of the salutogenic orientation – because it is indeed an understanding that flows from this orientation. Thinking pathogenically, one conducts studies and designs experiments testing hypotheses and stressors are pathogenic (sometimes adding "unless buffered"). Thinking salutogenically opens the way for studying the consequences of demands made on the organism to which there are no readily available or automatic adaptive responses – a generally accepted definition of a stressor – when there is good theoretical reason to predict positive health consequences.

It would, of course, be most valuable were studies designed in advance in these terms. But at the very least, surely researchers should be open to looking at their results with such a possibility in mind. Alas, this is seldom so, even when the data stare one in one's face. The illustration about shocked rats given at the opening of this chapter provides a case in point. My recalculation (1979, p. 167) of the data in the well-known Nuckolls, Cassel, and Kaplan (1972) study of complications in pregnancy suggests that "being high on stressors, given high social supports, is salutary," a point not noted by the authors. *Advances*, the journal of the Institute for the Advancement of Health, recently made its initial appearance and represents an outstanding scientific effort to further the understanding of mind/body interactions and their effects on health and disease. Each issue contains abstracts of more than a score of recently published studies. One reviews these in vain for more than one or two references to terms like *eustressor*, *potentiation*, or *activation response. Moderators, buffers, mitigators*, yes; but the stressor, the disturber of homeostasis, continues to be seen as inevitably unfortunate. True, Cannon, Selye, and many others called attention to the functional character of the stress response – that is, to mobilize the organism. But always, the stressor itself, though it may be prevented from causing damaging consequences, is unfortunate. Salutogenesis opens the way, as it were, for the rehabilitation of stressors in human life.

Adaptation or the Magic Bullet?

The second argument for the power of the salutogenic orientation focused on the question of etiology and diagnosis. By understanding the story of the person – note, not the patient, for salutogenesis constrains us to look at people on a continuum – rather than the germ or germs that caused a particular disease, I proposed, we can arrive at a more adequate diagnosis. I turn now to the implications of the two orientations for therapy. The pathogenic orientation leads researchers, practitioners, and policy makers to concentrate on the specific disease diagnosed or on prevention of specific diseases, particularly among high-risk individuals or groups. On the social level, it leads to mounting wars against disease X, Y, or Z. The ambience that comes into being is that which Dubos (1960) so cogently warned against, "the mirage of health." Salutogenesis, more pessimistic, leads us to focus on the overall problem of active adaptation to an inevitably stressor-rich environment. The key term becomes *negative entropy*, leading to a search for useful inputs into the social system, the physical environment, the organism, and lower-order systems down to the cellular level to counteract the immanent trend toward entropy. Not accidentally and of considerable import, it opens the way for cooperation between biological and psychosocial scientists. When one searches for cures of particular diseases, one bonds to stay within the confines of pathophysiology. When one searches for cures for particular diseases, one tends to stay within the confines of pathophysiology. When one searches for effective adaptation of the organism, one can move beyond post-Cartesian dualism and look to imagination, love, play, meaning, will, and the social structures that foster them. Or, as I would prefer to put it, to theories of successful coping.

Perhaps the best, and certainly the most dramatic, example I can given of this difference between the two orientations is, for this once, not in reference to scientific studies but to a personal experience. In November 1982 I was teaching interviewing to beginning medical students in Israel. The setting was a well-baby clinic, the reluctant interviewee a twenty-six-year-old mother who had brought her three-week-old infant, while her fourteen-month-old little girl trailed behind. Her reluctance, the nurse told us, was understandable: her four older children waited at home. After a few words about the uneventful delivery, she remained quiet in response to the student's next question, which referred to the presence of her husband at the delivery. Fortunately, he had learned how to wait patiently and use nonverbal expressions of concern. The woman then told him, in almost inaudible words, that her husband had been killed in the fighting in Lebanon some four months earlier. The rapport had been created, and she began to speak, going on for nearly an hour. At first, the picture that emerged was the one we had expected. The terrible blow could not be recalled. But the Rehabilitation Division of the Ministry of Defense had already arranged her move to a more spacious apartment, an adequate pension, financial assurance of her children's education, and the like. The diagnosis had been made, the therapy designed.

But the student, who had learned Cassell's concept of the story, had been taught to get a picture of the person's life, and patiently elicited what no one else had been successful in learning. As a child, Mrs. R. had been raped by her father. Pregnant at sixteen, she had no alternative but to marry the man whose death had made her a war heroine. She was often beaten, related to as a baby-making machine, and no more than occasionally provided for financially. The death had been the most fortunate thing that had ever happened to her. For the first time in her life, she now had the possibility – no more than that – of a decent human existence. Clearly, her strength was inadequate to transform this into a reality. Solution of financial problems, the assigned therapy, was necessary but far from sufficient. It was a magic bullet, not an adequate basis for active adaptation.

At this point, a parenthetical but crucial point is in order. I am fully aware that one implication of the salutogenic approach for the institutional organization of a society's health care system is the endless expansion of social control in the hands of those who dominate this system, a danger that Zola (1972) and others have called to our attention. As a behavioral science teacher of medical students, I have long been sensitive to the dangers of having them learn that just about everything in a patient's life is relevant to their functioning as physicians. I have no easy out in dealing with this intractable contradiction. The direction of the answer, to the extent that there is one, lies precisely in the question of who dominates the system, on the institutional as well as on the immediate, interpersonal level of the doctor/patient relationship. But, important as the issue is, I can do no more here than call attention to its existence.

The "Deviant Case" or Hypothesis Confirmation?

Finally, I would call attention to an unfortunate by-product of scientific methodology that is ignored by the pathogenic orientation. The good scientist formulates a hypothesis, when there is a basis for doing so, rigorously submits it to testing, and rejoices when it is supported in repeated testing. Having studied, repeatedly and in diverse ways, the relations between smoking and lung cancer, or race and hypertension, and having met the criterion of biological plausibility, we can speak of causality, identify high-risk groups, and propose solutions. Perhaps the most fruitful hypothesis of this sort in the psychosocial field is that linking the Type A behavior pattern to coronary disease.

And yet, no matter that the statistical relationship between risk factor and health outcome is shown by the computer printout to be $p = .0000$, only part of the variance is accounted for. The pathogenicist is content with hypothesis confirmation; the salutogenicist, without disdaining the importance of what has been learned, looks at the deviant case. Who are the blacks who do not have hypertension? Who are the Type A's who do not get coronary disease? Who are the smokers who do not get lung cancer?

The study by Shekelle and other (1981) is a classic pathogenic paper. I cite it precisely because I regard it as an important study, although further data are required before we can comfortably and fully accept its hypothesis. Depression, as measured by the Minnesota Multiphasic Personality Inventory, they proposed, is predictive of cancer mortality. Using data from a longitudinal, prospective seventeen-year study, they found that the subjects who had been classified as depressed were more than twice as likely to die of cancer as the nondepressed. The relative risks of the two groups are significantly different. But we are talking of cancer mortality of 7.1 and 3.4 percent, respectively. Of the 379 men defined as depressed, the great majority did not die of cancer or other causes. Thus the deviant case, as is so often true, is in the great majority. What protected him? Once we pose this question, I suggest, we can begin to generate hypotheses to explain salutogenesis and develop methodologies to test these hypotheses. Content with the most important confirmation of our initial hypothesis, however, we usually do not move ahead.

Pathogenesis and Salutogenesis: A Complementary Relationship

I can now summarize what is meant by the salutogenic orientation. It derives from the fundamental postulate that heterostasis, senescence, and increasing entropy are core characteristics of all living organisms. Thus: (1) It leads us to reject the dichotomous classification of people as healthy or diseased in favor of their location on a multidimensional health ease/dis-ease continuum. (2) It keeps us from falling into the trap of focusing solely on the etiology of a given disease rather than always searching for the total story of a human being, including his or her sickness. (3) Instead of asking, "What caused (or will cause, if one is prevention-oriented) a person to fall prey to a given disease?" – that is, instead of focusing on stressors – we are enjoined to ask, "What are the factors involved in at least maintaining one's location on the continuum or moving toward the healthy pole?"; that is, we come to focus on coping resources. (4) Stressors come to be seen not as a dirty word, always to be reduced, but as omnipresent. Moreover, the consequences of stressors are viewed not as necessarily pathological but as quite possibly salutary, contingent on the character of the stressor and the successful resolution of tension. (5) In contradistinction to the search for magic-bullet solutions, we are urged to search for all sources of negative entropy that may facilitate active adaptation of the organism to the environment. (6) Finally, the salutogenic orientation takes us beyond the data obtained from pathogenic inquiry by always looking at the deviant cases found in such inquiry.

I trust that this discussion and the examples given in each case have, at the very least, given food for thought to researcher and practitioner alike and indicated the basis for my contention that the salutogenic orientation is not just the other side of the coin and does meet the three tests proposed (looking at data in a different way; asking different questions; suggesting alternative hypotheses). I do think that the pathogenic orientation, which underlies many advances in knowledge and practice, cannot explain much of the data we have. Further, its near-total domination of our thinking has many limiting consequences. Having thus taken an unequivocal position, I would make it clear that I by no means advocate abandonment of the pathogenic orientation. It is important, for example, that work on the theory, prevention, and therapy of cancer continue; that the pathogenic consequences of stressors be considered; that we look for magic bullets. My plea, rather, is that we see the two orientations as complementary and that there be a more balanced allocation of intellectual and material resources than presently exists.

Notes

1   This is not nitpicking. Even in a journal presumably oriented toward health, encountered during the final drafting of this chapter, reference is made to the Laudenslager paper only to note immunosuppression, disregarding the issue I point out above (*Investigations*, 1984).
2   There is no reason to present additional data to those presented in chapter 1 of *Health, Stress, and Coping*, although such data are familiar to me. One could document decline in cardiovascular mortality (not necessarily in morbidity) but also make reference to AIDS, chronic pain, herpes, and violence. The thesis that deviance is "normal" (Antonovsky, 1979, p. 15) would remain.

References

Antonovsky, A. (1979). *Health, stress and coping: New perspectives on mental and physical well-being*. New York: Jossey-Bass.

Cassell, E. J. (1979). The Changing ideas of medicine. *Social Research*, 46, 728–43.

Coser, R. L. (1963). Alienation and the social structure. In E. Friedson (ed.) *The Hospital in Modern Society*. New York: Free Press.

Dirks, J. F., Schraa, J. C. and Robinson, S. K. (1982). Patient mislabelling of symptoms: Implications for patient-physician communication and medical outcome. *International Journal of Psychiatry*, 17, 15–17.

Dubos, R. J. (1960). *The mirage of health*. London: Allen and Unwin.

Gentry, W. D. (1984). (ed.). *Handbook of behavioral medicine*. New York: Guilford.

Holmes, T. H. and Rahe, R. H. (1967). The social readjustment rating scale. *Journal of Psychosomatic Research*, 11: 213–218.

Laudenslager, M. L., Ryan, S. M., Drugan, R. C., Hyson, R. L. and Maier, S. F. (1983). Coping and immunosuppression: Inescapable but not escapable shock suppresses lymphocyte proliferation, *Science*, 221: 568–70.

Matarazzo, J. D., Weiss, S. H., Herd, J. A., Miller, N. E., and Weiss, S. M. (1984). *Behavioural Health: A Handbook of Health Enhancement and Disease Prevention*. New York: Wiley.

Nuckolls, K. B., Cassel, J. and Kaplan B. H. (1972). Psychological assets, life crisis, and the progress of pregnancy. *American Journal of Epidemiology, 95,* 431–441.

Schwartz, G. (1979). The brain as a health care system. In G. C. Stone, F. Cohen, and N. E. Adler (eds), *Health Psychology: A handbook*. San Francisco: Jossey-Bass.

Shekelle, R. B., Rayner Jr, W. J., Ostfeld, A. M., Giarron, D. C., Bieliausksas, L. A., Lin, S.C., Maliza, C. and Paul, O. (1981) Psychological depression and 17-year risk of death from cancer. *Psychosomatic Medicine, 43,* 117–25.

Zimmerman, M. K. and Hartley, W. S. (1982). High blood pressure among employed women: A multi-factor discriminant analysis. *Journal of Health and Social Behaviour, 23,* 205–220.

Zola, I. K. (1972). Pathways to the doctor – From person to patient. *Social Science and Medicine, 7,* 677–689.

10 SOME OBSERVATIONS ON HEALTH AND SOCIO-ECONOMIC STATUS

Douglas Carroll, George Davey Smith and Paul Bennett

That health varies markedly with socio-economic status (SES) is now a commonplace. However, those concerned with the contribution of behavioural and psychological factors to health have, in general, either ignored SES completely or relegated it to the status of a control variable. Only recently has a case been made that they direct their attention to SES as an important health determinant in its own right (Adler *et al.*, 1994; Carroll, Bennett, and Davey Smith, 1993; Carroll, Davey Smith, and Bennett, 1994). There are at least four compelling reasons for doing so.

First, SES–health differentials are not transitory phenomena, but are evident throughout history; those in more favourable circumstances appear always to have enjoyed better health than those in less favourable circumstances. Second, present-day SES–health differentials are substantial; indeed, SES might be regarded as the major determinant of health status (Angell, 1993). Third, available evidence indicates that the association between SES and health is continuous; that is, it is not simply a matter of the most deprived suffering from exceedingly poor health but rather of continuous SES–health gradient. Fourth, and as a consequence of the continuous character to the SES–health gradient, explanations have to be cast wider than the obvious correlates of absolute poverty to embrace the possible involvement of psychological factors.

Historical Inequalities in Health

In the 15th century, the city of Florence operated a *Monte delle doti*, an endowment fund into which the relatively affluent fathers of female

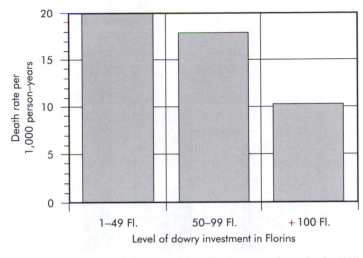

(Adapted from Morrison, Kirshner and Molho, 1977)

FIGURE 10.1   Deaths per 1,000 Person-years for Females Receiving Different Levels of Dowry Investment as Young Girls

offspring could deposit dowry investments, retrievable when their daughters married. Morrison, Krishner, and Molha (1977) compared the size of these investments with the subsequent ages at death of the women concerned. Figure 10.1 presents the outcome of an analysis derived from their data. It reveals a gradient of decreasing mortality from those women accompanied by a dowry of 49 florins or less to those with dowries greater than 100 florins.

Clearly, invention is required to obtain data from the past. Davey Smith, Carroll, Rankin and Rowan (1992) address the issue of SES–health stratification in Victorian Britain by taking advantage of the presence of commemorative obelisks in the 19th-century graveyards of Glasgow. Since the shape of these obelisks is uniform, height would have determined relative cost and, accordingly, reflect the SES of the decedents. The height of the obelisk was then compared with the age at death of the first generation of families commemorated. Figure 10.2 summarizes the outcome of the comparison; a reliable positive association between height of obelisk and age at death appears for both men and women.

Chapin (1924) calculated the death rates for taxpayers and non-taxpayers in Providence, Rhode Island, for the year 1865. Less than a quarter of the population were taxpayers, and they constituted the most affluent members of society, a state of affairs not necessarily echoed by current taxation arrangements. For taxpayers in the target year, the death rate was 10.8 per 1,000 of the population, whereas for non-taxpayers it was 24.8 per 1,000.

These studies of earlier eras are of more than archival interest. First, they argue that wherever you find socio-economic stratification you observe correlated health inequalities. Second, they indicate that even in earlier eras

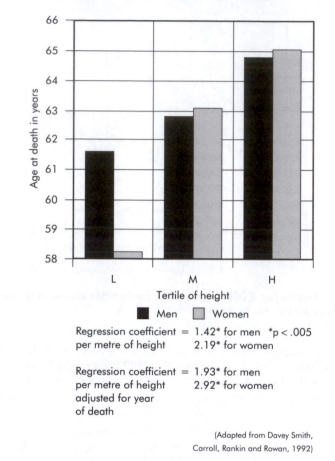

Regression coefficient = 1.42* for men   *p < .005
per metre of height   2.19* for women

Regression coefficient = 1.93* for men
per metre of height   2.92* for women
adjusted for year
of death

(Adapted from Davey Smith,
Carroll, Rankin and Rowan, 1992)

FIGURE 10.2   **Age at Death According to Height of Obelisk**

inequalities in health were not simply a matter of the most impoverished in society suffering exceedingly poor health. It was, after all, the prosperous in 15th-century Florence who attracted dowry investment and the relatively affluent citizens of Glasgow who were interred in its urban graveyards. On some of the obelisks occupations were recorded for the men commemorated; they were predominantly merchants and professionals, such as engineers, doctors and ministers. Further, the average age at death for the graveyards' sample during the period 1881–1900 was 65.4 for men and 63.3 for women. In contrast, in 1890, the midpoint of this range, the overall average age at death in Glasgow for people dying at 20 years or over was 50.1 for men and 52.4 for women. Finally, these studies of earlier times caution against explanations of present-day health inequalities which rely exclusively on contemporary concerns. For example, many of today's unhealthy behaviours most probably characterized the affluent of the 19th century rather than its poor.

Present-day Health Inequalities

Contemporary data confirm that health continues to vary strikingly with SES. In countries like the UK and US SES–related health inequalities proved resistant to phenomena such as post-World War II economic growth and, in the UK, the introduction of a National Health Service. There is now evidence that health inequalities have been increasing in recent years in both the UK and the US. This is a matter to which we return. For the moment it is suffi-cient to indicate that whether indexed by occupational status (e.g. Marmot, Shipley and Rose, 1984; Townsend and Davidson, 1982), or by income (e.g. Rogot, Sorlie, Johnson and Schmitt, 1993), or by material assets (e.g. Davey Smith, Shipley and Rose, 1970; Goldblatt, 1990), or by education (e.g. Kitagawa and Hauser, 1973; Pappas, Queen, Hadden and Fisher, 1993), or by area-level indices of deprivation/affluence (e.g. Carstairs and Morris, 1991; Davey Smith, Neaton, Stamler, and Wentworth, 1992), persons of higher SES suffer substantially less from premature mortality than do their lower SES counterparts.

Two examples serve to illustrate. The Whitehall 1 Study (e.g. Davey Smith et al., 1990; Marmot et al., 1984) examined, among other things, the associa-tion between occupational status at baseline and all-cause mortality during the subsequent 10 years for over 17,000 male British public servants. Employment grade was categorized in descending status order as adminis-trative, professional or executive, clerical and 'other grades' (messengers, porters and other unskilled manual workers). With controlling for age and setting the mortality rate of the administrators at unity, the relative risk of mortality for the other grades displayed an orderly linear pattern: 1.6 for the professional and executive grades, 2.2 for the clerical grades and 2.7 for the 'other grades'. Given the apparent homogeneous character of this popu-lation sharing a common employer, being domiciled in and around London, all having access to a national health-care system, the differences are indeed striking. In addition, when an asset marker, car ownership, is added to the analysis, the mortality gradient is even steeper (Davey Smith et al., 1990). The age-adjusted relative mortality risk between administrators who owned a car and other grade' employees who did not was 4.3.

Studies which adopted area-based indicators of SES tell a similar story. For example, a recent analysis of the Multiple Risk Factor Intervention Trial (MRFIT) screening sample of over 300,000 middle-aged American men reveals a linear relationship between the median income of area of residence at time of entry to the study and age-adjusted all-cause relative mortality risk (Davey Smith, Neaton et al., 1992). Figure 10.3 testifies to the regularity of the gradient.

The magnitude of these SES–mortality differentials are most easily illus-trated by considering the consequent variations in life expectancy. At the age of 20, given the mortality rates operating around 1980, social class I and II men in the UK can expect to live 5 years longer than social class IV and

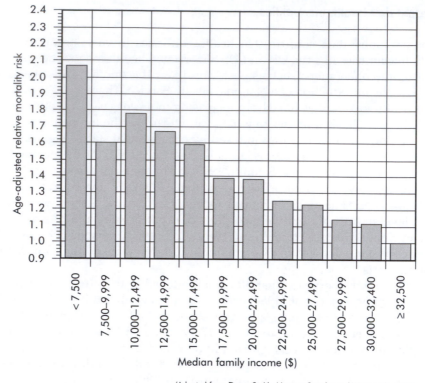

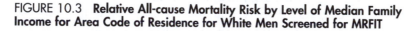

(Adapted from Davey Smith, Neaton, Stamler and Wentworth, 1992)

FIGURE 10.3 **Relative All-cause Mortality Risk by Level of Median Family Income for Area Code of Residence for White Men Screened for MRFIT**

V men (Haberman and Bloomfield, 1988). Even at age 65, there is still a 2.5 years' difference in life expectancy between these groups.

The relationship between SES status and mortality holds not only for all-cause mortality but for most of the major cause-of-death groupings (Townsend and Davidson, 1982). Various indices of morbidity display analogous patterns of stratification (Blaxter, 1990; Marmot et al., 1991). Further, health variations with SES appear to typify women as much as they do men (Arber, 1989), blacks as much as whites (Pappas et al., 1993), as well as appearing to be characteristic of all Western countries studied in this context (Fox, 1989).

The Continuous Character of SES–health Gradients

At least two inferences can be drawn from the examples of SES–health inequalities cited. First of all, the size and persistence of such health differentials, together with their robustness to the use of different measures of SES

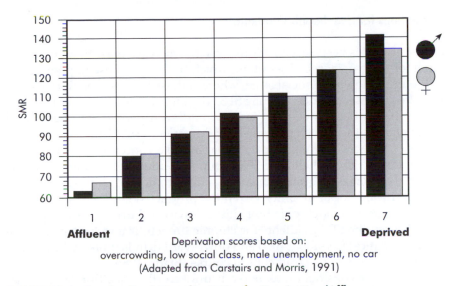

FIGURE 10.4   **Standardized Mortality Ratios for Deprivation/Affluence Categories (Ages 0–64)**

status and health outcome, defy their dismissal as artifactual. Second, SES differentials in health are not restricted to those suffering absolute immiseration but continue into the more privileged groups. What, in fact, emerges strikingly from recent studies is a fine stratification of mortality-risk contingent on SES. In the Longitudinal Study, which followed up the 1971 UK census data, non-manual workers who owned their own homes and had one car suffered considerably higher mortality risk than non-manual homeowners with two cars (Goldblatt, 1990). In an ecological study of mortality in Scotland, the SES of small postal-code areas was indexed by means of a composite deprivation/affluence score derived from the following components: social class, male unemployment, household overcrowding, access to a car. Areas were assigned a score of one to seven, where one signified the most affluent and seven the most deprived areas. The outcome of the analysis of mortality according to deprivation/ affluence is summarized in Figure 10.4, inspection of which reveals a continuous gradient of increasing mortality from the most affluent to the most deprived areas (Carstairs and Morris, 1991).

The explanatory power of this composite deprivation/affluence index can be seen when comparing regional mortality variations within the UK. For example, Scotland is cursed with decidedly higher rates of premature mortality than England is. In the age range 0–64 years, with the English mortality ratio set at 100, Scotland's standardized mortality ratio is 122. When deprivation/affluence scores are taken into account Scotland's relative disadvantage is substantially attenuated; with the English mortality ratio again set at 100, the comparable Scottish figure was now 105.

Explanations for SES–health Gradients

At the outset, it is necessary to address briefly one very parsimonious explanation for these data: social selection, which holds that those in poor health tend to move down the social scale, whereas those in good health move up. Thus , health is seen as determining SES. The most obvious manner in which health-related selection could operate would be if people who become ill having entered the labour market show downward SES drift, as a result of job loss or reduced earnings capacity, leading to a concentration of those at high mortality risk in the lower SES groups. Meadows (1961), for example, presented evidence suggesting that men with chronic bronchitis suffered just such downward social mobility. Given the protracted clinical course before death characteristic of chronic bronchitis, downward drift is clearly plausible. However, the SES gradients for chronic bronchitis and lung cancer are virtually identical (see Table 10.1) and downward drift is unlikely in the case of lung cancer, given its rapid clinical course (Blane, 1985).

Three further considerations make it unlikely that health-related social selection is a major contributor to SES–health gradients. First, in the Whitehall 1 study, mortality differentials remained when analysis focused only on those found at medical examination on entry to the study to have no detectable disease, that is, those for whom downward drift due to poor health was unlikely (Marmot et al., 1984). Second, in the Longitudinal Study, the mortality differentials among those not changing SES were similar to the overall mortality differentials (Goldblatt, 1988, 1989). Were social selection at work, differentials would be concentrated among the socially mobile. Finally, there is a mismatch between the years during which social mobility is most prevalent and those characterized by impaired health. While social mobility is most likely during the time between entry to the labour market and around 40 years of age, this is a time that is characterized by low morbidity.

If health-related social selection is little implicated, then it must be the characteristics of different SES locations or of those who populate them that determines health status. One obvious possibility is that SES constitutes a proxy for the propensity of different social groups to engage in unhealthy behaviours, such as smoking, poor diet and excessive alcohol consumption. Let us consider the case of cigarette-smoking.

Cigarette-Smoking

Of all the putative unhealthy behaviours, cigarette-smoking is the one which most profoundly compromises health (Doll and Peto, 1976; Reid, Hamilton, McCartney and Rose 1976). Further, smoking prevalence is linked to SES (Davey Smith and Shipley, 1991; Marmot et al., 1991; Pugh, Power, Goldblatt and Arber, 1991) and, since current rates of smoking cessation in countries like the UK and the USA are positively related to SES while rates of initiation

TABLE 10.1 **Social Class and Mortality from Lung Cancers and Bronchitis (England and Wales; 1979–80, 1982–83). Standardized Mortality Ratios for Men Aged 20–64**

	Social class					
	I	II	IIIN	IIIM	IV	V
Lung cancer	42	62	78	17	125	175
Bronchitis	34	49	84	109	134	208

I = Professional, II = Intermediate, IIIN = Skilled non-manual, IIIM = Skilled manual, IV = Semi-skilled, V = Unskilled

are negatively related, this SES–smoking gradient is likely to increase into the foreseeable future (Pugh et al., 1991).

Nevertheless, the available evidence suggests that unhealthy behaviours, such as cigarette-smoking, provide anything but a complete account. While statistically controlling for such behaviours may attenuate SES–health gradients, it in no way abolishes them. For example, in the Alameda County study (Berkman and Breslow, 1983; Hann, Kaplan and Camacho, 1987) the gradient of mortality with family income persisted when 13 health-risk factors, including smoking, diet alcohol consumption and exercise, were taken into account. Further, in the 10-year follow-up of British public servants that constituted the Whitehall 1 Study, the all-cause mortality differentials by occupational grade and car ownership for those men who had never smoked were much the same as those which characterized the whole cohort (Davey Smith et al., 1990; Davey Smith, Blane and Bartley, 1994). Figures 10.5a and 10.5b depict these analogous profiles. Further, large employment grade and car-ownership mortality differentials were still seen for causes of death not regarded as smoking-related (see Figure 10.6)

The available data on smoking should act as a caution in other areas of inference. We should not presume that the identification of a behavioural health risk and the observation of its preponderance in lower SES groups allow us to accord that risk a substantial role in mediating SES–health differentials.

If SES–health gradients are not, for the most part, attributable to variations in unhealthy behaviour, the major influences must reside in the broader fabric of people's lives. In addition, it is probably most fruitful to view poor health from the perspective of cumulative exposures to adversity, that is, to regard health as a matter of what occurs across the life course rather than as a consequence of exposures at one particular time in life, for example, in middle age or in early childhood (Ben-Shlomo and Davey Smith, 1991; Kuh and Davey Smith, 1993; Mare, 1990).

Chemicals and Environment

While the persistent ecologies of different SES groups undoubtedly vary in a number of ways, variations in exposure to physical pathogens are unlikely to be of negligible significance. For example, the health-damaging effects of

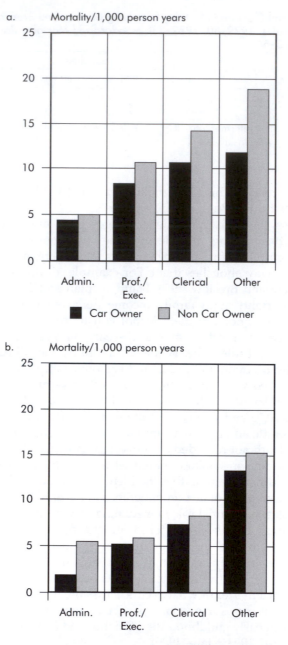

a. Mortality/1,000 person years

Car Owner   Non Car Owner

b. Mortality/1,000 person years

(Adapted from Carroll, Bennett
and Davey Smith, 1993)

FIGURE 10.5 a **All-cause Mortality by Occupational Grade and Car Ownership in the Whitehall 1 Study: Whole Sample.** b. **All-cause Mortality by Occupational Grade and Car Ownership in the Whitehall 1 Study: Never Smokers Only**

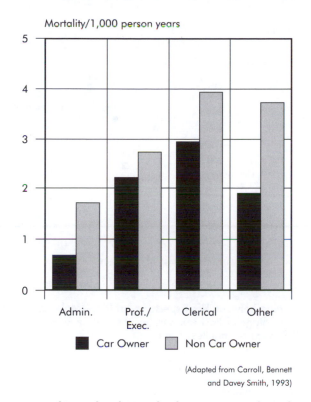

Mortality/1,000 person years

(Adapted from Carroll, Bennett
and Davey Smith, 1993)

FIGURE 10.6   **Non-smoking-related Mortality by Occupational Grade and Car Ownership**

exposure to physico-chemical hazards, primarily a feature of working-class occupations, have long been recognized (Hunter, 1995). Low-quality, damp accommodation has been found to be associated with poor health, particularly with higher prevalence rates for respiratory disease (Martin, Platt and Hunt, 1987; Platt, Martin, Hunt and Lewis, 1989). The strikingly higher rates of mortality suffered by the inhabitants of Glasgow relative to those of Edinburgh are paralleled by, among other things, stark differences in winter air-pollution levels. Concentrations of smoke and sulphur dioxide recorded in 1972–73 were almost twice as high in Glasgow (Watt and Ecob, 1992). While the physical correlates of morbidity and mortality have received substantially less attention in recent years than have the behavioural correlates, the available evidence suggests that physical influences are likely to be substantial.

Income and Class Structure

Two considerations suggest, however, that physical factors in adulthood afford an incomplete explanation of present-day SES–health inequalities. We have already considered the first of these: the persistence of health differentials into the materially better-off social strata. The second arises from recent

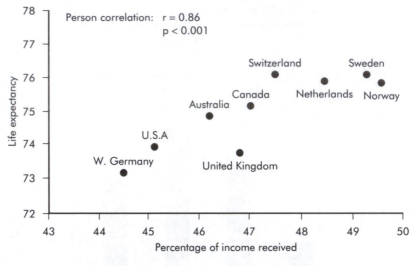

(Adapted from Wilkinson, 1990, 1992)

FIGURE 10.7 **Relation between Life Expectancy at Birth (Male and Female Combined) and Percentage of Past Tax and Benefit Income Received by the Least Well-off 70 Percent of Families, 1981**

analyses testifying to an association between overall life expectancy in Western countries and income distribution. Wilkinson (1990) compared data on income distribution and life expectancy for nine Western countries (Australia, Canada, Netherlands, Norway, Sweden, Switzerland, UK, US, West Germany). Whereas Gross National Product was poorly correlated with life expectancy at birth, income and benefit received by the least well-off 70 percent of 'families' yielded a substantial positive correlation ($r = .86$) (see Figure 10.7). It is interesting to note that Wilkinson's analysis did not include Japan. The Japanese now have the longest life expectancy in the world and also the most equitable distribution of income of any OECD (Organization for Economic Cooperation and Development) country (Marmot and Davey Smith, 1989).

Subsequent analyses of 12 European community countries (Wilkinson, 1992) indicate that for the years 1975–85, the annual rate of change in life expectancy was negatively correlated with the proportion of the population in relative poverty, defined as the proportion living on less than 50 percent of the national average disposable income. Again the correlation coefficient was substantial ($r = -.73$), indicating that a more rapid improvement in life expectancy was enjoyed by those countries which had registered a fall in the prevalence of relative poverty (see Figure 10.6). What these analyses appear to indicate is that for the majority of people in Western countries health hinges on relative as well as absolute living standards, implying that psychosocial processes may be at work. As Wilkinson (1990) concluded,

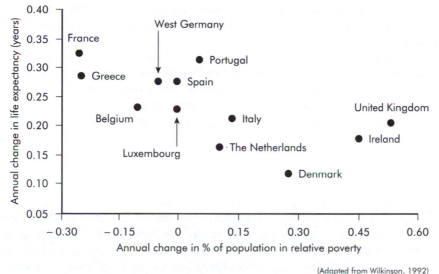

FIGURE 10.8 **Annual Rate of Change in Life Expectancy and in Proportion of the Population in Relative Poverty in 12 European Community Countries, 1975–85**

It looks as if what matters about our physical circumstances is not what they are in themselves, but where they stand in the scale of things in our society. The implication is that our environment and standard of living no longer impact on our health primarily through direct physical causes, regardless of our attitudes and perceptions, but have come to do so mainly through social and cognitively mediated processes. (p. 405)

Given the difficulties which attend life expectancy as a measure, that it is substantially influenced by infant mortality rates, Wilkinson's conclusion may be somewhat overstated. Nevertheless, his analysis and the continuous character of SES–health gradients invite a search for mediating processes of a psychosocial nature.

What might these psychosocial mediators be? We have, as yet only preliminary indications. Nevertheless, recent reviews identify psychological stress (Adler et al., 1994; Carroll et al., 1993; Williams, 1990); personal control (Carroll et al., 1993; Williams, 1990); social support (Adler et al., 1994; Carroll et al., 1993; Williams, 1990); hostility (Alder et al., 1994). In addition, evidence points to inequalities in the distribution of these psychosocial factors among different SES groups (Barefoot, Dodge, Peterson, Dahlstrom and Williams, 1989; Berkman and Breslow, 1983; Marmot et al., 1991). However, as we argued previously, the differential prevalence of a factor among different SES groups constitutes a necessary but far from sufficient condition for according it mediational status in this context. Further, many of the data which currently implicate these psychosocial factors in health are derived from either laboratory analogue studies or observational epidemiological research.

While the laboratory analogue study can be a useful tool for exploring the plausibility of putative psychobiological health mechanisms, this is a long way from establishing such mechanisms as determining SES–health variations. Observational epidemiological studies, on the other hand, are prone to yielding spurious associations through confounding (Davey Smith and Phillips, 1990).

Job Stress

Consider, for example the Karasek model of job stress (Karasek, Baker, Marxer, Ahlbom and Theorell, 1981; Karasek, Theorell, Schwartz, Pieper and Alfredsson, 1982), in which high job strain, resulting from the convergence of low-decision latitude (i.e. ability to control the nature of one's work) and high psychological demand, is considered to increase the risk of coronary heart disease. In a recent test of the Karasek model, the 25-year incidence of coronary-heart-disease mortality for 1683 men in the Chicago Western Electric Study was examined in terms of job-strain scores assigned on the basis of job titles at entry to the study (Alterman, Shekelle, Vernon and Burau, 1994). Adjusting for age, systolic blood pressure, serum cholesterol, smoking, alcohol consumption and family history of coronary heart disease, individuals with high job strain registered a relative risk of coronary-heart-disease mortality of 1.40. However, with additional adjustment for occupational class, the relative risk fell to 1.04.

Accordingly, high job strain might simply be a marker for lower SES and a generally unfavourable environment. Further testimony to difficulties of drawing causal inferences in this context emerges from consideration of their data on coronary heart disease and psychological demand, a component of the job-strain concept. Figure 10.9 reveals a U-shaped association between psychological demand and coronary-heart-disease risk; the Karasek model would predict a linear association. However, the source of the observed relationship is clear when one considers that psychological demand and occupational status are also linked in a U-shaped manner. In sum, what these data suggest is that job strain and the psychological demands of work may be no more than proxies for SES and not, as has been proposed, independent psychological coronary-heart-disease risk factors. At the very least, this study illustrates the difficulties involved in generating robust estimates of unconfounded associations from observational epidemiological research.

According to the principle of proximity, macro-social structures affect the individual by means of smaller, more proximal, mediating factors (Williams, 1990). Further, as we have indicated, it is unlikely, given the apparent significance of relative as well as absolute material circumstances implied by Wilkinson's (1990, 1992) analysis and the persistence of SES–health

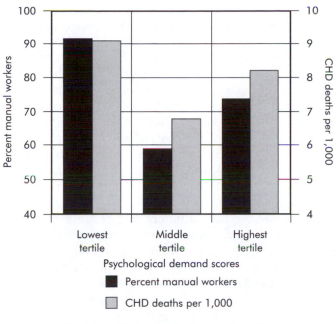

(Adapted from Alterman, Shekelle, Vernon and Burau, 1994)

FIGURE 10.9 **The Relationship of Psychological Demand to Coronary Heart Disease (CHD) and Occupational Status**

differentials into the relatively affluent sectors of society, that those physical factors which characterize absolute privation can afford a complete explanation. We almost certainly require a new conceptualization which, in addition to proximal influences from the physical infrastructure, allows for the possibility of psychosocial mediating factors. Again, we contend that, to the extent that they are implicated, psychosocial factors would exert an influence throughout the life course, rather than at some critical period.

Toward a Conceptual Model of SES–health Inequalities

The optimal conceptual framework for considering SES–health inequalities is one which regards exposure to adverse physical and psychosocial conditions over the life course as key. Further, while discrete factors may, by themselves, have only the most modest of impacts, a clustering of adverse factors over the life course may confer substantial health disadvantage. Davey Smith, Blane, and Bartley (1994) provide a discussion of how such longitudinal clustering can occur. A baby born to a lower-SES mother is more likely to register low birth weight or be premature or both. A child growing up in a low-SES household is more likely to be subject to a range of exposure: family instability, poor diet, damp and overcrowded accommodation and restricted educational opportunity. An adolescent from such a household is more likely to experience family strife, smoke cigarettes, leave school with few qualifications and experience unemployment before entering a low-paid and insecure occupation. As an adult this person is more likely to work in an arduous, hazardous occupation, endure periods of unemployment, suffer the stress of financial insecurity, enjoy few psychological uplifts, experience negative social interactions and be able to exercise little control over their lives. A retired person from this sort of background is unlikely to have an occupational pension, and will most likely have difficulties meeting the costs of adequate clothing, heating and diet and be more likely to experience social isolation. Thus, adverse factors may cluster over a life course, and while individually these factors may be only modestly associated with health, in combination they may make for considerable disadvantage.

It is possible to sketch a very different sort of life career: one of advantage, where none of these factors pertains. This sort of conceptualization, then allows the substantial health differentials between high- and low-SES groups to arise from the accumulated impact of what, in population terms, may be relatively weak individual health determinants. However, it would be wrong to leave the impression that people are either advantaged or disadvantaged in this context. For example, the career of clustered disadvantage that we plotted earlier may be interrupted in late adolescence by success in education and subsequent high-income employment.

In a study of mortality in Finland, Lynch et al. (1994) found that high earnings in adulthood off-set the disadvantage of low SES in childhood. Alternatively, disadvantage may begin in middle age with redundancy and jobs loss. A number of studies now attest to increases in morbidity and mortality consequent on unemployment (see, e.g., Bartley, 1994, for a scholarly review). The health-damaging effects of jobs loss would seem to extend to those without noticeable prior disadvantage. For example, Morris, Cook, and Shaper (1994) reported that men who experienced unemployment during a 5-year follow-up period in the early 1980s had a mortality risk of 2.1 relative to their continuously employed counterparts. Adjustment for SES, as well as unhealthy behaviours, reduced this relative risk only slightly to 1.95. Further, men who retired early for reasons other than ill health and who, in the majority, were not manual workers suffered an increased relative mortality risk of 1.87. Even the anticipation of job loss would seem to have negative health consequences that extend to previously privileged sections of population. Ferrie, Shipley, Marmot, Stansfeld, and Davey Smith 1995 found that self-rated health deteriorated in public servants anticipating privatization and possible job loss. Finally, at slightly higher socio-economic positions that the one described, fewer adverse factors will collide, yielding less overall disadvantage. Thus, consonant with the continuous SES gradients in mortality and morbidity, we would postulate fine gradations of advantage and disadvantage, that is, individuals will differ in the length and level of their exposure to physical and psychosocial adversity and in the number of adverse factors to which they are exposed.

This conceptual framework provides a direction for future research; it argues that studies need to be multifactorial and that they need to examine possible influences acting across the life course. In addition, consideration should be given to analytical strategies better suited to examining the interacting influences of combinations of variables. For example, Adler et al. (1994) advocate the application of tree-structured regression to handle such mulifactorial and multitemporal data. In contrast to the simple regression analysis that characterizes much of SES–health research to date, tree-structured regression partitions the study population into subgroups and then identifies different paths to given outcomes.

Increasing Differentials in Wealth and Health

Deciphering the key physical and psychosocial factors and the manner of their influence in this context is unlikely to be an easy task, given the interactions and overlaps which undoubtedly exist. As we argue elsewhere (Carroll et al., 1993), this can reasonably be regarded as one of the most telling challenges facing those concerned with SES–health inequalities. In responding to this challenge, however, we should not lose sight of the fact that the underlying pattern of health inequalities powerfully reflects inequalities in the distribution of material resources. Accordingly, the most compelling intervention strategies in this regard are unlikely to be psychological. Rather they will be those which directly counter material inequality (Carroll et al., 1993; Williams, 1990). This assertion is given particular weight by the findings of recent studies that increasing inequalities in income have been paralleled by increasing inequalities in mortality (Davey Smith and Egger, 1993).

Throughout the 1980s there was a massive increase in the numbers of households living in relative poverty in the UK. Millar (1993) details the trend, and Figure 10.10 is merely illustrative of the statistics she presents. It reveals that, in 1979, 9 percent of households existed on below half the average income, whereas, by 1990/91, 24 percent of households met this criterion of impoverishment. These percentages translate into 5 million households in 1979 and 13.5 million households in 1990/91. Other indices of poverty tell the same story. In 1983, 7.5 million people (14 percent of the population) were unable to afford at least three essential items (things such as heating, warm clothing, damp-free homes, hot meals); by 1990, the figure rose to 11 million (20 percent of the population). Not only have more people become impoverished during the 1980s in the UK, but the income gap between affluent and poor has widened considerably. For example, changes in taxation policy, including reductions in the top rate of income tax and shifts from direct to indirect taxation (indirect taxation bears more heavily on those with lower incomes) yielded an increase of £87 per week between 1979 and 1992 for the richest 10 percent of the population compared with a loss of £1 per week, for the poorest 10 percent. As these data indicate, it is not just that the poorest sections of the community have been subject to increasing

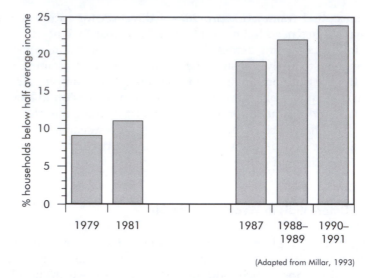

(Adapted from Millar, 1993)

FIGURE 10.10   **Percentage of Households Existing on Below Half-average Income, 1979 to 1990/91**

disadvantage in relative terms, they have also experienced a fall in income in real terms. Between 1979 and 1990/91 the poorest 10 percent of the population saw their real incomes fall by 14 percent after housing costs had been taken into account, whereas average incomes actually rose by 36 percent. Figure 10.11 illustrates this effect.

That these increasing disparities in wealth have clear consequences for SES–health gradients is demonstrated in two recent studies of regional mortality rates in the UK. In Glasgow, an affluence/deprivation index has been applied to classify small postal code areas of Glasgow, and standardized mortality ratios of these areas calculated for the years 1981 and 1989 (Forwell, 1993, McCarron, Davey Smith; and Wormsley, 1994). Figure 10.12 summarizes the findings. Differential mortality rates between the most affluent and most deprived areas were considerably greater in 1989 than in 1981.

Using the 1981 and 1991 census data, Philimore, Beattie, and Townsend (1994) apply the same deprivation index to rank small electoral areas (wards). Their geographical focus was the North East of England. Standardized mortality ratios were then calculated by ward using mortality data from the periods 1981–83 and 1989–91. Figure 10.13 depicts the outcome of their analyses. The mortality data from the two epochs pertaining to the most deprived fifth and most affluent fifth of wards are presented. A clear worsening in mortality relative to the national level is seen for the most deprived fifth of wards. Thus inequalities in mortality again appear to have widened over a decade in which the relative and absolute economic station of the poorest sections of the community deteriorated markedly.

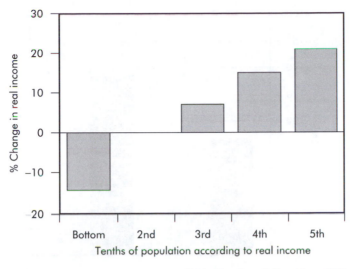

(Adapted from Davey Smith and Egger, 1993)

FIGURE 10.11   **Change in Real Income by Tenth of Income Distribution, 1979 to 1990/91**

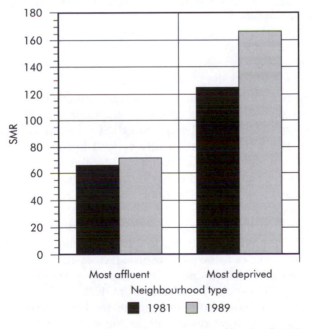

(Adapted from Forwell, 1993)

FIGURE 10.12   **Standardized Mortality Ratios (SMR) for Neighbourhood Types in Glasgow 1981 and 1989 (ages 0–64, Male and Female Combined)**

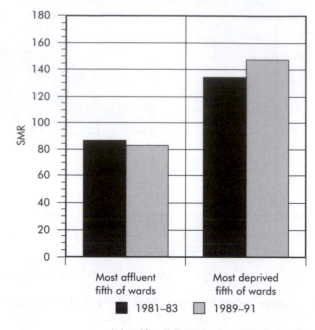

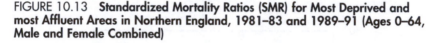

(Adapted from Phillimore, Beattie and Townsend, 1994)

FIGURE 10.13 **Standardized Mortality Ratios (SMR) for Most Deprived and most Affluent Areas in Northern England, 1981–83 and 1989–91 (Ages 0–64, Male and Female Combined)**

Concluding Remarks

The persistent and substantial inequalities in health contingent on SES present a formidable challenge to those concerned with putative health-related psychological processes (Adler et al., 1994). Indeed, SES–health gradients might be regarded as a key test of the frequently evoked but imperfectly articulated biopsychosocial model of health championed by the newly formalized disciplines of health psychology and behavioural medicine. Recent reviews identify psychological stress, social support, personal control and hostility as possible psychosocial mediators of SES–health effects. This list is undoubtedly preliminary, and further research is required to identify other candidates (Carroll et al., 1993; Williams, 1990). In addition, much needs to be done to clarify the precise role of those psychosocial factors already implicated.

Explanations of SES–health inequalities must pay attention to the physical as well as the psychosocial corollaries of material disadvantage and their interactions and combined influences across the life course. The model that we outline illustrates how exposures to physical and psychosocial challenges, which may be weakly implicated as individual health risks, can cluster over a life course to confer substantial health disadvantage. At the same time, though, we appreciate that, contingent on socio-economic position, individual exposure careers will vary in the level, length and number of exposures. We require not only conceptual models to do justice to this sort of complexity but analytical methods that can capture the complex and dynamic relationship among the many variables linking SES and health.

In turning our attention to research questions of this sort to achieve a fuller understanding of the mechanisms of SES influence, however, we must not let ourselves be distracted from the key fact of SES–health inequalities that: they are intimately bound up with material inequality. As inequalities in income have increased in societies such as the USA and the UK, so, too, have health inequalities (Davey Smith and Egger, 1993; Pappas et al., 1993). We submit that it is only through social and economic policies which counter gross material division that this trend will be reversed.

We already have evidence from small-scale studies of the health benefits that can derive from directly addressing material disadvantage. For example, Kehrer and Wolin (1979) reported a study in Gary, Indiana, of the effects of income supplementation through negative income tax on birth weight. Compared with low-income mothers who had not received income supplementation, the risk of low-birth-weight babies was reduced for those low-income mothers who were in receipt of such benefit. Analogous results emerged from a study in Alsace, France, in which income supplementation was used to compensate pregnant women for absence from physically arduous employment (Papiernik, Bouyer and Dreyfus, 1985). With supplementation, the incidence of very low birth weight in women at risk was substantially reduced. These results signal what might be achieved through progressive social and economic policies at a national level. As Wilkinson (1994) recently concluded, 'Policies intended to divorce health from deprivation have proved largely ineffective. Reducing the burden of excess mortality attributable to relative deprivation depends on reducing social and economic inequalities themselves' (p. 1114).

References

Adler, N. E., Boyce, T., Chesney, M. A., Cohen, S., Folkman, S., Kahn, R. L., and Syme, S. L. (1994) Socioeconomic status and health: The challenge of the gradient. *American Psychologist, 49,* 15–24.

Alterman, T., Shekelle, R. B., Vernon, S. W., and Burau, K. D. (1994) Decision latitude, psychological demand, job strain, and coronary heart disease in the Western Electric Study. *American Journal of Epidemiology, 139,* 620–627.

Angell, M. (1993) Privilege and health – What is the connection? *The New England Journal of Medicine, 329,* 126–127.

Arber, S. (1989) Gender and class inequalities in health: Understanding the differentials. In J. Fox (ed.), *Health inequalities in European countries.* (pp. 250–279). Aldershot: Gower.

Barefoot, J. C., Dodge, K. A., Peterson, B. L., Dahlstrom, W. G., and Williams, R. B., Jr. (1989) The Cook – Medley Hostility Scale: Item content and ability to predict survival. *Psychosomatic Medicine, 51,* 46–57.

Bartley, M. (1994) Unemployment and ill health: Understanding the relationship. *Journal of Epidemiology and Community Health, 48,* 333–337.

Ben-Shlomo, Y., and Davey Smith, G. (1991) Deprivation in infancy or in adult life: Which is more important for mortality risk? *Lancet, 337,* 530–534.

Berkman, L. F., and Breslow, L. (1983) *Health and ways of living: The Alameda County study.* Oxford: Oxford University Press.

Blane, D. (1985) An assessment of the Black Report's explanations of health inequalities. *Sociology of Health and Illness, 7,* 423–445.

Blaxter, M. (1990) *Health and lifestyle.* London: Tavistock.

Carroll, D., Davey Smith, G. and Bennett, P., (1993) Socio-economic health inequalities: Their origins and implications. *Psychology and Health, 8,* 295–316.

Carroll, D., Davey Smith, G., and Bennett, P. (1994) Health and Socio-economic status. *The Psychologists, 7,* 122–125.

Carstairs, V., and Morris, R. (1991) *Deprivation and health in Scotland.* Aberdeen: Aberdeen University Press.

Chapin, C. V. (1924) Deaths among taxpayers and non-taxpayers of income tax, Providence, 1865. *American Journal of Public Health, 14,* 647–651.

Davey Smith, G., Blane, D., and Bartley, M. (1994) Explanations for socioeconomic differentials in mortality. *European Journal of Public Health, 4,* 131–144.

Davey Smith, G., Carroll, D., Rankin, S., and Rowan, D. (1992) Socioeconomic differentials in mortality: Evidence from Glasgow graveyards. *British Medical Journal, 305,* 1554–1557.

Davey Smith, G., and Egger, M. (1993) Socioeconomic differentials in health and wealth: The legacy of the Thatcher years. *British Medical Journal, 307,* 1085–1086.

Davey Smith, G., Neaton, J. D., Stamler, J., and Wentworth, D. (1992) Income and mortality among 300,000 middle-aged men followed up for 12 years. Paper presented at the British Sociological Association/European Society of Medical Sociology Joint Conference, Edinburgh, Scotland.

Davey Smith, G., and Phillips, A. N. (1990) Declaring independence: Why we should be cautious. *Journal of Epidemiology and Community Health, 44,* 257–258.

Davey Smith, G., and Shipley, M. J. (1991) Confounding of occupation and smoking: Its magnitude and consequences. *Social Science and Medicine, 32,* 1297–1300.

Davey Smith, G., Shipley M. J., and Rose, G. (1990) The magnitude and causes of socioeconomic differentials in mortality: Further evidence from the Whitehall study. *Journal of Epidemiology and Community Health, 44,* 265–270.

Doll, R., and Peto, R. (1976) Mortality in relation to smoking: 20 years' observations on male doctors. *British Medical Journal, ii,* 469–473.

Ferrie, J., Shipley, M. J., Marmot, M. G., Stansfeld, S., and Davey Smith, G. (1995) Health effects of anticipation of job change and non-employment: longitudinal data from the Whitehall II study. *British Medical Journal, 311,* 1264–1269.

Forwell, G. D. (1993) Glasgow's health: Old problems – new opportunities. A report by the Director of Public Health, Department of Public Health, Glasgow.

Fox, J. (ed.). (1989) *Health inequalities in European countries,* Aldershot: Gower.

Goldblatt, P. (1988) Changes in social class between 1971 and 1981: Could these affect mortality differentials among men of working age? *Population Trends, 51,* 9–17.

Goldblatt, P. (1989) Mortality by social class, 1971–85. *Population Trends, 56,* 6–15.

Goldblatt, P. (ed.) (1990) *Longitudinal study: Morality and social organization.* London: HMSO.

Haan, M., Kaplan, G. A., and Camacho, T. (1987) Poverty and health: Prospective evidence from the Alameda County study. *American Journal of Epidemiology, 125,* 989–998.

Haberman, D., and Bloomfield, D. S. F. (1988) Social class differences in mortality in Great Britain around 1981. *Journal of the Institute of Actuaries, 115,* 495–517.

Hunter, D. (1955) *The diseases of occupations.* London: Hodder & Stoughton.

Karasek, R. A., Baker, D., Marxer, F., Ahlbom, A., and Theorell, T. (1981) Job decision latitude, job demands, and cardiovascular disease: A prospective study of Swedish men. *American Journal of Public Health, 71,* 694–705.

Karasek, R. A., Theorell, T. G., Schwartz, J. E., Pieper, C., and Alfredsson, L. (1982) Job, psychological factors and coronary heart disease: Swedish prospective findings and US prevalence findings using a new occupational inference method. *Advances in Cardiology, 29,* 62–67.

Kehrer, B. H., and Wolin, C. M. (1979) Impact of income maintenance on low birthweight. *Journal of Human Resources, 14,* 434–462.

Kitagawa, E. M., and Hauser, P. M. (1973) *Differential mortality in the United States: A Study of socioeconomic epidemiology.* Cambridge, MA: Harvard University Press.

Kuh, D., and Davey Smith, G. (1993) When is mortality risk determined? Historical insights into a current debate. *Social History of Medicine, 6,* 101–123.

Lynch, J. W., Kaplan, G. A., Cohen, R. D., Kauhanen J., Wilson, T. W., Smith, N. L., and Salonen, J. T. (1994) Childhood and adult socioeconomic status as predictors of mortality in Finland. *Lancet, 343,* 524–527.

Mare, R. D. (1990) Socio-economic careers and differential mortality among older men in the United States. In J. Vallin, S. D'Souza, and A. Palloni (eds), *Measurement and analysis of mortality: New approaches* (pp. 309–330). Oxford: Clarendon Press.

Marmot, M. G., and Davey Smith, G. (1989) Why are the Japanese living longer? *British Medical Journal, 299,* 1547–1551.

Marmot, M. G., and Davey Smith, G., Stansfeld, D., Patel, C., North, F., Head, J., White, I., Brunner, E., and Fenney, A. (1991) Health inequalities among British civil servants: The Whitehall 1 study. *Lancet, 337,* 1387–1392.

Marmot, M. G., Shipley, M. J., and Rose, G. (1984) Inequalities in health – Specific explanations of a general pattern? *Lancet, i,* 1003–1006.

Martin, C. J., Platt, S. D., and Hunt, S. (1987) Housing conditions and health. *British Medical Journal, 294,* 1125–1127.

McCarron, P., Davey Smith, G., and Wormsley, J. (1994) Deprivation and Mortality in Glasgow: changes from 1980 to 1992. *British Medical Journal, 309,* 1481–1482.

Meadows, S. H. (1961) Social class migration and chronic bronchitis. *Journal of Preventative and Social Medicine, 15,* 171–176.

Millar, J. (1993) The continuing trend in rising poverty. In A. Sinfield (ed.), *Poverty, inequality and justice.* Edinburgh: University of Edinburgh.

Morris, J. K., Cook, D. G., and Shaper, A. G. (1994) Loss of employment and mortality. *British Medical Journal, 308,* 1135–1139.

Morrison, A. S., Kirshner, J., and Molha, A. (1977) Life cycle events in 15th century Florence: Records of the Monte Delle Doti. *American Journal of Epidemiology, 106,* 487–492.

Papiernik, E., Bonyer, J., and Drefus, J. (1985) Risk factors from preterm births and results of a prevention policy. The Hagenau Perinatal Study, 1971–1982. In R. W. Beard, and F. Sharp (eds), *Preterm labour and its consequences* (pp. 15–20). Manchester: Richard Bates.

Pappas, G., Queen, S., Hadden, W., and Fisher, G. (1993) The increasing disparity in mortality between socioeconomic groups in the United States, 1960 and 1986. *The New England Journal of Medicine, 329*, 103–109.

Phillimore, P., Beattie, A., and Townsend, P. (1994) Widening inequalities of health in northern England, 1981–91. *British Medical Journal, 308*, 1125–1128.

Platt, S. D., Martin, C. J., Hunt, S., and Lewis, C. W. (1989) Damp housing, mould growth and symptomatic health state. *British Medical Journal, 298*, 1673–1678.

Pugh, H., Power, C., Goldblattt, P., and Arber, S. (1991) Women's lung cancer mortality, socioeconomic status and changing smoking patterns. *Social Science and Medicine, 32*, 1105–1110.

Reid, D. D., Hamilton, P. J. S., McCartney, P., and Rose, G. (1976) Smoking and other risk factors for coronary heart disease in British civil servants. *Lancet, ii*, 979–984.

Rogot, E., Sorlie, P. D., Johnson, N. J., and Schmitt, C. (1993) *A mortality study of 1.3 million persons by demographic, social, and economic factors: 1979–1985 follow-up US National Longitudinal Mortality study.* Washington DC: NIH.

Townsend, P., and Davidson, N. (1982) *The Black Report.* Harmonsworth: Penguin.

Watt, G. C. M., and Ecob, R. (1992) Mortality in Glasgow and Edinburgh: A paradigm of inequality in health. *Journal of Epidemiology and Community Health, 46*, 498–505.

Wilkinson, R. G. (1990) Income distribution and mortality: A 'natural' experiment *Sociology of Health and Illness, 12*, 391–412.

Wilkinson, R. G. (1992) Income distribution and life expectancy. *British Medical Journal, 304*, 165–168.

Wilkinson, R. G. (1994) Divided we fall: The poor pay the price of increased social inequality with their health. *British Medical Journal, 308*, 1113–1114.

Williams, D. R. (1990) Socioeconomic differentials in health: A review and redirection. *Social Psychology Quarterly, 53*, 81–99.

PART III

HEALTH BEHAVIOUR AND EXPERIENCE

THE READINGS

11 **Context and Coping: Toward a Unifying Conceptual Framework**
Rudolf H. Moos

12 **An 'Ecological' Approach to the Obesity Pandemic**
Garry Egger and Boyd Swinburn

13 **Moving Towards Active Living: Understanding the Contextual Nature of Barriers to Physical Activity**
Susan Drew

14 **Conditional Versus Unconditional Risk Estimates in Models of AIDS-Related Risk Behaviour**
Frank W. van der Velde, Christa Hooykaas and Joop van der Pligt

15 **Health and Romance: Understanding Unprotected Sex in Relationships between gay men.**
Paul Flowers, Jonathan A. Smith, Paschal Sheeran and Nigel Beail

Understanding the determinants of health-related behaviour and experience is a core part of health psychology. Individual behaviour was the primary focus in the latter half of the 20th century. However *behaviour does not occur in a vacuum*. A strong case can be made for including **context** and **culture** in all psychological analyses of behaviour. HPTRP advocates a social and cultural perspective using the '**onion model**' as a framework for understanding health behaviour and experience. This is reproduced in Figure 1.

In reading each article, one should be aware of which ring or rings of the onion are being dealt with. The first reading was an acceptance speech of the APA Division of Community Psychology's[1] Distinguished Contribution Award to Rudolf H. Moos (Reading 11). Moos offers an **ecological framework** for integrating the social context and human coping resources in human **adaptation** and growth. The framework proposed by Moos is described as transactional because there are influences in both directions between the environmental system and the personal system. Stresses, resources, cognitive and coping responses all contribute to health outcomes. Moos' research fits this framework rather well. He developed a variety of scales for the measurement of the relevant variables. Moos saw social network resources as including **social connectedness**, social activities with family and friends, cultural and recreational pursuits, religious concern and affiliation, and community club memberships. The report concludes with the idea that 'Broad social change occurs when many individuals who are each competent to cause such change band together with a common goal. The quest for a better society makes it possible to pursue objectives that are currently unattainable but that might become the birthright of all.'

Garry Egger and Boyd Swinburn (Reading 12) present an ecological model for **obesity** and fatness. They suggest that current strategies are not having any noticeable impact on the 'obesity pandemic' and argue for a shift from the traditional view of obesity as a personal weakness or disorder that requires treatment towards an ecological approach that regards obesity as a normal response to an abnormal environment. Egger and Swinburn argue that the fast food culture and sedentary environment of Western countries is 'obesogenic'. Interventions aimed at 'normalisation' of the environment are necessary to complement the health education and promotion aimed at the millions of affected individuals.

Susan Drew (Reading 13) is concerned with the barriers to physical activity. The data were drawn from semi-structured interviews and written histories coded and analysed using qualitative methods. Perceptions of physical activity as appropriate for the self were formed in relation to cultural stereotypes and comparisons of self with others. The participants' talk suggested that the social environment discourages physical activity, in agreement with Egger and Swinburn.

An important activity has been the testing of models concerning the prediction of health behaviours and intentions. In Reading 14, Frank van der Velde, Christa Hooykaas and Joop van der Pligt discuss the role of perceived risk in AIDS-related behaviour. The authors differentiate between conditional and unconditional **risk**. They argue that **conditional risk** estimates are more useful in predicting intentions using models such as the **health belief model** (Becker,

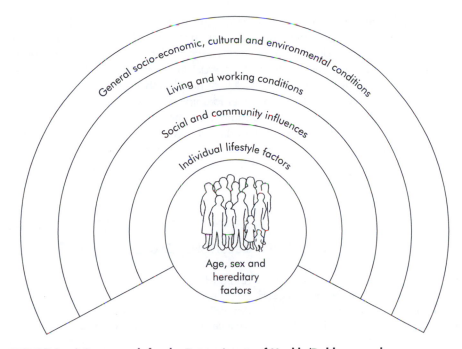

FIGURE 1   **A Framework for the Determinants of Health (Dahlgren and Whitehead, 1991, p. 23)**

1974) and the **protection motivation theory** (Rogers, 1975). Van der Velde and his colleagues found that estimates of **unconditional risk** were inconsistently related to behavioural intentions across different samples. This study illustrates several features about model testing. Firstly, the participants were a unique sample of voluntary heterosexual people older than 17 years attending a STD clinic in Amsterdam between October 1987 and December 1990, approximately half of those eligible to participate. The majority engaged in prostitution contacts. Can the findings be generalised beyond this time, place and sample? Secondly, the model assumes that decision-making is based on rational thought processes in the minds of sexually active and aroused adults. Emotional components of sexual encounters are overlooked? Thirdly, the amounts of variance in behavioural intentions that have been controlled[2] by the model variables about a quarter or less across the four analyses. This implies that about three-quarters of the variance remains uncontrolled by the model, meaning that the model provides a highly incomplete account of the participants' decision-making intentions. When we look at the participants' subsequent behaviour, the model is an even poorer fit to events. These limitations are typical of **quantitative approaches** to health behaviour analysis, opening the way to more exploratory approaches, e.g. **qualitative studies** from the perspective of the participants.

Paul Flowers, Jonathan Smith, Paschal Sheeran and Nigel Beail (Reading 15) explore the meanings of sex and relationships among gay men using **Interpretative Phenomenological Analysis**. The authors base their analysis on

20 in-depth interviews with working class gay men in a small South Yorkshire town. A set of meanings about love, trust, commitment and romance take priority over epidemiological admonitions to wear condoms. Flowers et al., call this set of meanings a 'romantic rationality' and contrast this with the 'health rationality' approach used in the conventional models of health behaviour.

Health psychology has focused on epidemiological imperatives concerning behaviours such as unconditional condom use, smoking cessation, jogging and the eating of five daily helpings of fruits and vegetables. This is a part of a grander vision for the field that deals with issues of meanings, **lived experience** and culture. The phenomenology of lived experience is the guiding light and behaviours, and talk, are tokens for expression.

HIGHLIGHTS, QUESTIONS, ISSUES

1 What is meant by an 'ecological' approach?
2 What is a 'transactional' model?
3 Why is 'social connectedness' a resource?
4 Think of three interventions to reduce the prevalence of obesity in the population.
5 How do stereotypes enter into people's decisions about indulging in physical activity?
6 What is the difference between 'conditional' and 'unconditional' risk?
7 Compare and contrast the quantitative and qualitative approaches to the study of sexual behaviour.
8 Romantic love is one interpretation in a sexual relationship. How might romantic love and commitment affect the partners' use of condoms?
9 How could sexual health promotion be made more effective?
10 What would a health psychology based on lived experience be like?

Notes

1 This is now the Society for Community Research and Action.
2 'controlled' is a more accurate term than 'explained' which implies causation.

11 CONTEXT AND COPING:
Toward A Unifying Conceptual Framework

Rudolf H. Moos

How can we understand the processes by which human contexts and coping resources promote human adaptation and growth? This problem provides the common thread that has unified my efforts over the past two decades. To deal with such an overarching question, my colleagues and I have addressed three component issues. What are the underlying characteristics of human contexts and how can such contexts be conceptualized as dynamic environmental systems? What are the major coping resources that help individuals to select and shape environmental contexts and how are such resources used to adapt to unavoidable life crises and inhumane settings? Finally, how can new knowledge in these areas be used to promote primary as well as secondary and tertiary prevention?

My work as a clinician and my knowledge of the detrimental effects of mental hospitals on long-term patients led me to focus first on psychiatric treatment settings. In this work, my colleagues and I developed methods by which the social environments or treatment atmospheres of such settings could be evaluated and changed to better suit their purposes (Moos, 1974). Subsequently, we expanded our efforts and explored the effects of learning environments in high school classrooms and university student living groups (Moos, 1979). Most recently, we have formulated measures to tap the underlying characteristics of family, work, and social group settings (Moos, 1981a, 1981b; Moos and Moos, 1981). As the findings from this work emerged, we found ourselves wondering how a particular social environment evolves from the discrete objects and people that comprise it. We became aware of the need for a more comprehensive formulation of environmental factors in order to understand the differential impacts of social settings and to develop more effective intervention strategies.

In a related endeavor, we began to examine the active ways in which individuals construct and cope with life transitions and acute health and other personal crises (Moos, 1977). Although stress typically takes its toll, we learned that most persons shape acceptable resolutions to difficult circumstances while some manage not only to survive but also to mature in the face of overwhelming hardships. This realization led us to consider the social network and coping resources that help individuals prevent and adapt to stressful life circumstances. Our most recent efforts are directed toward identifying how personal factors act in conjunction with environmental factors to affect adaptation. Overall, the thrust of our work highlights the value of an ongoing interplay between new concepts and measurement procedures as well as between basic social-psychological research and its applications.

Formulating an Integrative Conceptual Framework

My colleagues and I have formulated a general conceptual framework to guide us in addressing these issues. The model shown in Figure 11.1 considers the link between stressful life circumstances and adaptation to be affected by an environmental system (Panel I) and a personal system (Panel II), as well as by social network resources and appraisal and coping responses (Panels III and IV). The environmental system is composed of physical and architectural features, policy and program factors, and suprapersonal factors (that is, the aggregate characteristics of individuals in a setting), as well as social climate factors. The personal system included an individual's sociodemographic characteristics and such personal resources as self-esteem, cognitive ability, and general problem-solving skills, and health status and functional capacity. Stressful life circumstances encompass discrete events of short-term duration (such as a minor automobile accident in which no one is seriously hurt), as well as sequential combinations of such events (separation, divorce, child having problems at school), and chronic life strains (being in a confining marriage or being a parent of a severely handicapped child).

The conceptual model posits that life stressors (Panel III) and the environmental and personal factors related to such stressors (Panels I and II) can shape social network resources and coping responses (Panels III and IV), as well as their effectiveness (Panel V). In addition, factors in the environmental system (a high neighborhood crime rate) and the personal system (a vigilant perceptual style) can lead to cognitive appraisal (the perception of danger to personal safety) and coping responses (placing safety locks on windows and doors) that change the environmental system and reduce the probability of experiencing a stressful event (being robbed or burglarized). The fully nonrecursive nature of the model (that is, the bidirectional paths) reflects the fact that these processes are transactional and that reciprocal feedback can occur at each stage.

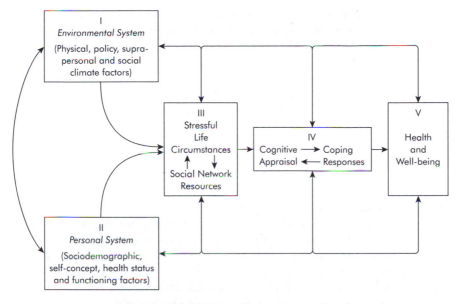

FIGURE 11.1 **A Model of the Relationship Between Personal and Environmental Factors and Adaptation**

Environmental Resources and Environmental Dynamics

Underlying Patterns of Social Climate

We began our work by developing a set of Social Climate Scales to tap three underlying domains of variables that characterize different types of settings. Relationship dimensions assess the extent to which people are involved with and supportive of one another. Personal growth or goal orientation dimensions assess the underlying goals toward which a setting is oriented; for instance, autonomy in psychiatric or medical treatment programs and task orientation in work groups. System maintenance and change dimensions deal with the degree of structure, clarity, and openness to change that characterize the setting. Dimensions drawn from these three categories have been related to a variety of indices of performance and well-being.

Family Environments and Children's Development One line of research has identified some links between child and adolescent behavior and the structure of the family environment. Cohesive and expressive families with relatively little conflict tend to have children who show fewer behavioral and emotional problems. Children in families oriented toward independence and achievement are likely to be more assertive and self-sufficient, while those in active, stimulating families (as indexed by intellectual and recreational orientation) show better perceptual and sensory-motor development and more adequate school adjustment. Finally, children in well-organized families tend to show better social and emotional adaptation, but overly rigid family structure may be associated with insecurity and less self-control (Gottfried and Gottfried, 1983; Moos and Moos, 1981, 1983; Nihira, Mink and Meyers, 1981).

Learning Environments and Student Growth   Another set of projects identified some of the learning environment factors that influence personal and academic growth among high school students. Positive relationships with teachers and peers and an emphasis on student participation in a well-organized classroom setting fosters student morale, interest in the subject matter, and sense of academic self-efficacy. Gains on standard achievement tests are most likely to occur in task-oriented classes that set specific academic goals in the context of supportive relationships and clear structure. Substantial achievement gains may occur in classes that stress task performance and are lower in warmth, but such classes are not as effective in fostering student interest or creativity. Moreover, we found sharply elevated student absenteeism rates in high school classes that are characterized by competition and teacher control but lack a moderating emphasis on student involvement and teacher support (Fraser and Fisher, 1982; Humphrey, 1984; Keyser and Barling, 1981; Moos, 1979).

Health Care Settings and Client Improvement   In a third set of studies, the treatment environments of hospital-based and community-based programs were related to indices of treatment outcome. Programs that emphasize practical task-oriented learning and encourage independence and personal responsibility enhance clients' self-care and community living skills. Conversely, clients are more likely to drop out of treatment programs that lack peer and staff support and that are disorganized and have unclear rules and procedures. Certain aspects of treatment settings may affect patients differentially, depending upon their level of emotional disturbance. Specifically, less disturbed patients tend to do better in programs with high expectations for independence and open sharing of personal problems in a relatively involving and expressive context. More disturbed patients need a tolerant and relatively structured setting that insulates them from too much interpersonal stimulation (Cronkite, Moos and Finney, 1983; Moos, 1974; Ryan and Bell, 1983).

Characteristics of Growth-promoting Environments

In conjunction with a considerable body of other research, such findings clarify some of the common consequences of conceptually similar social environmental factors (Cronkite et al., 1983; Moos, 1979; Moos and Spinrad, 1984). Most generally, the personal growth or goal orientation dimensions channel the direction of change, while the relationship and system maintenance dimensions influence the commitment to the environment as well as the extent of change and the personal costs involved (see Table 11.1). More specifically, environmental systems tend to maintain or accentuate

TABLE 11.1 **Some Links between Indices of Social Climate and Adaptation**

Type of setting	Relationship dimensions	Growth dimensions	Maintenance dimensions
Families			
Behavioral or emotional adjustment	Cohesion Expressiveness Conflict (Low)		Organization
Assertive, self-sufficient		Independence Achievement	
Intellectual development, school adjustment		Intellectual and social orientation	
Insecurity, lack of self-control			Rigid structure
Classrooms			
Morale and self-efficacy	Involvement Affiliation Teacher support		Organization
Academic achievement	Support	Task orientation	Organization
Absenteeism	Lack of support	Competition	Teacher control
Health Care Settings			
Self-care and community living skills	Involvement	Task orientation, autonomy	
Dropout	Lack of peer and staff support		Unclear, disorganized

individual characteristics congruent with their dominant aspects. Thus, patients located in programs that emphasize independence tend to improve in social and vocational functioning. Student achievement is enhanced by an emphasis on task performance and academic pursuits. Children located in families that value independence, achievement, and intellectual and recreational pursuits are likely to show more personal and social competence.

An emphasis on the relationship domain (that is, dimensions such as cohension, support, and expressiveness) is associated with morale and satisfaction. By fostering commitment and motivation, positive interpersonal relationships are linked to lower absenteeism and dropout rates and to the stable functioning of a setting. In addition, cohesive relationships amplify the influence of personal growth dimensions and moderate the problematic consequences of highly pressured, achievement-oriented environments. Conceptually similar findings have been identified in family and work settings, classrooms, student living groups, and psychiatric treatment programs, as well as in such task-oriented groups as neighborhood block organizations and high school basketball teams (Fisher, Mancini, Hirsch, Proulx and Staurowky, 1982; Giamartino and Wandersman, 1983; Moos, 1979; Moos and Moos, 1983). Such cross-situational generality indicates that social cohension and support can potentiate personal growth and have both direct and stress-buffering effects on adaptation.

Aside from regulating and organizing a setting, moderate emphasis on system maintenance factors promotes both personal growth and ego control. But strong emphasis on these factors (especially in the relative absence of cohesion) restricts individual development and may create anxiety or defiance. Notwithstanding such general relationships, there is also evidence that environmental structure may be more important for developmentally less mature or less competent individuals (Moos, 1979). Overall, the findings affirm the value of examining the interplay of relationship, personal growth, and system maintenance factors in searching out the consequences of varying social climates.

Exploring the Determinants of Social Climate

This body of work raises an intriguing question. Why do social environments develop in such disparate ways; that is, what factors affect the emergence of an emphasis on cohesion, or on autonomy, or on competition? How is social climate influenced by other domains of the environmental system (Panel I) and how are such domains related to personal well-being (Panel V)? To address this question, my colleagues and I have conceptualized the environment as a dynamic system composed of four domains: physical and architectural features, policy and program factors, suprapersonal factors, and social climate factors. We believe that physical, policy, and suprapersonal factors affect each other and the stress and resource characteristics of the social environment. In turn, these climate factors mediate and moderate the influence of the other three domains on health and adaptation.

Measuring the Environmental Domains   To examine these ideas, we used the perspective of four environmental domains to guide us in developing the Multiphasic Environmental Assessment Procedure (MEAP) to assess residential environments for older people. The MEAP consists of four main instruments, the content of which follows the conceptual organization of the four environmental domains. For example, the Physical and Architectural Features checklist (PAF) taps such physical resources as social-recreational aids, safety features, and space availability, while the Policy and Program Information Form (POLIF) covers program resources such as policy clarity, resident choice and control, and provisions for privacy. The Resident and Staff Information Form (RESIF) considers the residents' social backgrounds, degree of diversity, and functional abilities. The Sheltered Care Environment Scale (SCES) assesses residents' and staff members' perceptions of the facility social environment on dimensions such as cohesion, independence, and organization (Moos and Lemke, 1983).

Examining the Environmental Systems Model   We used data from the MEAP gathered on 90 residential care settings to identify the determinants of social climate. Cohesion among residents was more likely to develop in settings with more physical amenities (such as attractive decorations in the halls), better social-recreational aids (such as lounges furnished for casual conversation), and more available personal space. Such settings also tended to have policies that provided their residents with broader personal choice and more opportunity to participate in running the facility. A climate of independence was more likely to emerge in facilities that provided more social activities and allowed their residents more choice in organizing their daily lives and more control over certain aspects of facility policies. Such physical features as social-recreational aids and amenities contributed to resident independence by enabling facilities to select more socially competent residents who fostered more flexible autonomous policies.

Residents in settings that emphasized cohesion and autonomy were more involved in facility-based and community-based activities and showed less use of health and daily living assistance services, as well as lower 3-month turnover rates. Architectural and policy factors can promote supportive, independence-oriented social climates. In turn, these social climates can foster aspects of health-related functioning among older persons (Moos and Lemke, 1983). As noted earlier, cohesion can also amplify or offset the influence of other environmental factors, such as by augmenting the formation of committees that enable residents to participate in decision-making, or by promoting helping behavior in settings that lack orientational and prosthetic aids.

We have used these ideas to probe the links among the four environmental domains in classrooms and student living groups. For example, supportive-achievement oriented climates are more likely to develop in women's or coed living units with a high proportion of double rooms, better recreational facilities, and more scholarly and intellectual activities. In turn, these settings tend to promote students' academic and social development (Moos, 1979). Such findings begin to clarify cross-situational consistencies in the processes by which environments develop and influence the individuals who create them.

Coping Resources and Coping Processes

As our framework indicates, we visualize stressful life circumstances and social network resources as closely linked to each other, as well as to both the environmental and the personal systems. These systems influence the likelihood of exposure to life stressors and the selection of appraisal and coping processes used to adapt to them. Conversely, by affecting the environmental systems to which individuals are exposed, such processes can prevent the development of life stressors. Although they are placed as intervening or mediating factors in the model, the feedback loops indicate that one important function of social network and coping resources is to prevent stressors prior to their occurrence or, when stress is inevitable, to forestall a continuing sequence of strain that is ultimately debilitating.

We are pursuing these issues in a set of related projects on two groups of individuals who were randomly selected within specific census tracts in the San Francisco Bay Area. These samples were drawn to explore health and

TABLE 11.2 **Social Stress and Resource Indices**

Stressful life circumstances
  Negative life change events
  Ongoing family strain
    Spouse dysfunction (depression, physical symptoms)
    Children's health and behavioral problems
  Chronic work strain
    Work pressure and supervisor control
    Lack of autonomy and clarity
Social Network Resources
  Social connectedness
    Social activities with family and friends
    Cultural and recreational pursuits
    Religious concern and affiliation
    Community club memberships
  Quality of social relationships
    Family cohesion, expressiveness, conflict
    Work involvement, peer cohesion, supervisor support

adaptation among representative adult community groups, as well as to serve as demographically matched comparison groups for samples of treated psychiatric patients and their families. The patient and community families were assessed twice at approximately 12- to 15-month intervals with respect to variables included in four of the five sets of domains encompassed by the framework.

Measuring Life Stressors and Coping Resources

To facilitate our work, we developed indices of stressful life circumstances, of the quality of social network resources, and of appraisal and coping responses (Billings, Cronkite and Moos, 1983). In brief, stressful circumstances were measured by the occurrence of negative life change events as well as by indices of ongoing strain in family and work settings (see Table 11.2). We constructed indices of social network resources by tapping not only respondents' "connectedness" to family, friends, and community groups, but also the perceived quality of the social relationships in their family and work settings. For example, we considered the quality of family relationships and such work-related social resources as peer cohesion and supervisor support that may prevent the development of work stress or buffer its effects.

Our conceptual framework distinguishes between general cognitive styles or problem-solving strategies and the appraisal and coping responses involved in handling specific stressful situations. We have thus measured coping skills by asking individuals to describe how they dealt with a recent personal crisis or stressful life circumstance. One classification scheme involves dividing active attempts to resolve stressful circumstances into cognitive and behavioral strategies while separately clustering attempts to avoid the problem or reduce the emotional tension associated with the stressor. We have recently expanded this scheme and organized appraisal and coping responses into three domains. Appraisal-focused coping entails cognitive attempts to define the meaning of the situation while problem-focused coping involves taking action to modify or eliminate the source of stress or to deal with the tangible consequences of an unavoidable problem. Emotion-focused coping includes responses whose primary function is to manage the affect aroused by stressful situations (Moos and Billings, 1982; Billings and Moos, 1984).

Exploring the Stress and Coping Process

We are using these indices and our conceptual framework to guide us in exploring several issues involved in the stress and coping process. Selected findings are provided to exemplify such issues here.

Stress and Resource Predictors of Adaptation   Are life stressors and social network and coping resources predictively associated with health-related criteria? To address this issue, we controlled for initial levels of personal resources and functioning (variables in Panel II) and then examined relationships among variables in Panels III, IV, and V. Although the use of avoidance coping was linked to depression among both men and women, stressful events and decreases in the quality of family social resources were more closely related to depression among women than among men. In fact, lack of family and work resources was associated with depression among women after initial levels of depression and resources were considered. There was some evidence of a stress mastery effect among men in that a high initial level of stressful events was predictive of less subsequent depression than expected given the initial level of depressed mood and subsequent life events (Billings and Moos, 1982a, 1982b; Cronkite and Moos, 1983; Holahan and Moos, 1981).

Personal and Social Resources in Stress Prevention and Resistance   What is the preventive role of personal and social resources; for example, do persons who are functioning more adequately and who possess more coping resources subsequently experience fewer life events or strains? Consistent with the work of other investigators, we found that individuals of higher social status tend to function better, to be exposed to fewer stressors, to enjoy more social resources, and to use active-cognitive and active-behavioral rather than avoidance-oriented coping strategies. In terms of levels of functioning, the men in our community group who were initially less depressed experienced fewer stressors than expected in the subsequent 12- to 15-month interval. Married women who were initially less depressed subsequently experienced more family support and (for those who were employed) more interpersonal support at work (Billings and Moos, 1982a, 1982b; Cronkite and Moos, 1983).

We have recently focused on stress resistance by attempting to identify personal resources that offset the potential negative effects of life stress. Using data from our community sample, we found individuals who fell into a stress-resistant group, that is, who experienced high stress but few psychosomatic symptoms and little or no depression. In comparison to a distressed group (high stress, high distress), the stress-resistant individuals were more easygoing and less inclined to use avoidance coping methods. In addition, stress-resistant men were more self-confident and stress-resistant women enjoyed more family support than their counterparts in the distressed group. Such findings indicate that men and women may differ in the factors that are most helpful in enabling them to resist environmental stress (Holahan and Moss, 1983). In conjunction with the results presented earlier, they exemplify the bidirectional associations among the sets of factors in the framework.

Cross-situational Influences   The potential importance of cross-situational influences was suggested initially by our finding that work stressors were predictive of poorer adaptation among individuals who were not living in family settings, though they had no such effect among individuals who enjoyed family support. We also found that the quality of the family environment had a stronger influence on adaptation among married women who were homemakers than among those who were employed outside the home. We later obtained more direct evidence that work and family environments affect each other. Men who experienced more work stress also experienced less family support, while high stress in a married woman's job setting was associated with her husband's report of less family cohesion and more symptoms. Moreover, the stressful circumstances experienced by a wife contributed to her use of avoidance coping strategies, which were related to a lack of family social resources (Billings and Moos, 1982a, 1982c; Cronkite and Moos, 1983). In this way, individuals can be affected indirectly by settings in which they do not participate.

Implications for Evaluation and Intervention

My colleagues and I have used a general framework to conceptualize the domains of contextual and coping factors, and to explore their reciprocal links with social stressors and indices of health and illness. By depicting the connections among the sets of factors involved in adaptive functioning, the framework can help community psychologists design more effective evaluation and intervention procedures.

Conducting Conceptually Informed Evaluation Research

The idea of three domains of social climate factors can help to correct overly simplified views of environments and thereby to plan more informed intervention programs. For example, there is intense debate about whether learning environments should emphasize task performance and teacher control ("back to basics") or student relationships and innovative teaching practices. Some educators believe that strong classroom structure and organization are essential, while others argue that too much teacher control retards the development of independence and intrinsic motivation to learn. The fact is that basic skills programs would benefit from being supportive as well as oriented toward performance and structure, while open program or alternative classes could stand more emphasis on academic achievement and organization.

Intervention programs typically are neither implemented as planned nor delivered to recipients in a fixed, standard manner. A second area of importance entails using environmental assessment procedures to monitor the adequacy of program implementation. For instance, Felner, Ginter and Primaverra (1982) examined the implementation of a primary prevention project that sought to promote personal adjustment and school performance by increasing the level of peer and teacher support and clarity among students in transition to high school. As compared to matched controls, project participants in fact saw the school setting as clearer and more structured and reported higher levels of involvement and support. A similar approach was used by Steiner (1982) to show that a therapeutic community could be developed on an adolescent psychosomatic unit that combined a medical with a psychiatric treatment orientation. When the intervention is being delivered as intended, the relationship between specific program components (including the quality of the social environment) and individual outcomes can be explored. At this point an evaluator can help practitioners to reorient the program to concentrate its resources on those components that are associated with better outcome.

A social-ecological perspective also affirms the need for a fundamental shift in thinking about intervention programs and their effects (Moos and Finney, 1983). An intervention program is but one (indeed, a temporary one) of the multiple environmental microsystems or specific settings that influence personal growth and maturation. Other powerful current environments also shape individual mood and behavior; subsequently, the initial effects of an intervention can be augmented or nullified by new environmental factors. For instance, nonschool settings can influence school and classroom settings by inhibiting their effects (as when the family or peer group does not value an achievement oriented school), by augmenting their effects (as when home and family factors reinforce an achievement oriented learning environment), or by compensating for their lack of effects (as when children are taught skills at home that they have not learned in school).

The links among settings are important in regard to the probable stability of the effects of intervention programs. Many of the hard-won gains of social programs fade away over time. This is precisely as expected on the basis of our knowledge about environmental impact and the diversity of settings to which most individuals are exposed. Inherent in the belief that an intervention program can promote change is the assumption that other more recent environmental factors can modify such change. Conversely, if community settings can alter individuals, so can intervention programs. The "decay" in the effects of such programs may be due largely to the social ecological context of program recipients. The use of a systems framework to identify convergent cross-setting effects should make it possible to formulate more integrated and powerful social programs.

Changing and Improving Community Settings

Since each path in the framework identifies a process that is potentially alterable, the model is rich with implications for intervention at both the individual and the environmental level. At the individual level, the use of the framework can promote the integration of social-ecological formulations in clinical case descriptions and thereby augment the therapeutic process (Moos and Fuhr, 1982). At the environmental level, each of the four domains provides a different perspective on an environment (Otto and Moos, 1973) and each highlights specific techniques and strategies for implementing change. We have formulated a four-step process to promote change: assessment of the environment and of environmental preferences, feedback and discussion of the resulting information, planning and instituting specific changes, and reassessment. This process has been used to improve hospital-based and community-based treatment programs (Moos, 1974), correctional facilities for youthful offenders (O'Leary, Duffee and Wenk, 1977), and classrooms (Waters, 1982) and student living groups (Daher, Corazzini and McKinnon, 1977), as well as to design effective work climates for health care staff (Koran, Moos and Zasslow, 1983).

Information about the domains and dynamics of the environmental system can help individuals to formulate needed interventions and to monitor the results of an intervention program. For instance, our findings on the development of cohesion and independence in residential care settings provided administrators and staff guidelines with which to understand and modify the social milieu. Knowledge about the "determinants" of social stressors and coping resources identify directions in which change is likely to occur and highlight the types of person-setting combinations that are most amenable to change. A focus on all five sets of factors in the framework can help to develop conceptually integrated intervention strategies as well as to forecast the problems that may arise from using them.

Conceptual and Theoretical Issues

The framework I have described can help to guide and integrate research in what typically are separate lines of empirical work. The model can identify commonalities and gaps in our knowledge about the influence of contextual and coping factors in health care settings, group living facilities for students and older people, and family, classroom, and work environments. Moreover, the framework seems to apply to patients being treated for unipolar depression or alcohol abuse and their families and to persons with serious medical conditions, as well as to representative groups of "normal" men and women (Billings and Moos, 1984; Moos, 1984). In this regard, the stress and coping processes involved in the development of "diagnosable" disorders are likely to be similar (albeit accentuated) to those related to mood and adaptation among healthy individuals. At least three sets of conceptual and theoretical issues must be clarified in order to make fundamental progress in understanding these processes.

Understanding the Environmental System

We are beginning to comprehend the domains and dynamics of the environmental system. Aside from better integrated measures of contextual factors, more work is needed on identifying their connections to life stressors and coping resources, that is, on the links between Panel I and Panels III and IV in the model. Little is known about either the processes by which the broader environmental context affect the balance of stressors and social resources in an individual's life or the influence of contextual factors on the selection and efficacy of appraisal and coping responses.

Another point concerns the differential strength of contextual factors. The more intensive, committed, and socially integrated a setting, the greater its potential impact, particularly on personal factors that are undergoing developmental change. Cohesive homogenous settings tend to influence incongruent individuals to change in the direction of the majority, while those in the majority maintain or further accentuate their attitudes and behavior in the relevant areas. For instance, we found that college students who increased their alcohol consumption during their freshman year were likely to be located in cohesive living groups in which their peers drank more heavily. A heterogeneous setting has more diverse influences and provides each person with a wider choice of options. Individuals are more likely to find other persons with similar attitudes and values and less likely to experience consistent pressure to change in such a setting (Moos, 1979).

While powerful environments offer an unusual opportunity for effecting change, they also carry significant risks. Although such settings change most of the individuals who elect to stay in them, they have high turnover and "casualty" rates. For instance, concentrating high-ability students in certain classrooms can promote their aspiration and achievement levels. But social comparison processes often work to the detriment of the less able students, who may feel alienated and less competent in such classes. Group homes with high expectations for independent functioning tend to produce positive changes in social and vocational adaptation, but residents in such homes also have higher relapse and rehospitalization rates. Any setting that is powerful enough to promote constructive personal change is also powerful enough to induce some concomitant stress. Moreover, such settings can lead to significant problems, as when homogeneous cohesive living groups influence students to engage in social pursuits and neglect academic goals.

Both personal factors and other environmental factors can counteract the effects of powerful settings. For instance, young men who remained abstainers in "high risk" living groups were more self-confident and insulated themselves from peer group influences through their involvement in independent academic and athletic pursuits (Moos, 1979). As noted earlier, the interplay among settings can help to explain why stressful life events and work strains have fewer detrimental effects on individuals in supportive families. General cognitive and personal styles such as field independence and internal control and specific coping skills such as cognitive avoidance and behavioral withdrawal may also help to understand how individuals can encounter powerful environments without showing much change. Conversely, individuals who are open to change, concerned about social acceptance, and sensitive to normative pressure are more likely to be affected by environmental factors, for better and for worse.

Matching Persons and Environments

As our conceptual framework and foregoing considerations imply, the role of environmental factors and coping resources must be considered in light of the personal characteristics of the individuals involved. The heterogeneity of individuals' reactions to environmental contexts has led to some enthusiasm for matching different types of persons with "appropriate" environments. To learn more about person-environment matching, we need to examine the relationship of personal preferences to environmental provisions as well as that of personal competencies to environmental demands (Carp, 1978–79).

Personal Preferences and Environmental Provisions   One cornerstone of our work involves a focus on environmental preferences, this focus has broadened in line with our expanded view of environmental domains. Accordingly, we have constructed methods for tapping social climate preferences as well as preferences about physical design and program factors in group housing (Moos, Lemke and David, 1984). Some investigators have linked the congruence between individual preferences and environmental provisions to outcome criteria. In one such study, students who preferred more supportive, competitive, clear, and innovative learning environments developed more positive attitudes toward science when they were in classes that emphasized these specific areas (Fraser and Fisher, 1983). One effective (though not foolproof) way to achieve a suitable person–environment match is to enable individuals to adopt their preferences in selecting environments.

Personal Competence and Environmental Demand   Another general perspective assumes that competent people have greater latitude for person–environment congruence and are able to function effectively in a wide range of situations. Conversely, less competent individuals can function adequately in a relatively narrow range of settings. This idea is embodied in the environmental docility hypothesis, which proposes that the behavior of less competent persons is more molded by environmental factors than is behavior among more competent persons (Lawton, 1982). In this regard, we found that a reduction of physical barriers and an improvement in prosthetic aids (fewer environmental demands) fostered more diverse space utilization patterns among (less able) wheelchair residents but had no effect on (more able) ambulatory residents (Lemke and Moos, 1984).

Hunt's (1975) conceptual level (CL) matching model adds a useful developmental perspective to these ideas. Hunts posits that more mature individuals are able to organize their own environments, while those who are less mature need the stabilizing effect of a well-structured setting. In support of this model, Brill (1978) found that less mature boys who were placed in a structured residential treatment program showed satisfactory adjustment, but that those who were mismatched to unstructured programs did less well. Variations in structure were not as important for more mature boys, since they had sufficient personal resources to organize their behavior in either situation. The model is also consistent with the finding that variations in classroom environments are more strongly associated with adaptation among problem than among nonproblem students (Wright and Cowen, 1982), as well as with evidence that more academically mature students adjust and perform in less structured learning environments (Moos, 1979).

Unifying Perspectives of Stressors and Resources

Our current perspective tends to envision life stressors as problematic and social resources as beneficial. Although there is an association between stress and mental and physical dysfunction, most people adapt successfully to difficult circumstances and many show increased morale and life satisfaction when challenged by such circumstances. The effective resolution of stress often promotes long-term growth and augments self-esteem and personal maturity (Antonovsky, 1979; Elder, 1979). Men and women who experience more change during adolescence and the early adult years tend to be more empathic and tolerant of ambiguity in middle-age. Moral developmental in the preadult period may be fostered by ego processes that permit stress to be experienced and resolved rather than simply negated (Haan, 1977). Moreover, some persons report enhanced personal growth and integration and a "transcendental redirection" of their lives in the aftermath of an acute health crisis.

A related point involves the value of considering the problematic aspects of social ties (such as competition and conflict) and the potential negative concomitants of what are typically seen as social "resources." For example, cohesive relationships can place undue pressure on individuals to conform to normative expectations (such as to increase their alcohol consumption) and foster collective rejection and scapegoating. Group solidarity can help an individual handle a personal crisis, but it can also promote subservience to group norms that restricts an individual's independence or causes a "rebellious" person to feel isolated. Friends and relatives can precipitate and exacerbate as well as buffer life crises. Stressful life circumstances are an inherent part of the human condition and can lead to greater personal effectiveness as well as to illness and dysfunction; moreover, interpersonal relationships are a primary source of stress as well as support.

Future Directions

Community psychology stands at the interface of the individual and the environment. As such, it has much to contribute to collaborative work directed toward understanding the biopsychosocial processes involved in the impact of context and coping on health and adaptation. For instance, chronic strain can lead to the development of depression which may in turn affect the immune system and increase the risk of physical illness. Cohesion and social approval may promote stress-resistance and stress-buffering effects by stimulating neuroendocrine mechanisms to produce betaendorphin and other neuropeptides (Broadhead, Kaplan, James et al., 1983). Environmental factors can also affect well-being by altering health risk behaviors such as eating, smoking, and drinking patterns (Holroyd and Lazarus, 1982). By clarifying the dynamics of the environmental system, community psychologists can play a vital role in promoting a unified biopsychosocial perspective on health and illness.

More generally, the issues I have raised are relevant to humanizing community settings on a broad social scale. Learning to cope with one's external environment is a basic skill that generalizes from one setting to another. Broad social change occurs when many individuals who are each competent to cause such change band together with a common goal. The quest for a better society makes it possible to pursue objectives that are currently unattainable but that might become the birthright of all (Moos and Brownstein, 1977). It offers the opportunity to define the human species of the future by helping to shape the conditions under which that species will live. This task moves us beyond primary prevention. It provides a fitting challenge to spark the maturation of community psychology.

References

Antonovsky, A. *Health, stress and coping.* San Francisco: Jossey-Bass, 1979.
Billings, A., Cronkite, R., and Moos, R. Social-environmental factors in unipolar depression: Comparisons of depressed patients and nondepressed controls. *Journal of Abnormal Psychology*, 1983, 92, 119–133.

Billings, A., and Moos, R. Social support and functioning among community and clinical groups: A panel model. *Journal of Behavioral Medicine,* 1982, *5,* 295–311. (a)

Billings, A., and Moos, R. Stressful life events and symptoms: A longitudinal model. *Journal of Health Psychology* 1982, *1,* 99–117. (b)

Billings, A., and Moos, R. Work stress and the stress-buffering role of work and family resources. *Journal of Occupational Behaviour,* 1982, *3,* 215–232. (c)

Billings, A., and Moos, R. Coping, stress, and social resources among adults with unipolar depression. *Journal of Personality and Social Psychology,* 1984, *46,* 877–891.

Brill, R. Implications of the conceptual level matching model for treatment of delinquents. *Journal of Research in Crime and Delinquency,* 1978, *15,* 229–246.

Broadhead, W. E., Kaplan, B., James, S. et al. The epidemiologic evidence for a relationship between social support and health. *America Journal of Epidemiology,* 1983, *117,* 521–537.

Carp, F. M. Effects of the living environment on activity and use of time. *International Journal of Aging and Human Development,* 1978–1979, *9,* 75–91.

Cronkite, R., and Moos, R. *The role of predisposing and mediating factors in the stress-illness relationship.* Palo Alto: Social Ecology Laboratory, Stanford University and VA Medical Center, 1983.

Cronkite, R., Moos, R., and Finney, J. The context of adaptation: An integrative perspective on community and treatment environments. In W. A. O'Connor and Lubin (eds), *Ecological models in clinical and community mental health.* New York: Wisley, 1983.

Daher, D., Corazzini, J., and McKinnon, R. An environmental redesign program for residence halls. *Journal of Cottege Student Personnel,* 1977, *18,* 11–15.

Elder, G. Historical change in life patterns and personality. In P. B. Baltes and O. G. Brim (eds), *Life span development and behavior* (Vol. 2). New York: Academic Press, 1979.

Felner, R., Ginter, M., and Primaverra, J. Primary prevention during school transitions: Social support and environmental structure. *American Journal of Community Psychology,* 1982, *10,* 277–290.

Fisher, A., Mancini, V., Hirsch, R., Proulx, T., and Staurowsky, E. Coach-athlete interactions and team climate. *Journal of Sports Psychology,* 1982, *4,* 388–404.

Fraser, B., and Fisher, D. Predicting students' outcomes from their perceptions of classroom psychosocial environment. *American Educational Research Journal,* 1982, *19,* 498–518.

Fraser, B., and Fisher, D. Use of actual and preferred classroom environment scales in person-environment fit research. *Journal of Educational Psychology,* 1983, *75,* 303–313.

Giamartino, G., and Wandersman, A. Organizational climate correlates of viable urban block organizations. *American Journal of Community Psychology,* 1983, *11,* 529–541.

Gottfried, A. W., and Gottfried, A. E. Home environment and mental development in young children of middle class families In A. W. Gottfried (ed.), *Home environment and mental development: Longitudinal research.* New York: Academic Press, 1983.

Haan, N. *Coping and defending: Processes of self-environment organization.* New York: Academic Press, 1977.

Holahan, C. J., and Moos, R. Social support and psychological distress: A longitudinal analysis. *Journal of Abnormal Psychology,* 1981, *90,* 365–370.

Holahan, C. J., and Moos, R. *Life stress and health: Personality, coping, and family support in stress resistance* Palo Alto: Social Ecology Laboratory, Standford University and UA Medical Center, 1983.

Holroyd, K., and Lazarus, R. Stress, coping, and somatic adaptation. In L. Goldberger and S. Breznitz (eds), *Handbook of stress: Theoretical and clinical aspects*. New York: Macmillan, 1982.

Humphrey, L. Children's self-control in relation to perceived social environment. *Journal of Personality and Social Psychology*, 1984, 46, 178–188.

Hunt, D. Person-environment interaction: A challenge found wanting before it was tried. *Review of Educational Research*, 1975, 45, 209–230.

Keyser, V., and Barling, J. Determinants of children's self-efficacy beliefs in an academic environment. *Cognitive Therapy and Research*, 1981, 5, 29–40.

Koran, L., Moos, R., Moos, B., and Zasslow, M. Changing hospital work environments: An example of a burn unit. *General Hospital Psychiatry*, 1983, 5, 7–13.

Lawton, M. P. Competence, environmental press, and the adaptation of older people. In M. P. Lawton, P. G. Windley, and T. O. Byerts (eds), *Aging and the environment: Theoretical approaches*. New York: Springer, 1982.

Lemke, S., and Moos, R. Coping with an intra-institutional relocation. Behavioral change as a function of residents' personal resources. *Journal of Environmental Psychology*, 4, 137–151.

Moos, R. *Evaluating treatment environments*. New York: Wiley, 1974.

Moos, R. (ed.), *Coping with physical illness*. New York: Plenum Press, 1977.

Moos, R. *Evaluating educational environments: Procedures, methods, findings and policy implications*. San Francisco: Jossey-Bass, 1979.

Moos, R. *Group Environment Scale manual*. Palo Alto: Consulting Psychologists Press, 1981, (a).

Moss, R. *Work Environment Scale manual*. Palo Alto: Consulting Psychologists Press, 1981. (b).

Moos, R. Evaluating social resources in community and health care contexts. In P. Karoly (ed.), *Measurement strategies in health psychology*. New York: Wiley, 1984.

Moos, R., and Billings, A. Conceptualizing and measuring coping resources and processes. In L. Goldberger and S. Breznitz (eds), *Handbook of stress: Theoretical and clinical aspects*. New York: Macmillan, 1982.

Moos, R., and Brownstein, R. *Environmental and Utopia: A synthesis*. New York: Plenum Press, 1977.

Moos, R., and Finney, J. The expanding scope of alcoholism treatment evaluation. *American Psychologist*, 1983.

Moos, R., and Fuhr, R. The clinical use of social-environmental concepts: The case of an adolescent girl. *American Journal of Orthopsychiatry*, 1982, 52, 111–122.

Moos, R., and Lemke, S. Supportive residential settings for older people. In I. Altman, J. Wohlwill, and P. Lawton (eds), *Human behavior and the environment: The elderly and the physical environment*. New York: Plenum Press, 1983.

Moos, R., Lemke, S., and David, T. Environmental design and programming in residential settings for the elderly: Practices and preferences. In V. Regnier, and J. Pynoos (eds), *Housing in the elderly: Satisfactions and preferences*. New York: Garland, 1984.

Moos, R., and Moos, B. *Family Environment Scale manual*. Palo Alto: Consulting Psychologists Press, 1981.

Moos, R., and Moos, B. Adaptation and the quality of life in work and family settings. *Journal of Community Psychology*, 1983, *11*, 158–170.

Moos, R., and Spinrad, S. *The Social Climate Scales: An annotated bibliography update*. Palo Alto: Consulting Psychologists Press, 1984.

Nihira, K., Mink, I., and Meyers, C. Relationship between home environment and school adjustment of TMR children. *American Journal of Mental Deficiency*, 1981, *86*, 8–15.

O'Leary, V., Duffee, D., and Wenk, E. Developing relevant data for a prison organizational development program. *Journal of Criminal Justice*, 1977, *5*, 85–103.

Otto, J., and Moos, R. Evaluating descriptions of psychiatric treatment programs. *American Journal of Orthopsychiatry*, 1973, *43*, 401–410.

Ryan, E., and Bell, M. Follow-up from a long-term psychoanalytically oriented long-term treatment program for schizophrenic inpatients. *American Journal of Orthopsychiatry*, 1983, *53*, 730–9.

Steiner, H. The sociotherapeutic environment of a child psychosomatic ward. *Child Psychiatry and Human Development*, 1982, *13*, 71–78.

Waters, E. Evaluating and changing the social climate of an introductory sociology class. *Teaching Sociology*, 1982, *10*, 219–223.

Wright, S., and Cowen, E. Student perception of school environment and its relationship to mood, achievement, popularity, and adjustment. *American Journal of Community Psychology*, 1982, *10*, 687–703.

12 AN 'ECOLOGICAL' APPROACH TO THE OBESITY PANDEMIC

Garry Egger and Boyd Swinburn

The increasing prevalence of obesity in many countries means that it should now be considered a pandemic.[1] One estimate from Australia suggests that over the past decade the average adult has been adding 1 gram a day to body weight.[2] This has occurred in the face of increasing knowledge, awareness, and education about obesity, nutrition, and exercise. It has been suggested that a paradigm shift is necessary if future progress is to be made.[3]

Traditionally, weight gain was thought of as caused by eating too much or exercising too little, or both (changes in weight = energy intake – energy expenditure). This led to the search for small deficiencies in energy metabolism such as reduced thermic effect of food to explain obesity.[4] Treatment was dominated by calorie counting, and public health messages extolled people to balance their intake and output. This paradigm has changed with the increasing understanding of the dynamic relations between energy stores, appetite mechanisms, and energy metabolism and of the wider recognition of nutrient partitioning.[5,6] From studies which have shown that fat balance is equivalent to energy balance,[7] the fat balance equation was developed (rate of change of fat stores = rate of fat intake – rate of fat oxidation).[3] This equation is more dynamic than the original static equation and reflects energy balance under normal conditions of free access to food. Because fat intake and oxidation are not closely balanced,[8] this approach does not need metabolic abnormalities or genetic mutations to explain weight gain. Indeed, the differences in body fat between people living in the same environment could be better described as normal physiological variation. This paradigm is more helpful in explaining changes in body fat within an individual over time, but it does not account for the wider influences within and around individuals on obesity.

An Ecological Model

The model presented in Figure 12.1 proposes three main influences on equilibrium levels of body fat – biological, behavioural, and environmental– mediated through energy intake or energy expenditure, or both, but

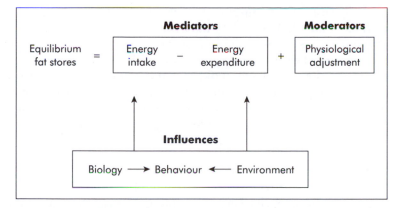

FIGURE 12.1   **An Ecological Paradigm for Understanding Overfatness and Obesity**

moderated by physiological adjustments during periods of energy imbalance. The level of body fat is seen not as a "set point" like a thermostat fixed on an exact temperature but as a "settling point" that depends on the net effects of the other components of the model and that changes as they change. This places obesity in an ecological context which calls for more than simple education about risk factors and needs a collaborative strategy with the multiple sectors which impact on the problem.[9]

Mediators

The ecological model uses total energy as mediator; for most conditions of human living it is interchangeable with fat energy. Fat intake is an important determinant of total energy intake, and for output, total energy expenditure is a major determinant of fat oxidation.

Energy Intake   Dietary fat is very energy dense and has a limited effect on suppressing appetite and enhancing fat oxidation.[10] This makes reducing dietary fat an obvious choice for reducing total energy to treat or prevent obesity. A reduction in dietary fat with an otherwise free choice of food promotes a modest weight loss which is initially less than that from a conventional low energy diet.[11] However, the longer term results are similar,[12] and the reduced fat regimen seems easier to maintain.[13] All weight loss programmes suffer from rebound weight gain, probably partly because of physiological defences against weight loss,[14] but ultimately weight loss is limited by the high settling point of fat stores for people living in an environment that promotes obesity. To keep fat stores below this point often requires considerable effort, which is difficult to maintain in an unsupportive "obesogenic" environment.

At a population level it seems that dietary fat and energy intake have not fallen as fast as energy output.[15] The results is a large energy imbalance, leading to obesity. On the input side of the equation, the strategy of reducing dietary fat within the diet (that is, changing the foods eaten and the composition of meals) seems a more realistic approach than reducing total energy (decreasing the size and frequency of meals). Large reductions in the content of the modern diet seem unlikely, and they may not be necessary for a population based approach, as small changes made by a large percentage of the populations often show up as greater improvements in a population's disease index than do large shifts made by only a few people.[16]

Energy Expenditure   The intensity of physical activity required for optimal oxidation of fat is controversial. Relative fat utilisation is higher during activity of moderate intensity such as walking, but absolute energy use is higher during vigorous exercise such as running. It has thus been suggested that vigorous exercise results in greater absolute fat oxidation.[17] This may be true for aerobically fit people, but unfit people tend to oxidise less fat at all levels of intensity. Hence, vigorous exercise – even if it could be carried out – is not likely to result in as much fat oxidation in unfit people as activity of more moderate intensity which can be comfortably sustained for longer periods. Obese people are usually unfit, and so moderately intense physical activity should be recommended for them.

As with fat intake population benefits are more likely to come from modest increases in activity of low or moderate intensity in many people than from increases in high intensity exercise in a few. Indeed, part of the secular increase in obesity is probably attributable to modest, population-wide reductions in physical activity of low to moderate intensity or to reduction in "incidental movement" due to the introduction of labour saving technology.[18]

Moderators

Physiological adjustment   refers to the metabolic and in some cases, behavioural changes that follow a disequilibrium in energy balance and that minimise large fluctuations in body weight. For example, in response to a negative energy balance, initially appetite may increase or physical activity may decrease[14]; then, with weight loss, fat oxidation and resting metabolic rate may decline until a new energy balance is achieved.[19] Physiological adjustment may be more vigorous in some people, as a result of biological factors such as sex, age, or genetic makeup.[20]

One implication of this is that frequent plateaus, or slowing of weight losses over time, are a normal physiological response to energy disequilibrium.[14] Adjustments seem to be more vigorous in response to weight loss than weight gain, especially in lean individual,[21] and they may also be more vigorous after rapid, rather than slow, changes. Hence the need to concentrate on long term loss of fat rather than short term, and usually temporary, loss of weight. This questions the ethics of programmes that advertise large weight losses in short periods.

Influences

Biological Influences   Biological factors known to influence body fat levels include age, sex, hormonal factors, and genetics,[22] all of which have been considered to be unalterable. The identification of the job gene and its product leptin in 1994 caused widespread optimism about unlocking the cause of obesity and developing successful treatments.[23] A greater understanding of appetite control will undoubtedly come from research on leptin, but no major effect of single gene defects has yet been identified, and it is likely that the genetic influences on body fat levels are polygenic.

There are also important sex differences in fat storage.[24] The differences between the sexes are apparent early in life, become greatest with the onset of menses, then tend to decrease with the changes in hormone status in post-menopausal women.[25] Fat loss and maintenance of lower equilibrium fat stores also becomes more difficult with age.[26] Finally, there is increasing evidence of racial influences on energy balance.[27] These biological influences explain much of the variance in body fat in individuals within a given environment, but they do not explain the large population increases which represent the epidemic itself.

Behavioural Influences   Behavioural factors typically thought to influence obesity are "sloth" and "gluttony", which imply a potential for willful control over the forces affecting body weight. Behaviours are the result of complex psychological factors, including habits, emotions, attitudes, beliefs, and cognitions developed through a background of learning history. Biological and environmental influences also affect behaviour, and, in turn energy balance. Cognitive factors (willpower based on knowledge, for example) may have only a minor effect on eventual behaviour, and this explains the limitations of education in the treatment and prevention of obesity. However, the causes and effects of behavioural factors do have to be considered,[28] and interventions to deal with these should be a part of any overall strategy.

Enviornmental Influences   Environment can be broadly categorised into "macro" (of the wider population) and "micro" (with close proximity to the individual). In general, the macro-environment determines the prevalence of obesity in a population and the micro-environment, along with biological and behavioural influences, determines whether an individual is obese. The environmental influences on the amount and type of food eaten and the amount and type of physical activity taken are vast and underrated; Table 12.1 shows some examples. A close examination of specific macro-environmental sectors (such as the fitness industry or the food service industry) or micro-environmental settings (such as the local gym or the workplace) will reveal many more interconnecting environmental influences than those listed. For example, food safety regulations, policies of food

TABLE 12.1 **Environmental Influences on Food Intake and Physical Activity**

Type of environment	Physical environment		Economic environment		Sociocultural environment	
	Food	Activity	Food	Activity	Food	Activity
Macro	Food laws and regulation Food technology Law fat foods Food industry policies	Labour saving devices Cycleways and walkways Fitness industry policies Transport system	Food taxes and subsidies Cost of food technology Marketing costs Food pricies	Cost of labour versus automation Investment in parks and recreational facilities Costs of petrol and cars Costs of cycleways	Traditional cuisine Migrant cuisines Consumer demand Food status	Attitudes to recreation National sports Participating versus watching culture Gadget status
Micro	Food in house Choices at school or work cafeterias Food in local shops Proximity of fast food outlets	Local recreation facilities Second cars Safe streets Household rules for watching TV and video	Family income Other household expenses Subsidised canteens Home grown foods	Gym or club fees Owning equipment Subsidised local events Costs of school sport	Family eating patterns Peer attitudes Pressure from food advertising Festivities	Peers' activities Family recreation School attitude to sports Safety fears

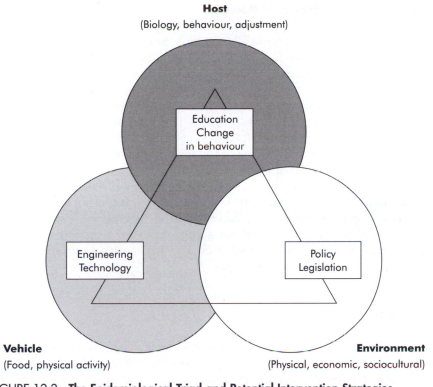

Host
(Biology, behaviour, adjustment)

Education
Change
in behaviour

Engineering
Technology

Policy
Legislation

Vehicle
(Food, physical activity)

Environment
(Physical, economic, sociocultural)

FIGURE 12.2 **The Epidemiological Triad and Potential Intervention Strategies for Obesity**

manufacturers, costs of cooking oils, and the availability of training programmes for food caterers can affect the choice, price, and quality of food at the work canteen.

Environmental influences represent the public health arm of the obesity problem. If the macro-environment is obesogenic, obesity will become more prevalent and programmes aimed at influencing individual behaviour can be expected to have only a limited effect. Historically, epidemics have been controlled only after environmental factors have been modified. Similarly, reductions in population levels of obesity seem unlikely until the environments which facilitate its development are modified. Yet this is often neglected in obesity management (as it was initially with tobacco control). Environmental change, such as regulation of the food industry or changes in building design, is likely to be unpopular. Although some changes may be overt, others – such as reductions of fat in the meat supply – may be more surreptitious.

Epidemiology of An Ecological Model

The model proposed in Figure 12.1 bears a resemblance to the epidemiological triad Figure 12.2 which has proved to be a robust model with epidemics such as infectious diseases, smoking, coronary heart disease, and, more recently, injuries.[29] For obesity "host" encompasses the biological and behavioural influences, plus physiological adjustment. "Environment" is similar in the two models, and "vehicle" is represented by energy intake (food) and energy expenditure (physical activity). Preventive interventions are superimposed on components of the triad in Figure 12.2. These provide some options for a wider approach to obesity.

Recent advances in obesity research (especially in molecular biology) may have an impact on treatment at the individual level. It is clear, however, that there is a major deficiency in research into the "obesogenic" environment and potential interventions. Without a supportive environment, treatment programmes are likely to be ineffectual and preventive programs will be restricted to mass education strategies.

Conclusion

Obesity presents us with two challenges: to treat people who are currently obese and to prevent obesity in people who are still lean. Neither of these challenges is currently being met; hence it is important to re-examine the paradigms on which treatment and prevention programmes are based. The model presented here suggests that the driving force for the increasing prevalence of obesity in populations is the increasingly obesogenic environment rather than any "pathology" in metabolic defects or genetic mutations within individuals. A paradigm shift to understanding obesity as "normal physiology within a pathological environment" signposts the directions for a wider public health approach to the obesity pandemic.

References

1   James WPT. Epidemiology of obesity. *Int J Obesity* 1992; 16 (suppl 2): S23–6.
2   Magnus P, Bennett S. Trends in cardiovascular risk factors in Australia. *Med J Aust* 1994; 161: 519–27.
3   Hawks SR, Richins P. Toward a new paradigm for the management of obesity. *J Health Educ* 1994; 25: 147–53.
4   Ravussin E, Swinburn B. Energy metabolism in obesity. In: Stunkard AJ, Waddin TA, eds. *Obesity: theory and therapy.* 2nd ed. New York: Raven, 1992: 97–124.
5   Swinburn B, Ravussin E. Energy balance or fat balance? *Am J Clin Nutr* 1993; 57 (suppl): 766–71S.

6   Stubbs RJ. Macronutrient effects on appetite. *Int J Obesity* 1995; 19 (suppl 5): S11–9.

7   Flatt JP. Importance of nutrient balance in body weight regulation. *Diab Met Rev* 1988; 4: 571–81.

8   Schutz Y, Flatt JP. Jequier E. Failure of dietary fat intake to promote fat oxidation: a factor favouring the development of obesity. *Am J Clin Nutr* 1989; 50: 307–14.

9   Kickbush I. Approaches to an ecological base for public health. *Health promotion* 1989; 4; 265–8.

10 Westrate JA. Fat and obesity. *Int J Obesity* 1995; 19 (suppl 5): S38–43.

11 Lissner L, Heitmen BL. Dietary fat and obesity; evidence from epidemiology. *Eur J Clin Nutr* 1995; 49: 79–90.

12 Prewitt TE, Schmeisser D, Bowen PE, Aye P, Dolecek TA, Langenberg P, et al. Changes in body weight, body composition, and energy intake in women fed high- and low-fat diets. *Am J Clin Nutr* 1991: 54: 304–10.

13 Lyon X-H, Di Vetta V, Milton H, Schutz Y. Compliance to dietary advice directed towards increasing the carbohydrate to fat ratio of the everyday diet. *Int J Obesity* 1995; 19: 260–9.

14 Prentice AM, Goldberg GR, Jebb SA, Black AE, Murgatrovd PR. Physiological responses to slimming. *Proc Nutr Soc* 1991; 50: 441–58.

15 Prentice AM, Jebb SA. Obesity in Britain: gluttony or sloth? *BMJ* 1995; 311: 437–9.

16 Rose G. *The strategy of preventive medicine.* Oxford: Oxford University Press, 1992.

17 Glasser GA. Burning carbohydrate to lose fat. *Sports Med Digest* 1995; March: 5

18 James WPT. A Public health approach to the problem of obesity. *Int J Obesity* 1995; 19 (suppl 3): S37–46.

19 Liebel RL, Rosenbaum M, Hirsch J. Changes in energy expenditure resulting from altered body weight. *N Engl J Med* 1995; 332: 621–8.

20 Heitmann BL, Lissner L, Sorensen TI, Bengtsson C. Dietary fat intake and weight gain in women genetically predisposed for obesity. *Am J Clin Nutr* 1995; 61: 1213–7.

21 Keys A, Brozek J, Kenschel A, Mickelsen O, Taylor HL. *The biology of human starvation.* Vol 1, Minneapolis: University of Minnesota Press. 1950.

22 Katahn M, McMinn MR. Obesity: a biobehavioral point of view. *Ann NY Acad Sci* 1990; 602: 189–204.

23 Zhang Y, Proenca R, Maffei M, Barone M, Leopold L, Friedman JM. Positional cloning of the mouse obese gene and its human homologue. *Nature* 1994; 372: 425–32.

24 Frisch RE. The right weight: body fat, menarche and fertility: *Proc Nutr Soc* 1994; 53: 113–29.

25 Rebuffe-Scrive M, Enk L, Crona N, Lonnroth P, Abrahamsson L, Smith U, et al. Fat cell metabolism in different regions in women; effect of menstrual cycle, pregnancy and lactation. *J Clin Invest* 1985; 75: 1973–6.

26 Bourdin M, Pastene J, Germain M, Lacour JR. Influence of training, sex, age and body mass on the energy costs of running. *Eur J Appl Physiol* 1993; 66: 439–44.

27 Tuten C, Petosa R, Sargent R, Weston A. Biracial differences in physical activity and body composition. *Obesity Res* 1995; 3: 313–8.

28   Brownell KD, Wadden TA. Etiology and treatment of obesity: understanding a serious, prevalent, and refractory disorder. *J Consult Clin Psychol* 1992; 60: 505–17.

29   Hadden W. Advances in the epidemiology of injuries as a basis for public policy. *Public Health Rep* 1980; 95: 411–21.

13 MOVING TOWARDS ACTIVE LIVING:

Understanding the Contextual Nature Of Barriers To Physical Activity

Susan Drew

The overwhelming evidence for the health benefits of physical activity (PA) and disturbingly low levels of fitness and activity in the population has promoted the inclusion of PA in the targets for the *Health of the Nation* (Bouchard et al., 1994; Blair, 1993; Activity and Health Research, 1993; Cale and Almond, 1992; Riddoch et al., 1991). Currently the Health Education Authority is concerned to find suitable strategies for raising PA in the population and promoting moderate level activity (Physical Activity Task Force, 1995).

This chapter reports on a study into some of the major factors which people identify as blocking or facilitating their participation in PA. It attempts to recognize and address some of the problems associated with understanding and changing inactivity.

Traditionally, research into exercise motivation has focused on personal attributes, or features of the environment or the activity itself (Bouchard et al., 1994; Dishman, 1994). Interventions have relied on the giving of information and exercise prescription, assuming that behaviour change is simply a matter of choice. What is not addressed in most research or interventions is the effect of the meanings which people attach to PA on their own motivation and the ways in which wider contextual factors operate in the process of human action.

The Study

The aim of the study was to explore participants' own accounts of their experience of physical activity and the perceptions of barriers to being active. This paper focuses on the two central themes of "barriers to PA", and transcripts of 42 semi-structured interviews and 51 written histories which were coded and analysed thematically using qualitative data software (Dey, 1993).

The participants were men and women employed in a variety of jobs at a university whose activity levels ranged from inactive to very active. Half of them were trying to raise their activity levels. This offered a chance to capture the dynamic nature of the change process and address the problem of only having retrospective data.

Exploring the Data

The two themes which emerged most frequently in the data centred on "self-perception" and "lack of time". In the interviews there were 267 and 197 separate episodes of speech devoted to these themes, respectively.

Most interesting are the *ways* in which people talked around these themes. There was a strong sense of people seeing their bodies and the action of taking time for PA as inappropriate.

I want to argue that this "talk" points to the ways that personal history and social and cultural images and pressures, form the basis for individuals' constructions of themselves in the physical activity context. Frequently the mediating factor in the process was the use of self-comparison (see Figure 13.1).

The Body as "Inappropriate"

Although participants were invited to write freely about past experience in the written histories, accounts of school experience dominated. Over half reported a very negative effect on attitudes, feelings and self-esteem. Many reports are vehement and very poignant. The first exemplifies talking about physical attributes:

> At school, I was very overweight and short-sighted; this meant school and games were an absolute torment. The consequence for my later life has been that I never had an interest in sport.

Similarly, people expressed feelings of timidity and being unskilled and a belief that PA was not for them, or beyond their capacity.

Many such extracts demonstrated how early experience contributed to a view of the self as inappropriate for PA. They also indicate the consequences for subsequent participation in PA:

> When I left school, I made a conscious decision never to do any sporting activity ever again. I am still a bit suspicious of people who are interested in sport.

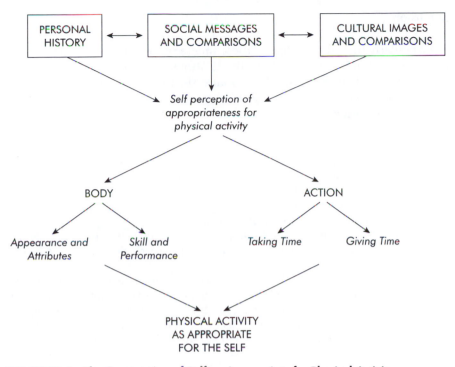

FIGURE 13.1   The Construction of Self as Appropriate for Physical Activity Based on Thematic analysis of the Data

Social and Cultural Comparison

The interviews showed that people were comparing their bodily appearance and performance both with other people's bodies and with the prevalent cultural stereotypes of the desirable body form. These contextual factors seem to serve as a locus of normality, creating a sense of what is appropriate. Perceiving themselves as different from this, many defined themselves as "inappropriate" in these contexts.

For some people these social and cultural images were inextricably linked with their perception of the purpose and effect of PA. Weight, shape, muscle tone and defeating ageing were prominent sub-themes in the body discourse. As were ageism and fatism also reflected in the way they felt some people treated them. The effects of comparison and context on a woman who enjoys swimming but perceived herself as fat are revealing:

> Swimming here is a nightmare, there is definitely a negative loop in my motivation. There's a wonderful pool in California where the women are all at least 14 stones and it's heaven for me. It's wonderful to feel almost thin.

Confusion

A particularly disturbing effect of these images and comparisons on motivation is confusion in thinking about the relationship of body, competence, fitness, health and "being sporty". For many, the purpose and effect of PA had
become totally confused with "what I look like", with a resultant negative
effect on motivation.

Interviewer: What does being physically active conjure up for you?

Participant: Very slim people in leotards, leggings and being fit and healthy. That
is how I would like to be. I've always wanted to be a sporty person
but never was very good at sport … I'd like to be a sporty person but
I don't think I ever will be really.

Interviewer: You seem to have been saying throughout the interview that you
have to be slim to be sporty. Is that the case, do you need to be slim
in your own eyes?

Participant: Yes, because I feel people who do enough will be. I feel if I did
enough exercise as I should then I would be slim. Sometimes the way
I feel about myself affects whether I go swimming. If I'm feeling low
about things and feeling really fat in my swimming costume there is
a high chance I won't go. It's completely ridiculous because I know
when I go swimming it isn't going to produce instant results, but if I
don't feel better after a couple of weeks I think, 'this isn't working',
and I give up.

Such examples signal the need, for all involved in activity promotion, to sort
out what are relevant messages about PA and challenge the social and cultural influences which shape this self-defeating way of constructing the self
in relation to PA. The problem is the hegemonous nature of the influences on
our thinking. People tend to accept the discourses of "physical activity" and
"the body" at face value, not as being socially constructed. Even the few who
had a political awareness confessed to being trapped by this way of viewing
themselves.

Is PA Appropriate for me?

An adjunct to personal appropriateness was the way people defined PA
itself. Experiential and cultural factors appeared to shape limited perceptions of its nature and scope. Mostly PA was defined as sport, aerobics or
using the gym. Hence identifying with PA was difficult for many, in the light
of their feelings of inadequacy. Enjoyment featured little and people seemed
at a loss to identify activities that might have been more appropriate in the
context of their own lives.

Interestingly, much PA is still marketed as sport of fitness merely reinforcing negative images of PA for many people. Imaginative ways of encouraging participation and the opportunity to re-think what PA could be are a necessary part of PA promotion.

"Taking Time" as Inappropriate

People talked of feeling desperate to have time for themselves. However, this was consistently viewed as an "inappropriate" use of time or "wasting time". Family, work and other caring duties were discussed at length as constraints on time.

For women particularly, all these aspects of their lives were prioritized over taking time for themselves. There was a tacit assumption that using time for others' benefit or "doing one's duty" was "appropriate" use of time. Taking "time for myself" therefore, carried the burden of feeling guilty. There were many behavioural consequences of this way of thinking. For example, women feeling guilty about leaving partners to "cope" while they went out. Hence if they did take time, they took only a little time, feeling the need to hurry back again. The reported consequence of this was to feel under pressure, even when the intended purpose of the activity was to unwind.

> Every minute counts, it's terrible.
> I feel I have to take as little time as possible.
> If you have to squeeze it in it becomes another thing to feel guilty about.

A number of women talked about putting off activity until it was more manageable in their lives. Health benefits, however come from current physical activity and relief from stress is needed when we are most pressed. Some women freed from the constraints of small children still found themselves in the caring role.

> My father-in-law had a stroke, needing constant caring. I'm the nearest female relative, my husband doesn't see it as his job.

Here the culturally embedded assumption that women are responsible for caring, surfaces.

Work and Time

Talk about work revealed similarly oppressive feelings. For example, people reported forgoing lunch breaks for meetings yet feeling guilty about taking a break to walk or join a lunchtime class even though they worked evenings and weekends. This was particularly so for those responsible for structuring their own time.

> I feel if I'm not actually working all the day I'm skiving. I know it's irrational because I take so much work home.

These ways of talking reflect the language of time used in our society. We talk of wasting time, losing time, spending it, or saving it, but never ask what we are saving it for.

Although most people were knowledgeable about the health risks of inactivity and in many cases felt that they wanted to exercise, these factors were not enough to change behaviour. (Many said this explicitly). Even those who reported enjoyment and experiencing positive benefits in the past from exercise were struggling to be regularly active. It was clear that the social pressures to prioritize using time in caring, working and other duties over their own well-being coupled with poor self image in the PA context mitigated against participation.

Discussion

There is clear evidence in this study for social, cultural and historical influences on people's beliefs and feelings about themselves and their actions, mediated by a human propensity to compare the self with others.

The frequently researched environmental factors such as access to facilities, instructor style, class atmosphere and the like, were discussed by some participants. However, they played a minor role in their accounts of barriers to PA compared with the major themes presented here. Social benefits and enjoyment were similarly discussed but positive motivational aspects of these were frequently contingent upon positive social comparisons or at least absence of negative ones; in effect, contingent on feelings about the self. Hence factors, often presented in correlational studies as having considerable significance in relation to motivation, played only a subsidiary role for these participants. This signals one problem with research or health interventions which de-contextualize motivation.

We must address factors outside of individuals which affect how they think about themselves, and the choices which they believe that they have, in relation to PA. An example would be the need for physical educationists to address the potentially negative affects of PE and sport teaching. Similarly the ways the media and the fitness and leisure industry portray and market physical activity and the way it is presented in health settings need radical re-thinking.

It is also necessary to pay greater attention to individual diversity. There is no suggestion that the themes in my research would necessarily occur in other groups, rather my argument is that the starting point for any intervention should be in uncovering the salient themes for the particular participants involved.

There is evidence from the "action" part of this research that well facilitated groups can help people re-evaluate their thinking about themselves and find personal solutions to the problem of attaining active living. This however needs to be pursued in further research.

References

Activity and Health Research (1992) *Allied Dunbar National Fitness Survey*. London: Sports Council/Health Education Authority.

Blair, S. N. (1993) C. H. McClay Research Lecture: Physical activity, physical fitness and health. *Research Quarterly for Exercise and Sport*, 64, 4, 365–376.

Bouchard, C., Shepard, R. J. and Stephens, T. (1994) *Physical Activity Fitness and Health*. Champaign, IL: Human Kinetics.

Cale, L. and Almond, L. (1992) Physical activity levels of secondary-aged children: a review. *Health Education Journal*, 51, 4, 192–197.

Dey, I. (1993) *Qualitative Data Analysis*. London: Routledge.

Dishman, R. K. (ed.) (1994) *Advances in Exercise Adherence*. Champaign, IL: Human Kinetics.

Physical Activity Task Force (1995) *More People More Active More Often: Physical Activity in England, A Consultation Paper*. London: Department of Health.

Riddoch, C., Mahoney, C., Murphy, N., Boreham, C. and Cran, G. (1991) The physical activity patterns of Northern Irish schoolchildren ages 11–16. *Pediatric Exercise Science*, 3, 300–309.

14 CONDITIONAL VERSUS UNCONDITIONAL RISK ESTIMATES IN MODELS OF AIDS-RELATED RISK BEHAVIOUR

*Frank W. van der Velde,
Christa Hooykaas,
and Joop van der Pligt*

With the introduction of models such as Becker's (1974) health belief model (HBM) and Rogers' (1975) protection motivation theory, subjective probability concepts such as perceived *susceptibility* and *vulnerability* appeared in the health literature (Sutton, 1982). The health belief model distinguishes five factors that influence the adoption of preventive, risk-reducing behavioural practices. These are (a) perceived susceptibility or vulnerability to developing a health problem, (b) perceived severity of the problem, (c) perceived benefits of changes in behaviour, (d) perceived barriers and/or possible negative consequences of these changes, and (e) specific cues to action, such as a symptom or a health communication (see Janz and Becker, 1984).

Rogers' protection motivation theory postulates that information about a health hazard stimulates a cognitive appraisal of the severity and probability of the negative event, and of the efficacy of the recommended preventive action. Both models thus assume that an individual's response to a health threat is (partially) determined by the subjective probability of the event's occurrence *and* the perceived severity of the depicted negative outcome (Sutton, 1982).

One of the assumptions of these models is a correspondence between objective probabilities and the subjective assessment of potential risks (Sutton, 1982). However, it is well established that the accuracy of perceptions of risk vary considerably among people and that they often show little correspondence to epidemiological findings (e.g. Slovic, Fischhoff and Lichtenstein, 1987). Errors in perceptions of risk are not random. Slovic et al.

(1987), for example, report that the probability of dramatic and sensational causes of death were likely to be overestimated, compared to more common causes. Another bias concerns what Weinstein termed "unrealistic optimism" i.e. the tendency of people to perceive themselves to be less at risk than others around them (Weinstein, 1980, 1982).

Much effort has been directed to understand the factors that shape beliefs about susceptibility, to describe errors and optimistic biases in these beliefs, and to unravel the relationship between perceived susceptibility and precautionary behaviour (Weinstein, 1989). Perceptions of risk are often found to be positively related to preventive health behaviour (see e.g. Cummings, Jette, Brock and Haefner, 1979; McCusker, Stoddard, Zapka, Zorn and Mayer, 1989). However, in some instances, measures of perceived risk are found to be negatively related to preventive behaviour or behavioural intentions (e.g. Joseph, Montgomery, Emmons, Kirscht, Kessler et al., 1987; Rogers and Mewborn, 1976), or not at all (e.g. Rippetoe and Rogers, 1987; Temoshok, Sweet and Zich, 1987). Research on the BHM also indicates that the relationship between perceived risk and behaviour can be opposite to the predicted direction (Becker, Kaback, Rosenstock, and Ruth, 1975; Becker, Nathanson, Drachman, and Kirscht, 1977; Langlie, 1977). Several findings suggest that an increased sense of risk – combined with low expectations of success in dealing with the risk – may provoke a helplessness reaction, and hence, decrease intentions to behave adaptively (Beck and Frankel, 1981). Indeed, in Rogers and Mewborn's (1976) study, a negative relation between perceived risk and behavioural intentions occurred *only* when recommendations for preventive behaviour were presented as relatively ineffective. Similar results were obtained in a study on cigarette smoking (Maddux and Rogers, 1983). Furthermore, Joseph et al. (1987) found that higher levels of perceived risk were related to both increased barriers to AIDS risk reduction, and to increased psychological and social distress.

In this context it seems necessary to distinguish between *unconditional* and *conditional* risk estimates. *Unconditional* risk estimates may be defined as the subjective probability that an event will occur based on whatever sets of factors individuals take into account (e.g. perceptions of control, the efficacy of preventive behaviours). Vulnerability or susceptibility is generally defined as the *conditional* probability that an event will occur provided no specific action is taken to reduce risks (see for example, Beck and Frankel, 1981; Sutton, 1982). Thus conditional risk refers to the probability of an event if no preventive action is taken, or the probability of an event if a specific (preventive) action is taken. A conditional risk estimate would require respondents to indicate their risk given their present behavioural practices. Similarly, one could also ask them to indicate their risk if they would change specific behaviours.

Although most models refer to *conditional* risk estimates, many operationalization are phrased in terms of an *unconditional* risk estimate (e.g. "How likely is it that you will get ...", followed by the health risk(s) under study).

Sometimes, different measures are combined into an index-score. In a study on AIDS, for example, Joseph et al. (1987) used a composite-scale based on two items. The first item asked participants to consider all factors that may contribute to AIDS, including their past and present behaviour (perceived risk), the second item asked participants to compare their risk to that of an average gay man (comparative risk). Most studies however, tend to rely on a general, unconditional risk estimate. Unfortunately it is unclear what set of factors participants take into account when answering this general question.

In a recent study Ronis (1992) combined the health belief model with the theory of subjective expected utility (SEU) to derive hypotheses about the conceptualization and measurement of health threats. Ronis argued that subjective expected utility theory complements the HBM and that it makes more specific predictions about the relations between beliefs and behaviours. SEU theory assumes that people assess the expected utility or desirability of alternative behavioural actions and select the option with the highest SEU. An important implication of this combination of theories concerns the necessity to measure health threats in ways that are clearly conditional on action. Ronis predicted that preventive behaviour and attitudes toward this behaviour would be more accurately predicted from conditional than from unconditional measures of health risks. He found support for his prediction in a study of judgments about a hypothetical disease and a study on dental flossing behaviour.

As mentioned before, most research testing protection motivation theory or the health belief model uses unconditional risk estimates. In the present study, we assessed both conditional and unconditional risk estimates, and related these measures to factors incorporated in protection motivation theory and/or the health belief model (perceived severity, response efficacy, and self-efficacy), and other factors (fear, psychological stress, personal control, and perceived risk status). Additionally, the two different measures of risk were examined in relation to previous (risk) behaviour, behavioural intentions, and subsequent risk behaviour.

In the present study we focus on risk estimates in relation to sexual behaviour. Previous research shows mixed findings concerning the relationship between these subjective estimates and behaviour or behavioural intentions. Interestingly, quite a few studies found lower risk estimates to be associated with higher intentions to engage in safe sex practices (Joseph et al., 1987; Otten and van der Pligt, 1992; van der Velde, van der Pligt, and Hooykaas, 1994). This counterintuitive finding may be the result of the use of an unconditional risk estimate. Respondents may well incorporate their behavioural intentions when assessing their own risk (e.g. "I am not going to change my behaviour, hence my risk is and will be relatively high", or "I intend to engage in safe sex practices, so my risk is rather low"). To assess the differential effects of conditional and unconditional risk estimates we included both in the present study and investigated their role in the context of factors from the HBM and protection motivation theory.

Method

Participants

Participants in this study were visitors of a STD clinic of the Municipal Health Service of Amsterdam. The study focused on sexually active hereosexual participants. Visitors of the clinic were asked to participate if they were older than 17 years of age, and if they had at least five sexual partners in the six months prior to the study.

Haemophiliacs, men with homosexual contacts and intravenous drug users were excluded from the study. Between October 1987 and December 1990, approximately half the people who met the entrance criteria decided to participate: 259 males and 343 females ($n = 602$). Visitors of the STD clinic most likely to refuse participation were younger males of ethnic minorities (see Van der Linden, Van der Velde, Hooykaas, Van Doornum, and Coutinho, 1990). Participants were asked to return to the clinic every four months; 61% ($n = 365$) returned for the first follow-up visit. After the first visit, the percentage of participants not returning for their follow-up visit dropped from 39% to 10–17% for every next visit. The majority engaged in prostitution contacts: 157 males (61%) visited prostitutes, 259 females (76%) worked as a prostitute. On average, male participants had 14 prostitution and seven private partners, female participants had a total of 524 prostitution and four private partners in the four months prior to the study. Furthermore, medical examination indicated that 25.6% had one or more STDs at entry of the study, 47.5% and 13.9% had a history of STDs in the preceding five years and the preceding four months respectively. Finally, 25.0% reported sexual contacts with AIDS-risk-groups in the five years prior to the study.

The present study was carried out in the later stages of this longitudinal research project; a total of 247 participants were approached at their follow-up visit to the clinic. Of these 147 participants engaged in prostitution contacts, 100 participants had private partners only. The questionnaire described below was administered for the first time in 1989 and 1990. Most participants (63.9%) had participated in the study for more than 16 months.

Measures

First, the interviewers asked questions about respondents' *reason for clinic visit* (STD-related complaints or not), their ethnicity, gender, age, and sexual practices in the four months preceding the study. *Sexual behaviour* consisted of number and type of partners (private or prostitution partners), frequency of various sexual techniques per type of partner, and condom use per technique and per type of partner. Responses for frequencies and condom use were made on a 5-point Likert-type scale; and end-points for both scales were *never* and *always*. A measure of previous risk behaviour was calculated by multiplying the number of partners per technique with the frequency of vaginal intercourse (multiplier 0 when technique was not practiced, via .25,

.50 and .75, to 1 if the technique was practiced with all sexual contacts). Finally, the resulting score was multiplied with the frequency of condom use (multiplier 1 if condoms were not used at all, via .75, .50, and .25 to 0 if condoms were always used). For example, a participant with five private partners and five prostitution partners who had often (.75) vaginal intercourse with private partners without using condoms (1), and who always (1) engaged in vaginal intercourse with prostitution partners while using condoms half of the time (.5), obtained a risk-score of (5 * .75 * 1) + (5 * 1 * .5) = 6.25. Because of skewed distributions, the resulting score was log-transformed afterwards. Sexual behaviour was assessed together with the other variables in one interview. In a subsequent follow-up study (approx. four months later) we again assessed sexual behaviour. Additionally, *STD-history* was assessed covering both the period of four months and the period of five years prior to the study.

All other measures were assessed by means of a questionnaire. Unless otherwise mentioned, responses were made on 5-point scales. *Behavioural intentions* were gauged by asking if participants intended to use condoms in the following four months, separately for various sexual techniques, and separately for private and prostitution contacts. Responses ranged from "definitely not" to "definitely yes". Summing yielded, separately for participants with prostitution partners and participants with exclusively private partners, an overall score for intentions. To assess the *unconditional* risk estimate, participants responded to the question "how do you estimate the chance that you will become infected with the AIDS-virus in the next two years, because of your sexual behaviour?" (own risk). The same probability estimation was asked for an average other of one's own age and gender (others' risk). This question was phrased "how do you estimate the chance that a man/woman of your age, chosen at random, becomes infected with the AIDS-virus in the next two years, because of his/her sexual behaviour?". Responses were made by setting a mark on a continuum ranging from 0 to 100% chance, with every 10% point marked. The *conditional* risk estimate was assessed using the same scale. This question was phrased "How do you estimate the chance that you will become infected with the AIDS-virus in the next two years, if you would not use condoms?". *Perceived risk status* was assessed by asking participants to rate the extent to which they felt they belonged to an AIDS-risk group, on a scale ranging from *absolutely not* (1) to *absolutely* (5).

Several other measures were included in the questionnaire. *Perceived severity* was assessed by rating the severity of an HIV infection on a scale ranging from *not at all severe* (1) to *very severe* (5), *personal control* was assessed by asking participants how much control they thought to have over avoiding an infection with HIV. Scores ranged from *no control* (1) to *complete control* (5). *Self-efficacy* was assessed by asking participants (a) if they thought they were able to use condoms effectively, (b) if they thought they would be able to propose condom use to future sexual partners and (c) to indicate the extent to which they would be able to insist on using a condom (scales for these items ranged from *not at all* to *very much*). Item-scores were summed to yield an index for self-efficacy. A measure for *response efficacy* was established by subtracting the perceived safety of sexual techniques with condoms from the perceived safety of the same techniques without condoms. Difference scores for these techniques were summed afterwards. Responses could range from *not at all safe* to *very safe*. *Fear* was assessed by six questions (e.g. "are you afraid you might already have been infected with HIV?"), participants rated to what extent they felt they worried about AIDS, responses ranged from *not at all* to *very much*. These items resulted in a Cronbach's alpha of .86. Psychological stress was assessed with an abbreviated and validated version of the *Voeg-Stress-scale* (Jansen and Sikkel, 1981). The reliability of the ten item scale was .83 (Cronbach's alpha), participants responded to the items by indicating whether they applied to them or not.

Results

Participants were split into two groups: those with prostitution partners, and those with private partners only. As shown in Table 14.1, participants with prostitution partners gave higher conditional risk estimates concerning a possible infection with HIV than participants with exclusively private partners ($F(1,238) = 4.3, p < .001$). *Unconditional* risks were, on average, perceived as somewhat lower by participants with private partners than by participants with prostitution partners. This difference did not reach statistical significance ($p = .12$). However, participants with prostitution partners acknowledged their belonging to an AIDS-risk group (risk status) more often than did participants with exclusively private partners ($F(1,238) = 5.9$, $p < .01$).

Furthermore, participants with prostitution partners reported lower levels of perceived control over an infection with HIV ($F(1,238) = 4.8, p < .05$), had higher levels of previous risk behaviour ($F(1,245) = 4.2, p < .05$), and, finally, had higher levels of subsequent risk behaviour ($F(1,218) = 4.1, p < .05$). Differences in self-efficacy, response efficacy, perceived severity, fear, and stress were not found between participants with prostitution partners and participants with exclusively private partners.

Perceptions of Risk and Behavioural Intentions

Overall, the unconditional risk measure was not significantly related to behavioural intentions ($r = -.08$, ns.). However, replicating earlier results (Van der Velde, Hooykaas and Van der Pligt, 1994), the relationship between the *unconditional* risk estimate and behavioural intentions varied with participants' type of partner. For participants with prostitution partners, higher levels of perceived own risk were related to lower intentions to engage in safe sex ($r = -.27, p < .001$). For participants with private partners perceived own risk was not related to intentions ($r = +.12$, ns.). Moreover, higher levels

TABLE 14.1 **Mean Scores on Perceptions of Risk and other Factors, for Subjects with Private Partners only, and Subjects with Prostitution Partners (N = 247)**

	Private partners n = 100		Prostitution partners n = 147	
	Mean	(sd.)	Mean	(sd.)
Unconditional risk[a]	16.18	(15.70)	17.82	(18.20)
Conditional risk[a]	34.74	(28.21)	52.43	(33.12)**
Perceived risk status[b]	2.18	(1.26)	2.60	(1.33)**
Personal control[b]	4.21	(0.76)	3.92	(1.13)*
Previous risk behavior[c]	1.02	(1.10)	1.59	(2.64)*
Subsequent risk behavior[c]	0.81	(1.18)	1.54	(3.31)*

Note: [a]Possible range of scores from 0% to 100% chance. [b]Scores could range from 1 (low) to 5 (high). [c]Scores ranged from 0 to the (log transformed) total number of sexual partners. *$p < .05$. **$p < .01$. ***$p < .001$.

of perceived risk *for others* were related to higher intentions ($r = +.17, p < .05$). These results seem to contradict theoretical assumptions: in general a positive relation is predicted between measures of perceived risk and intentions to reduce risks (see for example Sutton, 1982). Although conditional and unconditional risk are related concepts, their role in explaining behavioural intentions was found to be different. Regardless of participants' type of partner, the *conditional* risk estimate appeared to be positively related to behavioural intentions with private partners ($r = +.39, p <.001$) and prostitution partners ($r = +.29, p < .001$). Overall, the conditional risk estimate vulnerability correlated $+.33$ ($p < .001$) with behavioural intentions. Figure 14.1 illustrates these findings. We split up each sample by median split in a group with low and a group with high intentions to engage in safe sex practices. Results show that higher intentions were associated with higher levels of (conditional) risk but not with higher levels of (unconditional) risk. Analysis of variance testing the differences between the two groups confirmed the correlational analysis reported above. For both private and prostitution partners, high intention respondents estimated their risk to be higher than those with low intentions ($F(1,76) = 13.6, p < .001$, and $F(1,22) = 7.0, p < .01$). For private partners, the unconditional risk estimate did not differ for the two groups. For prostitution partners those with high intentions rated their (unconditional) risk to be lower than those with low intentions ($F(1,24) = 8.4, p < .01$).

Rogers and Mewborn (1976) and Maddux and Rogers (1983) found a negative relation between vulnerability and behavioural intentions *only* when participants perceived coping responses to be relatively ineffective. Additionally, Joseph et al. (1987) hypothesized that such a negative relation may have been caused by higher levels of stress. Although the present data do not provide a direct test of these explanations, the relation between the unconditional risk estimate and behavioural intentions was re-examined for participants with higher levels of response efficacy, higher levels of self-efficacy, and lower levels of stress (dichotomized by median split). For participants with prostitution partners, the relation between perceived risk and intentions remained negative for both participants with lower levels of

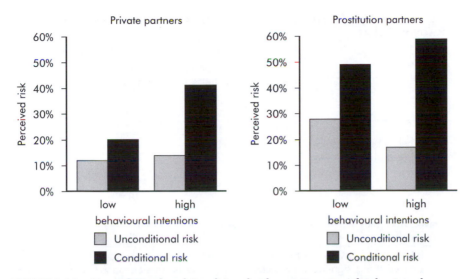

FIGURE 14.1 **Unconditional and Conditional risk as a Function of Behavioural Intentions, for Participants with (Exclusively) Private Partners and Participants with Prostitution Partners**

Notes:
1 Scores for perceived risk could from 0 to 100%.
2 Mean behavioural intention scores equaled 3.8 for participants with exclusively private partners and 4.6 for participants with prostitution partners (possible range of scores from 1 (low) to 5 (high)).

stress and higher levels of response efficacy ($r = -.27$ in both instances). Although controlling for levels of self-efficacy did decrease the strength of relationship between perceived risk and intentions significantly, this relationship remained negative ($r = -.07$, ns). Further (ANOVA) analysis did not reveal any interaction effects.

In conclusion, the conditional risk estimate seems to be a more stable factor in predicting behavioural intentions; whereas the relationship between perceived (unconditional) risk and intentions was dependent on the type of partner (private or prostitution), conditional risk was positively related to intentions *regardless* of the risk status of participants' partners. Additional analyses did not corroborate the findings of Maddux and Rogers (1983) and Joseph et al. (1987): the negative relation between perceived risk and intentions could not be explained by lower levels of self-efficacy and/or response efficacy, or by increased levels of stress.

Perceptions of Risk in Relation to Other Factors

Before examining the relations between perceptions of risk and behaviour, regression analyses (stepwise selection of independent variables) were performed to related perceptions of risk to factors incorporated in behavioural models such as protection motivation theory.

TABLE 14.2 **Multiple Regression Analyses: Factors Associated with Measures of Perceived Risks**[a]

	Unconditional risk		Conditional risk	
	private partners	prostitution partners	private partners	prostitution partners
	(R²)[b] Beta[c]	(R²) Beta	(R²) Beta	(R²) Beta
	(.57)***	(.40)***	(.48)***	(.50)****
Previous behavior	+.51***	+.19*	−.07	−.15
Perceived control	−.05	−.24***	+.05	−.01
Stress	+.21*	+.22***	+.11	+.16
Self-efficacy	−.04	−.10	+.30**	+.12
Fear	+.10	+.17	+.28**	+.33***
Perceived risk status	+.15	+.09	+.27**	+.21**
Responce efficacy	+.14	−.12	+.08	+.30***

Note: [a]Total $n = 247$, [b]Multiple R for the variables in the equation; multiple R's reported here were obtained using significant predictors only in the regression analysis. [c]Positive *Beta* weights indicate higher scores on the conditional and unconditional risk estimates. *$p < .05$, **$p < .01$, ***$p < .001$, ****$p < .0001$.

Multiple regression analyses were performed to find factors related to the conditional and the unconditional risk estimate, separately for participants with private and prostitution partners (see Table 14.2). For participants with private partners, higher levels of the *unconditional* risk estimate were predicted by higher levels of previous risk behaviour, and by higher levels of stress ($F(2,63) = 15.1$, $p < .001$, multiple $R = .57$). For participants with prostitution partners, higher levels of perceived risk were also predicted by higher levels of both previous risk behaviour and stress, and by lower levels of perceived control ($F(3,112) = 6.8$, $p < .001$, multiple $R = .40$). Higher levels of the *conditional* risk estimate for participants with private partners ($F(3,93) = 9.3$, $p < .001$, multiple $R = .48$) were predicted by higher levels of self-efficacy, higher levels of fear, and acknowledgement of belonging to a high-risk group. For participants with prostitution partners, higher levels of *conditional* risk or vulnerability were predicted by higher levels of fear, acknowledgement of belonging to a high-risk group, and, finally, by higher levels of response efficacy ($F(3,131) = 14.7$, $p < .001$, multiple $R = .50$).

Perceptions of Risk, Cognitive Mediators, and Behavioural Measures

The unconditional risk estimate was predicted primarily by factors associated with previous behaviour and stress, the conditional risk estimate was predicted primarily by fear, self-efficacy, response efficacy, and perceived risk status. Given these differences between the conditional and the unconditional measures of perceived risk, the relations between these measures and cognitive mediators of protection motivation theory are likely to be different as well. Figures 14.2 and 14.3 present the results of these analyses, LISREL VI was used to estimate the unknown coefficients. The

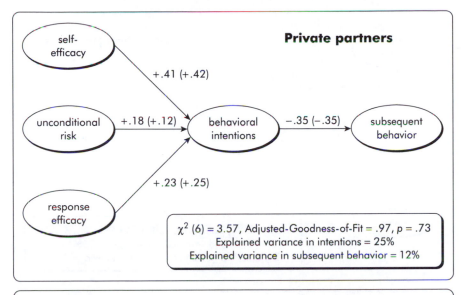

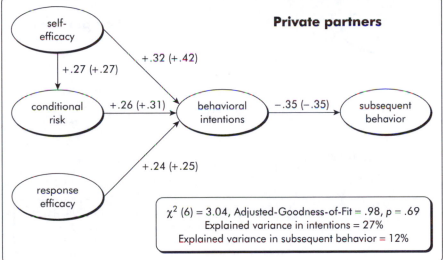

FIGURE 14.2   **LISREL Analyses for Unconditional and Conditional Risk (Participants with Private Partners, n = 100)**[a]

Note: [a] **Indices refer to ML-estimates, correlations are given in parentheses. All paths are significant at p < .05 except the path between unconditional risk and behavioral intentions.**

assumption of a multinormal probability density underlying the data was not violated, which enabled us to use LISRELS' Maximum-Likelihood (ML) estimates. Because these estimates do not, in general, coincide with coefficients of regression among observed variables, zero-order correlations are added in the figures in parentheses (Jöreskog and Sörbom, 1983).

Figures 14.2 and 14.3 present the relations of perceptions of risk, cognitive mediators of protection motivation theory, and behavioural measures. With

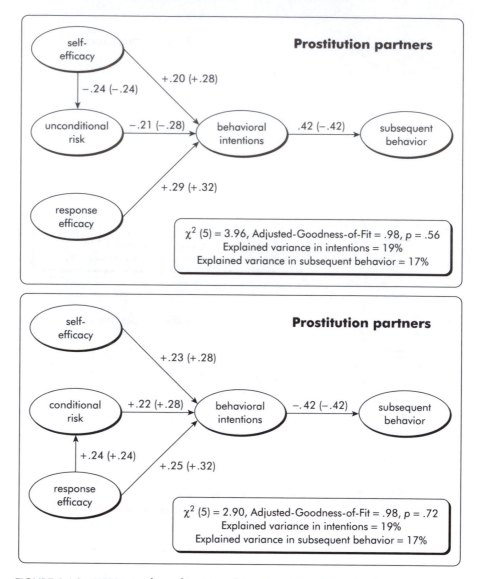

FIGURE 14.3 **LISREL Analyses for Unconditional and Conditional Risk (Participants with Prostitution Partners, *n* = 147)**[a]

Note: [a] Indices refer to ML-estimates, correlations are given in parentheses. All paths are significant at p < .05.

one exception, only the paths that were significant (*t*-value > 2.00) are shown in these figures (and were used to calculate the Chi-square and associated Adjusted-Goodness-of-Fit Index). In all analyses, severity was influenced by at least one of the mediators of protection motivation theory. Severity was, however, not incorporated in the analyses, since it was not significantly related to the behavioural measures.

As shown in Figure 14.2, for participants with exclusively *private* partners, two differences were found with regard to the two risk estimates. First, self-efficacy was significantly related to the conditional estimate: participants with higher levels of self-efficacy perceived the chance to become infected with HIV – if they would not use condoms – to be higher ($ML = .27$, $t = 2.27$). Second, the conditional risk estimate showed a significant positive relation to intentions ($ML = .26$, $t = 2.36$ as opposed to $ML = .18$, ns. for unconditional risk). As shown in Figure 14.3, neither the conditional, nor the unconditional risk estimate were independent of the other mediators of protection motivation theory for participants with *prostitution* partners. Higher levels of *self-efficacy* ($ML = -.24$, $t = 2.48$) were related to lower levels of *unconditional risk*, higher levels of *response efficacy* ($ML = +.24$, $t = 2.44$) were related to higher levels of *conditional risk*. Figure 14.3 clearly underlines the negative relationship between the unconditional risk measure and behavioural intentions for participants with prostitution partners ($ML = -.21$, $t = 2.28$). Again, the conditional estimate showed a positive relationship with behavioural intentions; higher levels of perceived vulnerability were related to higher levels of intentions $ML = +.26$, $t = 2.16$).

Differences in explained variance in intention and/or subsequent behaviour were not found (see Figure 14.3). However, comparing these models between both partner types, the explained variance in intentions was lower, and the explained variance in subsequent behaviour was higher for participants with private partners as opposed to participants with prostitution partners.

Discussion

Results presented in this article confirm earlier mixed findings concerning the relationship between perceived (unconditional) risk and behavioural intention. The literature shows both positive and negative relations between these measures (e.g. Joseph et al., 1987; Maddux and Rogers, 1983; Rogers and Mewborn, 1976; Van der Velde and Van der Pligt, 1991). We found only limited support for Beck and Frankel's (1981) and Joseph's et al. (1987) assumption that the counterintuitive negative relationship is due to inadequate responses, resulting in helplessness and (dis)stress.

A negative relation between perceived own (unconditional) risk and intentions was found only for participants with prostitution partners. For participants with (only) private partners, intentions were not related to the unconditional risk estimate. Although participants with prostitution partners experienced lower levels of personal control, they did not report lower levels of coping responses, nor higher levels of stress than participants with private partners. Considering the consistent positive relation between the *conditional* risk estimate and intentions, other explanations needed to be explored for the sample-differences with respect to the unconditional risk estimate.

In general, it is assumed that people are more willing to behave adaptively (or reduce their risks) once they perceive themselves to be higher at risk – provided that the threat is judged to be sufficiently severe. A negative relation between perceived risk and intentions would therefore imply that people willingly accept higher levels of risk, not planning to reduce risks in the future. Since an infection with HIV is seen as a severe event, they are, apparently, aware of factors that may hinder them to behave adaptively. Bauman and Siegel (1987), for example, found that "sexual impulse control difficulties" impeded participants to reduce their risk. In our sample, female participants with prostitution partners may engage in risky sexual practices, and hence, accept higher levels of risk for commercial reasons.

Another explanation for the differential relationship between unconditional risk and intentions may reside in the way participants perceive the consequences of maladaptive behaviour. Especially for participants relatively high at risk (e.g. participants with homosexual or prostitution partners), the same maladaptive behaviour is more likely to result in negative consequences than for participants with partners at relatively low-risk. Since unconditional risk and intentions were assessed simultaneously, a reversed causation effect between intentions and unconditional risk is not inconceivable. Therefore, when a strong relation is perceived between maladaptive behaviour and subsequent negative consequences, participants might attune their risk estimate to their behavioural intentions; lower levels of intentions thus resulting in higher levels of perceived (unconditional) risk.

Contrary to participants with prostitution partners, participants with exclusively private partners did not perceive a relationship between previous maladaptive behaviour and their level of risk in the future. Furthermore, these participants did not seem to acknowledge a direct link between (lower) intentions and (higher) perceptions of risk. In fact, in previous research (Van der Velde, Hooykaas, and Van der Pligt, 1992) concerning the same sample, perceived risk for *others* was found to be related to behavioural measures (including subsequent risk behaviour). It seems likely therefore, that participants in low-risk groups attune both their perceptions of risk *and* their intentions to an estimate of HIV prevalence rates in their social network (see also Van der Velde, Hooykaas, and Van der Pligt, 1994).

Conditional and unconditional risk estimates were also differentially related to other factors: whereas unconditional risk was found to be more closely related to factors associated with behaviour (previous risk behaviour and perceived stress), conditional risk was found to be more closely related to factors generally incorporated in models of health behaviour (self-efficacy and response efficacy). However, these differences between the two risk estimates and other factors barely influenced the results of the LISREL analyses: substituting the unconditional risk estimate with the conditional risk estimate in analyses including other mediators of protection motivation theory did not reveal marked differences. With one notable exception: regardless of type of partner, the conditional risk measure was found to be consistently (positive) related to intentions.

Given the lack of clarity concerning the causal relationship between the unconditional risk estimate and behavioural intentions, it would have been more correct to present a correlational rather than a causal relationship between these two variables. However, for the purpose of comparability, we decided to present a causal relationship.

In sum, using a *conditional* measure of perceived risk instead of an *unconditional* measure, has several advantages. First of all, a conditional measure more closely resembles the original construct as developed by Rogers (1975) and Becker (1974). Ronis (1992) also argued that the concept of perceived risk or susceptibility needs to be refined and suggested that it needs to be made conditional on the alternative actions or inaction. People are inclined to take preventive action if they believe that inaction significantly increases their risk as compared to taking preventive action. Thus, they perceive a high susceptibility to the disease given inaction. Similarly they would be less inclined to take action if they think they are likely to get the disease even if they would take action. In the latter case high perceived risk is not associated with preventive behaviour. General, unconditional risk measures do not provide the possibility to disentangle these mechanisms, hence the need for conditional measures of risk. Another drawback of the unconditional measure of risk concerns the direction of causality between unconditional risk estimates and behavioural intentions. This direction is unclear, since participants may use their behavioural intentions to anticipate future levels of risk. Finally – and most importantly – a conditional risk estimate seems to be less dependent upon differences in actual risk status, and is therefore more likely to be related to behavioural intentions in a consistent and interpretable manner.

References

Bauman, L.J. and Siegel, K. (1987) Risk perception among gay men of the risk of AIDS associated with their sexual behaviour. *Journal of Applied Social Psychology,* **17**, 329–350.

Beck, K.H. and Frankel, A. (1981) A conceptualization of threat communications and protective health behaviour. *Social Psychology Quarterly,* **44**, 204–217.

Becker, M.H. (1974) The health belief model and personal health behaviour. *Health Education Monographs,* **2**, 324–508.

Becker, M.H., Kaback, M., Rosenstock, I. and Ruth, M. (1975) Some influences on public participant in a genetic screening program. *Journal of Community Health,* **1**, 3–14.

Becker, M.H., Nathanson, C.A., Drachman, R.H. and Kirscht, J.P. (1977) Mothers' health beliefs and children's clinic visits: A prospective study. *Journal of Community Health,* **3**, 125–135.

Cummings, K.M., Jette, A.M., Brock, B.M. and Haefner, D.P. (1979) Psychological determinants of immunization behavior in a Swine Influenza campaign. *Medical Care,* **17**, 639–649.

Jansen, M.E. and Sikkel, D. (1981) Verkorte versies van de VOEG-schaal. *Gezondheid en Samenleving,* **2**, 78–82.

Janz, N.K. and Becker, M.H. (1984) The Health Belief Model: A decade later. *Health Education Quarterly,* **11**, 1–47.

Jöreskog, K.G. and Sörbom, D. (1983) LISREL VI: *Analysis of Linear Structural Relationships by the Method of Maximum Likelihood*. Department of Statistics, University of Uppsala, Uppsala.

Joseph, J.G., Montgomery, S.B., Emmons, C.A., Kirscht, J.P. and Kessler, R.C., et al. (1987). Perceived risk of AIDS: Assessing the behavioural and psychological consequences in a cohort of gay men. *Journal of Applied Social Psychology*, **17**, 321–250.

Langlie, J.K. (1977) Social networks, health beliefs, and preventive health behavior. *Journal of Health and Social Behavior*, **18**, 244–260.

Maddux, J.E. and Rogers, R.W. (1983) Protection motivation and self-efficacy: A revised theory of fear appears and attitude change. *Journal of Experimental Social Psychology*, **19**, 469–479.

McCusker, J., Stoddard, A.M., Zapka, J.G., Zorn, M. and Mayer, K.H. (1989) Predictors of AIDS-preventive behavior among homosexually active man: a longitudinal study. *AIDS*, **3**, 443–448.

Otten, W. and Van der Pligt, J. (1992) Risk and behavior: The mediating role of risk appraisal. *Acta Psychologica*, **80**, 325–346.

Rippetoe, P.A. and Rogers, R.W. (1987) Effects of components of protection-motivation theory on adaptive and maladaptive coping with a health threat. *Journal of Personality and Social Psychology*, **52**, 596–604.

Rogers, R.W. (1975) A protection motivation theory of fear appeals and attitudes change. *The Journal of Psychology*, **91**, 93–114.

Rogers, R.W. and Mewborn, C.R. (1976) Fear appeals and attitude change: Effects of a threat's noxiousness, probability of occurrence, and the efficacy of coping responses. *Journal of Personality and Social Psychology*, **34**, 54–61.

Ronis, D.L. (1992) Conditional health threats: Health beliefs, decisions, and behaviors among adults. *Health Psychology*, **11**, 127–134.

Slovic, P., Fischhoff, B. and Lichtenstein, S. (1987) Behavioral decision theory persepectives on protective behavior. In N.D. Weinstein (ed.), *Taking care: understanding and encouraging self-protective behavior* (pp. 14–41). Cambridge: Cambridge University Press.

Sutton, S.E. (1982) Fear arousing communications: A critical examination of theory and research. In J. R. Eiser (ed.), *Social Psychology and Behavioral Medicine* (pp. 303–337). New York: Wiley.

Temoshok, L., Sweet, D.M. and Zich, J. (1987) A three city comparison of the public's knowledge and attitudes about AIDS. *Psychology and Health*, **1**, 43–60.

van der Linden, M.M.D., Van der Velde, F.W., Hooykaas, C., Van Doornum, G.J.J., and Coutinho, R.A. (1990) HIV-prevalentie onder heterosexuelen met veel wisselende partners in Nederland. *Nederlands Tijdschrift Voor Geneeskunde*, **134**, 1361–1364.

van der Pligt, J., Otten, W., Richard, R. and van der Velde, F. (1993) Perceived risk of AIDS: Unrealistic optimism and self-protective action. In J.B. Pryor and G.D. Reeder (eds). *The Social Psychology of HIV infection* (pp. 39–58). Hillsdale NJ: Erlbaum.

van der Velde, F.W. and Ver der Pligt, J. (1991) AIDS-related health behavior: coping, protection motivation, and previous behavior. *Journal of Behavioral Medicine*, **14**, 429–451.

ver der Velde, F.W., Van der Pligt, J. and Hooykaas, C. (1992) Risk perception and behavior: Pessimism, realism, and optimism about AIDS related health behavior. *Psychology and Health*, **6**, 23–38.

ver der Velde, F.W., Hooykaas, C. and Van der Pligt, J., (1994) Perceiving AIDS-related risk: accuracy as a function of differences in actual risk. *Health Psychology*, **13**, 25–33.

Weinstein, N.D. (1980) Unrealistic optimism about future life events. *Journal of Personality and Social Psychology*, **5**, 806–820.

Weinstein, N.D. (1982). Unrealistic optimism about susceptibility to health problems. *Journal of Behavioral Medicine*, **5**, 441–460.

Weinstein, N.D. (1989) Perceptions of personal susceptibility to harm. In V.M. Mays, G.W. Albee, and S.F. Schneider (eds), *Primary prevention of AIDS: Psychological approaches* (pp. 142–167). Newbury Park, CA: Sage.

15 HEALTH AND ROMANCE:
Understanding unprotected sex in relationships between gay men

Paul Flowers, Jonathan A. Smith, Paschal Sheeran and Nigel Beail

... Even within the constraints of a concern for AIDS, a narrow view of sexual behaviour may be effective if all that we are concerned with is social book- keeping and epidemiological modelling, but it will be inadequate to the task of understanding behaviour in a way that results in behaviour change. Sex conduct is embedded in culture and in social relations – as we begin to deal with this dimension ... we will need to know a great deal more about the why (Gagnon, 1989, p. 500 as cited by Ingham and van Zessen, 1995).

Studies reporting increases in unprotected anal sex amongst gay men have caused lively debate regarding the applicability of the notion of 'relapse' (e.g. see Hart, Boulton, Fitzpatrick, McLean and Dawson, 1992). This issue is problematic because of the pejorative connotations of 'relapse' and the pathological implications for gay men 'failing' to respond to the threat of HIV with the appropriate adoption of consistent condom use. In contrast to their apparent 'failure', other research (e.g. Kippax, Crawford, Davis, Rodden and Dowsett, 1993; Schiltz and Adam, 1995) interprets these same findings as highlighting the adoption of strategic responses to the HIV epidemic, such as 'negotiated safety'. In 'negotiated safety' a couple undergo HIV testing and, if both are negative and remain mutually monogamous (at least in respect to unprotected anal intercourse), they can 'safely' stop using condoms. The recent promotion of such an alternative to condom use (e.g. Billington, Hickson and Maguire, 1996) has caused intense discussion in the British gay press and remains a contentious issue within the gay community.

One of the most surprising aspects of this whole issue has been the lack of psychological research specifically addressing unprotected anal intercourse between men in romantic relationships. The role of relationships is conspicuously lacking within psychological theory regarding gay men's sexual health. The potential theoretical significance of what is often described as 'relationship status' is anomalous to health psychology's present theoretical conception of sexual health. 'Relationship status' is not a psychological variable specified in sexual health applications of either the health belief model – HBM (Rosenstock, 1974), the theory of reasoned action – TRA (Fishbein and Ajzen, 1975) or protection motivation theory – PMT (Rogers, 1983), nor is it part of the most sophisticated and domain-specific model of sexual health, the AIDS risk reduction model – ARRM (Catania, Kegeles and Coates, 1990). Yet, as an atheoretical demographic variable employed in many studies of sexual health, it has proved to be significant, far more often and consistently than any of the traditional psychological constructs which occupy a central place within these theories (see Flowers, Sheeran, Beail and Smith, 1997).

Table 15.1 summarizes the existing literature regarding gay men in relationships and unprotected anal intercourse. Condoms are less likely to be used by primary regular sexual partners and more likely to be used with casual partners. This finding has also been reflected amongst heterosexuals (Dolcini et al., 1993; Peterson, Catania, Dolcini and Faigeles, 1993; Sabogal, Faigeles and Catania, 1993). This finding is important because it is so robust. There is a clear association between being in a romantic relationship and engaging in unprotected anal sex across the international literature.

This chapter represents an attempt to remedy the paucity of psychological research into gay men's relationships and unprotected anal sex. It seeks to address the theoretical gap between health psychology and the existing research findings. The sheer scale of this gap, one minor (atheoretical) variable proving more significant than any of the major psychological constructs (Flowers et al., 1997), highlights the need for a serious reconsideration of the possible determinants of unprotected anal sex between gay men in relationships. It appears these possible determinants are not necessarily to be found within existing theories of health psychology.

With such a broad and exploratory inquiry in mind, we employed qualitative methodology to gain theoretical insight into the occurrence of reported unprotected anal sex within relationships amongst gay men. Though there are many ways qualitative methods can inform health psychology theory, Interpretative Phenomenological Analysis IPA; see Smith, Flowers and Osborn, 1997) was chosen as the most appropriate approach with which to address this research question. Broadly speaking, IPA seeks to reflect the perspectives of the participants in a study. It seeks to engage with the way participants think and act. Furthermore, unlike some other current qualitative approaches (e.g. discourse analysis as employed by Potter and Wetherell, 1987) it is grounded within a 'realist' ontology (i.e. a belief in the chain of connection between account, cognition and behaviour) and was therefore appropriate to our study given our concern with the relationships between these domains (see Smith, 1996a).

In this study, rather than assume to know a priori how gay men thought of the connection between unprotected anal sex and relationships, we sought to discover how individual gay men thought about it, and to incorporate this insight into psychological theory concerning sexual health. This

TABLE 15.1 **The Association Between Relationship Status and the Adoption of Safer Sex**

Author(s)	Operationalization	Significance *p*
Cross-sectional studies		
Fitzpatrick et al. (1990)	Regular non-regular	.005 (+)
Hays, Kegeles and Coates (1990)	Having a lover	<.01 (+)
Doll et al. (1991)	Primary partner	
	San Francisco	<.05 (+)
	Chicago	<.0489 (+)
	Denver	<.0005 (+)
Connell et al. (1989)	Relationship status	<.0001 (+)
Schmidt et.al. (1992)	Steady partner	<.0005 (+)
Ekstrand and Coates (1990)	Monog/non-monogamous	<.05 (+)
Gold et al. (1991)	Lover/casual partner	<.01 (+)
Gold and Skinner (1992)	Lover/casual partner	n.s.
Fitzpatrick et al. (1989)	Monog/non-monogamous	<.05 (+)
Valdiserri et al. (1988)	Single	<.05 (+)
Longitudinal studies		
Fitzpatrick et al. (1991)	Regular non-regular	<.0001 (+)
Aspinwall et al. (1991)	Relationship status	n.s.
Catania et al. (1991)	Mutual monogamy	n.s.
Martin et al. (1989)	Primary partner	<.05 (+)
McKusick et al. (1990)	Monogamous/non-monogamous	<.05 (+)
Martin (1990)	Having a lover	
	(i) URAI	<.05 (+)
	(ii) UIAI	<.05 (+)

URAI = unprotected receptive anal intercourse; UIAI = unprotected insertive anal intercourse; (+) = the association of casual partners and safer sex.

insight cannot provide a veridical model of gay men's decision making regarding condom use in relationships, but can suggest an heuristic model which would be useful in directing both quantitative research and sexual health promotion practice. The inductive approach we are taking here stands in contrast to the deductive approach of quantitative research; the latter seeks to test and measure associations within a pre-defined framework. Qualitative research is most useful in this area, given the existence of a problematic and puzzling finding in the quantitative studies – the repeated association between relationship status and unprotected anal intercourse.

Method

Twenty interviews were conducted with men from a small town in South Yorkshire, England, who all identified themselves as being gay. All interviews were conducted by the first author and most were conducted in the interviewees' own homes. The names of all the men who took part in the study, and the people they have referred to, have been changed to ensure confidentiality. The men were recruited into the study through a 'snowballing' technique. Initial contacts were made through the first author's involvement in the local gay community. Subsequent contacts, from these initial key informants, traced gay men's social and sexual networks. None of the men approached to take part in this study refused, and in fact some men volunteered to take part.

It is worth noting that truly representative samples of men who have sex with men are almost impossible to attain and furthermore, sampling gay identified men also presents many problems (see Harry, 1986). The sample could be described as being broadly representative of gay men from a small town in South Yorkshire, consisting of predominantly working-class men and aged between 19 and 45, who in varying degrees, all used the local gay scene. Qualitative research has different conceptions of sampling than quantitative research. The aim of most qualitative research projects is to explore a small well-defined sample in detail. One then makes claims for that group which may be quite strong but one is cautious about generalizing to a wider population. This point is taken up in the discussion.

The interviews were recorded on audio cassette. They lasted between one and four hours. A general interview schedule was employed, consisting of open-ended questions. The interview style was non-directive, a process of reflecting and probing was employed (e.g. Could you tell me more about ... etc.). In this way, the content of each interview was dictated by the individual respondent; once rapport and trust were established the primary role of the interviewer was facilitating the disclosure of the interviewee's perspective.

The interviews were then transcribed verbatim. Following this, the transcripts were analysed for recurrent themes. Themes emerged within individual interviews and across different interviews. The process of identifying themes involved several steps. Throughout, the analyst attempted to acknowledge and suspend any existing knowledge of the field, and indeed, personal experiences within it. This was done in an attempt to 'see' the world as it is experienced by the respondent. Bearing this in mind, each transcript was repeatedly read. Following this, the analysis of each transcript began, in which both semantic content and language use were examined; key words, phrases or explanations which the respondent used were highlighted. These were then coded with a key word or phrase which captured the essence of the content. These represented emergent themes. The process was repeated with each transcript. Following this, repetitions of these emergent themes (between each individual transcript) were taken as indicative of their status as recurrent themes which reflect shared understandings. In this manner, for each theme, a file of transcript extracts was created. While an emphasis is placed here on themes emerging from the data, inevitably this selection process requires interpretation on the part of the analyst. One is attempting to capture the meaning of the phenomenon to the participant but this necessarily involves interpretative engagement with the respondent's text (Smith, 1995, 1996a).

In the following presentation of the analysis, extracts were chosen for being exemplary of the underlying recurrent theme. The extracts used represented the most articulate or powerful examples of an underlying common theme. It must be noted that not every man expressed the particular themes; some men presented a plurality of themes, some men described contradictory themes. However, rather than focus upon individual variability within accounts (e.g. Potter and Wetherell, 1987), the focus here is on similarity and the consistent way people think about, and give accounts concerning, particular issues. In this way, each theme does represent a distinctive representation of a way of thinking about an issue. A way which, we believe, reflects the causal role of these underlying cognitions in effecting sexual decision making.

A validation check was conducted by the second author who looked through five of the transcripts, alongside the relevant thematic items, to confirm the selected items did not misrepresent the participants. See Smith (1996b) and Yin (1989) for the discussion of alternative criterion for the validity and reliability of qualitative research.

Analysis

The analysis, presented below, focuses upon those themes relevant in understanding unprotected anal intercourse within relationships. It begins with a presentation of how gay men understood casual sex and describes the theme of detachment. In contrast to this, the rest of the analysis illustrates the way men thought of sex and HIV-related behaviours, within the context of romantic relationships. This begins with a presentation of how men described penetrative sex within relationships and the theme of self-involvement. Following this, the analysis specifically examines how they understood the issue of unprotected anal sex and the role of condoms and semen exchange therein.

Casual Sex and 'Detachment'

The very robust findings reported, from the quantitative literature (e.g. Table 15.1), showed that there were clear differences in reported sexual behaviour across different relationship contexts. This was also reflected throughout the interviews. Sex within relationships was understood to be different from casual sex. The differences were not described in terms of traditional constructs, such as physical sensation or self-efficacy. Instead the differences reported related very strongly to the meaning of the sex. There was a strong theme of 'detachment' (as opposed to 'involvement') linked with casual sex. The meaning of 'detachment' reflected a sense of minimal self-involvement in the sex, and an objectification of casual sexual partners who were characterized as sex objects lacking personhood. This was illustrated, for example, when 'he' could have been used to describe the partner and 'it' was substituted. Similarly, where 'anyone' could have been used 'anything' was used instead. As an example,

Andrew talked about 'old queens in cottages'. A queen is a colloquialism for a gay man and a cottage is a public toilet used for sex. Andrew said of the men:

> A: and you know they're never going to get off with anything unless they pay it.

This sense of detachment is also apparent in the way that people talked about themselves in casual sex. For example Dan said:

> D: That's the big thing, a lot of sort of casual sex where some people don't like snogging and they don't snog. It's like a lot of straight people use them (cottages) or whatever and it's a way of distancing, distancing yourself from it. Doing it with your body but not with your mind.

Dan noted the lack of 'snogging'[1] within casual sex in a cottage. Implicit in his account of why people do not 'snog' was the assumption that 'snogging' represented 'doing it' with your mind as well as your body. This was distinct from not snogging, which was doing it with your body but not your mind. 'Snogging' here signified some kind of involvement, as opposed to detachment. Stenner (1994) also identified the theme of differential 'involvement' across different sex acts amongst heterosexuals talking about oral sex. Similarly, Connell and Kippax (1990) explored patterns of sexual practice and pleasure among gay men. They found kissing along with sensual touching and anal intercourse without a condom, were the three most emotionally satisfying sex acts.

Penetrative Sex, Relationships and 'Self-involvement'

The 'detachment' illustrated in talking about casual sex is sharply contrasted with ideas linking romantic love to sex in relationships. These interviews and other research (e.g. Connell and Kippax, 1990; Davies, Hickson, Weatherburn and Hunt, 1993; Schmidt et al., 1992) showed that, for many men, there was a distinction between sex in relationships and casual sex. Some sexual acts, namely penetrative sex, were more likely to be part of their sexual repertoire within relationships and not outside of them. As Andrew said:

> A: I would not do it (getting fucked) purely to be fucked, that's against what I believe in.
> P:[2] What do you believe in?
> A: I suppose it's like putting on the same lines as sex within marriage and not before. It's like I said before I couldn't click off with somebody and be fucked, it just wouldn't be right.

Andrew appeared keen to reject the possibility of penetrative sex practised purely for the sexual pleasure. Instead, he stressed the role of penetration in the context of a relationship. In the interviews, men referred to the existence of a 'right' time, within a relationship, for penetrative sex. As Richard described it:

> R: It only happened when it felt right, I mean I wouldn't have allowed it to happen otherwise, you know, I couldn't have got into bed and done it straight away, not like I had done in the past.
> P: Did it change the relationship, when it became penetrative sex?
> R: It became closer, it became much closer.

It appears that penetrative sex, within a relationship context, sometimes functions as an expression of commitment to that relationship and thus penetrative sex was seen as a kind of milestone. It is in the context of relationship development that penetrative sex comes to function expressively. In this way, in the following extract Peter illustrates a possible function of receptive anal intercourse. Central to his account of the significance of penetrative sex in his relationship, was the assumption that through allowing himself to be penetrated he expressed his total commitment to his relationship and his total self-involvement. This relationship was different from others, because, this time, he did not 'hold a bit of himself back':

> Pe: It took me a long time to love John and that, I suppose for us to have anal sex it kind of, put the icing on the cake [pause] a sense, the relationship was complete because sexually we were ... I suppose sexually embarrassed to approach anal sex and then when we did do it, it got that obstacle out of the way. And also I wouldn't [pause] I've always held a bit of myself back, relationship-wise, because I've been dumped so many times [pause] so in order to [pause] with John, once we'd had anal sex, then I knew I'd given myself completely over, there was nothing else really I was holding back.
> P: And you did it without condoms?
> Pe: Yeah. Yeah.

Masturbation is a key part of most sexual sessions (Davies et al., 1993; Kippax et al., 1993), there is no differential use across casual and relationship contexts. As such, masturbation can carry little expressive potential with regards to relationship development or commitment. Penetration has historically been granted special status, in both definitions of virginity and of rape. Legislation condoning vaginal penetration and sanctioning other sexual acts stems from the reproductive potential of vaginal penetration. Anal penetration has its own specific historical legacy (Foucault, 1985; Gilbert, 1981; Morin, 1986). Furthermore, the insertive receptive dimensions can have their own distinct significance when practised between men, often relating to masculinity and male identity (Carrier, 1971, 1976; Lancaster, 1988; Murray, 1992, cited in Davies et al., 1993; Tapinc, 1992; Young, 1973). Clearly, penetrative sex can carry much symbolic weight, in terms of the physical act of joining, as well as being inside someone else's body, or letting someone else inside your body. As Phil put it:

> *Ph:* Actually him inside me, actually knowing that my boyfriend is inside me. Knowing that he's there, inside me, it's a lovely feeling. You know, a wanted. You know, he wants to be there for you and he wants to be for you, and I find if you're in a relationship, if the person that you're in a relationship with doesn't want to fuck you, it means they don't love you, it means they don't feel anything for you.

Or as Richard described his feelings regarding anal penetration within his relationship:

> *R:* If it's somebody casual, then a fuck's a fuck, isn't it? But like Bill and I, it's making love, because it's sort of like the most ultimate expression of closeness, yeah? Am I saying that right? Is it coming across? Do you know what I mean?
> *P:* Try and tell me some more?
> *R:* Well I think, when you're penetrating someone, you sort of become one piece, you're joined together aren't you and that's why I think it's more intimate than any other sexual experience that you can have between two people, you know a wank's a wank isn't it? You can have fun with a wank, but when you actually penetrate somebody, that's just like, the ultimate.

It would seem that the symbolic function of penetrative sex in a relationship may, perhaps, stem from the literal similarity between physical togetherness and psychological/emotional togetherness. A parallel was being made between physical and psychological intimacy. It is clear that penetrative sex can function expressively within a relationship to signify commitment to that relationship.

Unprotected Anal Penetration and the Romantic Rationality

Since the 1980s, with the identification of unprotected anal intercourse as a high-risk transmission route for HIV, penetrative sex has taken on an additional distinction from other sexual acts. The significance of penetration, and now the further significance of HIV risk in penetrative sex, has allowed the issues of penetration and condom use to become very powerful signifiers, signifiers which, like other symbols, can be used to represent quite specific meanings. Below, Dan introduces this issue:

> *D:* When I was going out with Simon, like before I weren't fucking, blah-de-blah just the general things, but like with Simon it were more like being there for each other and like wanting to be inside each other. Like I wanted him inside of me, and part of me inside of him and which in a relationship can also be a big thing with the sort of safe sex thing, of actually wanting to be so close to the other person, that you actually, you know, you know it carried all these risks and still you're having to put a barrier between you and someone

you love and even if it is only a few inches of barrier, if you like it's still something artificial that's there, which is otherwise a sort of spiritual, animal, type of thing.

Clearly, central to Dan's problematization of condom use was the symbolic barrier it presented. Condom use in a relationship juxtaposes individualistic health concerns upon what essentially is an experience of sharing. It can represent the threat of disease and death in the moment of celebrating life. It draws attention to the parameters of the individual body in an experience which is understood to be concerned with 'becoming one'.

Phil's account, below, gives an insight into the importance, and meaning, of exactly what condom use prevents, i.e. semen exchange. He describes how this relates to the context of a romantic relationship:

> *Ph:* He cummed inside me. A lovely feeling. You know, there's some'at there of someone that you care about, you love. I used to like it.
> *P:*   What is it about their cum that means so much?
> *Ph:* [sighs] It gives you a feeling. It gives you a buzz. You know, I've had his seed inside of me, things like that, just sit here thinking about it hours after. And then you go to the toilet and it goes Plop! Plop! Plop! [pause] Yeah me body sort of went 'oh he's gone now'. He's there, he's just like [pause] there. I'm still like it now.

In the same way in which penetration itself embodies the sharing of selves, so semen itself can be understood as representing a sexual partner. Earlier Dan described how condom use was problematic within romantic relationships. The issue of condom use has been appropriated, because of this, to express some very specific meanings, for example, trust. As Brent explains:

> *B:* It were different because we weren't using condoms and it were different because I love him. It's not such a rush job.
> *P:* What is different about it?
> *B:* No, it just feels better, it feels nice because he's trusting me. Like my life's in his hands and his life's in my hands and it's like that. If he cheats with anyone who dun't use owt and he gets some'at – I'll have it. That's the way it is, and if he does, I'll kill him.

The presence of HIV has accentuated some of the powerful pre-existing symbolic language of penetration. Peter said of receptive anal intercourse 'I knew I'd given myself completely over'; this directly related to the theme of self-involvement, of giving oneself, of letting oneself be taken, of somehow surrendering one's identity to one's partner. In the same way that penetration is important, because of the significance of joining which represents the centrality of the couple above and beyond the individual, Brent and Jake utilized the threat of HIV to illustrate the primacy of their relationship, literally putting their lives in each other's hands. This emphasis on trust, both in terms of emotions and disease prevention, hints at the possible role of condom use in quantifying trust. As Neil explained why people have penetrative sex:

> N: In a relationship is to show respect, is to show caring and love, right, there is a lot to say about penetrative sex when you're in a relationship and also you know you're showing the partner of how much you trust them, especially if you don't use a condom.

This shows clearly how a specific sexual act (the non-use of condoms in anal penetration) can enter the vocabulary of sexual acts which are utilized, quite actively, by gay men. Though penetration itself carries emotive and specific meanings, unprotected anal intercourse, because of HIV, has come to magnify many of these meanings, such as trust or as the next extract shows 'love':

> Ph: I just asked him one day, that were the day that I told him I loved him and he says 'Oh you can't love another man' I says 'I love you enough to fuck you without a condom on', 'yeah, yeah'. I says 'I want to fuck you without a condom on or you fuck me, I want you to come inside me or I'll fuck you and come inside you, and things like that. And he says 'Whatever takes your fancy but you can't tell me that you love another man'. I says 'Well you know in a few years time I'll probably be purely gay and you'll probably never even come out, you'll probably stop with your wife, you're happy, I'm not. He says 'whatever then'. So we did.

Philip's insistence on unsafe sex was based around his expression of love for his partner. This expression gains its magnitude because of the risks of HIV infection. It is only through his familiarity with the risks of HIV infection that Philip can show the measure of his feelings through unsafe sex and and semen exchange. Similarly Dan describes, once more, the privileging of the relationship above the self. This process is dependent upon knowledge of sexual health risks and in this case, HIV status. It is important to notice how he qualifies his remarks with a quantification of love, 'if we really loved somebody':

> D: I've not been in the situation, but if we really loved somebody and that's what you wanted to do, even if you knew they were HIV, I think that would even come into the equation, if you know, if you were wanting, you know, wanting to die with somebody, or even if you loved somebody that much I suppose, wanting somebody's virus inside'em. You know they've got it then you want it as well [pause] sort of thing.

Dan describes how HIV has shaped the meanings of sexual behaviour. Becoming infected knowingly is the ultimate expression of prioritizing the relationship above and beyond the individuals themselves and their own health concerns. This can also be described as the ultimate expression of love.[3]

Discussion

One central issue which runs throughout the analysis has been the way gay men understand sexual activity. Their understanding contrasts with the dominant mode of thinking within health psychology. Specific sexual activity emerges not as the end-point, or the result of sexual decision making but as a means to an end of achieving *other* aims or goals, which often relate directly to the social context of sexual activity (i.e. a romantic relationship).

Men's reported sexual decision making could be accurately described as individual calculated choice which relates directly to social motivation – to tell one's lover how much one loves them, or to tell one's casual sexual partner how little they mean to one. Throughout men's accounts of their sexual decision making, there seems to be a consistent awareness of sexual acts as being communicative, capable of capturing very powerful expressions (see Prieur, 1990). Semen exchange within a relationship highlights sharing bodies, whilst condom use in a relationship exemplifies keeping bodies separate and isolated. The threat of HIV and AIDS seems to have been incorporated within the existing 'language' of sexual acts.

This chapter has described a collection of motivations, within sexual decision making, which could be described as representing a 'romantic rationality' – a rationality which is distinct from that used in current sexual health psychology. Currently, our theoretical understandings of sexual behaviour, in the field of sexual health, has been borrowed from health psychology; they constitute what could be described as a 'health rationality'. Conceptual frameworks such as the health belief model (Rosenstock, 1974), the theory of planned behaviour (Ajzen, 1991), and the theory of reasoned action (Fishbein and Ajzen, 1975) were initially employed. Here, the most salient issue is the individual in pursuit of health and the avoidance of illness; behavioural change has the single function of maximizing health. In these models, the general heuristic of a costs and benefits analysis is central. Broadly speaking, in sexual health research, this is conceived in terms of an individual's disease prevention beliefs (condom use), weighted up against an individual's beliefs regarding sexual pleasure (loss of sensation). Sexual acts are understood to be the end-point of a calculated decision process – a decision process which can be targeted within sexual health promotion.

Health psychology, with its single 'health-rationality' perspective, highlights the utility of condom provision as an appropriate response for service providers, and points to the consistent use of condoms by gay men as an effective means of reducing HIV risk. In contrast, gay men in relationships may privilege the 'romantic rationality' and make informed decisions, in the light of HIV-risk taking, not to use condoms in order to show 'commitment', 'trust' or 'love'. In doing so, gay men may well be at risk of HIV infection. An approach is needed that reflects the plurality of possible rationalities and their hierarchical organization, rather than a specific focus upon any single rationality, as an explanatory tool for sexual decision making. Different 'rationalities' have different implications for service provision. In contrast to condom provision, as the sole means of responding to the dictates of a health rationality, a phenomenologically informed approach seeks to accommodate men's desire to engage in unprotected anal intercourse. Yet, as this paper describes, it was the expression of quite specific meanings that led to the occurrence of unprotected anal sex. 'Negotiated safety' (see Kippax et al., 1993), as an alternative to condom use, offers other means to quite specifically express these. In terms of the 'romantic rationality', 'commitment' is expressed through consistent condom use, across a three-month window period, with a mutual agreement for testing and counselling at the end of this period. 'Trust' is accomplished within counselling, wherein explicit agreements to limit unprotected anal intercourse to the relevant partner are made. Agreements must also be made regarding the possibility of sex outside the relationship and action plans must be drafted, for example with regard to the occurrence of condom breakage with other partners. Love is expressed through the couple's explicit commitment to each other, and their active negotiation of unprotected sex in the context of sexual health service providers. The special or exceptional nature of condoning unprotected anal intercourse is still dependent upon the context of HIV risk. It still employs the language of HIV-risk taking which men were using themselves. This approach seems useful for those men who share the same HIV status, though the literature is sparse regarding the danger of reinfection from other HIV-positive men. Yet, for those men in relationships whose HIV status are different, at present, there can be no alternative to condom use within penetrative sex, without risking HIV infection. Couple counselling can address sexual decision making for these men in terms of a plurality of rationalities; finding alternative expressions of commitment and love rather than focusing upon health, for example.

Models of sexual decision making should begin with some contextualizing of the sex, in terms of its function, or rationality, whether it be concerned with the dynamics of a relationship (as in this chapter), of power (e.g. Bloor, McKeganey, Finlay and Barnard, 1992; Holland, Ramazanoglu and Scott, 1990), economic exchange (Zalduondo and Bernard, 1995), identity (Ingham, Woodcock and Stenner, 1992; Flowers, Smith, Sheeran and Beail, 1997; Wight, 1993), religion (Cohen and Hubert, 1995) or solely of sexual pleasure. Furthermore, Bloor (1995) and Rhodes (1995) draw attention to the occasions in which habit, or constraints, preclude the possibility of calculated individual decision making.

It makes sense to theorize sexual activity as social activity, to acknowledge that an individual's choice of sexual acts may be determined as much by the social context of the activity, as by beliefs relating to both sensate pleasure and disease avoidance. Yet throughout, when an individual makes such calculated choices, decision-making processes are open to persuasion and change. Effective campaigns must address men's choice of sexual act in the appropriate terms, or 'rationality' employed by gay men themselves. Whether sexual acts are understood as means to expressive ends (e.g. to show love), or as pleasurable ends incorporating prophylactic means, provided there are limited constraints, there is scope for an approach which targets the individual and calculated decision making. Such a broad approach to understanding sexual acts, and their place within various rationalities, does not necessarily highlight condom use as the most appropriate target of sexual health promotion. For men who share the same HIV status, a strategic response like 'negotiated safety' offers a viable alternative to condom use which incorporates key elements from both the health and romantic rationalities.

This chapter has explored the phenomenon of unprotected anal intercourse in the context of relationships between gay men from Benton, a small town in South Yorkshire. The consistency of the account means that we are confident that our analysis speaks for the particular population from which our sample was drawn. At the same time, of course, the convergence between our results and those of the quantitative data set suggests a wider significance. That is, we believe our analysis has helped to illuminate what is a problematic but consistent finding across the literature. Thus it can be argued that the romantic rationality identified in this chapter as an explanation for the behaviour of this group of gay men may well also apply to other populations of gay men as well. Of course, at this stage we are only claiming this as a credible explanation. The degree of generalizability of any analysis will depend upon further qualitative studies being conducted with different groups of gay men.

Notes

1 'Snogging' is kissing with tongues.
2 p = the interviewer (first author).
3 The historical context of sex between men also seems important here. In the UK, and many other countries, relationships between same-sex couples have no legal credibility and often no social acceptance outside of local social networks (Kitzinger and Coyle, 1995). Heterosexuals have the available rituals and ceremonies of engagement, marriage and divorce to mark the development of their relationships; no such parallel exists in contemporary gay culture. This offers us further insight into the use of unsafe sex to chart the 'seriousness' of relationships between men.

References

Ajzen, I. (1991). The theory of planned behaviour: Some unresolved issues. *Organisational Behaviour and Human Decision Process*, **50**, 179–211.

Aspinwall, L. G., Kemeny, M. E., Taylor, S. E., Schneider, S. G. and Dudley, J. P. (1991). Psychosocial predictors of gay men's AIDS risk-reduction behaviour. *Health Psychology*, **10**, 432–444.

Billington, A., Hickson, F. and Maguire, M. (1996). Thinking it through: A new approach to sex, relationships and HIV for gay men. London: Camden and Islington Community Health Services NHS Trust.

Bloor, M. J., McKeganey, N. P., Finlay, A. and Barnard, M. A. (1992). The inappropriateness of psychosocial models of risk behaviour for understanding HIV related risk practices among Glasgow male prostitutes. *AIDS Care*, **4**, 131–137.

Bloor, M. (1995). *The Sociology of HIV Transmission*. London: Sage.

Carrier, J. M. (1971). Sex role preference as an explanatory variable in homosexual behaviour. *Archives of Sexual Behaviour*, **6**, 53–65.

Carrier, J. M. (1976). Cultural factors affecting urban Mexican male homosexual behaviour. *Archives of Sexual Behaviour*, **5**, 103–124.

Catania, J. A., Kegeles, S. M. and Coates, T. J. (1990). Towards an understanding of risk behaviour: An AIDS risk reduction model (ARRM). *Health Education Quarterly*, **17**, 53–72.

Catania, J. A., Coates, T. J., Stall, R., Bye, L., Kegeles, S. M., Capell, F., Henne, J., McKusick, L., Morin, S., Turner, H. and Pollack, L. (1991). Changes in condom use among homosexual men in San Francisco. *Health Psychology*, **10**, 190–199.

Cohen, M. and Hubert, M. (1995). The place of time in understanding sexual behaviour and designing HIV/AIDS prevention programs. In L. Van Campenhoudt, M. Cohen, G. Guizzardi and D. Hausser (eds), *Sexual Interactions and HIV Risk: New Conceptual Perspectives in European Research*. London: Taylor and Francis.

Connell, R. W., Crawford, J., Kippax, S., Dowsett, G. W., Baxter, D., Watson, L. and Berg, R. (1989). Facing the epidemic: Changes in the sexual lives of gay and bisexual men in Australia and their implications for AIDS prevention strategies. *Social Problems*, **36**, 384–402.

Connell, R. W. and Kippax, S. (1990). Sexuality in the AIDS crisis: Patterns of sexual practice and pleasure in a sample of Australian gay and bisexual men. *Journal of Sex Research*, **27**, 167–196.

Davies, P. M., Hickson, F. C. I., Weatherburn, P. and Hunt, A. J. (1993). *AIDS: Sex, Gay Men and AIDS*. London: Falmer Press.

Dolcini, M., Catania, J., Coates, T. J., Stall, R., Hudes, E., Gagnon, J. and Pollack, L. (1993). Demographic characteristics of heterosexuals with multiple partners: The national AIDS behavioural surveys (NABS). *Family Planning Perspectives*, **25**, 208–214.

Doll, L. S., Byers, R. H., Bolan, G., Douglas, I. M., Moss, P. M., Weller, P. D., Joy, D., Bartholow, B. N. and Harrison, J. S. (1991). Homosexual men who engage in high-risk sexual behaviour: A multicenter comparison. *Sexually Transmitted Diseases*, **18**, 170–175.

Ekstrand, M. L. and Coates, T. J. (1990). Maintenance of safer sexual behaviours and predictors of risky sex: The San Francisco men's health study. *American Journal of Public Health*, **80**, 973–977.

Fishbein, M. and Ajzen, I. (1975). *Belief, Attitude, Intent and Behavior: An Introduction to Theory and Research*. Reading, MA: Addison-Wesley.

Fitzpatrick, R., Boulton, M., Hart, G., Dawson, J. and McLean, J. (1989). High risk sexual behaviour and condom use in a sample of homosexual and bisexual men. *Health Trends*, **21**, 76–79.

Fitzpatrick, R., Dawson, J., Boulton, M., McLean, J. and Hart, G. (1991). Social psychological factors that may predict high risk sexual behaviour in gay men. *Health Education Journal,* **50,** 63–66.

Flowers, P., Sheeran, P., Beail, N. and Smith, J. A. (1997). The role of psychosocial factors in HIV risk reduction among gay and bisexual men: A quantitative review. *Psychology and Health,* **12,** 197–230.

Flowers, P., Smith, J. A., Sheeran, P. and Beail, N. (1997). Identities and gay men's sexual decision making. In P. Aggleton, P. Davies and G. Hart (eds), *AIDS: Activism and Alliances.* London: Taylor and Francis.

Foucault, M. (1985). *The Use of Pleasure: History of Sexuality,* vol. 2. New York: Random House.

Gagnon, J. H. (1989). Disease and desire. *Daedalus,* **118,** 47–77.

Gilbert, A. N. (1981). Conceptions of homosexuality and sodomy in western history. *Journal of Homosexuality,* **6,** 57–68.

Gold, R. S., Skinner, M. J., Grant, P. J. and Plummer, D. C. (1991). Situational factors and thought processes associated with unprotected intercourse in gay men. *Psychology and Health,* **5,** 259–278.

Gold, R. S. and Skinner, M. J. (1992). Situational factors and thought processes associated with unprotected intercourse in young gay men. *AIDS,* **6,** 1021–1030.

Hart, G., Boulton, M., Fitzpatrick, R., McLean, J. and Dawson, J. (1992). 'Relapse' to unsafe sexual behaviour among gay men: A critique of recent behavioural HIV/AIDS research. *Sociology of Health and Illness,* **14,** 217–232.

Harry, J. (1986). Sampling gay men. *Journal of Sex Research,* **22,** 1–34.

Hays, R. B., Kegeles, S. M. and Coates, T. J. (1990). High HIV risk taking among young gay men. *AIDS,* **4,** 901–907.

Holland, J., Ramazanoglu, C. and Scott, S. (1990). Managing risk and experiencing danger: Tensions between government AIDS health education policy and young women's sexuality. *Gender and Education,* **2,** 125–129.

Ingham, R., Woodcock, A. and Stenner, K. (1992). The limitations of rational decision-making models as applied to young people's sexual behaviour. In P. Aggleton, P. Davies, and G. Hart (eds), *AIDS: Rights, Risk and Reason,* pp. 163–173. London: Falmer Press.

Ingham, R. and van Zessen, G. (1995). Towards an alternative model of sexual behaviour: From individual properties to interactional processes. In L. Van Campenhoudt, M. Cohen, G. Guizzardi and D. Hausser (eds), *Sexual Interactions and HIV Risk: New Conceptual Perspectives in European Research.* London: Taylor and Francis.

Kippax, S., Crawford, J., Davis, M., Rodden, P. and Dowsett, G. (1993). Sustaining safe sex: A longitudinal study of a sample of homosexual men. *AIDS,* **7,** 257–263.

Kitzinger, C. and Coyle, A. (1995). Lesbian and gay couples: Speaking of difference. *The Psychologist,* February, 64–69.

Lancaster, R. N. (1988). Subject honour and object shame: The construction of male homosexuality and stigma in Nicaragua. *Ethnology,* **27,** 111–125.

Martin, J. L., Dean, L., Garcia, M. and Hall, W. (1989). The impact of AIDS on a gay community: Changes in sexual behaviour, substance use, and mental health. *American Journal of Community Psychology,* **17,** 269–293.

Martin, J. L. (1990). Drug use and unprotected anal intercourse among gay men. *Health Psychology,* **9,** 450–465.

McKusick, L., Coates, T. J., Morin, S. F., Pollack, L. and Hoff, C. (1990). Longitudinal predictors of reductions in unprotected anal intercourse among gay men in San Francisco. The AIDS behavioral research project. *American Journal of Public Health*, **80**, 978–983.

Morin, J. (1986). *Anal Pleasure and Health*. Burlingame, CA: Yes Press.

Murray, S. O. (1992). The 'underdevelopment' of modern gay homosexuality in Mesco-America. In K. Plummer (ed.), *Modern Homosexualities: Fragments of a Gay and Lesbian Experience*, pp. 29–38. London: Routledge.

Peterson, J., Catania, J., Dolcini, M. and Faigeles, B. (1993). Correlates of HIV risk behaviour in Black and White San Francisco heterosexuals: The population-based AIDS in multiethnic neighbourhoods (AMEN) study. *Ethnicity and Disease*, **2**, 361–370.

Potter, J. and Wetherell, M. (1987). *Discourse and Social Psychology: Beyond Attitudes and Behaviour*. London: Sage.

Prieur, A. (1990). Gay men: Reasons for continued practice of unsafe sex. *AIDS Education and Prevention*, **2**, 110–117.

Rhodes, T. (1995). Theorizing and researching 'risk': Notes on the social relations of risk in heroin users 'lifestyles'. In P. Aggleton, P. Davies and G. Hart (eds), *AIDS: Safety, Sexuality and Risk*. London: Taylor and Francis.

Rogers, R. W. (1983). Cognitive and physiological processes in fear appeals and attitude change: A revised theory of protection motivation. In J. R. Cacioppo and R. E. Petty (eds), *Social Psychology: A Source Book*, pp. 153–176. New York: Guilford.

Rosenstock, I. (1974). Historical origins of the health belief model. *Health Education Monographs*, **2**, 328–335.

Sabogal, F., Faigeles, B. and Catania, J. (1993). Multiple sexual partners among Hispanics in high-risk cities. *Family Planning Perspectives*, **25**, 257–262.

Schiltz, M. and Adam, P. (1995). Reputedly effective risk reduction strategies and gay men. In P. Aggleton, P. Davies and G. Hart (eds), *AIDS: Safety, Sexuality and Risk*. London: Taylor and Francis.

Schmidt, K. W., Fouchard, J. R., Krasnik, A., Zoffmann, H., Jacobsen, H. L. and Kreiner, S. (1992). Sexual behaviour related to psycho-social factors in a population of Danish homosexual and bisexual men. *Social Science and Medicine*, **34**, 1119–1127.

Smith, J. A. (1995). Semi-structured interviewing and qualitative analysis. In J. A. Smith, R. Harre and L. Van Langenhove (eds), *Rethinking Methods in Psychology*. London: Sage.

Smith, J. A. (1996a). Beyond the divide between cognition and discourse: Using interpretative phenomenological analysis in health psychology. *Psychology and Health*, **11**, 261–271.

Smith, J. A. (1996b). Evolving issues for qualitative psychology. In J. Richardson (ed.), *Handbook of Qualitative Research Methods for Psychology and the Social Sciences*. Leicester: The British Psychological Society.

Smith, J. A., Flowers, P. and Osborn, M. (1997). Interpretative phenomenological analysis and the psychology of health and illness. In L. Yardley (ed.), *Material Discourses of Health and Illness*. London: Routledge.

Stenner, K. (1994). Young people talking about oral sex. Paper presented at the BPS Health Psychology special interest group, University of Sheffield, Sheffield.

Tapinc, H. (1992). Masculinity, femininity and Turkish male homosexuality. In K. Plummer (ed.), *Modern Homosexualities: Fragments of a Gay and Lesbian Experience*. London: Routledge.

Valdiserri, R. O., Lyter, D., Leviton, L. C., Callahan, C. N., Kingsley, L. A. and Rinaldo, C. (1988). Variables influencing condom use in a cohort of gay and bisexual men. *American Journal of Public Health*, **78**, 801–805.

Wight, D. (1993). Assimilating 'safer sex': Young heterosexual men's understanding of 'safer sex'. Paper presented at the seventh conference on Social Aspects of AIDS, South Bank University, London.

Yin, R. (1989). *Case Study Research: Design and Methods*, revised (ed.) Newbury Park, CA: Sage.

Young, A. (1973). Gay gringo in Brazil. In *The Gay Liberation Book*, pp. 60–67. San Francisco: Ramparts Press.

Zalduondo, B. and Bernard, J. M. (1995). Meanings and consequences of sexual-economic exchange. Gender, poverty and sexual risk behaviour in urban Haiti. In R. Parker and J. H. Gagnon (eds), *Conceiving Sexuality: Approaches to Sex Research in a Post-modern World*. London: Routledge.

PART IV

HEALTH BELIEFS, EXPLANATIONS, COMMUNICATION, EDUCATION AND PROMOTION

THE READINGS

16 **Cultural Diversity in Causal Attributions for Illness: The Role of the Supernatural**
Hope Landrine and Elizabeth A. Klonoff

17 **Illness Perceptions: A New Paradigm for Psychosomatics?**
John Weinman and Keith J. Petrie

18 **Consumer/Provider Communication Research: A Personal Plea to Address Issues of Ecological Validity, Relational Development, Message Diversity, and Situational Constraints**
Gary L. Kreps

19 **From Analysis to Synthesis: Theories of Health Education**
Jeff French and Lee Adams

20 **A New Evidence Framework for Health Promotion Practice**
Gordon Macdonald

The analysis and understanding of lay beliefs about health and illness is a key topic in health psychology. There is diversity in beliefs about the causes of health and illness depending upon culture, gender, age, and education. The type of procedures used to elicit the beliefs is also likely to affect the impression given of a group's belief system. Landrine and Klonoff (Reading 16) studied the cultural diversity of beliefs among the white population and also among ethnic minority groups using two methods for eliciting participants' judgements. People tend to attribute health and illness to a variety of lifestyle and interpersonal issues including stress, but they may also think of supernatural causes of illness that previous studies overlooked. People are unwilling to volunteer beliefs that they believe the investigator does not endorse including various types of supernatural causes. Having an accurate knowledge of a community's health and illness beliefs is essential contextual information in health communication, education and promotion.

This theme is discussed in the next reading by John Weinman and Keith Petrie (Reading 17). Using the **Illness Perception Questionnaire** Weinman and Petrie explore patients' understandings and beliefs about their illnesses. These illness perceptions relate in meaningful ways to the patients' coping responses and outcomes in the form of adherence, distress and disability. Weinman and Petrie argue that identification of patients' beliefs should play a more significant role in health care in facilitating adherence to treatment or recommended behaviour change. This interest in the patients' views is part of a larger scale movement towards understanding patients known as 'patient-centred health care'.

Psychological studies of communication in health care settings have addressed principally the issues that clinical settings bring to light, particularly patients' consultations with their doctors, e.g. patients' **adherence** to doctors' prescriptions and advice. At the experiential level, the focus has been the satisfaction with the processes and outcomes of consultations as 'consumers' of services given by doctors and other providers. The next article by Gary L. Kreps (Reading 18) of the National Cancer Institute in the USA gives a clear statement concerning health communications research. Kreps advocates a consumer-orientation to health communication with a broad agenda across the whole range of consumers and providers. Kreps points to the need for a relational orientation that examines how communications affect and are affected by the development of interpersonal relationships. Kreps also discusses the importance of the non-verbal cues in communication and of situational factors such as setting, age, gender, culture, and the medium of communication. Kreps' timely statement on health communications research reflects the state of the art at the turn of the century.

Applying psychology to health education and promotion presents an exciting challenge. **The Ottawa Charter** defined **health promotion** as the process of enabling people to exert control over the determinants of health and thereby improve their health. Relatively few articles and books address this field from a psychological point of view (Bennett and Murphy, 1997). The evidence base for

health education and promotion is becoming stronger but it is still perceived by many as being rather weakly supported (IUHPE, 1999). The remaining two readings in this section attempt to map these two domains.

French and Adams (Reading 19) construct a framework for health education with three basic 'models' associated with the different phases through which any individual, group or organisation intent on health improvements is assumed to pass: behavioural change, self-empowerment, and collective action. French and Adams argue that behavioural change at an individual level is the least potent method of improving health and consequently health education that aims to change personal behaviour is seriously flawed. The authors justify their hierarchy on the grounds that 'the most significant determinant of health is social and economic circumstance, and the least important individual health behaviour.' French and Adams condemn behavioural change models on ethical grounds using the argument 'who decides what is healthy and which behaviour should be changed'. Readers can make their own judgement about this, but if population groups and individuals are allowed the freedom to make choices and are given resources to determine health priorities for themselves, this issue evaporates.

Finally in this part, Macdonald (Reading 20) discusses health promotion 14 years after French and Adams published their paper. Some things never change. Like French and Adams, Macdonald also states that the principal determinants of health are socially, economically and politically controlled. Macdonald candidly admits that health promotion is founded more on ideology than theory. The little theory there is comes from other more established disciplines, especially psychology. Macdonald places special emphasis on social learning theory (Reading 6) and the theory of reasoned action (Ajzen and Fishbein, 1980; Reading 8). Macdonald proposes a three-stage framework for collecting evidence on behalf of health promotion: (1) Theoretical justification (input); (2) Systems analysis for understanding the process; (3) Quasi-judicious approach to indicators of success.

A new community orientation to health psychology beckons (Winett, King and Altman, 1989). Approaches from **community psychology** are engaging a new generation of health psychologists working in communities and organisations where many of the principle determinants of health have their origins. Community health psychologists will become more involved in community research and action as well as continuing to work with individuals. These activities require a broadening of awareness, methods and training, and a willingness to form alliances with community organisations. Any large-scale shift towards a community approach will be made easier if psychologists develop more sophisticated and contextually sensitive theories and methods.

Thinking about global health, psychological research is relevant to the achievement of human rights, a more ecologically sustainable planet, and poverty reduction. Health psychologists can contribute to these causes through community research and action alongside activists with skills and knowledge acquired through life experience.

HIGHLIGHTS, QUESTIONS, ISSUES

1 What role does ethnicity play in health care?
2 Causal beliefs include the supernatural. What are the implications for health care?
3 Why do patients frequently not adhere to their prescribed treatments?
4 In what ways might a person's beliefs about the cause of an illness influence their illness behaviour?
5 What skills are necessary for a clinical health psychologist?
6 If social and economic circumstances are the principal determinants of health and illness, what role can health psychology, education or promotion hope to play in improving health?
7 Is it ethical for the health authorities to try to change the behaviour of a population?
8 What is meant by 'empowerment'?
9 What role do communities play in promoting good health?
10 What skills are necessary for a community health psychologist?

16 CULTURAL DIVERSITY IN CAUSAL ATTRIBUTIONS FOR ILLNESS:
The Role of the Supernatural

Hope Landrine and Elizabeth A. Klonoff

Health Psychology researchers have examined people's beliefs about the causes of illness because these appear to be important mediators of health-related behavior and of illness outcomes. On the whole, studies have found that people tend to attribute illness to diet, heredity, weight, smoking, alcohol use, stress, lack of exercise, and other intrapersonal, natural variables (Affleck *et al.*, 1987; Blaxter, 1983; Taylor *et al.*, 1984; Tennen *et al.*, 1984). However, because these studies typically have employed white subjects, we do not know if these causal attributions hold for ethnic-cultural minorities.

Research in anthropology and sociology suggests that there is consider-able cultural diversity in beliefs about the causes of illness (Murdock, 1980) and that people of color attribute illness to other variables. Specifically, these studies have found that African-Americans (Bailey, 1987, 1991; Jackson, 1981; Snow, 1974, 1977), Latino-Americans (Castro *et al.*, 1985; Chesney *et al.*, 1980; Maduro, 1983; Martinez, 1978), Asian-Americans (Gould-Martin, 1978; Gould-Martin and Ngin, 1981), and Native-Americans (Csordas, 1989; Kane and Kane, 1972; Kunitz, 1983) attribute illness not only to the intrapersonal, natural variables listed above, but also to supernatural variables. These supernatural causes are often viewed as more significant than the natural ones, and the belief in their primacy may account for the multitude of ethnic differences in health-related behavior (Landrine and Klonoff, 1992). Investigating cultural differences in causal attributions for illness then becomes essential to providing effective behavioral medicine interventions for our diverse population as well as to decreasing the health gap between minorities and Whites, and such investigations also may limit the generaliz-ability of findings from White samples.

Investigating cultural diversity in causal attributions for illness, how-ever, may necessitate a change from the current methodology in which people are asked to generate causes of illness. This is because ethnic-cultural minorities may be reluctant to volunteer supernatural causes (e.g., God's punishment, the Evil Eye, hexes, bad blood, sinful thoughts, the imbalance of hot and cold) to white, middle-class American researchers, who are likely to view such attributions as 'superstitious' (Landrine and Klonoff, 1992). Thus, both supernatural and natural causes may need to be provided for subjects for possible ethnic differences to emerge. One obvious source of concern raised by providing causes for subjects to rate in terms of their importance, however, is that doing so may render the causes more salient; people may rate a cause as important because the experimenter called attention to it by providing it. This possibility must be investigated empirically.

The purpose of this study was to investigate possible ethnic-cultural differences in causal attributions for illness and to examine the extent to which free-form methodologies (asking subjects to generate causes) inhibit minorities from revealing their beliefs. We hypothesized that, when asked to generate their own causes for illness (free-form method), ethnic-cultural minorities would not differ from Whites in causal attributions. We predicted that both groups would generate similar natural and intrapersonal causes and rate these similarly in importance. We also hypothesized that, when provided with supernatural and natural causes, ethnic-minorities and Whites would not differ in the ratings of importance they assigned to the natural, intrapersonal causes but would differ in the importance they attributed to supernatural causes, with minorities rating supernatural causes as significantly more important. Finally, we hypothesized that providing causes would not increase their salience; we predicted that causes provided by the experimenter would not to be rated as more important than when those same causes were generated by the subjects.

Method

Participants

One hundred forty-nine undergraduates participated in the study. These 74 women and 75 men ranged in age from 18 to 61 years (mean = 28.5, SD = 9.3). Sixty were traditional college-student age (18–22) and 89 were older (23–61). Seventy-nine were White and 70 were people of color (35 Blacks, 23 Latinos, 12 Asian/Pacific Islanders). Fifty-one were Protestant, 46 were Catholic, 22 were Moslem or Buddhist, 2 were Jewish, and 28 listed their religion as None.

Procedure

Each subject completed a two-part questionnaire. In the first part, subjects were instructed to list the things that they personally believe cause illness (cause people to get sick) and then to rate each of these causes in terms of its importance on a scale that ranged from 1 (not at all) to 7 (extremely). The second part of the questionnaire provided subjects with 37 possible causes of illness, covering a wide range of supernatural, interpersonal, intrapersonal, and natural causes. Subjects were instructed to rate these experimenter-provided causes in terms of how important the subject personally believed them to be as causes of illness in general; these ratings were on the same 7-point scale.

Results

Subject-Generated Causes

Examples of subject-generated causes are shown in Table 16.1, along with the 25 categories into which such responses were coded. Subject-generated causes were coded by two researchers independently, with an inter-rater agreement of 99.97%.

Subject freely generated an average of 6 (± 3) causes of illness (Table 16.2), and there were no ethnic or gender differences in the total number of causes generated. The most frequently generated causes were diet (69.8%), stress (60.4%), contagion (40.9%), virus (40.3%), environment/pollution (36.2%), emotions (43.2%), Smoking (32.9%), drug use (32.9%), exposure to cold/weather (31.5%), and alcohol use (30.9%). These causes are similar to those found in the studies reviewed here, albeit those studies employed patient samples. Causes rated as most important (mean importance rating on a 7-point scale) were drug use (6.44), sexual activity (6.22), alcohol use (6.21), weight (6.14), lifestyle (6.13), stress (6.12), virus (6.12), smoking (6.07), lack of exercise (5.66), social status (5.55), and diet (5.54). Thus, causes generated by large percentages of the sample were not necessarily rated as the most important causes; the relationship between the number of subjects who generated the cause and the rating of importance they gave it appeared to be neither strong, linear, nor direct. For example, while diet was the most frequently generated cause, its rating of importance was relatively low. Similarly, while only 16.8% of the sample generated sexual activity as a cause of illness, its importance rating was high. This suggests caution in using the percentage of people who generate a cause as an indication of the cause's importance. Causes generated by most of the sample may not be those viewed as most important, but rather, those that the experimenter expects. We return to this point later in the analyses.

A series of chi-square analyses was run to assess ethnic differences in generating specific types of causes. As predicted, none of these 25 chi-squares was significant; minorities and Whites did not differ in the types of causes they freely generated. However, there were gender, age, and religion differences in the kinds of causes generated. Women were more likely than men to list specific stressors (e.g., a demanding boss, sexual harassment; $\chi^2 = 4.17$,

TABLE 16.1   **Coding Categories for Causes Generated by Subjects**

Stress	Specific stressors	Smoking	Alcohol use	Drug use
Stress Pressure	School Finals Work Demanding boss	Smoking Smoke Tobacco use	Drinking Booze	Drugs Taking drugs

Exercise	Lack of rest	Contagion	Virus/bacteria	Heredity
Lack of exercise Sedentary life	Improper sleep Not enough sleep Exhaustion Fatigue	People sneezing Kissing sick people Hanging around sick people	Virus Bacteria Nosocomial Infections	Genes Genetics Inherited Heredity

Emotions	Personality	Vitamins	Diet	Environmental
Loneliness Anxiety Worry Depression	Attitude Low self-esteem Hypochondria Type A Retentive	Vitamin deficiency	Eating junk Improper diet Eating eggs and red meat	Pollution Smog Pesticides/DDT Toxic waste Radioactivity Noise Pollen/ allergy

Weather/cold	Other natural	Unclassifiable	Status	Weight
Weather Climate Damp Catching a draft Getting wet Exposure to cold	Lack of immunity Vectors Bodily injury Toilet seats Chemical imbalances Accidents/trauma	Smells Social issues Body on rust Tongue depressors Fomites	Poverty Homelessness Sex Aging Poor housing	Beging fat Overweight Obesity Weight

Supernatural	Lifestyles	Sex	Hygiene	Relationships
Bad luck Fate Voodoo Religious guilt	Bad habits Partying Lifestyle	Anal sex Unsafe sex Unprotected sex Illicit sex Sex (STDs)	Cleanliness Not bathing Not brushing teeth Bad hygiene Not washing hands before eating	Marital disputes Bad kids Family trouble

$p < .04$), lack of rest ($\chi^2 = 3.60$, $p < .05$), heredity ($\chi^2 = 4.90$, $p < .02$), and emotions (e.g., anger, depression; $\chi^2 = 3.84$, $p < .05$), as cause of illness. Young people (18–22) were more likely than older people (233–61) to list emotions (e.g., anxiety; $\chi^2 = 3.69$, $p < .05$), lack of vitamins ($\chi^2 = 3.60$, $p < .02$), and cold weather ($\chi^2 = 10.64$, $p < .001$) as causes of illness. Finally, Protestants were more likely than others to list lack of exercise as a cause of illness ($\chi^2 = 13.32$, $p < .004$).

TABLE 16.2 Number of Causes Generated

Generated by	N	Mode	Median	Mean	σ	Range
Sample	149	6	5	6.42	2.89	0–16
Women	74	5	6	6.70	3.13	0–16
Men	75	6	6	6.13	2.62	1–14
Whites	79	4	6	6.58	2.87	0–15
Blacks	35	4,5	5	6.20	3.23	1–16
Latinos	23	5	6	6.57	2.94	2–14
Age 18–22	60	6	6	6.70	2.69	3–13
Age 23–61	89	5	5	6.22	3.01	0–16

Causes generated = 6 ± 3

Women vs men:	$t = 1.20$, ns
Whites vs Latinos:	$t = .02$, ns
Blacks vs Latinos:	$t = -.44$, ns
Whites vs Blacks:	$t = .63$, ns
Young vs older:	$t = .99$, ns

A MANOVA was run to assess ethnic differences in the importance ratings that subjects assigned to their own generated causes. The MANOVA for ethnicity (White vs Non-White) was not significant [$T^2 = 22.49$, $F(25,122) = 00.75$, $p < .79$]. As predicted, ethnic minorities did not differ from Whites in the importance that they attributed to any of the generated causes, including the supernatural causes. No gender differences were found [$T^2 = 44.92$, $F(25,122) = 1.50$, $p < .08$]. Thus, as hypothesized, no ethnic differences of any sort emerged when subjects were asked to generate their own causes of illness and to rate these in terms of their importance.

Experimenter-provided Causes

The 37 causes provided by the experimenters were factor analyzed using a principal-components analysis with an oblique rotation for simple factor loadings. Factors were retained on the basis of an eigenvalue ≥ 1.00, and items were retained on a factor if their loading was > 0.5; items with lower factor loadings were not retained in the factors. These results are shown in Table 16.3. Eight factors, accounting for 66.4% of the variance, emerged. These eight factors, rather than the 37 variables, were used as dependent variables in the analysis of possible ethnic differences in causal attributions.

MANOVA and follow-up ANOVAs for ethnic differences (White vs Non-White) on the experimenter-provided causes were conducted. For each subject, a total factor score for each of the eight factors was calculated by summing the ratings the subject had given to each cause in that factor. Table 16.4 shows those results along with the mean total factor score on each of the eight factors for Whites and people of color. As predicted, the only ethnic difference in causal attributions that emerged was on the supernatural factor. People of color rated causes as significantly more important than did Whites.

Table 16.5 presents a more detailed analysis of ethnic differences in making attributions for illness. The percentage of subjects who rated each

TABLE 16.3 Rotated Sorted Factors: Experimenter-Provided Causes

Causes	
I. Supernatural, 26.67% of variance	
Sinful thoughts	.871
Punishment from God	.869
The Evil Eye	.747
Sinful acts	.728
Lack of faith	.643
Hexes	.600
Payback	.549
Thin blood	.539
II. Interpersonal stress, 13.84%	
Emotions	.794
Relationships	.788
Worry	.654
Lack of harmony with nature	.623
Lack of harmony with others	.563
Envy	.526
III. Lifestyles, 6.25%	
Diet	.764
Hygiene	.759
Exercise	.694
Lack of rest	.555
Exhaustion	.544
IV. Personality, 4.49%	
Ambition	.873
Anger	.759
Anxiety	.640
V. Chance, 4.23%	
Bad luck	.830
Fate	.522
VI. Substance use, 3.84%	
Drinking	.793
Smoking	.789
VII. Natural, 3.65%	
Genes	.659
Sex	.606
VIII. Weather, 3.44%	
Weather	.781

supernatural cause as "important" (a rating ≥ 4) is shown, along with the mean ratings for Whites and people, of color and the ANOVA chi-square analyses are also shown in Table 16.5. As predicted (ANOVAs) people of color rated nearly all of the supernatural causes as more important than did Whites. The means for both groups, however, are low, which might imply that neither Whites nor people of color saw supernatural causes as important. The chi-square analyses indicate that this is not the case. For five of the eight supernatural causes, significantly more people of color than Whites rated these causes as important (a rating ≥ 4).

TABLE 16.4 **MANOVA and ANOVA of Ethnic Differences on Experimenter-Provided Causes: MANOVA, $T^2 = 17.83$, $F(8,132) = 2.12$, $p = .04$**

	Factor	Whites	People of color	SS	$F(1,139)$	p
I.	Supernatural	12.05	16.28	629.03	11.03	.001
II.	Interpersonal Stress	21.86	22.54	15.90	.23	–
III.	Lifestyles	26.45	25.79	15.08	.50	–
IV.	Personality	12.68	12.75	.18	.01	–
V.	Chance	3.79	3.91	.45	.08	–
VI.	Substance use	12.09	12.07	.01	.00	–
VII.	Natural	9.50	9.89	5.50	.63	–
VIII.	Weather	4.03	4.25	1.81	.64	–

Twelve of the causes generated by the sample matched causes provided by the experimenters. Table 16.6 compares the importance rating assigned to each of these 12 causes when the experimenter provided them versus when the subjects generated them (these are repeated measures). If providing a cause increases its salience, then causes should be rated more important when the experimenter provides them. As shown in Table 16.6, on the whole, this was not the case. Rather, for 6 of these 12 causes, there were no significant differences in mean importance ratings; for the remaining 6 causes, subjects rated the cause significantly more important when the experimenters provided it than when they generated it. While these six means differed significantly, the differences between the means were small (average difference, .46). Thus, no clear support for the salience hypothesis was found. In addition, while only 4.7% of the sample generated supernatural causes, large percentages of Whites and people of color alike rated these causes as important (a rating ≥ 4) when we provided them. Given that subjects do not appear to rate a cause as important simply because the experimenter provided it, these data probably reflect the importance that subjects attribute to these supernatural causes. Thus, these data suggest that people are reluctant to generate or volunteer causes that they believe the experimenter does not endorse, despite their belief that these causes are important.

Discussion

This study has four important results. First, as predicted and indicated in the literature of other social sciences, people of color endorsed more supernatural causes of illness than did Whites, and their tendency to endorse these causes – in addition to the natural ones – was the only difference between the two groups. This suggests considerable cultural diversity in causal attributions and so the need to be sensitive to these beliefs and their role in health-related behavior. While people of color rated supernatural causes as significantly more important than did Whites (Table 16.5), the

TABLE 16.5 ANOVAs and Chi-Square Values of Variables Constituting the Supernatural Factor

| ANOVA | Mean importance rating | | | | |
	Whites	People of color	SS	F^a	p
Sinful thoughts	1.39	2.13	19.38	11.85	.0008
Punishment from God	1.46	2.37	29.35	10.91	.001
The Evil Eye	1.20	1.81	12.79	10.56	.001
Payback for wrongdoing	1.51	2.15	14.21	7.08	.009
Hexes	1.38	1.81	6.43	4.52	.04
Sinful acts	2.34	3.03	16.84	3.94	.05
Thin blood	2.53	3.11	11.73	3.20	—
Lack of faith	2.58	2.91	3.82	1.18	—

| Supernatural cause | Rating | | | |
	High (≥ 4)	Low (< 4)	χ^{2b}	p
Sinful thoughts				
Whites	5 (6.3%)	74	6.24	.02
Minorities	14 (20%)	56		
Punishment from God				
Whites	5 (6.3%)	74	10.68	.01
Minorities	18 (25.7%)	52		
The Evil Eye				
Whites	1 (1.3%)	78	6.75	.01
Minorities	8 (11.4%)	62		
Payback for wrongdoing				
Whites	4 (5.1%)	75	6.70	.01
Minorities	13 (18.6%)	57		
Hexes				
Whites	4 (5.1%)	75	2.83	—
Minorities	9 (12.9%)	61		
Sinful acts				
Whites	19 (24.1%)	60	3.67	—
Minorities	27 (38.6%)	43		
Thin blood				
Whites	18 (22.8%)	61	7.77	.01
Minorities	31 (44.3%)	39		
Lack of faith				
Whites	24 (30.4%)	55	0.11	—
Minorities	23 (32.9%)	47		

^{a}df = 1,139 for each F.
^{b}df = 1 for each χ^2 value.

mean importance ratings for both groups were low (1–2 on a 7-point scale), suggesting that neither Whites nor people of color saw supernatural causes as important. On the other hand, however, the chi-squares (Table 16.6) indicated that more people of color than Whites rated these causes as important (a rating ≥ 4). Taken together, these findings suggest that there is not only considerable cultural diversity in causal attributions for illness, but also considerable diversity among minorities; some minorities view supernatural causes as very important, while others reject such attributions. These

TABLE 16.6 **Differences in Importance Ratings for Subject-Generated vs Experimenter-Provided Causes**

| | Mean rating | | | |
	Subject-generated	Experimenter-provided	Difference between means	Wilcoxon's T (2-tailed)
Diet (N = 103)	5.52	6.03	.51	435.00**
Virus (N = 59)	6.18	6.51	.33	135.00*
Drug use (N = 48)	6.42	6.39	.03	73.00
Smoking (N = 48)	6.10	6.08	.02	128.50
Weather (N = 47)	4.39	4.85	.46	86.50*
Alcohol use (N = 44)	6.11	6.38	.27	39.00
Exercise (N = 44)	5.60	6.11	.51	42.50**
Lack of rest (N = 39)	5.18	5.62	.44	50.00*
Heredity (N = 30)	5.28	5.80	.52	18.00*
Sex (N = 25)	6.35	6.24	.11	42.50
Relationships (N = 11)	5.23	5.27	.04	10.50
Lack of vitamins (N = 8)	4.38	4.38	.00	10.50

% of total sample rating each supernatural cause as important ($\geq$4)	
Bad blood	66.4
Lack of harmony w/ nature	44.3
Thin blood	32.9
Sinful acts	30.9
Selfishness	28.9
Lack of faith	22.8
Disobeying family	20.1
Punishment from God	15.4
Fate	14.8
Bad luck	14.1
Sinful thoughts	12.8
Payback for things done wrong	11.4
Hexes	8.7
The Evil Eye	6.0

*p < .05.
** p < .01.

differences cannot be attributed to education (because they were all college students) and so probably reflect acculturation, as well as membership in specific minority groups. It is important to note that large percentages of these minority, college-educated subjects endorsed supernatural causes and to consider the possibility that such beliefs may be largely independent of education.

The second finding was that reasonable numbers of the White college students in the sample also endorsed supernatural causes of illness (e.g., 30.4% rated lack of faith as 4 or higher in importance as a cause). This suggests that such health-related beliefs may hold for many Whites as well as for many people of color and, thereby, highlights the need for health psychology to begin to investigate such beliefs. If supernatural causes are inherently uncontrollable, the belief in them has important implications for help-seeking and symptom-reporting behaviors.

The third finding was that the methodology used to examine people's causal attributions for illness in part determines the nature of the results. Whites and people of color alike appear to be reluctant to generate supernatural causes for researchers who are likely to view such attributions as mere superstition; both groups fail to generate these, despite seeing such causes as very important. Thus, while only 4.7% of the total sample generated any type of supernatural cause, up to 66.4% rated such causes as very important (ratings > 4) when these were provided. This implies that the results in the literature regarding people's beliefs about the causes of illness may in part represent socially desirable rather than truthful answers; subjects may be telling us what they believe we believe and want to hear. Thus, data on health beliefs may need to be collected differently (*viz.*, by providing causes), not only to allow cultural diversity to manifest itself but also to acquire more accurate data.

The fourth finding was that providing such causes does not appear to increase their salience or importance, i.e., subjects did not uniformly attribute greater importance to causes simply because we provided them. Thus, providing causes does not appear to communicate that the experimenter views these as important (and so subjects rate them as important); rather, it may communicate that the experimenter views such cases to be acceptable, reasonable attributions and, so, facilitate honest responding.

This study is limited by the use of college students and must be replicated with medical patients to assess the generalizability of these findings. We do note that the literature reviewed here on minorities' supernatural attributions was based on medical patients [e.g., Bailey's (1991) sample of Black hypertensives and Csordas' (1989) Navajo cancer patients] as well as on normals. This suggests that such beliefs may hold irrespective of health status and that the beliefs then may be less of a reaction to illness and more of a manifestation of cultural concepts. Likewise this study is limited by the small numbers of subjects in each of the minority groups and did not permit an analysis of possible differences among the various minority groups. Replication with larger samples to permit such comparisons, as well as with medical patients, will clarify the generalizability of these results. In addition, many statistical tests were run, and this raises the possibility that at least a few of the differences found might be spurious: those differences, however, were predicted and, so, may argue against this possibility. Yet in light of such limitations, as we can at best only tentatively suggest that (a) generalizations regarding people's health beliefs, based on White samples, are inappropriate and (b) the methodologies we use to examine those beliefs may have contributed to our findings and obscured cultural differences.

References

Affleck, G., Tennen, H., and Croog, S. (1987). Causal attribution, perceived control, and recovery from a heart attack. *J. Soc. Clin. Psychol.* 5(3): 339–355.

Bailey, E. (1987). Sociocultural factors and health care seeking behavior among Black Americans. *J. Natl. Med. Assoc.* 79: 389–392.

Bailey, E. (1991). *Urban African-American Health Care.* University Press of America, Lanham, MD.

Blaxter, M. (1983). The causes of disease: Women talking. *Soc. Sci. Med.* 17(2): 59–69.

Castro, F. G., Furth, P., and Karlow, H. (1985). The health beliefs of Mexican, Mexican-American, and Anglo-American women. *Hispan. J. Behav. Sci.* 6(4): 365–383.

Chesney, M., Thompson, B., Guevara, A., *et al.* (1980). Mexican-American folk medicine. *J. Family Pract.* 11: 567–574.

Csordas, T. J. (1989). The sore that does not heal: Cause and concept in the Navajo experience of cancer. *J. Anthropol, Res.* 457–485.

Gould-Martin, K. (1978). Hot, cold, clean, poison and dirt: Chinese fold medical categories. *Soc. Sci. Med.* 12: 39–46.

Gould-Martin, K., and Ngin, C. (1981). Chinese Americans. In Harwood, A. (ed.), *Ethnicity and Medical Care.* Harvard University Press, Cambridge, MA, pp. 130–171.

Jackson, J. J. (1981). Urban Black Americans. In Harwood, A. (ed.), *Ethnicity and Medical Care,* Harvard University Press, Cambridge, MA, pp. 37–129.

Kane, R., and Kane, R. (1972). Determination of health care expectations among Navajo consumers. *Med. Care* 10: 421–429.

Kunitz, S. J. (1983). *Disease Change and the Role of Medicine: The Navajo Experience,* University of California Press, Berkeley.

Landrine, H., and Klonoff, E. A. (1992). Culture and health-related schemas: A review and proposal for interdisciplinary integration. *Health Psychol.* 11(4): 267–276.

Maduro, R. (1983). Curanderismo and Latino views of disease and curing. *West. J. Med.* 139: 868–874.

Martinez, R. A. (1978). *Hispanic Culture and Health Care,* C. V. Mosby, St. Louis, MO.

Murdock, G. P. (1980). *Theories of Illness: A World Survey,* University of Pittsburgh Press. Pittsburgh.

Snow, L. (1974). Folk medical beliefs and their implications for the care of patients. *Ann. Intern. Med.* 81: 82–96.

Snow, L. (1977). Popular medicine in a Black neighborhood. In Spicer, E. H. (ed.), *Ethnic Medicine in the Southwest,* University of Arizona Press, Tucson, pp. 19–95.

Taylor, S., Lichtman, R., and Wood, J. (1984). Attributions, beliefs about control, and adjustment to breast cancer. *J. Personal. Soc. Psychol.* 47: 489–502.

Tennen, H., Affleck, G., Allen, D., McGrade, B., and Ratzan, S. (1984). Causal attributions and coping with insulin-dependent diabetes. *Basic Appl. Soc. Psychol.* 5: 131–142.

17 ILLNESS PERCEPTIONS:
A New Paradigm for Psychosomatics?

John Weinman and
Keith J. Petrie

Typically, psychosomatic medicine has seen disease as an endpoint and has focused on the role of psychological factors in etiology or on the psychopathological consequences of illness. In contrast, the illness perception approach begins with the patient's experience of their illness and the main emphasis is on the patient's own model of their condition. Just as people construct representations of the external world to explain and predict events, patients develop similar cognitive models of the bodily changes that reflect either transient symptoms or more long-term illness. We believe that this approach has a widespread application in psychosomatic medicine, because all patients will construct working representations of their illness, and is therefore not limited to those who are regarded as having a pathological response to their condition.

The illness perception approach can be best understood in the context of wider changes in psychology. Since the emergence of contemporary cognitive psychology about 40 years ago [1], the focus on cognition and cognitive approaches has dominated all areas of psychological research and theory. For example, social cognition theories have been extremely influential in social psychology [2] and cognitive behavioral methods are now predominant in clinical psychology [3, 4]. Similarly, social cognition models are central to much research in health psychology as a basis for understanding health related behavior [5]. At the core of the cognitive approach is the view that individuals construct models, internal representations, or schema, which reflect their pooled understanding of previous experiences and are used for interpreting new ones and planning their behavior.

Early work on the perception of physical symptoms identified personal schema, selective attention, and the role of interpretive processes as important in making sense of both normal physiological changes [6] and the symptoms of illnesses such as diabetes [7]. Studies by Leventhal showed that patients' emotional response to changes in tumor size following chemotherapy for lymphoma were a function of their own personal cognitive model of the illness. From this and other studies Leventhal developed a self-regulatory model whereby patients construct their own representations or models which help them make sense of their experience and provide a basis for their own coping responses [8]. This representation contains core components, beliefs about the etiology of the illness, its symptoms and label, the personal consequences of the illness, how long it will last, and the extent to which the illness is amenable to control or cure. These components show logical inter-relationships. For example, a strong belief that the illness can be cured or controlled is typically associated with a short perceived illness duration and relatively minor consequences.

Patient models of their illness are, by their nature, private. In medical consultations patients are often reluctant to discuss their beliefs about their illness because they fear conflict with their doctor or risk being thought of as stupid or misinformed. Until recently, the assessment of illness perceptions has been by open-ended interviews designed to encourage patients to elaborate their own ideas about their illness. We have developed a new scale called the Illness Perception Questionnaire that can be used in a variety of physical illnesses and should make assessment more efficient for researchers [9]. Other recent developments have included scales for specific illnesses such as diabetes [10] and a scale to assess specific beliefs about medication [11].

In our work we have found patient models to vary widely across a number of chronic illnesses, even among individuals with the same disease severity [9]. For one person, diabetes may be seen as a relatively minor, time-limited condition caused by a diet high in sugar, whereas another with equivalent disease may see it as a genetic condition lasting for the rest of their life and with catastrophic consequences. From a clini-cian's perspective it may be very difficult to detect these differences in routine consultations, but they will become apparent in later responses to illness and compliance with treatment. Whereas most current research has focused on coping as a way of explaining illness adjustment and outcome, we believe that illness perceptions may not only explain the variety of coping responses to the same illness but also be more directly related to such outcomes as adherence, emotional distress, and illness-related disability [11, 12].

Some clear examples of the importance of patient models of illness in directing health-protective behavior, recovery, and disability can be seen in recent work on women with breast cancer in remission, myocardial infarc-tion patients, and chronic fatigue syndrome sufferers. Cameron [13] found, in a clinical placebo-controlled trial of tamoxifen, that the side effects of the active treatment served as a reminder of cancer risk and that by activating these illness representations they triggered associated worries about cancer, resulting in higher levels of breast self examination. A recent study that we conducted showed that patients' beliefs about their heart attack soon after admission to hospital predicted later attendance at a rehabilitation program and also how quickly patients returned to work and regained normal functioning [14]. The illness perception component most closely related to return to work and functioning was the perceived consequences of the heart attack. Those patients who believed that the illness would have a serious effect on their lives were slower to return to work regardless of the severity of the MI. We have found a similar pattern in chronic fatigue syndrome (CFS) sufferers. Those who catastrophized about the consequences of pushing themselves beyond their present physical state were more likely to report higher levels of fatigue and to be impaired in their ability to work and in their daily functioning [15].

Illness perceptions are central not only for understanding responses to specific diseases but also can be used to interpret patients reactions to genetic testing and health screening data, such as the results of cholesterol tests. Research on the understanding of genetic testing suggests that individuals have quite complex models of the risk of disease and find a simple genetically determined illness hard to conceptualize. More often people see the development of a genetic disease ultimately determined not only by their genetic make-up but also by lifestyle factors such as stress [16]. Much of the current evidence also points to the fact that systematic cognitive biases are employed by individuals to minimize the threatening nature of health information either by downplaying the seriousness of the test result, discrediting the accuracy of the test, or distorting the prevalence of a positive result. Recent work has also shown that memory for health information, such as the results of cholesterol testing was biased in a positive direction with individuals more likely to have reported their cholesterol level as being lower than it actually was, particularly if they had an unacceptably higher cholesterol level [17].

Many interventions currently used in the psychosomatic area such as cardiac rehabilitation and pain management programs, have been developed empirically and are not based on a sound theoretical understanding of underlying psychological processes. In our work to date we have identified a number of specific patient cognitions that can act as either a help or a hindrance to illness adjustment. We believe this approach offers an opportunity for researchers to identify the critical factors in patients' adaptation to illness. Furthermore, this approach can facilitate the development of interventions that modify or take account of specific patient cognitions such as beliefs about the cause or potential for control/cure of an illness. This view of the patient is compatible with the emerging view of health care that sees the patient as taking a more active and informed role. Patients are now requesting a more collaborative relationship in which their beliefs and expectations are acknowledged in consultations and treatment. Early exploration and identification of patients' perceptions offers the opportunity of minimizing or avoiding later difficulties such as nonadherence to treatment or recommended behavior changes. An understanding of illness perceptions is essential for effective patient management, and we believe that this approach has enormous potential for research and practice in the area of psychosomatic research.

References

1   Gardner H. The minds new science: a history of the cognitive revolution. New York: Basic Books 1985.
2   Fiske ST. Taylor SE. Social cognition. New York: McGraw-Hill 1991.
3   Beck AT, Emery G. Anxiety disorders and phobias: a cognitive perspective. New York: Basic Books 1985.
4   Hawton K, Salkovskis PM, Kirk J, Clark DM. Cognitive behaviour therapy for psychiatric problems: a practical guide. Oxford: Oxford University Press 1989.
5   Conner M, Norman P. Predicting health behaviour. Buckingham: Open University Press 1996.
6   Pennebaker JW. The psychology of physical symptoms. New York: Springer 1982.
7   Gonder-Frederick L, Cox DJ. Symptom perception, symptom beliefs and blood glucose discrimination in the self treatment of insulin dependent diabetes. In: Skelton JA, Croyle RT (eds). Mental representations in health and illness. New York: Springer Verlag 1991.
8   Leventhal H, Nerenz D, Steele DJ. Illness representations and coping with health threats. In: Baum A, Taylor SE, Singer JE (eds). Handbook of psychology and health. Hillsdale, New Jersey: Erlbaum 1984: 219–252.
9   Weinman J, Petrie KJ, Moss-Morris R, Horne R. The Illness Perception Questionnarie: a new method for assessing the cognitive representation of illness. Psychol Health 1996; 11: 431–446.
10 Hampson SE, Glasgow RE. Dimensional complexity of representations of diabetes and arthritis. Basic Appl Soc Psychol 1996; 18: 45–59.
11 Horne R, Representations of medication and treatment: advances in theory and measurement. In Petrie KJ, Weinman J (eds). Preceptions of health and illness: current research and applications. London: Harwood Academic Press 1997.
12 Moss-Morris R, Petrie KJ, Weinman J. Functioning in chronic fatigue syndrome: do illness perceptions play a regulatory role? Br J of Health Psychol 1996; 1: 15–26.
13 Cameron LD, Screening for cancer: illness perceptions and worry. In Petrie KJ, Weinman J (eds). Perceptions of health and illness: current research and applications. London: Harwood Academic Press 1997.
14 Petrie KJ, Weinman J, Sharpe N, Buckley J. Role of patients view of their illness in predicting return to work and functioning after myocardial infarction: longitudinal study. BrMJ 1996; 312: 1191–1194.
15 Petrie KJ, Moss-Morris R, Weinman J. The impact of catastrophic beliefs on functioning in chronic fatigue syndrome. J Psychosom Res 1995; 39: 31–37.

16　Michie S, McDonald V, Marteau T. Understanding responses to predictive genetic testing: a grounded theory approach. Psychol Health 1996; 11: 455–470.

17　Croyle RT, Sun YC, Hart M. Processing risk factor information: defensive biases in health related judgements and memory. In: Petrie KJ, Weinman J (eds). Perceptions of health and illness: current research and applications. London: Harwood Academic Press 1997.

18 CONSUMER/PROVIDER COMMUNICATION RESEARCH:

A Personal Plea to Address Issues of Ecological Validity, Relational Development, Message Diversity, and Situational Constraints

Gary L. Kreps

The Role of Interpersonal Communication in Health Care Delivery

I am pleased to see research attention being paid to the study of consumer/provider communication. I strategically use the terms 'provider' and 'consumer' here to encourage expansion of research attention to include the variety of health care delivery professionals and lay health care providers who work with patients, family members, and other concerned parties and advocates for patients. Too often, perhaps due to a medical bias, health care services research focuses myopically on only physicians' communication (Kreps, 2001). Not often enough, health services research also includes examinations of patients' communication. I list the consumer first in consumer/provider communication, to indicate the importance of recognizing the centrality of consumers in health care, advocating a consumer-orientation to health communication inquiry (Kreps, 1996).

I suggest a broad communication research agenda that examines the communication patterns and interactions of the wide range of relevant health care consumers and providers. Snetsinger vividly describes the many communication interactions that influenced her advocacy for her daughter, Clare, during treatment for cancer:

> The interactions extended from my immediate family, other relatives and friends to the medical community, including doctors and nurses, lab technicians, nutritionists, home health-care product suppliers, pharmacists, social workers, psychologists, support groups, various agencies, exercises and fitness trainers, yoga teachers, school personnel, religious advisors, counselors, and on to insurance

agents, bill collectors, bank-loan officers and even elected government officials. (1996, p. 400)

This is indicative of the many important interpersonal interactions that influence modern health care delivery and demand attention in consumer/ provider research.

Consumer/provider communication is an extremely important, complex, and growing topic for health care services research. (See Arora, 2001 for a state-of-the-art review of current consumer/provider communication research.) Interpersonal interaction between consumers and providers of health care is a primary channel used to develop and exchange relevant health information in the modern health care system. Relevant and timely health information is, perhaps, the most critical health care resource needed by both health care consumers and providers because accurate information is essential for guiding strategic health behavior, treatment, decision-making, and influencing psycho-social adaptation (Freimuth, Stein and Kean, 1989; Johnson, 1997; Kreps, 1988a; 2001).

> Health information includes the knowledge gleaned from patient interviews and laboratory tests used to diagnose health problems, the precedents developed from clinical research and practice used to determine the best available treatment strategies for a specific health threat, the data gathered in check-ups used to assess the efficacy of health care treatments, the input needed to evaluate bioethical issues and weigh consequences in making complex health care decisions, the recognition of warning signs needed to detect imminent health risks and direct health behaviors that have been determined to help individuals avoid these risks. (Kreps, 2001, p. 237)

Health care consumers and providers depend on communication to generate, access, and exchange relevant health information for making important treatment decisions, for adjusting to changing health conditions, and for coordinating health-preserving activities.

The quality of interaction between health care consumers and providers has direct influences on many important health care outcomes (Arora, 2000; Kreps and O'Hair, 1995). For example, at the onset of treatment, interpersonal communication is used to gather relevant information for accurate diagnoses. (Advanced health care equipment and technologies alone generally do not provide all the information needed to effectively diagnose health care problems.) Providers depend upon unique information provided by consumers about idiosyncratic symptoms, ailments, and history of care. Interpersonal communication is a critical process needed to effectively provide patients with informed consent when selecting appropriate treatment strategies. Interpersonal communication is the primary social process used to describe specific health care strategies to patients and to encourage patients to follow suggested treatment regimens. Interpersonal communication is also the process consumers and providers use to gather information needed to monitor responses to treatment and make decisions about refining care strategies over time. Consumer/provider communication is clearly an important health care delivery process that merits systematic investigation by health services researchers.

Sophisticated Consumer/Provider Communication Inquiry

I commend De Valck, Bensing, Bruynooghe, Kerssens, and Hulsmen (2001) for their fascinating research report examining the ways physicians break bad news to patients. This is a very important area of inquiry, that can help guide providers' communication during one of the more complex and challenging parts of health care practice (Buckman, 1984). Yet, after reading this research report, I am concerned that this study is indicative of the need to expand the depth of communication analysis in consumer/provider interaction research. In this chapter I provide some strategies for increasing the sophistication of the study of consumer/provider communication in health care. I strongly recommend researchers recognize the many complexities of interpersonal interaction in health care and endeavor to develop research designs and strategies that will enhance both the internal and external validity of research in this important domain.

Ecological Validity

Ecological validity is a primary research design issue that is essential to conducting rigorous and meaningful consumer/provider communication research. This involves faithfully operationalizing key variables and study conditions to mirror (as much as possible) the realities of health care delivery. 'Ecological validity refers to research that describes what actually occurs in real-life circumstances. To the extent that research procedures reflect what people do in the contexts in which their behavior normally occurs, confidence in the generalizability of findings to other people and situations is increased' (Frey, Botan and Kreps, 2000, p. 133). Patient/provider interactions occur within unique cultural frames, that need to be faithfully replicated in communication research for accurate examination (Cline and McKenzie, 1998). Artificial and contrived situations are used too often to study provider/patient communication research studies. Whenever possible, it is recommended that researchers study real health care providers in actual health care contexts, providing care to real patients, as opposed to examining student responses to manufactured health care situations. The ecological validity of research designs and the operationalization of key variables is crucial to the validity of health communication research.

Relational Orientation

Scholars are encouraged to adopt a relational orientation to consumer/ provider communication research that recognizes the evolutionary process of mutual influence, adaptation, and relational accommodation in human communication (DiMatteo and Lepper, 1998; Kreps, 1988b; Query and Kreps, 1996). Interpersonal communication is an ongoing developmental process and not just a set of discrete interactions. Past message exchanges inevitably influence future exchanges as they transactionally define and redefine interpersonal relationships (Cline and McKenzie, 1998). This relational process needs to be carefully examined in consumer/provider communication research.

Consumers and providers develop interpersonal relationships that define the ways they interact with one another. These relationships guide individual responses to communications. We must adopt a relational orientation to the study of consumer/provider communication to examine the ways the exchange of messages influence the establishment, development, and maintenance of interpersonal relationships in health care. This suggests that we must examine the perspectives of both consumers and providers in health communication research, and resist the tendency to glorify provider's communication, while ignoring the consumer's communication perspective.

There are many important relational communication issues that merit careful examination in consumer/provider interactions. For example, relational control and dominance are critical communication issues in health care delivery that must be better understood (Kreps, 2001; Thompson, 1998). Closely related to the issues of dominance and control is the way relational conflict is expressed and managed communicatively in health care (DiMatteo and Lepper, 1998). It is also imperative that the expression and relational development of empathy, therapeutic communication, social support, and psychosocial adjustment be examined in consumer/provider interactions (Thompson, 1998).

Verbal and Nonverbal Messages

It is most important for health communication scholars to focus broadly on the wide range of interpersonal messages health care consumers and providers exchange. Too often, consumer/provider research is limited to analysis of written transcripts of subject utterances. By examining only the words used in health care encounters, researchers are likely to lose critically important data about the richness of interpersonal communication exchanges and are likely to misinterpret the influences of the messages exchanged. Every verbal message used in health care encounters is surrounded and qualified by the use of nonverbal cues, such as vocal inflections, tone, and volume, as well as by eye-contact, body orientation, proxemics, and touching behaviors (Kreps and Thornton, 1992). These pervasive nonverbal cues are most important in interpreting the emotional tone of health care encounters; they are essential cues to understanding the quality of interpersonal communications.

Situational Constraints

Too often, consumer/provider communications is investigated without close attention to the unique social, historical, and environmental contexts in which they occur and that define the nature of health care interactions (Kreps, 1988b; Query and Kreps, 1996). Communication between consumers and providers in critical emergency care situations certainly differs from routine clinic visits. Private face-to-face interactions in a doctor's office are very different to more public interactions in a busy hospital ward during medical rounds. The nature of the health problem being attended to is also a distinguishing factor that defines the nature of health care interactions. Providing a diagnosis of advanced lung cancer or AIDS is certainly quite different than discussing more benign and routine health threats. Even the physical position of consumers and providers will influence the nature of health care interactions. Are the consumer and provider sitting across from each other at a desk? Is the patient in a prone position, lying in a hospital bed with I.V. and catheter tubes attached, while the health care provider looms above in a standing position? Is the female patient partially disrobed, vulnerable, and in an uncomfortable position on an examining table, while the gynecological conducts a pelvic examination and poses questions and asks for responses? These situational factors have dramatic influences on consumer/provider interactions.

A wide range of health communicator demographic factors, such as the age, gender, and cultural backgrounds of consumers and providers, significantly influence the nature of interpersonal health communications (Cline and McKenzie, 1998; Kreps and Kunimoto, 1994; Thompson, 1998). Attention to the specific channels and media used for interpersonal communication are also important consumer/provider interaction variables, especially as new communication technologies diffuse into society and influence modern health care delivery (Kreps, 2001). Are consumers and providers communicating face to face, over the telephone, via computer, with notes and letters? These are all critical situational factors that must be taken into account when conducting sophisticated consumer/provider communication studies.

Concluding Remarks

Investigations of the process of interpersonal communication between consumers and providers of health care are most important to evaluating and increasing understanding of modern health care delivery. This chapter is not meant to denigrate current consumer/provider communication research efforts; I celebrate the conduct of research in this rich and relevant area of inquiry. My purpose here is to encourage closer attention, greater sophistication, and in-depth analysis of communication between consumers and providers of health care. There is much to learn and much to be gained by such sophisticated health communication inquiry.

References

Arora, N.K. (2000). Impact of physician behaviors on patient outcomes: An evaluation of the patient's perceptions. Unpublished doctoral dissertation, University of Wisconsin, Madison.

Arora, N.K. (2001). Impact of physicians' communication behaviors on patient health outcomes: A critical examination of existing research. Unpublished research report, National Cancer Institute, Outcomes Research Branch, order # 263 SVP97196.

Buckman, R. (1984). Breaking bad news: Why is it still so difficult? *British Medical Journal, 288*, 1597–1599.

Cline, R.J., and McKenzie, N.J. (1998). The many cultures of health care: Difference, dominance, and distance in physician-patient communication. In L.D. Jackson and B.K. Duffy (eds), *Health communication research: A guide to developments and directions*. (pp. 57–74). Westport, CT: Greenwood Press.

De Valck, C., Bruynooghe, R., Bensing, J.M., Kerssens, J.J., and Hulsmen, R.L. (2001). Cue responding in a simulated bad news situation: exploring a stress hypothesis. *Journal of Health Psychology, 6* (5), 585–96.

DiMatteo, M.R., and Lepper, H.S. (1998). Promoting adherence to courses of treatment: Mutual collaboration in the physician-patient relationship. In L.D. Jackson and B.K. Duffy (eds), *Health communication research: A guide to developments and directions*. (pp. 75–86). Westport, CT: Greenwood Press.

Freimuth, V.S., Stein, J.A., and Kean, T.J. (1989). *Searching for health information: The Cancer Information Service model*. Philadelphia, PA: University of Pennsylvania Press.

Frey, L.R., Botan, C.H., and Kreps, G.L. (2000). *Investigating communication: An introduction to research methods*, 2nd edition. Boston: Allyn & Bacon.

Johnson, J.D. (1997). *Cancer related information seeking*. Cresskill, NJ: Hampton Press.

Kreps, G.L. (1996). Promoting a consumer orientation to health care and health promotion. *Journal of Health Psychology, 1* (1): 41–48.

Kreps, G.L. (1988a). The pervasive role of information in health and health care: Implications for health communication policy. In J. Anderson (ed.), *Communication Yearbook 11* (pp. 238–276). Newbury Park, CA: Sage.

Kreps, G.L. (1988b). Relational communication in health care. *Southern Speech Communication Journal, 53,* 344–359.

Kreps, G.L. (2001). The evolution and advancement of health communication inquiry. In W.B. Gudykunst (ed.), *Communication Yearbook 24* (pp. 232–254). Newbury Park, CA: Sage.

Kreps, G.L., and Kunimoto, E. (1994). *Effective communication in multicultural health care settings*. Newbury Park, CA: Sage Publications.

Kreps, G.L., and O'Hair, D. (eds) (1995). *Communication and health outcomes.* Cresskill, NJ: Hampton Press.

Kreps, G.L., and Thornton, B.C. (1992). *Health communication: Theory and practice* (2nd edition). Prospect Heights, IL: Waveland Press.

Query, J.L., and Kreps, G.L. (1996). Testing a relational model of health communication competence among caregivers for individuals with Alzheimer's disease. *Journal of Health Psychology*, 1(3), 1(3), 335–352.

Snetsinger, W.R. (1996). Communication and critical illness: A narrative account. *Journal of Health Psychology*, 1, 399–403.

Thompson, T.L. (1998). The patient/health professional relationship. In L.D. Jackson and B.K. Duffy (eds). *Health communication research: A guide to developments and directions.* (pp. 37–55). Westport, CT: Greenwood Press.

19 FROM ANALYSIS TO SYNTHESIS: Theories of Health Education

Jeff French and Lee Adams

Health education has developed somewhat untraditionally with problem solving and application preceding theory. (Dwore and Matarazzo, 1981)[1]

The vast majority of people involved in its practice realise that a clear understanding of the aims and nature of health education is vital if we are to be effective. In addition, a clear understanding of our purpose and methodology is essential if we are to communicate effectively with each other, and with people unfamiliar with the discipline.

One of the first tasks, if a way is to be found through the maze of health education theory, is to be clear about terminology. It is worth, briefly, exploring what is meant here by theory, model and ideology. For the purposes of our discussion, these three terms are defined as follows:

"An ideology is the science of ideas, ideas at the base of some economic or political theory."[2]

"A theory is an explanation or system of anything, an exposition of the abstract principles of a science or art speculation, a hypothesis, a reasoned explanation."[3]

"A model delineates a conceptual framework, identifying appropriate methods for the achievement of defined goals."[4]

Models by this definition are underlined and based on theories, which in turn are based on ideologies. Thus the sequence: ideology – theory – model can be identified.

To complicate matters even further, within health education two kinds of models can be identified – theoretical models and planning models. Here we concentrate on theoretical models but by planning models we mean those constructs which outline steps or sequences that health educators carry out in order to identify or fulfil stated aims. Planning models arise from theoretical models. Examples of planning models would be the OPT-EVAL model[5] and the PRECEDE model.[6] It is interesting to note that so far planning models have been developed for only one theoretical model, the behavioural change model. One task of health education is to develop other planning models for other theoretical positions.

Confusion over theory is made acute by the fact that those authors who have published papers use a plethora of terms when describing essentially similar positions. In addition, authors seldom make distinctions between theoretical and planning models of health education.

We should, then, ask ourselves whether with sufficient work it might be possible to establish a reasonably simple yet sound theoretical base upon which good practice in health education can be built? The answer to this quesiton is, we think, a tentative yes. Already the theoretical base of health education is more developed than many people realise. One of the main problems, however, is that because so little has been published, few people are aware of this groundwork.

Models of health education that have been developed to date encompass a wide range of approaches to enhancing health, but most have been descriptive in that they reflect current assumptions and practice rather than act as guidelines to new ways of working and thinking about health education. This latter role must begin to be fulfilled if theory is ever to become a positive stimulating force rather than a purely reactive and analytical position. Progress in health education can only be brought about if the symbiotic nature of theory and practice is recognised, and the fact that progress in one sphere will not be achieved without and through progress in the other.

Whilst we believe that it is possible to establish a sound theoretical base for health education, it is also probable that this base will never solidify into an unmoving foundation. This position is due to the nature of the underlying influences on health education, theoretical models of humanity, society, health and education, which are all "fundamentally contested issues".[7] The direct and cumulative influences of these elements would appear to indicate that we are extremely unlikely to reach a point, or even a plateau, now or at any time in the future when a definitive map of health education will be possible.

Theoretical Mapping

Since 1972, attempts to produce conceptual maps of health education have been based on one of six approaches. These approaches range through typologies based on models of health;[8,9] those that focus on the process of health education;[10,11,12,13] those that categorise health education in terms of its content;[14,15] typologies based on theories of communication;[16] typologies that seek to match models of health and models of education;[17] and typologies based on levels of intervention and the locus of power and control.[18] It has also been argued[19] that the phrase health education is a generic term like medicine, and it is suggested that specific approaches to various health education issues need to be developed individually and that the degree of overlap between approaches to different topics may be small. In a chapter of this length it is not possible to give a fuller account of the usefulness of each of these methods of mapping health education. After detailed consideration[20,21] we consider that the most practical solution is one that focuses on the ultimate aim of the model and its processes.

A Tri-phasic Map of Health Education

Set out in Table 19.1 are three health education models derived from a critical analysis of previously published typologies,[20,21] and also through discussion and consideration with a wide range of colleagues. This typology is not offered as a definitive map but rather as an aid to discussion and to facilitate a common set of terms for use by health educators when describing their own theoretical position.

Previous attempts to map health education have been largely confined to producing lists or typologies of various approaches to health education without exploring the nature of the relationships between the different approaches. It is interesting to note that in the two attempts[17,18] that have been made to explore these relationships, a similar mapping method, namely the use of two pairs of bi-polar co-ordinates to construct a quadrant map in which various models can be located, have been used. These attempts to map the interrelationship between various models of health education are useful in that they illustrate how a conception of health education relates to a number of selected co-ordinates. However, if we are to rely on this mapping method, it would be necessary to produce numerous maps in order to cover the many philosophical and methodological issues affecting the nature and practice of health education. In addition, these and other attempts to map health education theory fail to find a theoretical rationale for the relationships that exist between the various approaches to health education chosen, and the authors fail to state their own positions, preferring instead to portray health education as an eclectic or selective field of study. This eclectic position adopted by all authors to date is challenged by the authors of this paper, for we feel that all models of health education theory or practice are not equal or equally valid.

Health education lacks, therefore, a theoretical map which sets out the range of health education practice, that illustrates the nature of the relationship between various approaches to practice, and which is supported by a theoretical rationale.

We have attempted to construct such a theoretical map, based on the three models of health education depicted in Table 19.1. Figure 19.1 depicts a methodological continuum of health education practice. Implicit is the acceptance that generally to be healthy and educated leads to increasing degrees of autonomy and to be unhealthy and uneducated leads to decreasing autonomy, and consequently loss of power and control over one's health status.

The three levels of health education depicted in Figure 19.1 serve to represent phases through which an individual, group, or organisation may

TABLE 19.1

Model of health education	Behavioural change	Self-empowerment	Collective action
Aim	To improve health by changing people's behaviour.	To improve health by developing people's ability to understand and control their health status to whatever extent is possible within their environmental circumstances.	To improve health or changing environmental, social, and economic factors through community involvement and action.
Model of health	Optimum biological functioning and role performance.	Spiritual physical mental environmental and social harmony, Individual feeling of active well-being. Adaptation, happiness, high self-esteem and positive self-concept.	Health is a socially defined concept related to individual and group norms. Health is a symptom of the interplay between enviromental, social, economic, influences on the population.
Model of humanity (Women/Men)	Rational decision-maker. Mechanistic, knowable animal. Elitist. People are innately bad.	People are spiritual entities struggling for personal fulfilment and are innately good.	People are social animals and rational problem-solvers. People are born value neutral.
Model of Society	Positivist, Hierarchical and stratified. Ordered by consensus and conformity. Mechanistic in functioning. Operates according to universal mechanistic laws. Elitist groups guard and develop the society's high culture. Change brought about through slow evolution.	Society is organic plant or animal-like in nature. Society interacts with the environment and varies with time and place. Society is in a state of constant change and review and is not governed by universal laws. Humanist.	Materialist. Conflict between factions and various interests is the driving force of society. Society is dynamic and ever-changing.

(Continued)

TABLE 19.1 (Continued)

Model of health education	Behavioural change	Self-empowerment	Collective action
Model of education	Classical humanist. Education is an assimilative process and is geared to the acceptance of pre-defined knowledge values and standards. Educated people contribute to the ordered development of society.	Progressivist. Education is primarily about discovery and experience, through which growth is attained. Education should encourage people to question, reform and change their society.	Reconstructionist. Education is one of the main agents of change in society, and is concerned with the development of better citizens. Education is a social process pursued through projects problem-solving and discovery Education aims to renew society.
Example of methods	Propaganda. Mass media and mass participation. Attitude modification. Behaviour modification. Self-management techniques. Administrative and legislative change.	Lifeskills training. Value clarification. Self-help groups (coping). Counselling. Pastoral care and the promotion of self-esteem.	Advocacy. Knowledge and consciousness-raising compaigns Self-help groups (campaigning). Community action. Pressure groups. Popular legislation Administrative change Economic change.
Examples of evaluation criteria	Compliance rates, mortality and morbidity rates Knowledge increase attitude change, behavioural change Externally assessed.	Improved self-esteem. Improved lifeskills improved understanding improved decision-making improvement often self-assessed.	Morbidity and mortality rates. Knowledge increase attitude change increased involvement in action for health Externally assessed.

Phase three   Collective action model
                   of health education.

Phase two   Self-empowerment model of
                   health education.

Phase one   Behavioural change model of
                   health eduction.

FIGURE 19.1   **A Triphasic Map of Health Education**

pass as they become, or seek to help others become, more empowered in relation to their health status. Each of the three phases has its own ideological stance regarding the nature of health education, people and society (see Table 19.1). The ideologies behind each phase and the associated methodologies all seek ultimately to improve health, but at each phase "improved health" is defined in very different terms. Blocks may be encountered between each phase of the hierarchy. These blocks arise out of the reluctance on the part of a group or organisation to accept new or different systems of beliefs or ways of working, or because of structural or administrative constraints. It is unlikely that beliefs will be drastically and suddenly changed and a new set assimilated; rather health educators should seek to bring about a gradual shift from one level to the next. The hierarchy should not be interpreted as a fixed set of stages through which it is necessary to pass; it may be possible to miss or jump a particular phase.

Justifying the Hierarchy

The three models of health education proposed are set out in a hierarchy, because we believe that the most significant determinant of health is social and economic circumstance, and the least important individual health behaviour. This assertion is backed by a wealth of evidence, linking health status to issues, such as poverty,[22] employment,[28] low income,[23] and social class.[24] We place self-empowerment next in our hierarchy because we believe that personal, psychological well-being is the next most important determinant of health status.[25,26] In addition, self-empowerment approaches to health education are also ethically more justifiable than those based on behavioural change. Finally, we place behavioural change methods of health education at the bottom of our hierarchy for three reasons. First, there is growing evidence to contradict the assumption that individual behaviour is the primary determinant of health status. Whilst it is true that habits like lack of exercise, cigarette smoking, over-eating, or excess alcohol consumption do lead to death and disability, research suggests that more basic social, economic and environmental factors are both the direct cause of some diseases and important determinants of the health-damaging behaviour that leads to other ill-nesses. Social stress, economic crisis, community disruption, environmental and occupational pollution have all been linked with outcomes of such diseases as hypertension, mental illness, cardiovascular disease cancer, murder, suicide and accidents.[27,28,29,30,31]

A second weakness of behavioural change methods of health education is their lack of effectiveness.[32,33,34,35] Health education programmes that have tried to get people to stop smoking, drink less alcohol, use contraception, or avail themselves of preventive health services have been at best only partially successful. With a few notable exceptions, health educators have had little success in bringing about lasting behavioural changes, even among groups of voluntary subjects. In addition, the ultimate criteria by which such a model of health education should be judged is its contribution to the decrease in morbidity and mortality for a particular condition. By this measure we lack any convincing evidence that changes in individual behaviours brought about by health education have had any effect on public health.

Finally, there are ethical objections to behavioural change models of health education. Who decides what constitutes healthy behaviour? And who decides which behaviours should be changed? Even when health education of this type proceeds with people's consent, the very approach dictates that the health problem is located within the individual. In other words, the victim is blamed for the condition.

In summary, health education which aims to change personal behaviour has serious flaws. It is often based on a superficial analysis of what causes health and disease; it is based on dubious ethical assumptions; and it has not been shown to be a particularly effective strategy for public health.

Conclusion

The triphasic map of health education described above has resulted from a critical analysis of previous attempts to map health education. The map serves to indicate the nature and scope of health education, but also puts forward the notion of a hierarchical relationship between models based on the philosophical premise that health education should ultimately seek to promote the maximum possible autonomy and control of health status by individuals and groups.

References

1 Dwore R. Matarazzo J. The behavioural sciences and health education. *Health Education* 1981; May/June: 4–7.
2 *Chambers Dictionary,* Edinburgh: WR Chambers, 1979.
3 *Chambers Everyday Dictionary.* Revised edition. Edinburgh: WR Chambers, 1979.
4 Baric L. 1982. A new ecological perspective emerging for health education. *Journal of the Institute of Health Education.* 1982; **20 (4)**: 5–21.

5   Edward L. Delivering health education programmes. A model *Health Values*. 1982; **6 (6)**: November/December: 13–19.

6   Green LW, et al. *Health education planning: A diagnostic approach*. California; May field Publishing Co, 1980.

7   Gallie WB. *Essentially contested concepts*. Report of Meeting of the Aristotelian Society at 21 Bedford Square, London. March 12th, 1956.

8   Burkett A. Models of health. In *Reading in community health*. Ed. J Clark London: Churchill Livingstone, 1983.

9   Collins LF. Concepts of health education: a study of four professional groups. PhD Thesis. University of Southampton, 1983.

10 Tones, BK. Health education: prevention or subversion? *Journal of the Royal Society of Health*. 1981; **3**: 114–117.

11 Grigg, C. Ideas towards a procedural checklist for performance indicators in health education. Unpublished paper Polytechnic of the South Bank. Health Education Research Project. January, 1985.

12 Hornsey E. Health education in pre-retirement education: a question of relevance. *Health Education Journal* 1982; **41 (4)**: 107–113.

13 Seymour H. Health education versus health promotion – a practitioner's view. *Health Education Journal*. *1984*; **43 (2&3)**: 37–38.

14 Draper P. Three types of health education. *British Medical Journal*, 1980; **281**: 493–495.

15 Draper P. Tackling the diseases of ignorance. *Journal of the College of Health* 1983; **1**: 23–25.

16 Dorn N. First working paper on types of health education *Collaborative work on health education*. London: ISDD, 1981.

17 Beattie A. The Repertoire of health education. Seminar paper. Institute of Education. 25th March, 1980.

18 Nutbeam D. Health education in the NHS: The differing perceptions of community physicians and health education officers. *Health Education Journal*. 1984; **43 (4)**: 115–119.

19 Baric L. *Measuring family competence in the health maintenance and health education of children*. WHO, Geneva, 1982. IEH/HED/82.I.

20 French J. *A review of contemporary health education models*. M.Sc. Dissertation. Chelsea College, University of London, 1984.

21 Adams L. Health education in whose interest? MA Dissertation, Kings College, University of London, 1984.

22 Layard R. *The causes of poverty*. Royal Commission of the distribution of income and wealth. Paper No. 5, London: HMSO, 1978.

23 Le Grand J. 1982. *Strategy for equality*. London: Allen & Unwin, 1982.

24 Townsend P. *Inequalities in health. The Black Report*. London: Penguin Books, 1982.

25 Jourard S. Landsman T. *Healthy personality*. 4th edition. London: Macmillan Press, 1980.

26 Claxton G. Swami A. *Wholly Human*. RK Press, 1981.

27 Eyer J. Hypertension as a disease of modern society Int. *J. Health Service*. 1975; **5**: 539–558.

28 Brennet MH. Economic change and heart disease mortality. *Am. J. Public Health* 1971; **61**: 606–611.

29 Brenner MH. *Mental illness and the economy*. Cambridge: Harvard University Press, 1973.

30 Winkelstein W. Contemporary perspectives on prevention. *Bull N. Y., Acad. Med* 1975; **51**: 27–38.

31 Waldron I. Eyer J. Socioeconomic causes of the recent rise in death rates for 15–24-year-olds. *Soc. Sci & Med.* 1975, **9**: 283–396.

32 Cohen CI, Cohen EJ. Health education: Panacea, pernicious or pointless? *New England Journal of Medicine* 1978; **299**: 718–720.

33 Freunberg N. *Shaping the future of health education: from behavioural change to social change*. Health Education monograph, 1978.

34 Milio N. A framework for prevention: changing health-damaging to health-promoting life patterns. *Am. J. Public Health.* 1976; **66**: 435–439.

35 Gatherer A. *Is health education effective*? Monograph No. 2. London: Health Education Council, 1979.

A NEW EVIDENCE FRAMEWORK FOR HEALTH PROMOTION PRACTICE

Gordon Macdonald

If we are to achieve things never before accomplished, we must employ methods never before attempted (Francis Bacon, 1618)

Concern for the effectiveness of health promotion is not new. Debates and opinions about it go back more than a quarter of a century.[1] More recently there has been a mushrooming of publications concerned with the evidence base for health promotion interventions and the need to establish a new framework for measuring effectiveness.[2-4] Most of the discussion, however, focusses on the need to establish an alternative to the traditional approach that views the randomised control trail as the gold standard for health-related research.[5] Academics and researchers have tended to argue that experimental-design methodology is not usually appropriate for public health and health promotion research since many of the dependent variables cannot be controlled for, and with community- and population-based studies, there is the further problem of 'contamination' between intervention and control groups. They have argued, and there is a degree of consensus, that non-experimental designs and/or phenomenological qualitative research provides us with a better understanding of the attitudes and values that people attach to health, and give a much better understanding of the process that leads (or not, as the case may be) to change at the individual, community or policy level.

However, this polemic debate about evaluative methodology falls far short of a comprehensive approach to effectiveness which rests on a more fundamental principle. What academics and researchers in health promotion have to grapple with is a realisation that evaluation of interventions, while critical and important, do no more than tinker with the margins of health care and health status. The determinants of health are considered to be socially, economically and politically controlled[6] and what we need to construct is an approach to effectiveness that takes into account the emerging evidence that supports this broader agenda. It is necessary to re-design the evidence framework, to recognise the structures and systems that militate against health, but also to place greater emphasis on the theoretical bases for interventions and to produce novel indicators of sucess. While such a new re-designed evidence base of effectiveness may be conclusive, it is possible to construct a 'best evidence scenario' for success, that acknowledges the wider picture of health (and disease) and offers a chance to address the World Health Organization's 'core issue' of equity and how best to tackle the growing inequalities in health status.

This chapter sets out a re-designed framework with three distinct elements for the collection of best evidence. This framework takes into account the work of researchers in public health and health promotion, but also includes work from other related disciplines and fields. It argues that this evidence collection can in turn identify and correlate with the three stages of a typical health promotion or public health intervention, namely the *input*, *implementation* and *output* stages. The three phases of evidence collection collaed with these stages are then *theories* to support intervention type (*input*), *systems analysis* to understand the process of change (*implementation*) and finally the *judicious use of 'best evidence'* to help assess the *output* (Table 20.1).

Theories to Justify Input

Because the debate on the status of health promotion as a distinct discipline is still inconclusive, the theoretical bases for much of its work remains with other more established disciplines.[7,8] Generally writers acknowledge this, and consequently tend to justify interventions on the basis of ideology rather than theory.[9] Theory is concerned with making sense in some systematized way of observable phenomena, such that it can predict future changes and/or outcomes. However, the phenomena being observed in normal health promotion work are very difficult to control for. How can we differentiate between relevant and non-relevant phenomena when we are uncertain about dependent variables, especially in the community and population health arenas? We must nevertheless begin to make sense of the phenomena under investigation and build a framework for further observation such that we have, eventually, a kind of 'tower block' of phenomenological understanding in which we can start developing theoretical assumptions about how best to promote population health.

It is only by first understanding phenomenological relationship that we can then go on to develop models, which in turn inform embryonic health promotion theories. It is the theory that should drive the intervention, not the research method. The research method should be informed by the embryonic theory. The results of the intervention developed this way can then go on to embellish or reinforce the theory. Unless we have sound theory, we cannot really assess the evidence, since evidence is based on

TABLE 20.1 **Collecting Evidence for Health Promotion: a Three-stage Model**

Stage 1 Theoretical justification for approach (Input)
Stage 2 Systems analyses for process understanding (Implementation)
Stage 3 Quasi-judicious approach to indicators of success (Output)

method and outcome, and method should rely on theory. The old adage, 'there is nothing so practical as a good theory', is true.

However, despite these misgivings about the theoretical base to health promotion and its lack of a unifying theory to help understand social and community phenomena, some theories, typically from other disciplines, are used to help develop our understanding of individual behavioural change, community change and organisational change.

Individual Behavioural-change Theories

Social learning theory is perhaps the widest applied and most accepted 'feeder' theory for health promotion practice at the individual level. It builds on multidisciplinary observations between an individual and his or her environment, and has developed as a theory through positing and testing ideas on why individuals behave in ways they do, given certain social and environmental norms. It is a theory developed by researchers from many different backgrounds but has been applied to health, principally by Bandura.[10] Examination of the theory in detail is not the purpose of this paper, but key components of the theory help to inform health promotion practice. The notion of *reciprocal determinism*, whereby an individual learns continuously to assess his or her interaction with society and the environment, and sub-consciously to accept behavioural influence, is central to health promotion practice. Bandura further develops this idea through the notion of *self-efficacy*, which proposes that individuals will undertake certain behaviour changes only if there is a belief in them being successful. This links to both the health belief model and the stages of (behavioural) change model, both of which reinforce social learning theory.

The *theory of reasoned action* first proposed by Ajzen and Fishbein,[11] is predicated on the assumption that the intention to act (the *conative* domain) is the best way to determine action or behaviour in the future. This intention to behave is in turn regulated by attitudes and beliefs about behavioural change (will the change be of benefit?) and by behavioural controls (the development of self-esteem or internal locus of control) which determine the degree to which individuals feel that they have control over a behaviour and which is closely linked to *self-efficacy* (outlined above).

Both of these theories have influenced health promotion and public health interventions in relation to alcohol, smoking and drug-taking education[12] and been part of broader community-based interventions that also rely on theories to do with community change.[8]

Theories to Inform Community Change

Innovation diffusion theory, or *communication of innovations,* is one of the most tested theories that helps predict how a new product, idea or practice will be disseminated within a given community. Rogers[13] claims that it can substantiate some 103 generalisations about how and why communities change or adopt an innovation. It has been widely used in planning health education and health promotion research and interventions[14,15] and is potentially the most useful community-focused theory.

Coleman[16] provides public health with another less-tested theory but one which is currently at the top of the policy agenda in the developed industralised world, namely a *theory for collective decision-making.* This theory includes the notion of social capital, which refers to the norms and relationships in a community, characterised by trust, co-operation and civic engagement for mutual benefit. Investment in social capital is considered to be a public health benefit for a given community[17,18] and is a topical issue for debate and research.[19]

Theories to Inform Organisational Change

Theories that predict patterns in organisational change are less well-developed than behavioural- and community-based theories but are nevertheless of interest to the public health specialist. The origins of theory in this area are in schools of management and the driving force behind them was to improve organisational performance in the commercial sector. Increasingly however, they are being translated into theories or more appropriately models for organisational change.[20] Some of the theory in this area links to innovation diffusion theory and its application to adoption of innovations in organisations. Fullan[21] for example identifies three main phases in the change process in schools as organisations. Firstly the *initiation* phase, which includes the mobilisation of staff and resources and the adoption of decision-making processes; secondly the implementation phase which is characterised by putting the changes into place; and thirdly the *institutionalising* phase which means embedding the changes into the organisational system.

Coalition theory[22] adds an extra dimension to theories linked to organisational change and alliances in that it proposes four hypothetical parameters for effective organisational collaboration across sectors.

1 Resource allocation and size by specific alliance organisations predicts the commitment to coalition.
2 Reward for organisations from coalitions should be greater than if they were to act alone.
3 Organisations will coalesce often for the sake of non-utilitarian links if the links or ties produce positive benefits for individuals creating them.
4 Resource allocation may well decide the format for decision-making, with the largest contributor calling the loudest shots!

Coalition theory and theories of organisational change help to provide an understanding of how organisations and agencies might respond to interventions and programmes and help share the intervention type.

Systems Analyses to Aid Process and Implementation

All of us live in some form of social and economic system. There is growing evidence that it is the system or social and economic structure that affects the way we live and work and consequently our health.[23] The World Health Organization[24] produced a booklet highlighting ten structural social determinants of health that illustrated the power of the system in producing (ill) health. These determinants include work (and unemployment), transport, income distribution, poverty, social cohesion and social organisations. Many of the aspects of the 'system' have been researched and analysed, and a convincing case for demonstrating the effect the system has on health has been made.[6] However, more work is needed to elicit the many systemic causes of ill health. This needs to be done at both the social-system level and the organisational level since both contribute individually and synergistically to ill health and health inequalities.

Systems research and analysis could focus on, and in some cases build on, the evidence surrounding sustained stress on individual and social health, and the impact of welfare policies on the life course, from early childhood to the 'oldest' elderly. It could focus on the effect of unemployment in an economy that values work, employment status and material rewards. More research is needed on the relationship between income distribution, income inequalities, relative poverty and health although many researchers are making justified claims in this area.[25]

In a much more difficult area, more detailed scientific research is needed on the impact of social support or its absence on health. How do we define social support and how do we measure it? How is social support related to social cohesion? Is it a form of social capital? Mustard[18] and Stansfield[26] address many of these questions but are the first to recognise that further research and evidence is needed. The Health Education Authority[27] has recently commissioned a large-scale study and review of research in this vital area.

Organisations are central to many social systems and play a critical role in policy development and indeed in public health and health promotion practice.[28] While organisational change theory is critical for informing *input* in an intervention, it is also of crucial importance in understanding the *process*. Organisations are after all a potential setting for health promotion. Indeed, the whole settings approach to health promotion is predicated on the power and influence of organisations; yet we know little about how organisations are structured, about how decisions are made within them, or about how they have an impact on health. What little work has been done in health promotion tends to focus on the take-up of innovations, particularly in school.[14] However, Grossman and Scala[29] have developed a scheme for understanding the role of health promotion in organisational settings and argued persuasively that although we have organisations that deal with illness we have nothing structured in organisational or social-system terms for health. Theory generation and applied research as outlined above would undoubtedly help our understanding of how interventions are *processed* through organisations and systems. Health promotion must play a key role in developing a system or systems for health. At the moment we have systems that are designed to tackle ill health (social security, national health *care*, sickness benefits, etc) but no structures to tackle and promote health. Systems and organisations need to become health 'competent' so that they may be incorporated into a society that sustains health in the course of everyday interactions, and is not dependent on responsive or reactive interventions by agencies and professionals charged with promoting health.[29]

Best Evidence to Support Output

The area that has received the most attention and debate concerning effectiveness and evidence is that concerned with output or outcome.[5,30-32] Most researchers and academics have either analysed research methodology to improve output effectiveness or have suggested ways of developing new output indicators. There now seems to be a growing consensus that traditional approaches to public health and health promotion research that mimic experimental research designs associated with biomedicine are inappropriate. The favoured alternatives are methods associated with phenomenological research designs, that are qualitative and interpretative, or, even better, employ triangulation methodology.[33]

What is needed, however, within this new consensual framework is an agreed and rigorous set of indicators that help, directly and indirectly, to assess effectiveness and therefore contribute to the evidence base for health promotion. Direct indicators may be considered those that are a direct result of an intervention. They may occur immediately following the programme, for example a change in knowledge, or they may occur some time later, for example a change in morbidity or indeed mortality. This is sometimes considered to be the difference between output (immediate) indicators and outcome (longer-term) indicators. Tones[33] has used *proximal* (immediate) and *distal* (longer-term) to differentiate between the two. Examples of these differences are discussed elsewhere,[30] but it seems more than reasonable to suggest and apply the use of direct, immediate and longer-term indicators, to measure the success or otherwise of a public health intervention. This was certainly the case with national HIV/AIDS interventions in the 1980s, where change in knowledge was, in this particular health area, a precursor to a change in practice, which in turn led to changes in morbidity and mortality, at least in the gay communities.[34]

However, many health promotion interventions have unintended consequences that may have an effect on the public health in both the immediate, intermediate and longer term but were not planned at the outset (or the *input* stage) of the intervention. For example, a programme designed to get young people more physically active could be promoted through schools, clubs and the wider community. It may have both an immediate and longer-term effect on young people's fitness levels, and perhaps weight, but it may also encourage *indirectly* and *incidentally*, community participation and social networking. This could lead to an increased sense of belonging and social cohesion which, in turn, could improve the community's social capital, a major contemporary issue for research into health determinants. This by-product of an intervention may be called an *indirect proxy* indicator. That is, indicators could be developed and measured that were unintended outputs at the start of a particular programme, but which produced some health-status change in the longer term. This has happened frequently in the area of clinical medicine (witness the accidental discovery of viagra as a treatment for impotence). The difficulty would be in recognising the emergence of health-status change as a result of these indirect proxy indicators.

A second type of proxy indicator is one where an indicator is used deliberately, but instead of the primary indicator of change, as a measure that the intervention may be having an effect. For example, a new policy to improve public transport in order to reduce traffic congestion (the primary indicator) may also have an effect on respiratory diseases. Reductions in respiratory illness may then be a possible *direct proxy indicator* for reduction in traffic congestion.

Proxy indicators (direct and indirect) and output and outcome indicators may help to provide a much sounder base for evidence of effect in health promotion and public health, but that evidence still needs to be assessed. Although effectiveness reviews have developed as a 'science' and produced a hierarchy of evidence for therapeutic interventions, with randomised controlled trials at the top of the hierarchy,[35] the assessment is still just that. It involves making decisions about 'good' and 'bad' evidence based on what is available and accessible. The same can be said about assessing health promotion effectiveness. We have to make a decision about effectiveness based on the best available evidence in much the same way as a judge or jury decides the merits of a prosecutor's case. This quasi-judicious method, first developed by Bromley[36] to help analyse case studies in psychology, has been developed by Tones[33] in relation to health promotion. We may not be able to *prove* effectiveness absolutely, but we may be able to assess effectiveness, using various research methodologies, identifying best practice and utilising primary and proxy indicators, to the point of pulling the case 'beyond reasonable doubt', or proved 'on the balance of probabilities'. This best-case or best-evidence scenario is one that should not be discounted on the basis of being 'unscientific': it is making best use of the science and best use of judgement and experience. It is in essence a new form of methodological triangulation.

Conclusion

Health promotion is still a relatively young discipline, but its theoretical base, its increasing emphasis on understanding the process that interventions go through, and the search for meaningful indicators of success, only help it to mature and gain acceptance. It will have to be more ready, however, to recognise explicitly; the growing theoretical evidence for determining the nature of an intervention; the value of acknowledging the power and influence of social systems and organisations in determining health; and the importance of using quasi-judicious approaches to assessing primary and proxy indicators of success.

This chapter has demonstrated a three-stage model for a new evidence framework for health promotion that will, it is hoped, help to develop the discussion around evaluation and effectiveness. New methods are needed to address new concepts and practices. Bacon's words are still very apt.

References

1 Gathere A, Parfitt J, Porter E, and Vessey M. *Is Health Education Effective?* Health Education Monograph 2. London: Health Education Council. 1979.

2 Perkins E, Simnett I, and Wright I (eds). *Evidence Based Health Promotion.* Chichester: John Wiley and Sons, 1999.

3 Scott D, and Weston R (eds). *Evaluating Health Promotion.* Cheltenham: Stanley Thornes. 1998.

4 Davies J, and Macdonald G (eds). *Quality, Evidence and Effectiveness in Health Promotion: Striving for Certainties.* London: Routledge, 1998.

5 Speller V, Learnmouth A, and Harrison D. The search for evidence of effective health promotion. *British Medical Journal* 1997: **315**: 361–3.

6 Blane D, Brunner E, Wilkinson R. *Health and Social Organization.* London: Routledge, 1996.

7 Bunton R, and Macdonald G (eds). *Health Promotion: Disciplines and Diversity.* London: Routledge, 1993.

8 Glanz K, Lewis F, and Rimer B. *Health Behaviour and Health Education: Theory Research and Practice.* San Francisco: Jossey-Bass, 1997.

9 McQueen D. The search for theory in health behaviour and health promotion. *Health Promotion International* 1999: **11**(1): 27–36.

10 Bandura A. *Social Foundations of Thought and Action: a Social Cognitive Theory.* Englewood Cliffs, NJ: Prentice Hall, 1986.

11 Ajzen I, and Fishbein M. *Understanding Attitudes and Predicting Social Behaviour.* Englewood-Cliffs, NJ: Prentice Hall, 1980.

12 Bennet P, and Murphy S. *Psychology and Health Promotion.* Milton Keynes: Open University Press, 1997.

13 Rogers E. *Diffusion of Innovations.* New York: Free Press, 1983.

14 Macdonald G. Innovation diffusion theory and its application to health education in schools. In: Siddell M, Jones L, Katz J, Peberdy A (eds). *Debates and Dilemmas in Promoting Health*. London: Macmillan, 1997.

15 Parcel G, Perry C, and Taylor W. Beyond demonstration: diffusion of health promotion innovations. In: Bracht N (ed), *Health Promotion at the Community Level*. Newbury Park, CA: Sage, 1990.

16 Coleman J, Katz E, and Menzel, H. The diffusion of innovations amongst physicians. *Sociometry* 1957: **20**(4): 48–63.

17 Putnam RD. The prosperous community: social capital and public life. *American Prospect* 1993: **13**: 35–42.

18 Mustard J. Health and social capital. In Blane D, Brunner E, Wilkinson R (eds) *Health and Social Organisation*. London: Routledge, 1996.

19 Campbell C, Wood R, and Kelly M. *Social Capital and Health*. London: HEA, 1999.

20 Goodman RM, Steckler A, and Kegler MC. Mobilising organisations for health enhancement: theories of organisational change. In: Glanz K, Lewis F, Rimer B. *Health Behaviour and Health Education: Theory Research and Practice*. San Francisco: Jossey-Bass, 1997.

21 Fullan M. Change processes and strategies at the local level. *Elementary School Journal* 1985: **85**(3): 24–9.

22 O'Neill M, Lemieux V, and Groleau G. Coalition theory as a framework for understanding and implementing inter-sectoral health related interventions. *Health Promotion International* 1997: **12**(1): 79–85.

23 Marmot M, and Wilkinson R (eds). *Social Determinants of Health*. London: Routledge, 1999.

24 World Health Organisation. 1998.

25 Bartley M, Ferrie J, and Montgomery S. Living in an high unemployment economy: understanding the health consequences. In: Marmot M, Wilkinson R (eds), *Social Determinants of Health*. London: Routledge, 1999.

26 Stansfield S. Social support and social cohesion. In: Marmot M, Wilkinson R (eds), *Social Determinants of Health*. London: Routledge, 1999.

27 Health Education Authority. *Evaluation of a Social Action Research Project: Tackling Inequalities in Health*. London: HEA, 1999.

28 Harrison D. Social system intervention. In: Perkins E, Simnet I, Wright L (eds), *Evidence-Based Health Promotion*. Chichester: John Wiley and Sons, 1998.

29 Grossman R, and Scala K. *Health Promotion and Organisational Development. Developing Settings for Health*. Vienna: IFF/WHO, 1993.

30 Macdonald G, Veen, C, and Tones K. Evidence for success in health promotion: suggestions for improvement. *Health Education Research* 1997: **11**(3): 367–76.

31 Green J, and Tones K. Towards a secure evidence base for health promotion. *Journal of Public Health Medicine* 1999: **21**(2): 133–9.

32 Nutbeam D. *Health Promotion Effectiveness – the Questions to be Answered*. International Union for Health Promotion and Education/Commission of the European Union, 1999.

33 Tones K. Beyond the randomised control trail: a case for judicial review. *Health Education Research* 1997: **12**(2): i–iv.

34 Aggleton P, Oliver C, and Rivers, K. *The Implications of Research into Young People. Sex, Sexuality and Relationships*. London: HEA, 1998.
35 Sheldon T, Song F, and Davery-Smith, G. *Purchasing and Providing Health Care*. Edinburgh: Churchill-Livingstone, 1993.
36 Bromley DB. *A Case Study Method in Psychology and Related Disciplines*. Chichester: John Wiley and Sons, 1986.

PART V

CRITICAL HEALTH PSYCHOLOGY

THE READINGS

21 **Critical Approaches to Health Psychology**
    Wendy Stainton Rogers
22 **Theorizing Health and Illness: Functionalism, Subjectivity and Reflexivity**
    Henderikus J. Stam
23 **A Discourse-dynamic Approach to the Study of Subjectivity in Health Psychology**
    Carla Willig
24 **Health Psychology, Embodiment and the Question of Vulnerability**
    Alan Radley
25 **Possible Contributions of a Psychology of Liberation: Whither Health and Human Rights?**
    M. Brinton Lykes

The Reader has taken a journey through the more significant regions of **mainstream health psychology**. We have explored the definition and scope of health psychology, sampled the main theoretical ideas, and looked at how people's health behaviour, and beliefs influence the impact of health communication, education and promotion. With the exception of the study of 'romantic rationality', everything so far has been within the positivist tradition of theory or model testing using quantitative measurement and empirical methods.

There is no question that we have been journeying through a dynamic and fast-growing field. The early explorers have avidly worked within the terms of the biopsychosocial model using the methods of the natural sciences, namely, experimental and quasi-experimental observational methods in the laboratory or clinic and the hypothetico-deductive method. Methods and theories have been drawn from Western experimental social and cognitive psychology of the 1960s and 1970s. We have seen also that, while all the time wearing the mantle of science, a morality of individual responsibility for health has been woven into the definition of behavioural health, recently mooted in revised form as a new definition for health psychology.

When an area grows as rapidly as health psychology, it is not surprising that diverse and conflicting views are expressed about the direction and shape of the field. In this final part, we enter new territory, that occupied by those authors and workers who are critical of the mainstream and who propose some radically different approaches. These authors argue for new agendas, theories and methods. As we explore some of the pools and eddies that have sprung up in opposition, we discover that the mainstream is contestable, as much for its practice as for its theoretical assumptions.

Wendy Stainton Rogers (Reading 21) challenges the mainstream by heralding an interpretative, social constructionist, **critical health psychology.** Stainton Rogers discusses the radical and humanistic influences on a view of health and illness that recognises 'a multiplicity of alternative realities'. She argues that we need to analyse the **discourse** of people's accounts of reality as they talk about it, not try to discover a single, fixed reality because there is probably no such thing as far as psychological reality, or realities, are concerned. Stainton Rogers introduces different versions of discourse analysis based on the level and kind of analysis that is performed: meaning, use or function. That familiar target, the biomedical model, then surfaces again. Stainton Rogers challenges biomedicine's claim to having a superior source of knowledge or **epistemology**. *Both biomedicine and health psychology are ideological and ethnocentric in nature.*

Henderikus Stam (Reading 22) makes a passionate plea for theory, which he states: 'is not a luxury or what one does in one's armchair after a hard day of collecting data' ... it is one of the most crucial steps of our entry into the world of health, disease and illness precisely because it establishes nothing less than our political, epistemological and moral grounding'. (305) Stam addresses problems of vagueness and lack of definition with the biopsychosocial model (see also Part I). He draws attention to the dramatic organisational and sociological changes occurring in the health care systems of Western countries about which mainstream health psychologists remain silent. Stam then discusses the conditions that are necessary to make health psychology a responsible profession, especially foresight and truth within a collective activity that defines a universe of outcomes. No prescriptions for how mainstream health psychology should try to reform itself are on offer, except to say that Stam sees no progress following prescriptive lists of methods or formulas!

Carla Willig (Reading 22) focuses her criticism on the mainstream theories of health beliefs and behaviour (reviewed in Part II). Willig argues that people's accounts about health and illness are attempts to make sense of experiences using culturally available accounts that do not have to be either rational or predictive of behaviour. Thus **discourse analysis** is an alternative approach to the study of beliefs as stable, rational, cognitive units. Willig describes two principal kinds of discourse analysis, discourse as performative practice, and Foucauldian discourse analysis that is concerned with power and 'ways-of-being'. In this reading, discourse and subjectivity are shown to be interrelated within both the discourse of experts (focus 1) and lay people (focus 2). Willig argues for a new **social constructionism** health psychology which moves beyond the assumption that beliefs about the self are entirely transient, will-of-the-wisp phenomena. She argues that people internalise and reify our bodily and mental experiences so that labels that we apply become frameworks for interpreting how we subjectively feel. Discourse, subjectivity and practice are necessarily bound together. Discourse, subjectivity and practice interplay to produce a positioning that allows behaviour change. This provides an alternative reading to that of the mainstream models.

Alan Radley (Reading 24) argues that health psychology essentially agrees with the assumption in biomedicine that the body is the substrate of the mind with a Cartesian body-mind divide. We have an embodied mind, not a body and mind. The concept of the 'self' as an entity is equally artificial (see Part II). 'Health psychology's *assumptions about the body are shaped by the moral and ethical values that medicine has adopted*'. Specifically, medicine, and psychology, are constituted in difference, in separation, of doctor from patient and of person from body, Radley believes. Morality and vulnerabilty then become marginalised and not studied. Radley argues that psychology, like medicine, has 'married its scientific objectivity to the clinical gaze of the doctor'. The argument urges a radical re-reading of what it means to evaluate a patient in diagnosis or treatment. If these activities are to be truly caring as well as technical feats, then it is the vulnerability and fragility of the patient as a person just like oneself that have to be given priority.

Our final reading by M. Brinton Lykes (Reading 25) explores the potential contributions of a psychology of liberation for the practice of health psychology. The context for this paper is the abject poverty of a large proportion of the human population. To quote the World Development Report (2000/2001), Attacking Poverty:

> The world has deep poverty among plenty. Of the world's 6 billion people, 2.8 billion – almost half – live on less than $2 a day, and 1.2 billion – a fifth – live on less than $1 a day, with 44 percent living in South Asia ... In rich countries fewer than

1 child in 100 does not reach its fifth birthday, while in the poorest countries as many as a fifth of children do not. And while in rich countries fewer than 5 percent of all children under five are malnourished, in poor countries as many as 50 percent are. (p. 3)

The context of M. Brinton Lykes' work, which she terms **participatory action research**, is the intense social and psychological devastation and anomie among Mayan women in rural Guatemala following several decades of violent struggle and civil war. Lykes follows the principles of **liberation psychology** as practised by Ignacio Martin-Baro (1994), a Jesuit priest who worked until his assassination among the dispossessed victims of violence and poverty in war-torn Guatemala. In the West, the 1948 United Nations Declaration of Human Rights is seen as a mark of achievement in the field of human rights. However, Lykes points out that this convention is itself embedded within individualistic ideology, making no reference to the collective rights of indigenous peoples whose rights are held by the total community: 'Social context, that is culture, the environment, and history, are key to the very definition of human rights and to whom they adhere'. Lykes gives a moving and inspiring account that should be a valuable resource and a stimulus to others.

Health psychology in the 21st century, whether mainstream or critical, clinical, public, community or liberatory, promises to be ever more challenging. In Lykes' words, the challenge 'is to be, to do and to think among those whom we seek to understand, with those with whom we seek to speak truth to empower, among those with whom we seek to create greater economic justice and social equality'. Like water flowing down a mountain, this great field has the potential to follow multiple streams, falls and rivulets, each seeking its ultimate path of service and truth. Beware those who say they have found the only way or the only truth. There will always be another and another.

HIGHLIGHTS, QUESTIONS AND ISSUES

1 Stainton Rogers argues that mainstream health psychology is ideological? What reasons does she give for this statement?
2 List some problems with the positivist approach to health psychology.
3 Stam is critical of the mainstream. List three of his main criticisms.
4 Willig produces a new approach to the understanding of health behaviour, discourse-dynamic theory. Describe three key features of this theory and contrast these with the mainstream approach.
5 Design a hypothetical intervention for any familiar health issue based on Willig's discourse-dynamic approach.
6 Why is health psychology a moral activity as much as a technical one?
7 Radley discusses the relationship of patients with their doctors and psychologists as one of 'difference'. What does he mean by this?
8 What does Radley's paper tell us about the nature of caring?

9 What does Lykes mean by 'liberatory psychology'?
10 How could ideas from liberatory psychology be applied in Western industrialised countries?

21 CRITICAL APPROACHES TO HEALTH PSYCHOLOGY

Wendy Stainton Rogers

Because psychology as a discipline sits (some would say uncomfortably) between the biological and the social, its scope is incredibly broad-ranging. Its 'hardest', most biological subdisciplines (such as psychopharmacology and psychophysiology) are worlds apart from its 'softest' (such as psychodynamics or humanistic psychology). But the latter apart, the 'glue' that generally holds the discipline together is a prioritization of scientific method as its means of enquiry, and positivism as its theoretical foundation. Within the mainstream, this applies as much to social as to other kinds of psychology. Up until quite recently the vast bulk of work done under the heading of 'social psychology' has been experimentally based. It adopts an hypothetico-deductive approach to addressing the social aspects of behaviour and experience which parallels that used to address the study of cognitive processes (such as memory and perception), and indeed other areas such as developmental and clinical psychology. As a result, health psychology (whether it is regarded as a subdiscipline of social or clinical psychology) tends almost exclusively to draw upon scientific method to pursue its research questions.

In the broader domain of social psychology, however, things are changing. We are now seeing the emergence of a new paradigm, which can be loosely termed *critical social psychology*. My purpose in this chapter is to describe what is meant by critical social psychology, how it differs from the mainstream and examine some of its implications for health psychology. I also describe some recent work in medical sociology and anthropology which is pursuing a similar line, especially in its use of postmodern theorization to challenge positivistic approaches in those disciplines. However, to understand the implications of this new critical movement for health psychology, we need to know something about its historical origins. It is with this that I begin.

Interpretative Social Psychology

Paradigm innovation in psychology is nothing new. Just as the term *nouvelle cuisine* has been used repeatedly for at least 200 years to describe whatever was the latest fashion in cookery, psychology (even in its much shorter history) has continually been challenged by 'new paradigms'. Each one is presented as a dramatic refutation of a worn-out previous order, offering fresh insights and innovative solutions. It is almost as though theories – like computers – have built-in obsolescence. After a while they are superseded by new, improved models, offering greater power and more efficiency.

Up until about 10 years ago, the most ubiquitous 'new paradigm' in social psychology was that of 'interpretational social psychology', offered in slightly different versions by people like Ken Gergen and Edward Samson in the USA, and Rom Harré in Britain. Their 'new improved model' of psychology was most notable in its critique of the methods used for studying the social. First, they argued against experimentation, claiming that what goes on in the laboratory tells us little of any significance about the social aspects of how people think, act and feel in real-life settings. This, they asserted, in viewing people as 'idealized automata' which could be studied 'in bland, anomic environments' (Harré, 1979), profoundly undervalues the inventiveness and subtlety of the way people make sense of their social world, and the critical importance of the sociocultural context within which they commonly do so. Equally they criticized conventional qualitative approaches (such as interviews) pointing out that these are social events 'heavy with ambiguity, and shot-through with efforts at self-presentation by both the interviewer and interviewee' (Harré, 1979). Psychometric methods fared no better under their critique; so far as these are concerned, Harré argues:

> The use of questionnaires with limited range questions … which effectively preclude elaborations and reinterpretations … means that the concepts deployed are predetermined. The effect of this is to produce not a representation of the social world being studied, but the representation of the shadow cast upon the social world by the prior conceptual apparatus deployed by the person who constructed the questionnaire. (Harré, 1979, p. 115)

They therefore proposed a 'new psychology' which stresses the interpretational nature of human meaning-making and which investigates the purposive, rule-making and rule-following, constructive aspects of personhood and social interaction. With hindsight even its originators now admit that the main impact of this 'new paradigm' was on theory. Apart from a few exceptions (see, e.g. Antaki, 1981), for all the criticism directed against mainstream methodology, there was no immediate spate of methodological innovation. This early challenge to the mainstream, however, did set the scene for what was to come later – a much more fundamental shift towards the study of discourse, and the drawing of postmodern theorizing (at that time only really being seen as relevant in disciplines such as art history, film theory and literature) into the field of psychology.

This new 'interpretative social psychology', though only fully developed some 10 years later, was first launched in the late 1960s and early 1970s at a time of a more general social upheaval in Western society; an upheaval comprised of somewhat paradoxical tensions between:

- *a radical challenge,* based upon a renewed interest in the broader sociological and cultural influences upon behaviour and a commitment to social responsibility.
- *a humanistic challenge,* based upon an increasing interest in the uniqueness of each individual's humanity and a commitment to self-expression and self-actualization.

The Radical Challenge

In the first of these, emergent feminist, Marxist, politically radical and civil-rights groups were drawing attention to the way that the mainstream approach constituted a 'psychology of the "good guys"' (Moscovici, 1981) – that is, one which assumes that the values, abilities and understandings of white, middle-class men are universal and normative compared with those of, say, women, ethnic minorities and the poor (which are, thereby, cast as 'deviant'). By this account, orthodox social psychology fails to acknowledge (let alone do anything to help) the effects of inequality, disadvantage and oppression. It treats these as no more than variables (such as 'social class') which, via intervening variables (such as 'fatalistic' attitudes), lead to dysfunctional behaviour (such as unhealthy lifestyles).

In this way mainstream social psychology was seen to collude with – if not actively promote – a victim-blaming ideology and to bolster the status and power of dominant groups in society. Probably the best account of this perspective is Parker's (1988) *The Crisis in Modern Social Psychology, and How To End It.* Within this movement there was a call to make social psychology more accountable to and enabling of those over whom it holds power (such as the children it tested and the clients it therapized); less ethnocentric, homophobic and misogynist; and more willing to acknowledge the impact of social, economic and cultural influences.

The Humanistic Challenge

The other influential challenge to social psychology at this time arose from the humanistic movement and ideas coming out of self-actualization and personal construct theories. They were most disturbed by the mechanistic aspects of behaviourism, which they saw as dominating social psychology at the time. They saw it as portraying people as passive and mindless, denying the individual creativity, spiritual values and human ingenuity which they saw as most crucial to what being human is all about. Probably the most influential text here is Reason and Rowan's (1981) *Human Inquiry: A Source-book for New Paradigm Research*. Within this movement there was a call to make social psychology more respectful of individuals' self-determinacy and capacity for self-definition; less dehumanizing; and more willing to acknowledge the value of spiritual experience and its meaning in people's lives.

Modernism and Postmodernism

For some time, these two challenges pulled psychology in rather different directions. More recently, however, they have been superseded by what has been variously termed the *discursive turn*, postmodernism and 'a climate of perturbation' (cf. Stainton Rogers, R., Stenner, Gleeson, and Stainton Rogers, W., 1995). The last is probably the least contentious, since it implies no more than a manifold of intellectual movements engaged in troubling, shaking-up and generally undermining orthodox social psychological approaches, in particular their Modernist foundations.

Ibañez (1991) defines 'Modernity' as 'the joint outcome of the technical achievements of scientific knowledge, and the rhetoric of scientific truth'. (It may be worth noting that this is not a consensual definition, its meaning being different, for example, within the study of literature). Modernity, by Ibañez's definition, began in the West in the 16th and 17th centuries at the time historians call 'the Enlightenment'. Modernity can be viewed as the product of the post-Enlightenment project, a social movement intended to replace irrationality with reason, superstition with empirically validated 'true knowledge', and thereby to pursue human betterment. Throughout the 18th and 19th centuries the Modernist world-view was socially and culturally legitimated, not just in the domain of science itself but more broadly by the promotion of ideas of progress, democracy and individual freedom through the institutions of society such as education and the law.

The human sciences were both central products of Modernism, and have played a significant role in constructing the Modern worlds in which we live today. Our Modern 'industrial' and 'postindustrial' worlds are strongly influenced by ideas drawn from the biological and social sciences. Notions of individuals-in-society, of interpersonal relations, of 'selves', social forces and so on – which were constructed by and through Modernism – are now so established, so taken-for-granted, that we have become beguiled into seeing them as 'natural'. It feels to us as though the world as we experience it is the one 'real' world – a world in which personality, attitudes, cognition, affect and behaviour are 'real things', and other things which are meaningless to us (such as magic, curses, divine intervention) are mere phantoms of an earlier consciousness from which rationality and science liberated us.

A central tenet of Modernism (particularly the High Modernism of the 19th century) is that it represents the end-state in a three-stage developmental theory of civilization, namely:

First of all there was:	**a primitive world** understood in terms of a belief in magic and superstition.
This was superseded by:	**a pre-Modern world** understood by way of religious belief, where an all-knowing God was viewed as the sole authority of what constitutes true knowledge.
Which was itself then superseded by:	**a Modern world** understood through science and rationality, where science is held to be the sole source of objective, empirical knowledge.

This 'up the mountain' tale of human progress (cf. Kitzinger, 1987) thus prioritizes science as a superior form of knowledge, all other forms (such as magic, religion and traditional folklore) being (within Modernism) regarded as invalid – not really knowledge at all, but merely 'beliefs' and 'myths'. At the very core of Modernity is thus a rhetoric of scientific truth.

Within its own theorizing it is a distortion to think of 'postmodernism' as simply a further, fourth stage in the progression – though, at first sight, this is what the term seems to imply. However, it does challenge the central claim of Modernism to have access to a single, coherent, real world of nature which lies 'out there' waiting to be discovered; and it denies that science is the sole authority over what constitutes knowledge. Postmodernists contend, instead, that there is a multiplicity of alternative realities, of which each one is made – and made real – by way of human meaning-making. Another way of putting this is that our realities are the products of 'representational labour'. In broad terms, this is what is implied by Berger and Luckmann's (1967) 'social construction of reality'. A central concept is that of 'reification' – the process by which ideas (ideas like 'attitudes', 'personality', 'the self' and 'intelligence') become 'thingified' – that is, accorded a material existence as 'things-in-the-world'.

We need to recognize what is being argued here. Postmodernism is not simply a matter of viewing different individuals or collectives as having different perspectives on the world, which make them interpret it in diverse ways. This still implies there is a single 'world' (i.e. an objective, physically present, real world) on which it is possible to have different perspectives. Rather postmodernists assert that every world – as each individual and collective knows it and interprets it – is always a product of representational labour, constituted out of the meanings and understandings which this labour has brought into being.

What are the Implications for Health Psychology?

The postmodern challenge to orthodox, scientistic social psychology, therefore, has profound implications for how we think and theorize about notions like health and illness. This is elegantly illustrated by Sedgwick (1982), when he argues that

> The fracture of a septuagenarian's femur has, within the world of nature, no more significance than the snapping of an autumn leaf from its twig: the invasion of a human organism by cholera germs carries with it no more the stamp of 'illness' than does the souring of milk by other forms of bacteria.

From this theoretical stance, apparently real things like 'health' and 'illness' are not the naturally occurring biological events and phenomena we commonly assume them to be, however much they may appear to be so. Rather, they gain their compelling sense of being 'really there', having real existence, through the ways in which we constitute our social and cultural understandings.

Seen this way, a disease like cholera only exists – has thinghood – within a world-view steeped in the ideas of Western biomedicine. From within another world-view – such as a 'primitive' one (where, e.g. the bodily experience we call *cholera* might be seen as the manifestation of a curse) or pre-modern one (where, e.g. the distress, discomfort and possibly death we would see as caused by cholera would be regarded as a punishment from God) – the entity of 'cholera' simply does not exist. Two highly readable and accessible accounts of such 'alternative worlds' within which illness is differently constituted are Dingwall's *Aspects of Illness* (1976) and Herzlich and Pierret's *Illness in Self and Society* (1987). Less accessible is Foucault's work on this topic, especially *The Order of Things (Les Mots et les choses)* (1970), although this is generally regarded as the classic text.

Another 'take' on this way of conceptualizing illness is to consider the transient 'reality' of diseases which have only recently entered into our consciousness such as anorexia, repetitive strain injury and post-traumatic stress disorder; or others – such as hysteria – which have lost their meaning for us within our contemporary world-view. Difficult as it may be to resist the 'enchantment' by which our taken-for-granted world has constructed for us a potent sense of reality, historical analyses such as Herzlich and Pierret's can help to disenchant us; so too can cross-cultural analyses (Currer and Stacey's 1986 collection *Concepts of Health, Illness and Disease* is a good example). Both help us to see that 'illnesses' are cultural products of particular times and/or particular locations.

The notion that disease only exists in some places and has only existed in a recent historical period is not simply cultural or historical relativism. The argument is not that there *really* is an entity which we call 'cholera' (which is *really* real and *really* exists), which simply gets interpreted in different ways in different places and different times. The assumption is not that cholera is a disease from a medical point of view, but, say, a manifestation of a curse from another point of view; nor is the argument that (in some meaning of the words) cholera microbes are mere figments of our imagination. The argument is that we have to be agnostic over its 'reality' because it is (and is only) what we think it is – what we have made it to mean and made it to matter – no more and no less. Cholera microbes therefore have real existence, but only to the extent that human beings have developed concepts like 'microbes', and they cause illness only to the extent that concepts such as 'illness' and 'cause' have gained currency within human meaning-making.

The word *currency* is a good one, since the analogy with money works well. If I try to buy things in the UK with, say, Slovak crowns, I would not get very far. They operate as currency only in Slovakia. Yet Slovak crowns are perfectly 'real'; I have some in my desk drawer, and I will use them when I go next to Bratislava – indeed, I would be lost without them. But their currency is local and contingent. The analogy can be taken a bit further by observing that US dollars and German marks currently do have currency in parts of Slovakia – which says something about the relative status of the different currencies. Knowledge too can be limited in its currency or be more global. The knowledge-base of Ayurvedic medicine, for example, tends to have currency only within the Indian subcontinent, whereas biomedical knowledge has currency pretty well worldwide.

Another way of looking at this is to consider how the proverbial Martian might understand disease. It could, for instance, view microbes as a functional component of a system which requires all living organisms on our planet to die and decay in order to regenerate the life-system of Gaia. If so, the Martian would not constitute what we humans see as disease as dis-ease at all, but as a natural and normal – indeed life-enhancing – process.

Thus within postmodern theorizing, cholera as a disease has a *practical* reality. Its assumed 'thinghood' serves pragmatic purposes – from a human perspective. It allows us (within the technology of the medical system that we humans have developed) to view it as a 'cause' of illness, theorize about how it operates, find out how to prevent it from operating and, therefore, to 'treat' it (i.e. to ameliorate its effects on human bodies and thus prevent people from dying from it). The ability to diagnose it and to treat it does not make cholera an objective 'real-thing'. It merely means that, as a concept – as a way of making sense of the world – it serves a particular purpose from a human point of view.

When we apply this agnosticism over the 'real' to health psychology (psychology in general) we are faced with a serious problem. Conventionally, we assume that all psychology needs to do is to strip off a thin, social, group-specific and/or culture-specific veneer to uncover universal 'laws of human nature' (e.g. about how people compute the pay-offs of different courses of action, such as compliance or non-compliance with a medical treatment programme). Once we come to regard such laws as *only* social-group-specific or culture-specific – as always 'local' (only applicable in certain social spaces) and always 'time-contingent' (only operating in certain historical times) – then the search for universal 'laws of human nature' becomes as pointless as the alchemists attempts to turn lead into gold. In different times and different places quite other laws will apply. The corollary is that all that psychology can ever discover are local and contingent operating rules. This is not the impression one gets by looking at social psychology textbooks.

They are packed full of empirical 'demonstrations' of such laws: the fundamental attribution error; cognitive dissonance; learned helplessness (the list, if not endless, is certainly a long one). The obvious reaction is that if these are no more than the manifestations of local and contingent operating rules, why, then, can they so easily be demonstrated in the laboratory? The answer a postmodernist would give is that whenever a social psychological experiment 'works' (i.e. its experimental hypothesis is given support by the data obtained) what we are seeing is not some revelation of a general principle of how the social 'works'. All that is going on is a demonstration that the experimenter and the subjects of her or his experiment share a common set of operating rules. How else could the experimenter come up with a plausible hypothesis in the first place?

Postmodernism thus offers a profound challenge to everything that traditional, scientistic social psychology holds dear. It is an heretical position, since it challenges the foundations (empiricism, objectivity, hypothetico-deductive methods) upon which mainstream psychology is constructed. It operates on the principle that psychologists cannot discover 'objective facts' because there are no such facts – no timeless, naturally occurring psychological phenomena (such as 'attitudes' and 'beliefs') – to be 'discovered'.

Should We All Pack Up and Go Home?

Because of the aforementioned kinds of denial, postmodernism is often seen as nihilistic. Agnosticism over an objective reality, however, does not mean that there is nothing left to study. Rather, it means changing what gets studied and asking rather different research questions. Instead of trying to find out about the 'facts' of how social life and social processes operate, postmodernists examine the very thing that gives rise to the scientists' problem: the representational systems (the term generally used is *discourse*) by and through which our 'realities' are constituted.

A growing number of social psychologists have turned to investigating discourse, drawing from literary, hermeneutic and semiotic theorizing to find out about how knowledge is 'storied into being' (cf. Curt, 1994). As examples, Sarbin (1986) proposes the use of narrative as a 'root metaphor' for psychological analysis; literary techniques (such as dialogue between a formal cast of dramatis personae) have come (back) into vogue as critical teaching devices (e.g. Edwards and Potter, 1992; Woolgar, 1988); Shotter and Gergen (1989) adopt a textual analytic for exploring identity; Parker (1992) argues for examining the dynamics of discourse as a means to investigate the social world; and Billig and colleagues (1988) explore what they call new forms of 'dilemmatics'.

Discursive Approaches

Discourse is an increasingly popular term which, although drawn originally from linguistics, has, within in postmodern theorizing, acquired a wider meaning than simply a section of speech or writing. It is used by post-modern researchers to address the constructive, productive and pragmatic aspects of language use, rather than its merely descriptive or representational aspects. This shift of focus comes about through the recognition that language can never neutrally describe the world, because language itself is an active part of making the world. The analysis of discourse, however, is not a search 'behind' the words people use for their cognitions, motivations or other psychological entities – which, from a positivistic perspective, would be seen as underlying language. Rather, talk and other texts are seen as social practices which are productive of experience and which construct the realities in which we live. Potter, Edwards and Wetherell (1993) see discourse analysis as being 'the theory of, and method of studying, social practices and the actions that constitute them' (p. 383). Probably the best entrée into this kind of work is Ian Parker's (1992) *Discourse Dynamics: Critical Analysis for Social and Individual Psychology*. However, it has become so popular recently and is used for such a wide range of different purposes and in so many different ways, it is worth spending a little time examining precisely what is meant by 'discourse analysis'.

Discourse Analysis

A discourse analytic approach to studying how people, say, understand and take action towards health and illness does not – as would a mainstream approach – assume that what is at stake is an investigation of, say, the beliefs that individuals hold (about, say, the causes of illness). Rather, it seeks to find out about the different discourses which are available to people and which enable them to make sense of (in this case) why people get ill. In this it is very different from approaches such as personal construct theory, as it is concerned with what is 'common property' (albeit in a particular socio-cultural setting, at a particular point in history).

The kinds of question asked about discourses are:

- What are the discourses that are available?
- Where are these discourses coming from? How and from where were they 'knowledged into being'?
- For what purposes are they – and can they be – used? What conduct do they prescribe, and what conduct do they prohibit?

- Whose purposes do they serve?
- How do they impact upon each other? Which one is dominant? Which ones are thereby 'covered up'?

These are very different research questions. No longer is there any concern about whether the knowledge promoted by each discourse is 'true' or not (given there is no benchmark against which to judge 'the truth'). There is no attempt to distinguish fact from fiction. Instead, the interest lies in the relationship, in particular, between power and knowledge – in who gains (and gains what) and who loses (and loses what) when, say, one particular discourse gains dominance over all the others. Curt (1994) terms this aspect of discourse analysis 'tectonics', which draws attention to the way in which discourses are seen as actively impinging upon each other and, as they clash together (with first one and then another gaining ascendancy) constantly moving the 'cultural lithosphere' of discursive space.

A good illustration of this kind of approach is an anthropological study by Helman (1978) entitled 'Feed a Cold and Starve a Fever.' In this piece of research, Helman examines the way in which 'folk wisdom' about ordinary, everyday illnesses like colds and flu intersect with the medical knowledge of doctors. He looks at how the understandings of lay people are influenced by popular science (e.g. as written about in magazines) and how the conceptions of disease of GPs are influenced by 'folk wisdom'.

By examining the extent to which GPs and their patients share a common understanding and a common language, he was able to theorize about the ways in which knowledge can be deployed – for example, not just to manage disease but to manage doctors' workloads and their interpersonal relationships with their patients. Helman argues that we are seeing not just an interface between biomedical and lay discourses about illness but a process whereby each is made to flow into and mould the other to achieve particular outcomes.

For instance, by using the lay notion of 'a bug going around' the GP can avoid the costly and time-consuming process of trying to identify the particular microbe which may be causing a patient's symptoms. As patients become more sophisticated (i.e. gain greater access to a clinical, biomedical discourse), however, they can resist what they see as being 'fobbed off' and demand more tests. The outcome can be a growing battle over scarce resources.

Probably the best known proponents of discursive approaches in psychology are Potter and Wetherell (1987); their *Discourse and Social Psychology* has become something of a 'bible' for initiates. Many psychologists make the assumption that discourse analysis à la Potter and Wetherell is the only version around. It has, however, a much longer history, and comes in a number of versions. These can be conceived of as falling along three main strands: *verstehen* approaches, micro-discourse analysis and macro-discourse analysis.

Verstehen Approaches These have strong links to methods used in anthropology, phenomenological sociology and humanistic psychology. The goal of research is to gain 'understanding' (*verstehen*) by attending to how sense is made of a topic or issue *by the account-giver*. Researchers seek to avoid imposing interpretation, but rather aspire to 'give voice' to the views being expressed. A good example is the notion of 'reflective research', as described by Shakespeare, Atkinson and French (1993), where researchers see themselves as seeking to engage others in the research endeavour in a more participative, less exploitative manner than is the case with traditional psychological methods. In other words, it is discursive to the extent that it centres on trying to gain access, in a non-intrusive manner, to the ways in which people formulate their beliefs, understandings and representations of their world and the significant events in their lives. We can see here a continuation of the earlier humanistic challenge, described at the beginning of this article.

Micro-discourse Analysis This is the UK-based approach of Potter and Wetherell (1987) and Billig and colleagues (1988). It focuses on language, since it regards this as central to all social activities, and draws extensively from semiotics, speech-act theory and ethnomethodology. It is more theoretically radical and overtly interpretative than the *verstehen* approach in that it is sited more explicitly within a social constructionist theory of knowledge (cf. Berger and Luckmann, 1967), and seeks to explore the discursive functions to which language is put in different situations. The 'discourse' studied is usually talk (e.g. transcriptions of meetings or counselling sessions). The things people say in such conversations are viewed as constructed from a pre-existing, shared manifold of 'linguistic repertoires', predicated upon collective ideas (i.e. discourses). These are seen to act as resources from which people weave arguments, explanations, descriptions and so on to meet different rhetorical purposes and functions – which shift as the conversation progresses. There is (though Potter and Wetherell deny it) considerable theoretical overlap with the social representations theory of Moscovici (see, for example, 1981). However, this approach can be thought of as the micro level of discourse analysis, in that the focus of interest is generally on very fine-grained scrutiny of short extracts of talk. The research questions being posed are 'What is *this* person, in *this* part of the conversation, seeking to achieve?' and 'What discourse(s) are they drawing on to do so?'

Macro-discourse Analysis Of the three approaches, macro-discourse analytic work is located most specifically within postmodern theorizing. It draws extensively from French theory, especially the work of Foucault and his concern with the relationships between power and knowledge. The analysis is far more macro in its focus, attending primarily to the collective nature of discourse. Here, there is concern with both the 'textuality' of discourse (i.e. its functions, uses and ability to wield power) and its sociocultural 'tectonics' (i.e. the ways in which discourse is produced, and how discourses impinge upon one another). The approach is less concerned with what particular individuals say in particular settings than with the way in which discourse operates more generally and more globally as a social and cultural resource to be used in human activities and endeavours. Thus, rather than fine-grained analysis of, say, segments of conversation, the methods used are more taxonomic, seeking to identify and describe, for any particular topic or issue, the main discourses in play. These include forms of cultural analysis (e.g. the scrutiny of media such as movies, television programmes and newspaper articles) and Q methodology (see, e.g. Curt, 1994; Stainton Rogers, R. et al., 1995; Stainton Rogers, W., 1991). The kind of research question being posed is: 'In respect to this topic, what discourses are available, how are they deployed and what can they be used to achieve?'

The Implications of a Discursive Approach for Health Psychology

Thus, a discursive approach to health psychology changes the research questions asked and adopts rather different research methods to do so. However, at least as important is the way in which it is reflexive; that is, it reflects back upon the endeavour of the discipline itself and subjects its own discourses to scrutiny. As a consequence, it opens to question a number of the basic assumptions on which health psychology is founded. In conclusion, let us look at two of these:

- Its challenge to biomedicine's claim to be epistemologically superior.
- Its exposure of the way in which health psychology promotes a particular ideology.

Challenging Biomedicine's Claim to Superior Epistemology

A key issue for health psychology emerging from discourse-analytic studies of this kind (which are found far more frequently in medical sociology and anthropology) is the way in which medical science has come, in Western culture particularly, to be regarded as the basis of *superior* knowledge – as having the status of 'fact', in contrast with the status of 'belief' accorded to all other forms of knowledge. The sociologist Friedson (1970) described this well when he wrote of the medical profession as the 'architects of medical knowledge'. With respect to health and illness they (and only they) are accorded the power to determine what constitutes 'real illness' (as opposed, say, to hypochondria or malingering).

This assumes that there is an epistemological distinction between scientific 'facts' upon which biomedical knowledge about health and illness is based and the lay beliefs, old wives' tales and popular misunderstandings held by ordinary people. A good example is work by Furnham (1993) where he lists a number of 'factual errors' that ordinary people make (e.g. agreeing with statements like 'alcohol is a stimulant' and 'alcohol can help a person sleep more soundly') and then he comments disparagingly:

> A surprising number of people would endorse these statements as true despite the fact that they are all demonstrably false. If their knowledge is so patchy, if not downright wrong, it is perhaps, therefore not surprising that their explanations of, or theories for, alcoholism are simple or misguided. (p. 79)

Another reading of the situation is that the statements in question have quite different meanings within popular discourse compared with how they are constituted within biomedical discourse. In everyday terms, being *stimulated* is about how one behaves (i.e. more gregariously, in a less inhibited manner, becoming louder, taking more risks) and has nothing to do with the actions of chemical processes within the nervous system. A case can be made that it is the medical sciences that have appropriated common, everyday terms like *stimulant* into their technical language – and, in the process of redefining them, have converted them into a 'medicalese' which is inherently confusing to ordinary people. So, what Furnham shows (and all that he has shown) is that ordinary people in ordinary situations understand the effects of alcohol by way of a quite different discourse from that used by medical experts in medical settings (and it is worth adding that no doubt most medical experts turn to popular discourse once they start partying!).

Yet whereas this epistemological equivalence between the 'different universes of meaning' of popular and professional discourse has been extensively argued in the fields of medical sociology and anthropology, there continues to exist among some health psychologists a continuing conviction of the superiority of biomedical epistemology. Upon this basis they set out to study things like 'health beliefs' within contexts such as attribution theory (see, e.g. King, 1983), models of cognitive algebra such as the health beliefs model (Rosenstock, 1974), and constructs such as 'locus of control' (cf. Rotter, 1966, though the 1976 work of Wallston, B., Wallston, K., Kaplan, and Maides is the best-known application to the field of health). Each of these 'take for granted' the veracity of biomedical knowledge and regard the cognitions of ordinary people as beset by error and distortion.

Yet, denying that biomedicine offers the only 'true' knowledge is precisely what critical psychology seeks to do. This is not, as has been stressed before, an outright denial of the pragmatic usefulness of biomedical science altogether. When critical psychologists challenge *scientism* they have no problems at all in seeing science – as an endeavour – as a patently powerful and serviceable technology for solving practical problems. This is notably the case in the field of biomedicine, where Western medical science undoubtedly offers immense benefits to humankind in alleviating pain and discomfort and saving lives. What is being challenged is not its utility but its claims to superiority at an epistemological level and to ethical or ideological neutrality.

The anthropologist Taussig (1980) views biomedicine as 'reproducing a political ideology in the guise of a science of (apparently) "real things"'. The sociologist Crawford (1984) regards biomedicine as ideologically motivated, in that its explanations of illness (especially those attributable to 'modern life') tend to locate the blame for patients' health problems in their own lifestyle and habits. 'This emphasis on individual responsibility for health', he argues, 'mystifies the social production of disease and undermines demands for rights and entitlements to medical care.' A similar case is made by the anthropologist Young (1980) with regard to 'stress' (p. 75). This way of making sense of a collection of bodily and psychological discomforts serves, Young argues, the ideology of liberal capitalism. It beguiles us into thinking of them as a personal problem, requiring the sufferer to seek for solutions (e.g. programmes of stress-reduction). In so doing it diverts our attention away from other potential culprits, such as poor living and working conditions, unemployment and poverty.

Health Psychology as Ideology

If we define *ideology* as 'the use of knowledge to promote the power of certain groups', then psychology is pre-eminently ideological – a discipline where knowledge is 'sought' not for its own sake but to achieve certain goals. These goals have always been made quite explicit. Take, for example, the following 'mission statement' presented by three early psychologists, Tiffin, Knight and Josey (1940):

> The value of learning more about ourselves and human nature is obvious. Our social, political and economic theories rest ultimately upon our understanding of human nature. Upon sound knowledge of human nature depends the possibility of directing social changes, so as to make social institutions and practices better suited to human needs. As citizens, then, we need to make our beliefs about human nature as sound and rational as possible. The nineteenth century was marked by great achievements in engineering. Advances in psychology, sociology, and physiology should lead to as striking advances in 'humaneering' during the twentieth century. (pp. 23–24)

This quest – 'to boldly go' and seek out 'sound knowledge of human nature' to 'make social institutions and practices better suited to human needs' – is woven intimately into what a majority of health psychologists do. The topics they identify to study, the knowledge they seek to obtain and the theories they construct are all 'shot through' (as a fabric may be 'shot through' with elastic thread) with this pursuit of human betterment. Far from being 'mere scholarship', health psychology is a profoundly value-laden, ideological endeavour, with a far-reaching commitment to human betterment.

Another way of describing this is to suggest that what is going on is missionary evangelizing, promoting the 'true faith' of liberal humanism (see

Stainton Rogers, R., et al., 1995, for a fuller treatment of this argument). 'So what's the harm in that?' you might argue. The harm, as critical psychologists see it, is that liberal-humanism is not half as benign or egalitarian as it is often made out to be. It can be profoundly ethnocentric, and it can serve to bolster the power injustices that run through the relationships between men and women, the rich and the poor, indeed anywhere where there are differentials of power.

A good illustration of the liberal-humanistic agenda of health psychology is the locus of control construct as it has been amended for use in the field – the health locus of control (HLC) construct (Wallston, B., et al., 1976). In my own work, I used Q-analysis and Q-methodology (see Stainton Rogers, W., 1991, for further detail) to deconstruct its liberal-humanistic claims. The results I obtained question the whole monolithic basis of the locus of control construct – that individuals make sense of the world according to a small set of general, consistent, causal explanations derived from social learning in childhood. My results suggest that explanation is instead a flexible process in which attribution is applied differently, according to a variety of situational and other demands, and is highly influenced by culture and religious belief.

To give just one example, locus of control elides together ideas about 'fate' and 'chance', rendering people whose responses favour such explanations as 'fatalistic'. Yet the patterns of response from one participant in the study – a Hindu – show a quite different pattern of response from 'chance' items (which he strongly rejected) compared with 'fate' items (which he strongly endorsed). It does not take much cultural sensitivity to view this as reflecting a world-view in which *fate* and *chance* hold quite different meanings, both from each other and from those held within Western consciousness. Certainly, it would be quite wrong to see such a person as 'fatalistic'!

The preceding and other data that I obtained in my study, I believe, offer strong evidence of the ideological basis of the locus of control construct. It sites explanation within a positivist and mechanistic mould and assumes that the kind of understanding of causality salient to a small group of Western psychologists at a particular historical period would be sufficiently robust and comprehensive to explain why people in general act in particular ways, or why they construe the world in the way that they do. The Health Locus of Control scale, by imposing this conceptual strait-jacket upon people's explanations of health and illness, failed (see Stainton Rogers, W., 1991, chap. 7, for a review of its poor performance as an either independent or dependent variable in studies of health-related behaviour). It failed, I believe, not just because its construct validity is suspect (because of its ethnocentricity apart from anything else) but because when people seek to make sense of the world, far more is involved than a simplistic attempt to explain cause-and-effect within a very limited domain of variables.

People, I maintain, are artful and insightful negotiators of social reality (within their own thinking and in their conversations with others). When they attribute control over health and illness, their thinking is no knee-jerk affair, with beliefs somehow acting as an internal lever pushing them into action. Rather, they make sense of their worlds by weaving understanding out of the discourses made available to them in their culture; discourses which tell a diversity of different stories about where control over health can be located (such as in God's will or patriarchy). To argue that these under-standings are somehow inferior to biomedical knowledge is, I contend, an ideological endeavour. With all ideological endeavours, we have to ask: Whose interests are at stake? In other words, a critical approach imposes a demand to consider not matters of veracity but matters of ethics and, cru-cially, issues of power, especially who has the power to construct, distribute and legitimate knowledge.

Conclusions

In this chapter I have argued that the approach generally taken by health psychology is far too constrained by its preoccupation with traditional, scientistic psychology. While there are certainly areas in which science – as a practical endeavour – offers a fruitful means to pursue a number of ques-tions which health psychology must address. I believe that we need to break out of the conceptual and methodological straitjackets which a monolithic devotion to scientism imposes. In particular, I contest, health psychology has much to gain and to learn from discursive and postmodern approaches to psychology and from critical work more generally, particularly that emerg-ing in the domains of medical sociology and anthropology. These offer fer-tile grounds waiting to be explored, which can but open up and enlarge whole new and exciting vistas of possibility. These possibilities, I hope, will be taken up. To end on an 'up note', it says something about the growing open-mindedness of health psychology that, at last, critical work is being brought in from the cold and welcomed into the academic arena. It should, I hope, make for some interesting arguments – but then, that is what true scholarship is all about.

References

Antaki, C. (1981). *The psychology of ordinary explanations of social behaviour.* London: Academic Press.

Berger, P., and Luckmann, T. (1967). *The social construction of reality.* Harmondsworth: Penguin.

Billig, M., Condor, S., Edwards, D., Gane, M., Middleton, D., and Radley, A. (1988). *Ideological dilemmas.* London: Sage.

Crawford, R. (1984). A cultural account of 'health': Control, release and the social body. In J. B. McKinlay (ed.) *Issues in the political economy of health care.* London: Tavistock.

Currer, C., and Stacey, M. (1986). *Concepts of health, illness and disease.* Leamington Spa: Berg.

Curt, B. (1994). *Textuality and tectonics: troubling social and psychological science.* Buckingham: Open University Press.

Dingwall, R. (1976). *Aspects of illness.* London: Martin Robertson.

Edwards, D., and Potter, J. (1992). *Discursive psychology.* London: Sage.

Foucault, M. (1970). *The order of things.* London: Tavistock.

Friedson, E. (1970). *The profession of medicine: A study of the sociology of applied knowledge.* New York: Dodd Mead.

Furnham, A. (1993). *Lay theories – everyday understanding of problems in the social sciences.* Oxford: Pergamon.

Harré, R. (1979). *Social being: A theory for social psychology.* Oxford: Blackwell.

Helman, C. G. (1978). 'Feed a cold and starve a fever' – Folk models of infection in an English suburban community, and their relation to medical treatment'. *Culture, Medicine and Psychiatry, 2,* 107–137.

Herzlich, C., and Pierret, J. (1987). *Illness in self and society.* (E. Foster, Trans.). Baltimore, MD: Johns Hopkins University Press.

Ibañez, T. (1991). Social psychology and the rhetoric of truth. *Theory and Psychology, 2,* 187–202.

King, J. (1983). Attribution theory and the health beliefs model. In M. Hewstone (ed.), *Attribution theory: Social and functional extensions.* Oxford: Blackwell.

Kitzinger, C. (1987). *The social construction of lesbianism.* London: Sage.

Moscovici, S. (1981). The phenomenon of social representations. In R. M. Farr and S. Moscovici (eds), *Social Representations.* Cambridge: Cambridge University Press.

Parker, I. (1988). *The crisis in modern social psychology, and how to end it.* London: Routledge.

Parker, I. (1992). *Discourse dynamics: Critical analysis for social and individual psychology.* London: Routledge.

Potter, J., Edwards, D., and Wetherell, M. (1993). A model of discourse in action. *American Behavioral Scientist, 36*(3), 383–401.

Potter, J., and Wetherell, M. (1987). *Discourse and social psychology: Beyond attitudes and behaviour.* London: Sage.

Reason, P., and Rowan, J. (1981). *Human inquiry: A sourcebook for new paradigm research.* Chichester: Wiley.

Rosenstock, I. M. (1974). Historical origins of the health belief model. *Health Education Monographs, 2,* 328–335.

Rotter, J. B. (1966). Generalised expectancies for internal versus external control of reinforcement. *Psychological Monographs, 80*(1).

Sarbin, T. (1986). *Narrative psychology: The storied nature of human conduct.* New York: Praeger.

Sedgwick, P. (1982). *Psychopolitics.* London: Pluto Press.

Shakespeare, P., Atkinson, D., and French, S. (eds). (1993). *Reflecting of research practice.* Buckingham: Open University Press.

Shotter, J., and Gergen, K. J. (1989). *Deconstructing social psychology.* London: Routledge.

Stainton Rogers, R., Stenner, P., Gleeson, K., and Stainton Rogers, W. (1995). *Social psychology: A critical agenda.* Cambridge: Polity.

Stainton Rogers, W. (1991). *Explaining health and illness: An exploration of diversity.* Hemel Hempstead: Harvester Wheatsheaf.

Taussig, M. (1980). Reification and the consciousness of the patient. *Social Science and Medicine, 14b,* 3–13.

Tiffin, J., Knight, F. B., and Josey, C. C. (1940). *The psychology of normal people.* Boston: Health.

Wallston, B. S., Wallston, K. A., Kaplan, G. D., and Maides, S. A. (1976). Development and validation of the health locus of control (HLC) scale. *Journal of Consulting and Clinical Psychology, 44,* 580–585.

Woolgar, S. (1988). *Science: The very idea.* Chichester: Ellis Harwood.

Young, A. (1980). The discourse on stress and the reproduction of conventional knowledge. *Social Science and Medicine, 14b,* 133–146.

22 THEORIZING HEALTH AND ILLNESS:
Functionalism, Subjectivity and Reflexivity

Henderikus J. Stam

This article is, simply put, a plea for theory. One of the reasons for propagating the work of theorizing came out of my own practice as a psychologist, now a decade ago, of working in a cancer treatment setting as both a clinical and a research psychologist. It is I, think, not necessary to enumerate the kinds of personal, institutional and political problems one is confronted with in such settings to say that there was a wide gulf between practice and the literature on health psychology or behavioural medicine (cf. Stam, 1988, 1992). Although I eventually decided that my contributions to a 'politics of care' could be more effectively made outside rather than inside biomedicine, I have continued to remain involved in health care institutions and research in peripheral ways. I should note here that Health Psychology is (and can be) far more than what is covered by the clinical focus of what is sometimes referred to as Clinical Health Psychology. Although heavily involved in and influenced by clinical issues for reasons having to do with the social and economic organization of clinical psychology, health psychology includes studies and problems that range from community research and studies that have implications for health policy to considerations of individual problems of adjustment to illness. What I have to say about theory is generally relevant to all of these dimensions even though I chose examples that come predominantly from the latter domain (see also Marks, 1996; Spicer and Chamberlain, 1996; Stainton Rogers, 1996).

As will become clear below, by theory I do not have in mind a conception based on the traditional notions of reductionism, instrumentalism or realism in the philosophy of science. Indeed, neither do most psychologists for that matter, who treat theory as mere variants of functionalist claims that resemble hypotheses but whose actual foundations are left somewhere floating in mid-air (see Stam, 1996, for a discussion). My conception of theory is primarily governed by its reflexive properties or the claim that the researcher shares in a non-trivial way the practices of the community that he or she investigates, practices that are premised on shared linguistic and cultural customs. I will draw out several implications of this for theory and practice below.

By referring to a politics of care, above, I mean just those aspects of health care which are contested and configured in the activities of those who make up, provide and use biomedicine. These activities are constituted discursively and an exploration of care-talk necessarily leads to a deconstruction of traditional categories of health care as well as an invocation of understanding such categories in terms of subjectivities, power and knowledge (see Fox, 1994). In addition, these activities are constituted collectively and an exclusive focus on individual actors usually obfuscates the complex moral/power relations involved.

These concerns seem a long way from the 'worlds' created or constructed by contemporary health psychology around a set of limited professional topics, but the connection between a politics of care and these topics I wish to draw here is precisely by way of the problems of theory. In short, I want to make the case that theory is not a luxury or what one does in one's armchair after a hard day of collecting data. On the contrary, it is one of the most crucial steps of our entry into the world of health, disease and illness precisely because it establishes nothing less than our political, epistemological and moral grounding. It also establishes our responsibility as professionals who intervene in the lives of others even if done at the level of research. At the same time, it announces our commitments in advance, locating us as professionals among other professions and clients. As such we had best try to get clear the grounds of our interventions. In addition, we do not, and I would argue we cannot, do this alone.

I am now not only making claims that are relevant to health psychology; disciplinary boundary maintenance is particularly troublesome for any critical project that seeks to open for investigation the grounds of its own practice. Moreover, other social scientific disciplines similarly involved in the health care system have engaged in serious theoretical work for many years. Certainly sociologists, anthropologists and some psychologists are a case in point; it is difficult to imagine, for example, a Bryan Turner, an Emily Martin or an Alan Radley seriously proposing the kind of claim that one author in *Health Psychology* made recently. He said at the conclusion of a long and complex empirical study on a chronic illness that the theoretical significance of his study was that stress and coping variables are related in different ways to various dimensions of adjustments.[1] Since such 'findings' are entirely obvious, and indeed, may not require empirical research at all (cf. Smedslund, 2000 and commentaries), the practice of research has more to do with institutional and career progress than the generation of new knowledge.

The Discipline of Health Psychology

The hegemonic position of clinical psychology and the vast extension of biomedicine following the Second World War in the North-Atlantic world, and especially the English-speaking part of that world, has led to an unprecedented domination of health topics in the social sciences by psychologists. The emergence of Managed Care in the USA and the related move to provide empirically validated treatments, supported by the American Psychological Association among others, means that the dominance of what I will call 'mainstream health psychology' will continue. In addition, health psychology remains a growing area of academic and applied psychology in North America as well as one of the more common areas where many psychologists find employment (Stone et al., 1987; Taylor, 1999). The mission statement of Division 38 (Health Psychology) of the American Psychological Association (1996) contains the following: 'Psychologists are in increasing demand in health and medical settings. The single largest area of placement of psychologists in recent years has been in medical centers'. Through the use of licensing, continuing education and the like, the dominance of a mainstream perspective is institutionally defined and maintained. There are two obvious consequences of this:

1 For health psychology, biomedical authority and all its related social, financial and institutional supports remains a benign provider of health care and a duly constituted authority on health and illness. The contested and shifting political, social and economic forces engaged in and by the health care systems and their profound consequences for the clients of that system are, to health psychology, psychologically uninteresting and unimportant.
2 A singular form of research is treated as the ultimate tool of knowledge, and this research is presented in terms of its adherence to a methodologically fixed set of principles that suppress the discursive, social constitution of health care and its hierarchical allocation of resources, as well as the negotiated and collective constitution of 'health' and 'illness'.

I do not wish to argue that mainstream health psychology has no theory, but instead that it is theory of a particular kind. Although health psychologists claim to rely on several models, including systems theory, biopsychosocial theory and self-regulatory theories, among others, these are all variants of functionalism. For example, systems theory has been espoused as providing a foundation for understanding adaptive mechanisms (e.g. Stone, 1980, Taylor, 1999). However, systems theory, especially the version that circulates in health psychology, adheres in practice to the three necessary conditions for a functionalist model (Evans-Pritchard, 1951): first, systems are natural phenomena with interdependent levels that serve to maintain the systems; second, within systems theory social events are reduced to empirical relationships that are predictable; and third, systems theory is ahistorical about the makeup of systems. In this sense systems theory is neutral about the nature of biomedical systems. Within the context of health and health care, such a functional view espouses a concept of persons as well-turned machines (rather than sentient beings) whose actions are intelligible in larger control systems. Self-regulatory models are likewise driven by functional considerations; the 'self', however conceived, is entirely absent in these formulations.

The Biopsychosocial Model

The 'biopsychosocial' position and related concepts have a unique role in health psychology. Engel's original publication in *Science* in 1977, where the term originated, was primarily a critique of biomedicine. Only the latter half of his article concerned itself with the biopsychosocial model proper and most of this is by way of example rather than the development of a model, theory or position. In fact he does not even define the term but argues that the 'model must ... take into account the patient, the social context in which he [or she] lives, and the complementary system devised by society to deal with the disruptive effects of illness, that is, the physician's role and health care system' (p. 132). Furthermore, argues Engel, the dichotomy between 'disease' and certain 'problems of living' is clear neither for patient nor for physician. As an example he describes the case of grief. It exemplifies a phenomenon in which psychological factors are primary yet it constitutes a discrete syndrome with a relatively predictable symptomatology which includes bodily and psychological disturbances. A biopsychosocial model would merely take all of these factors into account, and Engel alludes in his conclusion to the relationship between the biopsychosocial model and systems theories.

It is an interesting phenomenon in its own right that such a loose formulation has become the rhetorical mainstay of theory in health psychology (see Stam, 1988). I surveyed five recent health psychology textbooks and found that the term 'biopsychosocial' is now thoroughly embedded in the discipline. Indeed it appeared almost obligatory to mention the model although none of the texts cite papers beyond the original formulations by Engel (e.g. 1977) or the revision published by Schwartz in 1982. The 'model' has simply been taken for granted and, remarkably, there is absolutely no discussion of what this term could mean other than the 'interplay' or 'interaction' of biological, psychological and social factors. Taylor (1999) is even less committed by noting that these three factors are merely 'involved' in the model. No author notes that this is neither a theory nor a model.[2] Indeed, I think it is sufficient to say that it is a clever neologism masquerading as a model and its naive distribution to undergraduates ought to lead us to urge publishers to place a warning label on textbooks indicating that they are a danger to the health of one's theoretical education.[3] On the other hand, the absence of theory and the vagueness of the model can be construed as a useful ploy because anything can be covered by it: anything remotely relevant counts as a topic under 'health'. As Shelley Taylor pronounces in the last sentence of her textbook on health psychology 'the opportunities for the fledgling health psychologist are boundless' (1999, p. 489). Opportunities indeed, so long as they don't interfere with institutional privileges. In short, the functionalist prescriptiveness and lofty inclusiveness of the biopsychosocial 'model' make it a useful rhetorical device for the appropriation of a set of topics in health and illness into psychological practice and research.

From the perspective of professionalization, this is an exercise of 'social closure' (Turner, 1986) wherein a profession's knowledge base serves as a strategy of market regulation. Although such a view might be construed as strictly concerned with the political and social role played by health psychology, it is not entirely surprising given that psychology is continually in competition with neighbouring disciplines for the same territory. Family medicine, community medicine, nursing, social work, epidemiology, sociology of health and other health-related disciplines have marked as their domain certain problems and topics in health care that are also part of the practice and research repertoire of health psychologists. These include topics such as family, living with chronic illness, prevention of diseases, and so on. In that sense, part of health psychology's success is derived from its capacity to innovate and to secure new markets, clients and rewards.

In a related sense it is strange, if not suspicious, that discussions of the deeply contested, political and social issues that make up health care today are absent from health psychology. One of the major expenses of Western governments, individuals and families is health and health care. Dominated by mixed models of physicians as private entrepreneurs/public servants who work within both private and public medical facilities, health care has been (in the post-war period) and still is, in a constant state of crisis and restructuring. The biomedical model has been challenged on many fronts and a steady growth and proliferation in health professions and specialties (within medicine but also in dentistry, pharmacy, and so on) and complementary occupations (nursing, physiotherapy, laboratory specialists) have transformed the health labour force. As other groups have joined this labour force through a strategy of professionalization (among others, psychologists, chiropractors and nurses), and administrative and support services have proliferated, the medical domain has become a contested and fragmented one (see Aries and Kennedy, 1990; Burke and Stevenson, 1993). As if this is occurring in another world, psychologists ignore and suppress these events and their impact on their own research and practices, their conceptions of health and illness and, perhaps fatally, the importance of these considerations for their intended end-users, the research participants and the ill.[4]

However, despite the crucial importance of the structural background to health psychology, this appears to me to be an incomplete picture. It paints psychologists as ignorant of the world they inhabit or as ruthless entrepreneurs in the same way that some critiques of medicine paint physicians as heartless technocrats. Such one-dimensional caricatures may make sense of the background activities that make a profession possible; what is at stake, however, is not the individual motivation of psychologists but the constitution of health psychology as a collective practice. What functionalist theory allows is the discursive construction of health and illness as a set of *variables* whose identification is obvious and whose analysis requires no more than the use of aggregate statistics that allow one to make simple yes/no judgments. I wish to say a few words about this which I hope will clarify my understanding of theory when I return to the question of theory as a moral project.

Methodology and the Constraints on Theory

Like theory in psychology generally, what passes for theory in health psychology is loosely related to a version of positivism (modelled on the philosophical version of logical positivism) that has dominated psychology since mid-century. According to the *philosophical* version of logical positivism, a theory is no more than an axiomatized collection of sentences that has a specified relationship to a set of observables. This relationship (dependent on a theory of verification) was much in dispute for the life of logical positivism. Psychology generally by-passed this view (and the concomitant debate). Instead, it has relied on the 19th-century positivism of Ernst Mach that was gradually modified and introduced into psychological research through behaviourism with an explicit emphasis on observation as the key element of scientific research (Danziger, 1990; Mills, 1998; O'Neil, 1995). On this view observations were separate from theory, and gradually came to rely on models, such as Hull's, which were 'deductive-nomonological' in nature. Theories in this context came to mean statements that had a specific relationship to the events to be explained, a deductive-nomonological relationship. In the ideal case the theory was a universal law that could act as a 'covering law' that explains the events under consideration.

For all its elegance, the model can be seen in very little research after that of Clark Hull. Practically, the development of inferential statistics and the demise of behaviourism as an all-encompassing theory for psychology led to a much more liberal approach in understanding theoretical claims. Although the emphases on observation and quantification persisted and were strengthened by post-war generations psychologists, inferential statistics encouraged the wider use of theoretical models or 'hypotheses' in psychology and discouraged formal theorization (with the exception of some areas such as mathematical psychology). It has only been the advent of cognitivism in the last 40 years that has gradually reintroduced theory in a more formal manner by way of (cognitive) functional analyses, analyses that have come to rely on and require the kind of statistical averaging used in tests of statistical inference.

Among the many consequences of the widespread adoption of statistical inference techniques in psychology, the most deleterious was their restriction of theoretical developments in the discipline (Gigerenzer, 1993; Stam and Pasay, 1998). Kurt Danziger (1990) gives an account of how, in response to the demand for an applied knowledge, research came to be conducted on groups that were constituted so that they could be contrasted on an abstract variable. For example, research in intelligence demanded some conception of normative levels for the development of intelligence tests. Individual scores came to be reported in the aggregate and deviations were construed as 'error'. Aggregate scores, however, make it difficult to develop concepts about intra-individual processes and these were the most important to the development of the discipline. The introduction of inferential statistics solved this problem for psychologists, namely, it allowed the identification of psychological properties with the hypothetical distributions of statistical analyses. In other words, individual scores no longer mattered but rather the distribution of scores came to represent the theoretical processes at hand. For example, such processes as memory could be captured not by studying individual acts of remembering but by comparing how different groups ('experimental conditions') of individuals performed on some restricted tasks such as learning and recalling a list of nonsense syllables. The resulting, functional theoretical notion was one that no longer referred to any single participant in the experiment but instead to an abstract property of 'memory'.

Methodological prescriptions, including the requirements of confirmation through observations analysed using statistical inference techniques, severely constricted the possibilities of theory development. However sophisticated one's psychological notions, the indiscriminate use of tests of statistical inference led to a mechanical and routine use of the technique that by its very nature foreclosed rather than advanced theory (Gigerenzer, 1993). Psychological theory remains relatively simple because the techniques of adjudication between theories require uncomplicated, elementary and simplified models and hypotheses.[5]

More important yet for health psychology, the restriction of theory and the absence of a strong theoretical foundation allows the practices of psychologists to coincide with those of biomedicine. I do not claim that this is necessarily or always intentional; institutional prerogatives and agendas rarely are in any case. With its focus on prevention, adjustment and coping, health psychology considers 'healthy' the patient who has regained the ability to perform. Health in this sense is a functional entity, not one negotiated in a shifting discourse of health and illness encompassing the activities of falling ill or becoming well (see also Spicer and Chamberlain's notion of 'flow-charting', 1996). I would argue, however, that any substantial theorization of the psychology of health and illness and its subjectivization must begin by taking a critical distance from the discourse of biomedicine. This distancing is almost impossible to do in mainstream health psychology. Discursively and methodologically it is tied to a single simplified model, the very maintenance of which is also a strategic discursive act even as it masquerades as scientifically pure.

There are obviously occasions and questions associated with health that demand an empirical descriptive strategy. For example, we might want to know the motives for condom use among young adults (e.g. Cooper, Agocha and Powers, 1999) or the relations among ethnicity, wealth and health (e.g. Ostrove, Feldman and Adler, 1999). Note, however, that many such questions are broadly epidemiological or social and not just psychological. That is, they concern social and community health questions, precisely the kinds of questions to which one wants to have descriptive data so that policy and practice issues can be brought to the fore. They do not even begin to address what is psychological about such issues.

What remains as theorizing in the mainstream of health psychology hides the professional and authorial source of knowledge, makes reciprocity between the source and the production of knowledge impossible, and treats the producers of that knowledge as professionals carrying out a job in the name of science. It is unreflexive about its knowledge production, namely that of constituent players engaged in the construction of health and illness. Behind its universalism lies an individualism that characterizes much of psychology; what the scientific knower knows is independent of who the knower happens to be, the knower's social position, and the use to which such knowledge is put.

I will not rehearse the multiple antidotes to this form of knowledge production that have been prescribed over the last four decades by theorists and methodologies in the name of various emancipatory or post-positivist projects. Feminism, critical theory, postmodernisms of various kinds as well as the wide prevalence of qualitative methods have sought to reclaim territory from the wider fields of health sciences just as these have pervaded other domains of psychology (e.g. Stainton Rogers, 1996). Nevertheless, qualitative research does not, in itself, guarantee an escape from more traditional mainstream forms of knowledge production. It is an easy step to reformulate qualitative research so that it is yet another neutral method of inquiry that captures better, and implicitly, more faithful and true characterizations of health and illness.[6]

Responsible Health Professionals

What multiple critical perspectives have foregrounded, however, is the place *from* which we do research or *from* which we practise. Feminist philosopher Kathryn Addelson has argued that as professionals, 'being morally responsible requires foresight in acting from *one's place*, foresight on the outcomes of collective activity in which one takes part' (Addelson, 1994, p. 18, original emphasis). This means that we devise 'theories and practices that can make explicit what the collective activity is' and what the outcomes of that activity might be (p. 18). In other words, our interventions in health do not arise *de novo* from rational objective theories but always first and foremost from a discursive position within such seemingly objective theories that have as their ends the production of certain 'goods', be they function, adaptation, understanding, insight, and so on.

In addition, what the new epistemologies have taken from us is the possibility of a fixed, certain or rational standpoint from which to engage in professional activities. Instead, our activities are always politically engaged because of our positions as professionals in the social order. Reflexivity then means recognizing not only the inevitability of being so positioned but deciding what moral goods we will pursue in our activities.

Our cognitive authority as professionals is granted to us by the institutions that employ us. Indeed, Addelson argues that all professions, and this certainly includes the service professions, are obliged to have knowledge makers providing that 'difficult body of knowledge' that legitimates their professional status. And it is this body of knowledge that distinguishes professionals, such as health psychologists, from workers in other occupations. As health psychologists we use this knowledge to define more clearly the need that we in turn service.[7] Hence there is an intimate relationship between our knowledge base and our practical endeavours. If we define needs in terms of abstract functional variables such as coping and adjustments, or in terms of DSM criteria, our research priorities will reflect the objective and abstract definitions of those needs. That makes the service and research context simpler and more manageable. If, on the other hand, we negotiate these needs in the terms that the ill give us, in terms of their own life histories and in terms of their needs to negotiate a complex health system, then we also create more responsible but less comfortable service positions for ourselves.

However, it is not only needs and practices that we establish; we also have a hand in defining outcomes. When these are to be constituted as empirically verifiable constructs such as adjustment, 'quality of life' objectively defined or compliance with a medical regime, we deny that we are collectively, as a profession, defining a set of outcomes for others. The process of objectification denies the historical constitution of those outcomes. Historical constitution here means simply that outcomes always take place in collectives whether these range from the conversation between two people to the discussions that take place in a conference on health psychology (cf. Addelson, 1994). Professional accounts of outcomes are special kinds of outcomes, produced in the context of and supporting existing social, political and economic orders.

To return for a moment to Kathryn Addelson's work. I would like to pursue her general proposal that 'truth' is always enacted in collective action. Our claims as professionals, even as critical or qualitative researchers, make sense so long as others recognize the talk. As collectives (such as at a conference or writing for, and reading, specialized journals) we then elaborate on, seek out further clarification of, and redefine our professional talk. But in our interactions with the ill or with other health care professionals we also come prepared and sensitized to the setting. Working on a defined terrain, we know *how*, from within our professional activities. Addelson argues that we are socially embodied actors who not only do professional work but in doing so are also significant moral and political actors. We are taken to be 'trustworthy instruments of governance' (1994, p. 208).

What can be Done

At this juncture it is not an unreasonable obligation on the critic that he or she should proffer some alternative to the problems here enumerated. I have two objections to this request: first, there is already sufficient critical, theoretical, morally informed research and writing in various literatures related to health. Large numbers of studies have been conducted inspired by a host of approaches that cover a wide range of phenomena and problems, albeit largely outside psychology (but see, for example, articles in the *Journal of Health Psychology*, the journal *Health*, or such examples – among many others – as Blair, 1993; Kleinman, 1996; Kugelmann, 1992; Mathieson and Stam, 1995; Radley, 1994; Toombs, 1992; Wennemo, 1993; Williams, 1993). Such examples typically begin by conceptualizing the problems of health/illness outside the domains of biomedicine, locating it in lives as they are understood by the ill, in class consciousness, in culture and talk, and so on. What marks this literature is the separation of the institutional agenda from the experiential, the social and the access issues governing health care.

There seems to me a second, more compelling reason not to provide lists of problems and the manner in which I wish to see them addressed with appropriate methods/attitudes and the like. My concerns about the nature of functional theory, aggregate statistics and the need for moral reflexivity is to open up and create new possibilities for understanding health and illness that are not constrained by the turgid strictures of methodocentric preoccupations whose purpose appears sometimes limited to helping its authors become published and promote careers but do not fundamentally involve our understanding of the problems at hand. Or, as Daniel Robinson recently argued so elegantly, 'progress in science is won by the application of an informed imagination to a problem of genuine consequence; not by the habitual application of some formulaic mode of inquiry to a set of quasi-problems chosen chiefly because of their compatibility with the adopted method' (2000, p. 41). However we conceive of science and its relation to health psychology, it is not going to progress in any sense of that word by following lists of prescribed formulations, even if those formulations come from well-meaning critical theorists.

Theorizing health and illness in psychology is not an abstract activity but one permanently embedded in how we approach our research and practice settings, participants and colleagues, how we conduct ourselves in those settings, and how we read the outcomes of those activities. At each stage we are engaged in the negotiation of health, disease and illness through a complex moral and social process. Our theories are, if you will, not only 'observation-laden' but also dependent on the place from which we theorize and generate knowledge.

To bring this into some kind of perspective, allow me to give two case studies that focus on the subtle relationship that exists between institutional commitments and knowledge claims. I am not giving examples of either research or how one ought to proceed. I want simply to locate the problem of the relationship between the professional, institutional context of our activities and our rational considerations of health and illness. The first case comes from Ruth Miltenburg, a Dutch health care activist and organizational consultant who has a debilitating chronic illness herself. Her understanding of being ill has been shaped by her conception of illness as a 'job' or 'profession'. Just like other jobs, one must learn it well in order to carry it off. But it is a difficult profession because it covers so many terrains that we normally do not have to deal with when we are not ill, including doctors and hospitals but also relationships, death, and so on (Miltenburg, 1998). At a recent conference on nursing care she said that 'nursing care ... is occupied with tasks that are better known at the United Nations as torture, namely, the systematic and organized deprivation of sleep and proper feeding ... [the] disturbance of biorhythms, deprivation of freedoms, dehumanization and so on' (Miltenburg, 1997). By juxtaposing the UN definition of torture with normal nursing care she brought the problem of 'care' into the moral, everyday domain and demanded that care at the very least requires the skill to think from two perspectives, not only from that of one's own profession but also from the persepctive of the ill. Or, more precisely, the professional orientation so common to nursing frequently equates care with efficiency, time spent in hospital, physiological healing and the like. Such simple matters as obtaining sufficient sleep and a reasonable meal, which may be paramount to the patient, are not part of the nursing definition of 'care' and hence simply don't come to matter to institutional agendas.

Finally, I recently had the opportunity to sit on the medical admissions committe of my home university and witness more clearly how professional sensitivities operate. I initially thought that my early experience in the hospital would prime me for seeking out particularly good candidates for the medical profession. Confronted by the applications, however, I quickly realized that the lore and lure of professional medicine is such that it draws a relatively homogenous set of applicants. Virtually all of them are high achievers, many have had experiences with illness and death, have extensive volunteer experience and most are idealistic and express altruistic motives, at least their applications are rhetorically structured in such a way that they give the appearance of a relatively unique group of similar young adults. Once certain obvious (to the committee) candidates were excluded, one might think that the remainder were virtually chosen by lottery (as is the case in some countries). What I recognized among my own choices and those of my colleagues on the committe, however, was that these were far from random but gradually revealed a set of professional and personal concerns never articulated by the committee and not present in the admission criteria. We were sensitized by insiders' and professional concerns, capable of making judgments in the abstract about individuals we had never met, on the basis of fine details in their biographical reports or their application information. And although my own sensitivity was different from the physicians', it was there nonetheless, recognizable by the criteria that gradually came to make a difference to my judgments of 'yes' or 'no'.

The point of this story is *not* that the medical admissions committee should change its criteria or make its application process more effective or transparent. This would be merely to assume that fully rational and objective decisions about who can or cannot become a doctor are available. Indeed, medical schools present just such a face to the world, complete with discussions of criteria and their evaluation via research published in medical journals. Hence the process appears justifiably rational. My point, however, is only that such professional sensitivities are inevitable and ever-present in all our activities inside institutions, including medical ones. We never leave our moral commitments behind at the breakfast table, they follow us into the consulting room, the meeting room and the classroom. Furthermore, we negotiate them in practice so I am not advocating that we merely meditate on their implications. Instead, as we are doing in print, here, we work them out in action. It is for these reasons that our theoretical commitments are so crucial to our considerations of health and illness, for I see them as nothing less than an articulation of our political, epistemological and moral grounding.

Notes

1   This author is not alone or unique and I do not wish to single him out except that he was in a recent issue of the journal in question. This strategy of theorizing is ubiquitous, inside health psychology and out, and its historical and institutional foundations are sufficiently complex that I can only note this here (cf. Stam, 1996).

2   Models in science are normally taken to be partial simulations derived from a theory and hence a limited test of a more advanced and developed theoretical formulation (Suppe, 1989). In the social sciences, however, the term 'model' is often used loosely to describe a guiding formulation that is not related to a particular theory but is associated instead with functional properties. My argument here is that the 'biopsychosocial model' doesn't even approximate this looser use of the term 'model'.

3   An adaptation of an idea from Ian Lubek (1993) who has argued that social psychology textbooks should, like cigarettes, carry a warning about their potential hazards.

4   In health psychology there is almost no discussion of the ethical and economic limits of biomedicine that have become so apparent in the past decade and

no recognition that the struggle to change life-styles is at its worst a 'hypochondriacal narcissism of a privileged class shutting its eyes to the deterioration of the rest of the world' (Renaud, 1993).

5 In less official publications, health psychologists acknowledge this problem. For example, using his presidential column in the APA Division 38 newsletter, Howard Leventhal remarked that 'many of our theories are little more than broad themes that guide but do not constrain our thinking; they are frames of reference rather than theories' (1996, p. 1). Unfortunately, Leventhal had no solution to this problem.

6 See the special issue of this journal edited by Murray and Chamberlain (1998) for a discussion of these problems.

7 By 'need' I do not mean just clinical need. I also mean the 'need' for more research that is opened up by any extant 'finding.'

References

Addelson, K. P. (1994). *Moral passages: Toward a collectivist moral theory*. New York: Routledge.

American Psychological Association, Division 38, (1996). *Mission statement* [On-line]. Available: [http://freud.apa.org/divisions/div38/mission.html].

Aries, N., and Kennedy, L. (1990). The health labor force: The effects of change. In P. Conrad and R. Kern (eds), *The sociology of health and illness: Critical perspectives* (3rd ed.) (pp. 195–206). New York: St Martin's.

Blair, A. (1993). Social class and the contextualization of illness experience. In A. Radley (ed.), *Worlds of illness* (pp. 27–48). London: Routledge.

Burke, M., and Stevenson, H. M. (1993). Fiscal crisis and restructuring in Medicare: The politics and political science of health in Canada. *Health and Canadian Society, 1*, 51–80.

Cooper, M. L., Agocha, V. B., and Powers, A. M. (1999). Motivations for condom use: Do pregnancy prevention goals undermine disease prevention among heterosexual young adults? *Health Psychology, 18*, 464–474.

Danziger, K. (1990). *Constructing the subject: Historical origins of psychological research*. New York: Cambridge University Press.

Engel, G. L. (1977). The need for a new medical model: A challenge for biomedicine. *Science, 196*, 129–136.

Evans-Pritchard, E. E. (1951). *Social anthropology*. London: Cohen & West.

Fox, N. J. (1994). *Postmodernism, sociology and health*. Toronto: University of Toronto Press.

Gigerenzer, G. (1993). The superego, the ego, and the id in statistical reasoning. In G. Keren and C. Lewis (eds), *A handbook for data analysis in the behavioral sciences: Methodological issues*. Hillsdale, NJ: Erlbaum.

Kleinman, A. (1996). Suffering, ethics, and the politics of moral life. *Culture, Medicine and Psychiatry, 20*, 287–290.

Kugelmann, R. (1992). *Stress: The nature and history of engineered grief*. Westport, CT: Praeger.

Leventhal, H. (1996) President's column. *The Health Psychologist, 18*(4), 1, 22.

Lubek, I. (1993). Social psychology textbooks: An historical and social psychological analysis of conceptual filtering, consensus formation, career gatekeeping and conservatism in science. In H. J. Stam, L. P. Mos, W. Thorngate, and B. Kaplan (eds), *Recent trends in theoretical psychology* (Vol. III) (pp. 359–378). New York: Springer Verlag.

Marks, D. F. (1996). Health psychology in context. *Journal of Health Psychology, 1,* 7–21.

Mathieson, C. M. and Stam, H. J. (1995). Renegotiating identity: Cancer narratives. *Sociology of Health & Illness, 17,* 283–306.

Mills, J. A. (1998). *Control: A history of behavioral psychology.* New York: New York University Press.

Miltenburg, R. (1997). *De verpleegkundige praktijk in Nederland: Een geval van neglect voor 'zorg'.* [Nursing practice in the Netherlands: A case of the neglect of 'care'.] Paper presented at Netwerk IPB Verpleegkundige Kwaliteitszorg, November.

Miltenburg, R. (1998). *Over ziek zijn* [On being ill]. Utrecht/Antwerp: Kosmos-Z & K.

Murray, M., and Chamberlain, K. (1998). Qualitative research in health psychology: Developments and directions. *Journal of Health Psychology, 3,* 291–295.

O'Neil, W. M. (1995). American behaviorism: A historical and critical analysis. *Theory & Psychology, 5,* 285–306.

Ostrove, J. M., Feldman, P., and Adler, N. E. (1999). Relations among socio-economic status indicators and health for African-Americans and whites. *Journal of Health Psychology, 4,* 451–463.

Radley, A. (1994). Making sense of illness: *The social psychology of health and illness.* London: Sage.

Renaud, M. (1993). Social sciences and medicine: Hygeia versus Panakeia? *Health and Canadian Society, 1,* 229–247.

Robinson, D. N. (2000). Paradigms and 'the myth of framework': How science progresses. *Theory & Psychology, 10,* 39–47.

Schwartz, G. E. (1982). Testing the biopsychosocial model: The ultimate challenge facing behavioral medicine. *Journal of Counsulting and Clinical Psychology, 50,* 1040–1053.

Smedslund, G. (2000). A pragmatic basis for judging models and theories in health psychology: The axiomatic method. *Journal of Health Psychology, 5,* 133–149.

Spicer, J., and Chamberlain, K. (1996). Developing psychosocial theory in health psychology. *Journal of Health Psychology, 1,* 161–171.

Stainton Rogers, W. (1996). Critical approaches to health psychology. *Journal of Health Psychology, 1,* 65–77.

Stam, H. J. (1988). The practice of health psychology and behavioral medicine: Whither theory? In W. J. Baker, L. P. Mos, H. V. Rappard, and H. J. Stam (eds), *Recent trends in theoretical psychology* (pp. 313–325). New York: Springer Verlag.

Stam, H. J. (1992). Troublesome bodies. *Disability Studies Quarterly, 12* (2), 31–36.

Stam,, H. J. (1996). Theory and practice. In C. Tolman, F. Cherry, R. V. Hezewijk, and I. Lubek (eds), *Problems of theoretical psychology* (pp. 24–32). Toronto: Captus Press.

Stam, H. J. (in press). Theoretical psychology. In K. Pawlik and M. Rosenzweig (eds), *International handbook of psychology.* London: Sage.

Stam, H. J., and Pasay, G. A. (1998). The historical case against null-hypothesis significance testing. *Behavioral and Brain Sciences, 21,* 219–220.

Stone, G. C. (1980. Psychology and the health system. In G. C. Stone, F. Cohen, and N. E. Adler (eds), *Health psychology – A handbook* (pp. 47–75). San Francisco: Jossey-Bass.

Stone, G. C., Weiss, S. M., Matarazzo, J. D., Miller, N. E., Rodin, J., Belar, C. D., Follick, M. J., and Singer, J. E. (1987). *Health psychology: A discipline and a profession*. Chicago: University of Chicago Press.

Suppe, F. (1989). *The semantic conception of theories and scientific realism*. Urbana, IL: University of Illinois Press.

Taylor, S. E. (1999). *Health psychology*. Boston: McGraw Hill.

Toombs, S. K. (1992). *The meaning of illness*. Dordrecht: Kluwer.

Turner, B. S. (1986). Sociology as an academic trade: Some reflections on centre and periphery in the sociology market. *Australian and New Zealand Journal of Sociology, 22*, 272–282.

Wennemo, I. (1993). Infant mortality, public policy, and inequality – A comparison of 18 industrialized countries, 1950–85. *Sociology of Health and Illness, 15*, 429–446.

Williams, G. (1993). Chronic illness and the pursuit of virtue in everyday life. In A. Radley (ed.), *Worlds of illness* (pp. 92–108). London: Routledge.

23 A DISCOURSE-DYNAMIC APPROACH TO THE STUDY OF SUBJECTIVITY IN HEALTH PSYCHOLOGY

Carla Willig

One of the concerns of contemporary health psychology is the relationship between health beliefs and health behaviours. This is because health behaviours impact upon quality of life, morbidity and mortality. For example, the risk of contracting a life-threatening disease or of being seriously hurt in an accident can be reduced through the adoption of health-protective behaviours such as the use of seatbelts, giving up smoking or using condoms. Health psychologists who wish to explore the relationship between health beliefs and health behaviours frequently draw on social psychological theories. The most widely used approaches include attribution theory, health locus of control, social learning theory and various social cognition models such as the theory of planned behaviour (see Ogden, 1996, for an overview). Despite important differences between these theoretical frameworks, they all share the view that individuals acquire a set of assumptions and expectations in relation to health and illness which in turn shape their health-related behaviours. For example, a person with an internal health locus of control is described as someone who believes that their health is controllable by themselves and that their actions will have predictable consequences for their health. Such an individual would be expected to be able to implement behavioural changes (e.g. to adopt a low-cholesterol diet) successfully. Social constructionist critics of psychological research into health beliefs (e.g. Radley, 1994; Stainton Rogers, 1991) have argued that such work over-emphasizes the role of cognitions and neglects the social context within which health-related behaviours take place. They argue that 'health' and 'illness' are not 'fixed entities in the minds of the people concerned' (Radley, 1994, p. 55), and that health-related cognitions are not consistent, stable and predictive of behaviour. Instead, talk about health and illness is seen as a social practice which is inextricably bound up with other areas of people's lives. Here, people's statements about health and illness are not an expression of their inner thoughts on the subject but rather the mobilization of culturally available explanations. This means that any one individual speaker is likely to draw on different and often contradictory arguments in order to make sense of their experiences in different social contexts. Thus, according to social constructionist critics, health psychologists ought to study the explanations of health and illness which are available within a culture and not just the individuals who happen to use them at a particular point in time.

Social constructionist approaches to the study of 'health' and 'illness' have been successful in developing our understanding of the social, cultural and historical situatedness of these constructs. As one of the key tools of social constructionist research, discourse analysis has allowed us to explore the ways in which 'health' and 'illness' are constructed through language.

The analysis of discourse plays an important role in a range of diverse disciplines, including linguistics, sociology and psychology. Furthermore, discourse analysts can work with different epistemological and methodological frameworks even within the same academic discipline (see Parker, 1998). A distinction can be made between discourse analysts who are concerned with discourse practices, or the performative qualities of discourse, and those who seek to explore the role of discourse in the constitution of subjectivity, selfhood and power relations (for helpful discussions of this distinction, see Burr, 1995; Potter and Wetherell, 1995; Potter, Wetherell, Gill, and Edwards, 1990).[1] The former approach has its roots in ethnomethodology and conversation analysis, whereas much of the latter work has been inspired by the writings of Foucault and post-structuralism. Discourse analysts who are primarily concerned with discourse practices (e.g. Edwards and Potter, 1992) emphasize the variability and fluidity of discourse and draw attention to the ways in which speakers use discursive resources in order to achieve interpersonal objectives in social interaction. According to this version of discourse analysis, 'subjectivities' and 'identities' are transient products of particular localized discursive formations. They are continually renegotiated as speakers move across discursive contexts. By contrast, Foucauldian discourse analysts emphasize the role of discourse in wider social processes of legitimation and power. Part of such a project is an exploration of the availability of subject positions in discourse and their implications for possibilities of selfhood and subjective experience for different groups of people. In this chapter, I am concerned with the relationship between discourse and subjectivity and with how discursive constructions and practices may be implicated in the ways in which we experience ourselves and our bodies (e.g. as 'sick' or 'healthy', as 'fit' or 'unfit'). My discussion of the literature in the remainder of this chapter is, therefore, limited to discourse analytic work which seeks to describe and critique the discursive worlds people inhabit and to explore their implications for possible ways-of-being.

There are two major ways in which discourse analysis has been applied within this context. First, discourse analysis has been used to deconstruct expert discourses of health and illness. This work has tended to take a critical turn whereby dominant discourses are subjected to a careful examination of the ways in which their use of linguistic categories and discursive constructions legitimates a particular version of reality and experience, thereby excluding alternative versions. This application of discourse analysis shall be referred to as Focus 1. The second way in which discourse analysis has been used, Focus 2, involves the analysis of non-expert texts in order to determine the extent to which dominant discourses are reflected in lay people's talk about health and illness. Both Focus 1 and Focus 2 have generated research which provides valuable insights into the ways in which the categories of 'health' and 'illness' are discursively constructed, maintained and deployed within a range of contexts. They have also suggested that health-related discourses and practices may have implications for how particular health-related conditions may be experienced by those to whom they have been ascribed. However, in this chapter, I shall argue that in order to progress our understanding of the subjective experience of our bodies as 'healthy' or 'sick', discourse analytic work needs to develop Focus 2.

In the following sections, Focus 1 and Focus 2 will be discussed in more detail and their limitations identified. Attempts to theorize subjectivity will be introduced and the role of positioning theory in the development of discourse analytic studies of health and illness will be outlined. The chapter concludes by sketching a research programme for a discourse-dynamic[2] approach to the study of subjectivity in health psychology.

Focus 1: Expert Discourse

This involves the exploration of contemporary expert discourses and institutional practices (e.g. pain management, health promotion, sex education) and the ways in which these construct and position subjects (e.g. as 'at risk', as responsible, as passive). Data for this type of analysis are texts such as expert writings, official publications, specialist literature, the media, as well as institutional practices such as education methods, or diagnostic and treatment techniques. Yardley (1997a) describes these as 'macro-level discourses' (p. 42).

Much of this work has been influenced by Foucault, who strove to 'create a history of the different modes by which, in our culture, human beings are made subjects' (1982, p. 208, cited in Bunton and Petersen, 1997, p. 3). For example, Lupton (1995) discusses the ways in which health promotion discourse constructs people as permanently 'at risk' and simultaneously in charge of their physical and mental well-being. Ogden (1995) traces the ways in which contemporary psychological theory constructs the 'intraactive subject' and thus constitutes the self-controlling individual. Kugelmann (1997) explores the ways in which biopsychosocial theories of pain, together with their concomitant practices (pain management) and institutions (the pain clinic), position chronic pain patients as 'partners in healing', as self-disciplining and therefore personally responsible for their pain and its treatment. Brown (1999) examines the narratives and rhetorical devices which constitute 'stress as regimen' in a corpus of self-help texts and shows how these construct the psychological subject as a 'serviceable self', in charge of and responsible for maintaining and upgrading itself. Glassner (1989) draws attention to the ways in which contemporary fitness discourse and practice provide a space for the construction of a self which is protected through regimen from the influence of the ills of modern culture (such as drug abuse, depression and eating disorders).

A key theme which has emerged from these studies is that contemporary health discourses are characterized by an emphasis on self-control. Direct institutional surveillance and coercion are being replaced and/or complemented by technologies for self-monitoring, risk assessment and preventive practices. In this way, it can be argued, responsibility for public health is shifted away from the state and its institutions and on to individual citizens.

Focus 2: Everyday Talk

This work aims to assess to what extent expert discourses are reflected in lay people's accounts. Here, analysis of expert discourses is followed by an examination of texts generated by respondents through methods such as interviews, diaries or group discussions.

For example, Yardley (1997b) discusses the ways in which 'disorientation' has been constructed in medical, scientific, literary and philosophical writings in past and present. She then traces the deployment of discursive themes identified in the analysis of these texts in interviews with sufferers of 'disorientation'. Similarly, Woollett and Marshall (1997) analyse information booklets distributed to pregnant women in order to identify 'official' discourses of pregnancy and childbirth. This is followed by an analysis of interviews with mothers and mothers-to-be. Biological-medical discourses are identified in both sources, whereas psychological discourses are used by the women as an alternative, and in addition, to biomedical constructions. Howson's (1998) analysis of documentary sources such as medical journals and official reports concerned with the development of cervical screening is followed by an analysis of women's accounts of their experience of cervical screening. Howson observes that whilst expert discourse constructs 'objective risk categories' related to age and lifestyle, the women themselves articulate personalized risks which emerged from their own experience of screening participation, including timing, reliability and trustworthiness of the process. Taylor (1997) explores the ways in which psychological discourses impact upon individuals' talk about their SM (sadomasochistic) identities and practices. Following a review and critique of the essentialist construction of SM within sexological and psychological writings, Taylor identifies eight common interpretive repertoires used by SM devotees in order to make sense of their SM within the context of a research interview. These repertoires included (e.g. SM as pathology, SM as learned behaviour) but also went beyond (e.g. SM as dissidence, SM as transcendence) the psychological discourses identified in the literature.

Some researchers have taken the reverse approach: having identified prevalent discursive constructions in lay people's talk about health issues, they have then attempted to ground them in expert discourses. For example, Gillies and Willig (1997) identified discourses of physiological and psychological addiction in women smokers' accounts of cigarette smoking. These discourses were then culturally located within the disciplines and practices of medicine and health education.

It is important to acknowledge that a focus on lay people's uptake of expert discourse (Focus 2) need not imply passivity on the part of lay people. Researchers who work around Focus 2 often draw attention to the tensions and contradictions created by the multiple meanings which coexist within people's accounts, and to their subversive potential (e.g. Burman et al., 1996). Whilst expert discourses are clearly present in people's accounts, they are also challenged and disclaimed by those who use them. For example, Hunter and O'Dea (1997) show how menopausal women used biomedical discourse in order to define themselves in relation to the menopause (i.e. as undergoing certain bodily changes and thus as 'menopausal'), but then went on to disclaim a menopausal identity by minimizing the impact the menopause had upon their lives (e.g. as opposed to other women and contrary to expectation). So whilst the women positioned themselves *in relation to* expert discourses, they did not necessarily construct themselves *in accordance with* them.

Related Literature

There is a large body of literature which addresses social constructionist concerns in relation to health-related discourse and practice without necessarily adopting an explicitly discursive methodology. Using historical and cross-cultural perspectives, social scientists have been able to critically interrogate contemporary ways of defining and regulating bodily states and experiences. Stainton Rogers (1991) reviews the work of medical anthropologists such as Young (1980) and Taussig (1980) who have written about biomedicine's construction of reality and its sociocultural effects. For example, 'compliance' has been identified as a problematic concept which functions as a historically specific ideology which assumes and perpetuates a certain type of (paternalistic, authoritarian) relationship between physician and patient (Trostle, 1988). Qualitative research using methods such as grounded theory, phenomenology and ethnography has drawn attention to the role of cultural and linguistic practices in framing our experiences of 'health' and 'illness' (e.g. Morse, 1992). Medical sociologists (e.g. Dingwall, 1976) have for some time been looking at the ways in which ordinary people make sense of their experiences of health and illness within the context of social norms and culturally available commonsense knowledges. Recently, a constructionist version of the grounded theory method has also begun to be used to study both participants' and researchers' construction of meanings around health and illness (see Annells, 1996, and Chamberlain, 1999, for a discussion of this, and other, versions of grounded theory). For example, Charmaz (1990) used grounded theory in order to explore how chronic illness affects ill people's self-concepts. She paid close attention to respondents' use of language, which, she suggests, 'can help you bridge your participants' lived experience with your research question' (Charmaz, 1995, p. 36). Although this interdisciplinary and diverse literature has undoubtedly had, and continues to have, a significant influence upon discursive work in this area, I shall not return to it in the remainder of this article. This is because this chapter is concerned with the relationship between discourse, subjectivity and experience, and it seeks to identify ways in which this relationship may be theorized, explicitly and directly, within a discourse analytic frame.

Limitations

Focus I has been adopted by researchers within a number of different academic disciplines, including medical sociology (e.g. Lupton, 1994, 1995) and psychology (e.g. Stainton Rogers, 1991). An increasing number of critical analyses of discourses of health and illness continue to be published. However, Bunton (1997) draws attention to the fact that much of this work focuses on expert discourses of one sort or another and, as a result, neglects the study of everyday knowledge and popular culture. Lupton (1997), too, points out that Foucauldian analyses tend

> ... to neglect examination of the ways that hegemonic medical discourses and practices are variously taken up, negotiated or transformed by members of the lay population in their quest to maximize their health status and avoid physical distress and pain. (pp. 94–95)

Focus I has facilitated an extensive discussion of the discursive economy within which individuals live, and it has allowed us to speculate about its implications for individuals' subjective experiences. Authors have invoked the emergence of culturally and historically specific states of mind such as 'risk consciousness' and an 'awareness of responsibility' to care for themselves (e.g. Howson, 1998). It has been argued that contemporary surveillance techniques such as health risk assessments, screening and health promotion construct contemporary self-monitoring subjectivities (see Petersen and Bunton, 1997). It has also been suggested that health-related discourses and practices shape the ways in which we experience our bodies and ourselves (e.g. Yardley, 1997b). However, there has been little discussion of exactly *how* discourse may be implicated in subjectivity and *how* experience may be mediated by discourse. Howson (1998) points out that within sociology 'the content and consequences of the "risky self" in the context of specific forms of prevention tend to be assumed' (p. 197). In other words, Focus 1 invokes but fails to theorize the relationship between discourse, subjectivity and experience. I would argue that in order to fill this gap a more dynamic approach is required which takes as its object the individual as constituted by discourses and practices, and yet as uniquely purposive and reflective. A number of authors, including Foucault, have called for a deeper exploration of individual subjectivity, an 'ontology of experience', as Lupton (1997, p. 104) calls it.

Fox (1997) draws on Foucault's later writings in order to argue that 'Foucault's project is with how we become "desiring subjects"; in other words, how we articulate our bodies and desires within a subjectivity capable of reflection' (p. 42). This process of becoming-a-subject involves practices, or technologies, of the self. Foucault himself identified the need to shift from Focus 1 to Focus 2:

> I've insisted too much on the technology of domination and power. I am more and more interested in the interaction between oneself and others and in the technologies of individual domination, the history of how an individual acts upon himself, in the technology of the self. (Foucault, 1988, p. 19, cited in Fox, 1997, p. 42)

Such a focus upon self-formation also allows us to acknowledge and explore the tensions and contradictions which characterize the subject status (e.g. Schrift, 1995). A move towards a 'phenomenology of everyday life and subjectivity' (Lupton, 1997, p. 104), therefore, allows us to study individuals' resistance to dominant discourses, and the emergence of alternative subject positions as well as subversive practices.

Focus 2 has the potential to take up the challenge of theorizing how available discourses and practices constitute subjectivity. For example, Radley (1994, 1997) discusses the social negotiation of the sick role and its implications for the subjective experience of symptoms through the giving of meaning to bodily signs. Thus, the decision to 'give up' in the face of bodily signs and to define oneself as 'ill' actually changes the experience of these signs: it constitutes a 'redeployment of bodily potential' which allows the individual to 're-experienc[e] signs of bodily disturbance as symptoms of disease' (Radley, 1997, p. 58). There are, however, limitations to the way in which Focus 2 has been operationalized, and these will be discussed later in this chapter.

Implications for Social Constructionist Health Psychology

I would argue that social constructionist health psychology needs to move beyond critical deconstruction of health-related discourses and practices and begin to explore the ways in which these are appropriated, modified and challenged by individuals 'in their quest to maximize their health status and avoid physical distress and pain' (Lupton, 1997, pp. 94–95). That is to say, it needs to theorize the relationship between discourse, practice, subjectivity and experience.

In my view, social constructionist health psychology also needs to move beyond a concern with discourse practices and a conceptualization of 'selves' as purely contextual and transient discursive formations. This is because the experience of our bodies as 'sick', 'healthy', 'disabled', 'able-bodied', 'fit', 'fat', and so on, though undoubtedly subject to shifts and variation across discursive contexts, can become internalized and reified. Discursive constructions of what it means to be chronically ill, pregnant, menopausal, or whatever, and narratives of illness and/or recovery (including associated practices such as diagnostic and treatment regimens) provide a framework for the ways in which we are able to experience ourselves and our bodies over time (see also Frank, 1998; Murray, 1997). Social constructionist health psychology needs to find ways of studying embodied subjectivities and their discursive frames.

Theorizing Subjectivity

A number of social constructionist phychologists have attempted to theorize subjectivity. Positioning theory has been influential in this area. Memory work constitutes a more recent and less widely used approach. A concern with 'embodiment' represents the latest development in the study of subjectivity. In the following sections, I aim to outline the basic premises of these three approaches and to illustrate their relevance to social constructionist health psychology.

Memory Work

Memory work is a method of inquiry developed by the German feminist scholar Frigga Haug (1987) in order to study the sexualization of women's bodies. Haug was interested in the part played by women in their own subordination, in the 'self-construction of the prison of gender' (backcover). She proposed that memories play a key role in the construction of the self, and that an analysis of memories of how the (female) body is imbued with meaning allows us to explore the historical process of the constitution of the self. Memory work involves the collective analysis of participants' memories. It has affinities with discourse analysis in that it explores the ways in which memories invoke sociocultural meanings and positionings. However, memory work goes further than most discourse analytic work because it attempts to understand how discursive meanings, over time, constitute subjectivity, that is, a sense of self, including the experience of an emotional self (Crawford, Kippax, Onyx, Gault, and Benton, 1992) and a bodily self (Haug, 1987).

In memory work, the distinction between 'researcher' and 'researched' disappears. Participants collectively analyse their own memories in order to identify the discourses and social practices which have made them who they are today. The process of constructing and reconstructing the self is, of course, never complete, and the experience of memory work itself is likely to lead to reappraisals and changes in participants. Memory work uses memories of contradictory, unfamiliar or otherwise problematic episodes in order to uncover the ways in which meanings are negotiated in interaction with others, and how such meanings support the construction of the self. The collective analysis of a pool of memories allows participants to focus on the commonality of experience and to explore the role of social factors and processes in the construction of the self.

Though a fairly recent development and currently not widely used, I would argue that memory work is a promising point of departure for the study of subjectivity. It works with participants' sense of self and continuity whilst reflexively tracing how their subjectivities may have become constituted over time. Thus, unlike qualitative research methods such as focus groups where the split between researcher and researched is maintained, memory work mobilizes the tensions between our subjective accounts as participants and our analytic 'insights' as researchers in order to understand the processes by which we become 'selves'. Since memory work allows researchers to work with their own memories, they are directly confronted with the (emotional, bodily, psychological) consequences of the various discursive constructions and subject positions they themselves occupy. They have immediate access to the quality of experience associated with the various ways-of-being afforded by contemporary discourses. For example, emotions such as shame or pride can be experienced by participants as they share their memories with the group. This, I would argue, enables memory workers to explore the relationship between the discursive spaces they inhabit and the ways in which they experience themselves within them.

Memory work research to date has been primarily concerned with women's (and more recently also men's – see Pease, 2000) relationships with their bodies (e.g. Haug, 1987), with emotions (e.g. Crawford et al., 1992; Kippax, Crawford, Benton, Gault, and Noesjirwan, 1988) and with sexual practice (e.g. Harden and Willig, 1998; Kippax, Crawford, Waldy, and Benton, 1990). Thus, the ways in which we experience our bodies has been the focus of much memory work research. In line with the objectives of social constructionist health psychology outlined earlier, memory work therefore provides us with a suitable research method with which to study embodied subjectivities.

Positioning Theory

A number of social constructionist psychologists have utilized the concept of the 'subject position' in order to develop an account of subjectivity. Here, persons are seen to be constituted by positionings in discourse. 'Positioning theory' is by no means a unified account of self and personal agency; rather, it provides a set of conceptual tools with which to explore the relationship between discourse and subjectivity. There are various versions of positioning theory (e.g. Davies and Harré, 1990; Fahy and Smith, 1999; Hollway, 1989), all of which are continuously being modified and extended (e.g. Howie and Peters, 1996; Jones, 1997; Larner, 1998). Wendy Hollway (Henriques, Hollway, Urwin, Venn, and Walkerdine, 1984; Hollway, 1989) and Rom Harré (Davies and Harré, 1990; Harré and Gillett, 1994) have provided two of the most developed and detailed accounts of positioning theory. These will be discussed in the remainder of this section.

Wendy Hollway (1984, 1989) analysed heterosexual couples' talk about intimate relationships and identified a range of available subject positions. For example, the 'Discourse of Male Sexual Drive' prescribes and legitimates a biological, asocial expression of male sexuality. Within this discourse, the only subject position available to men is that of the instinct-driven sexual predator. Hollway argues that available positionings are not only deployed strategically in order to achieve particular social objectives (e.g. to excuse aggressive sexual behaviour), but that they actually structure the individual's private experience itself. In other words, discourses constitute subjectivities.

However, Henriques et al. (1984) as well as Hollway (1989) argue that discursive work on its own is not capable of theorizing subjectivity satisfactorily. Psychoanalytic concepts are mobilized in order to account for the motivational basis upon which particular positions in discourse are taken up, as well as to explain the individual's emotional investment in such positionings. For example, Hollway (1989, p. 64) refers to projection as a defence mechanism against threatening emotions in order to explain why one of her respondents positioned himself as the object, rather than the subject, of a have/hold discourse from within which sex should only take place within the framework of a lasting relationship.

Rom Harré's work is concerned with individual cognition as privatized discourse (e.g. Harré, 1997). Here, subjectivity as well as emotions are underpinned by positionings in discourse. Harré and Gillett (1994) argue that:

> Many psychological phenomena are to be interpreted as properties or features of discourse, and that discourse might be public or private. As public, it is behaviour; as private, it is thought. (p. 26)

Unlike most discourse analysts, Harré does not reject the notion of 'cognition'. Rather, he proposes to reconceptualize cognition in terms of the internalization of public discourses. Subjectivity, therefore, arises in public discourse but it need not be expressed publicly.

Consequently, positioning theory provides a way of accounting for the continuity of our experience of ourselves *as selves*. Though many subject positions which are taken up in discourse are temporary and fleeting (e.g. being positioned as a 'fare dodger' when caught travelling without a valid ticket), others are more permanent and therefore become internalized (e.g. being positioned as mother or father, man or woman, black or white) (see Burr, 1995, p. 145). Such positionings constitute ways-of-being through placing the subject within a network of meanings and social relations which facilitate as well as constrain what can be thought, said and done by someone so positioned. What originates in the social reality of language use becomes an internal subjective orientation. This is what Harré and Gillett (1994) mean when they talk about psychological phenomena as 'features or properties of discourse' (p. 26).

I would argue that if our aim is to study discourse as a way of mapping an'ontology of experience', as suggested by Lupton (1997, p. 104), positioning theory provides us with a suitable theoretical and methodological framework. Whilst approaches to positioning theory differ in their orientation to existing psychological frameworks, most notably psychoanalysis, they all attempt to make a connection between language and experience, between how subjects and objects are constructed through discourse and what it feels like to be constructed and positioned in particular ways. Like memory work, positioning theory recognizes continuity and it allows for an exploration of internal(ized) discourse. Consequently, positioning theory offers a way of conceptualizing the processes by which the experience of our bodies as 'sick', 'healthy', 'disabled', 'able-bodied', 'fit', 'fat', and so on, can become internalized and reified, thus defining (and constraining) possible ways-of-being. Researchers who want to explore how categories such as 'health' and 'illness' can become 'real' in the experience of those who are positioned within them may look to positioning theory as a suitable framework.

Embodiment

In an attempt to overcome dualistic conceptions of mind–body which have survived the social constructionist turn in psychology, attention has been focused on 'embodiment' (e.g. Bayer and Shotter, 1997; Stam, 1997). 'Embodiment' refers to the body's direct and immediate involvement in the social construction of meanings, collectively and individually. It has implications for both subjective experience and interpersonal communication. Embodiment moves beyond what Sampson (1996, p. 603) refers to as the 'object-body', that is, the body as perceived and studied from the outside. The study of embodiment is concerned with the bodily as well as linguistic practices which constitute human subjectivity. That is to say, the way we do things, as well as what we say and how we say it, 'makes certain social worlds appear' (Radley, 1996, p. 566). For example, gestures, posture and movements are part of the embodied discourse of gender difference.

Such a notion of 'embodiment' constitutes a challenge to many social constructionist accounts. Baerveldt and Voestermans (1996) discuss the ways in which social constructionists have theorized 'the body' and come to the conclusion that neither 'weak' nor 'strong' forms of social contructionism grant the body a role in the production of meaning. Instead, the body is seen to merely enact or dramatize discursively constructed cultural resources. The body itself is a blank to which meaning is added or attached; Baerveldt and Voestermans (1996, p. 696) refer to this as the 'mannequin' body. What is missing from such a conceptualization of 'the body' is its role in the constitution of subjectivity, or what Baerveldt and Voestermans (1996, p. 709) call the 'selfing process'. In other words, social constructionists need to concern themselves with what it means to 'be a body' rather than to 'have a body', with the experiential and expressive qualities of the body rather than merely with its communicative and symbolic functions. I would argue that a full understanding of the social construction of 'health' and 'illness' must include an account of how we 'become' sick and/or healthy bodies, that is, how discourses of health and illness are interleaved with our material bodies, how this is reflected in our subjective experience of these bodies (see also Grosz, 1994; Yardley, 1996, 1997c).

A concern with 'embodiment' raises methodological questions. The most widely used and best developed social constructionist research methods work with texts. Texts may be generated through interviews, focus group discussions, naturally occurring conversations, diaries or other documents. Analysis involves an exploration of the social construction of meaning through language. However, once the body is conceptualized as 'a meaning-producing device' (Baerveldt and Voestermans, 1996, p. 700) other methods may be required to study embodiment. We need to find ways in which bodily meaning production may be researched which do not rely upon textual material alone.

Embodiment is a relatively recent theoretical construct which requires further elaboration and development. Those who argue the case for embodiment tend to present detailed critiques of dualist approaches to the embodied person, followed by a rough outline of what the study of embodiment may entail. Illustrations of the application of such a theoretical framework are supplied by reference to sociological, historical or anthropological research. The relationship between discourse, embodiment and subjectivity needs to be theorized and researched more fully.

From Positionings to Selves

Having identified approaches to the study of subjectivity which are compatible with and conducive to the aims of social constructionist health psychology (see p. 530), I want to propose their extension in order to take account of personal histories, practice and change.

There seems little doubt that memories, discursive positionings and embodiment play a role in the constitution of subjectivity. However, research attempting to explore subjectivity has remained constrained by a number of limitations: first, such attempts tend to be concerned with discourse produced at one point in time rather than discursive change over time; second, they have concerned themselves almost exclusively with discourse rather than with the relationship between discourse, practice and experience;[3] and, third, they tend to sideline the question of motivation and continuity in relation to the take-up of discursive positions. In the remainder of this chapter, I shall discuss these three claims in more detail. I aim to build on the approaches to subjectivity introduced above and to sketch a research programme for the discourse-dynamic study of subjectivity which takes account of history, practice and change.

Personal History

I would argue that future research into the constitution of subjectivity needs to proceed in a 'bottom-up' fashion. In this sense, I endorse Focus 2. However, there are limitations to research which aims to identify official and/or expert discourses in lay people's talk. Even though such work focuses upon subjectivity, it tends to use lay people's utterances simply to illustrate the availability of official and/or expert discourses. It fails to explore, and theorize, how discursive constructions are used and by whom, in what combinations, within which contexts and with what consequences for subjectivity and experience. Much current writing about 'subjectivity' tends to remain at a descriptive level. This is to say, authors identify and describe subject positions offered by contemporary discourses and practices. However, what has been missing from this literature is an account of exactly *how* discourse is implicated in the constitution of subjectivity, in the 'fabrication of individual experience and identity' (Armstrong, 1997, p. 22). In other words, our focus needs to shift from the *availability* of discursive resources in the culture to the individual's *appropriation* of (some of) these over time. Hojholt (1997) describes the problem thus:

> When we look at individuals in their social contexts we should not let the context itself, the social discourse, interaction or culture be the active subject in our analysis. That easily happens when we take as our point of reference one single isolated context. When we look at social contexts in isolation they are in danger of losing their meaning for participants. Social contexts get their social meaning through their connection with other contexts, their connections with something more comprehensive. Furthermore, in a context the participants act on the basis of their participation in other contexts and what kind of meaning participation here has to them. (p. 1)

Hojholt makes the important point that individual subjectivity is a historical as well as a social product. Here, she echoes Foucault's reference to the importance of 'the *history* of how an individual acts upon himself' (Foucault, 1988, p. 19, cited in Fox, 1997, p. 42, my emphasis). Consequently, it is not enough to examine the extent to which individuals position themselves within dominant discourses in a one-off interview. Any real understanding of subjectivity needs to pay attention to the individual's personal history. As Hojholt (1997) puts it, 'we need theorizing about how individuals live their lives in trajectories of social practice' (p. 9) and, we may add, discursive practice.[4]

Practice

Most versions of discourse analysis recognize the performative nature of talk. They take into account the action orientation of talk and text, and thereby conceptualize discourse as a form of practice. People do things with words (e.g. blame, accuse, excuse, disclaim, etc.) and they construct versions of reality in conversation with others. Furthermore positioning theory is concerned with the ways in which available discursive resources can constrain as well as enable what can be thought, said and done by individuals (e.g. Harré and Gillett, 1994; Parker, 1992). Here, internalized discursive positionings set the limits to what a person is able to do and feel, even when they are alone. For example, Harré and Gillett (1994) argue that the 'sense of agentic position, the sense that one is the agent of one's actions and responsible to others for them' (p. 111), is acquired through language and cultural conventions and is expressed in the indexical grammar of 'I' (not available in all cultures). Thus, discursive resources facilitate access to some ways of being but not others, including emotions and non-verbal practices. For example, Willig (1995, 1997, 1998) and Gillies and Willig (1997) explored the relationship between discursive positionings and health practices. This research identified ways in which discursive constructions (of trust and addiction, respectively) positioned respondents in such a way (as trusting spouse, as addict) as to facilitate, or even require, potentially health-damaging practices (unsafe sex, cigarette smoking). In this research, discourse is seen as primary in the sense that discursive resources open up (or close down) possibilities for action. However, little research has been carried out into the ways in which practices may, in turn, constrain discourse. In other words, access to discursive resources including positionings may be limited by institutionalized or otherwise regulated practices. Harré and Gillett (1994) point out that

> ... to act with freedom, the discursive possibilities that are potentially available to an individual must be affirmed, owned and used in some practice.... Given that a person is always trying to make sense of their life and the situations around them, they cannot just abandon their established discursive positionings and put nothing in their place. Alternative meanings have to arise and be validated in some way. (p. 127)

A discourse-dynamic approach to the study of subjectivity would have to acknowledge that discourse and practice are bound up with each other. Parker (1992) reminds us that discourses are grounded in social and material structures, such as institutions and their practices, and that, therefore, 'discourse analysis needs to attend to the conditions which make the meanings of texts possible' (p. 28). For example, upon hospitalization it may become virtually impossible *not* to position oneself as 'patient' within a biomedical discourse. Thus, our study of subjectivity must include an analysis of the social and material practices which mediate access to discourses and the availability of discursive positionings.

Change

Both memory work and positioning theory acknowledge the importance of personal history. Memory work does it most obviously by exploring the relationship between past events, memories and the construction of the self. Hollway addresses personal histories though her use of psycho-analytic categories. Harré's notion of 'cognition as privatized discourse' is informed by Vygotsky's developmental psychology, according to which children become persons through the appropriation practice such of social language. This requires the practice of joint action, since 'all the higher mental functions originate as actual relations between people' (Vygotsky, 1987, p. 57, cited in Newman and Holzman, 1997, p. 44). According to Vygotsky, speaking completes thinking, thus allowing children, and, Newman and Holzman (1997) would argue, also adults, to continuously become other through communication with others.

The objective of a discourse-dynamic study of subjectivity is to explore the ways in which people's subjectivities undergo change through their engage-ment with their material, social and discursive environments. Both memory work and positioning theory offer the theoretical tools with which to trace such change.

Whereto Now? Directions for Health Psychology Research

There are examples of recent work in the social study of health and illness which incorporate some of the ideas developed in this chapter. In order to provide a sense of the kind of health psychology research I have in mind, in this final section I shall draw attention to two projects which have attempted to locate an account of subjectivity within a trajectory of discursive and bodily change.

Selfing Through Stories

Arthur Frank (1998) is concerned with the ways in which first-person illness narratives can transform the self by resisting an institutionalized process of medical standardization. Illness narratives allow the individual to inter-rogate the kind of self they want to be:

> Against the medical standardization of disease, the personal story claims its unique way of being ill.... More than disease itself, medical diagnosis and treatment, with their enforced routinization of the patient's life, threatens the differences between human beings on which moral significance depends. (p. 340)

Frank acknowledges that illness narratives constitute not only a 'care of the self', that is, an opportunity to 'reclaim a voice' for oneself, but also a 'technology of the self', that is, the legitimation of certain social knowl-edges. He argues that, within this space, individuals can resist the threat to the self posed by illness and 'refashion experience to reassert individu-ality' (p. 341). In *The Wounded Storyteller* (1995), Frank draws on published and unpublished first-person accounts in order to demonstrate how dif-ferent illness narratives are implicated in different illness experiences.

He identifies three major narratives: restitution, chaos and quest. The restitution narrative tells the story of illness as a temporary abberation, a mechanical fault in the body machine which can, and ought, to be fixed in order to return the individual to their previous (healthy) condition. The chaos narrative, by contrast, tells the story of life never getting better. It reflects the teller's experience of life as lacking in order, causality or coherent sequencing, and their sense of being trapped in a present of endless suffering. The quest narrative talks about illness as an occasion for personal growth; here, the crisis is the start of a journey which offers an opportunity for self-transformation and change, and where illness is no longer pointless. Frank argues that the availability of narratives has implications for the individual's experience of illness. For example, the restitution narrative does not make mortality available to experience. Those whom Frank describes as being 'captured by the exclusivity of the restitution narrative' (p. 94) find themselves with nothing left to say when restitution is not an option. Here, 'the tragedy is not death but having the self-story end before the life is over' (p. 96). Similarly, those who live with chronic illness and/or disability are not well served by the restitution narrative. They require narratives which 'affirm life beyond restitution' (p. 96). Frank explicitly connects language with experience and subjectivity. His work is concerned with the ways in which narratives make available certain kinds of experience and shape selves over time. It is also concerned with practice, since stories are not only told but also 'enacted' (p. 116). Finally, Frank's notion of 'narrative ethics' revolves around 'personal becoming' (p. 158), that is, self-conscious change through telling certain kinds of stories.

Subject Positions and Experience

Kathleen Fahy and Philip Smith's (1999) paper traces the subject positions through which a midwife researcher and a pregnant teenager move in negotiating medical encounters, and their implications for subjectivity and experience. Within the framework of a critical feminist ethnography project, the midwife researcher provided a midwifery service for adolescents aged 12–15. She also acted as support person for the young women during medical encounters. The analysis presented in Fahy and Smith's paper uses subject positions theory in order to better understand the ways in which one young woman and the midwife researcher managed and experienced two critical incidents: a vaginal ultrasound and the birth. Fahy and Smith identify a range of subject positions, including those of the 'nurse', the 'advocate', and of 'good' and 'bad' doctors and patients. They trace the consequences of the performance of these varied subject positions for the unfolding of the interactions between participants and for participants' subjective experience of the situation. For example, enacting the subject position of 'nurse' can feel comfortable and unambiguous, whereas the subject position of 'advocate' can create fear and ambivalence on the part of the midwife researcher. Fahy and Smith show how medical power is reproduced and challenged through 'the interplay of the repertoire of subject positions mobilized in specific event sequences' (pp. 89–90). Fahy and Smith's exploration of the relationship between positions in discourse, their enactment and the individual's subjective experience of a situation provides an illustration of how we may begin to research our discursive and embodied subjectivities.

Conclusion

I have argued that social constructionist research with relevance to health-related subjectivation has been primarily concerned with the identification of 'macro-level discourses' of health and illness (Focus 1). Work which has used everyday talk as data has tended to look for the presence of dominant discourses in lay people's talk (Focus 2). In addition, most discourse analytic research in this area has been content to analyse one-off interviews with individuals, and its emphasis has been on the availability of discursive repertoires to participants. I proposed an extension of Focus 2 in order to allow for the discourse-dynamic study of subjectivity. This requires that we take the individual as our subject of inquiry within a longitudinal design. The theoretical framework for such an approach is provided by positioning theory.

There is a practical reason for developing a discourse-dynamic research programme for the study of subjectivity in health psychology. Social constructionists have successfully criticized psychological theories of health behaviour for their insensitivity to the importance of the cultural and discursive meanings of health practices (e.g. Ingham, Woodcock, and Stenner, 1991, 1992; Maticka-Tyndale, 1992). They have produced powerful accounts of why individuals find it difficult or impossible to comply with health education messages which are in conflict with such meanings and practices; however, there has been little discussion of how people *do* change and become able to adopt healthful practices. A discourse-dynamic approach to the study of subjectivity would enable us to explore the relationship between health-related discourses, available positionings within such discourses, and the practices which they facilitate or even command. A better understanding of this relationship could then open up opportunities for interventions which aim to facilitate empowerment through the repositioning of the subject (see also Willig, 1999). For example, if health promotion discourse and practice position smokers as 'addicts' within a discourse of physical and psychological addiction, and if such positionings are experienced as disempowering, then those who want to support smokers in their attempts to quit smoking need to provide opportunities for access to alternative, and arguably more empowering, subject positions (Gillies, 1999). One aim of such an intervention could be to replace the passive positioning as 'nicotine addict' with the active positioning of 'activist against multinational tobacco companies' by involving smokers in campaigns against the tobacco industry.[5]

Notes

1 Wetherell (1998), however, has challenged this distinction. She argues that the 'division of labour' (p. 405) created by the two approaches is not helpful, and that a more synthetic approach to discourse analysis is required.

2 I am using the term 'discourse-dynamic' in line with Parker's (1992) emphasis upon the role of discourse in reproducing and transforming the material world as well as its inhabitants' subjectivities.

3 As pointed out in the introductory pages, in this chapter I am concerned with the relationship between discursive constructions and the ways in which we experience ourselves and our bodies. My discussion of the literature, including critique, is therefore confined to those authors who share this concern. My comments are not directed at those discourse analysts who question the value of the category 'experience' and who conceptualize it as a purely discursive move instead. They do not aim to theorize 'experience' (or subjectivity) and are therefore excluded from my discussion. To take issue with the aims and objectives of their brand of discourse analysis would constitute the subject matter of another chapter.

4 An awareness of the importance of personal history, and its absence from social constructionist theorizing, has motivated a growing interest in psychoanalytic concepts among Foucauldian discourse analysts in recent years. Even though psychoanalysis provides us with a way of connecting the social construction of meaning with individual life histories, there are problems with its uncritical use of explanatory constructs such as 'repression', 'projection', and so on, which, from a social constructionist point of view, ought themselves to be understood as social and discursive constructions.

5 An example of such activism is the Australian Billboard-Utilizing Graffitists Against Unhealthy Promotions (BUGA UP), who used spraycans to 'reface' hoardings carrying cigarette advertisements (Hewat, 1991).

References

Annells, M. (1996). Grounded theory method: Philosophical perspectives, paradigm of inquiry, and postmodernism. *Qualitative Health Research, 6*(3), 379–393.

Armstrong, D. (1997). Foucault and the sociology of health and illness: A prismatic reading. In A. Petersen and R. Bunton (ed.), *Foucault, health and medicine* (pp. 15–30). London: Routledge.

Baerveldt, C., and Voestermans, P. (1996). The body as a selfing device: The case of anorexia nervosa. *Theory & Psychology, 6*(4), 693–713.

Bayer, B.M., and Shotter, J. (1997). *Reconstructing the psychological subject: Bodies, practices and technologies*. London: Sage.

Brown, S.D. (1999). Stress as regimen: Critical readings of selp-help literature. In C. Willig (ed.), *Applied discourse analysis: Social and psychological interventions* (pp. 22–43). Buckingham: Open University Press.

Bunton, R. (1997). Popular health, advanced liberalism and *Good Housekeeping* magazine. In A. Petersen and R. Bunton (eds), *Foucault, health and medicine* (pp. 223–248). London: Routledge.

Bunton, R., and Petersen, A. (1997). Foucault's medicine. In A. Petersen and R. Bunton (eds), *Foucault, health and medicine* (pp. 1–11). London: Routledge.

Burman, E., Aitken, G., Alldred, P., Allwood, R., Billington, T., Goldberg, B., Gordo Lopez, A.J., Heenan, C., Marks, D., and Warner, S. (eds). (1996). *Psychology, discourse and social practice: From regulation to resistance.* London: Taylor & Francis.

Burr, V. (1995). *An introduction to social constructionism.* London: Routledge.

Chamberlain, K. (1999). Using grounded theory in health psychology. In M. Murray and K. Chamberlain (eds), *Qualitative health psychology: Theories and methods* (pp. 183–201). London: Sage.

Charmaz, K. (1990). 'Discovering' chronic illness: Using grounded theory. *Social Science and Medicine, 30*(11), 1161–1172.

Charmaz, K. (1995). Grounded theory. In J.A. Smith, R. Harré, and L. van Langenhove (eds), *Rethinking methods in psychology* (pp. 27–49). London: Sage.

Crawford, J., Kippax, S., Onyx, J., Gault, U., and Benton, P. (1992). *Emotion and gender: Constructing meaning from memory.* London: Sage.

Davies, B., and Harré, R. (1990). Positioning: The discursive production of selves. *Journal for the Theory of Social Behaviour, 20*(1), 43–64.

Dingwall, R. (1976). *Aspects of illness.* London: Martin Robertson.

Edwards, D., and Potter, J. (1992). *Discursive psychology.* London: Sage.

Fahy, K., and Smith, P. (1999). From the sick role to subject positions: A new approach to the medical encounter. *Health, 3*(1), 71–93.

Foucault, M. (1988). The dangerous individual. In L.D. Kritzman (ed.), *Michel Foucault: Politics, philosophy, culture.* New York: Routledge.

Fox, N.J. (1997). Is there life after Foucault? Texts, frames and differends. In A. Petersen and R. Bunton (eds), *Foucault, health and medicine* (pp. 31–50). London: Routledge.

Frank, A.W. (1995). *The wounded storyteller: Body, illness, and ethics.* London: University of Chicago Press.

Frank, A.W. (1998). Stories of illness as care of the self: A Foucauldian dialogue. *Health, 2*(3), 329–348.

Gillies, V. (1999). An analysis of the discursive positions of women smokers: Implications for practical interventions. In C. Willig (ed.), *Applied discourse analysis: Social and psychological interventions* (pp. 66–86). Buckingham: Open University Press.

Gillies, V., and Willig, C. (1997). 'You get the nicotine and that in your blood': Constructions of addiction and control in women's accounts of cigarette smoking. *Journal of Community and Applied Social Psychology, 7*, 285–301.

Glassner, B. (1989). Fitness and the postmodern self. *Journal of Health and Social Behaviour, 30*, 180–191.

Grosz, E. (1994). *Volatile bodies: Toward a corporeal feminism.* Bloomington/Indianapolis: Indiana University Press.

Harden, A., and Willig, C. (1998). An exploration of the discursive constructions used in young adults' memories and accounts of contraception. *Journal of Health Psychology, 3*(3), 429–445.

Harré, R. (1997, 29–31 August). *The ontological status of persons.* Paper presented at the Inaugural Conference of the Centre for Critical Realism, University of Warwick.

Harré, R., and Gillett, G. (1994). *The discursive mind*. London: Sage.

Haug, F. (ed.). (1987). *Female sexualization: A collective work of memory* (E. Carter, Trans.). London: Verso.

Henriques, J., Hollway, W., Urwin, C., Venn, C., and Walkerdine, V. (eds). (1984). *Changing the subject: Psychology, social regulation and subjectivity*. London: Methuen.

Hewat, T. (1991). *Modern merchants of death*. Victoria: Wrightbooks.

Hojholt, C. (1997, 27 April–2 May). *Child development trajectories in social practice*. Paper presented at the Berlin Conference of the International Society for Theoretical Psychology, Berlin.

Hollway, W. (1984). Gender difference and the production of subjectivity. In J. Henriques, W. Hollway, C. Urwin, C. Venn, and V. Walkerdine (eds), *Changing the subject: Psychology, social regulation and subjectivity* (pp. 227–263). London: Methuen.

Hollway, W. (1989). *Subjectivity and method in psychology: Gender, meaning and science*. London: Sage.

Howie, D., and Peters, M. (1996). Positioning theory: Vygotsky, Wittgenstein and social constructionist psychology. *Journal for the Theory of Social Behaviour, 26*(1), 51–64.

Howson, A. (1998). Surveillance, knowledge and risk: The embodied experience of cervical screening. *Health, 2*(2), 195–215.

Hunter, M.S., and O'Dea, I. (1997). Menopause: Bodily changes and multiple meanings. In J.M. Ussher (ed.), *Body talk: The material and discursive regulation of sexuality, madness and reproduction* (pp. 199–222). London: Routledge.

Ingham, R., Woodcock, A., and Stenner, K. (1991). Getting to know you … : Young people's knowledge of their partners at first intercourse. *Journal of Community & Applied Social Psychology, 1*(2), 117–132.

Ingham, R., Woodcock, A., and Stenner, K. (1992). The limitations of rational decision-making models as applied to young people's sexual behaviour. In P. Aggleton, P. Davies, and G. Hart (eds), *AIDS: Rights, risk and reason* (pp. 163–173). London: Falmer.

Jones, R. (1997). The presence of self in the person: Reflexive positioning and personal constructs psychology. *Journal for the Theory of Social Behaviour, 27*(4), 453–471.

Kippax, S., Crawford, J., Benton, P., Gault, U., and Noesjirwan, J. (1988). Constructing emotions: Weaving meaning from memory. *British Journal of Social Psychology, 27*, 19–33.

Kippax, S., Crawford, J., Waldy, C., and Benton, P. (1990). Women negotiating heterosex: Implications for AIDS prevention. *Women's Studies International Forum, 13*(6), 533–542.

Kugelmann, R. (1997). The psychology and management of pain: Gate control as theory and symbol. *Theory & Psychology, 7*(1), 43–65.

Larner, G. (1998). Through a glass darkly: Narrative as destiny. *Theory & Psychology, 8*(4), 549–572.

Lupton, D. (1994). *Medicine as culture: Illness, disease and the body in western societies*. London: Sage.

Lupton, D. (1995). *The imperative of health: Public health and the regulated body*. London: Sage.

Lupton, D. (1997). Foucault and the medicalization critique. In A. Petersen and R. Bunton (eds), *Foucault, health and medicine* (pp. 94–110). London: Routledge.

Maticka-Tyndale, E. (1992). Social construction of HIV transmission and prevention among young heterosexual adults. *Social Problems, 39*(3), 238–252.

Morse, J.M. (ed.). (1992). *Qualitative health research.* London: Sage.

Murray, M. (1997). A narrative approach to health psychology: Background and potential. *Journal of Health Psychology, 2,* 9–20.

Newman, F., and Holzman, L. (1997). *The end of knowing: A new developmental way of learning.* London: Routledge.

Ogden, J. (1995). Changing the subject of health psychology. *Psychology and Health, 10,* 257–265.

Ogden, J. (1996). *Health psychology: A textbook.* Buckingham: Open University Press.

Parker, I. (1992). *Discourse dynamics: Critical analysis for social and individual psychology.* London: Routledge.

Parker, I. (Ed.). (1998). *Social constructionism, discourse and realism.* London: Sage.

Pease, B. (2000). *Recreating Men. Postmodern Masculinity Politics.* London: Sage.

Petersen, A., and Bunton, R. (eds). (1997). *Foucault, health and medicine.* London: Routledge.

Potter, J., and Wetherell, M. (1995). Discourse analysis. In J.A. Smith, R. Harré, and L. van Langenhove (eds), *Rethinking methods in psychology* (pp. 80–92). London: Sage.

Potter, J., Wetherell, M., Gill, R., and Edwards, D. (1990). Discourse: Noun, verb or social practice? *Philosophical Psychology, 3*(2), 205–217.

Radley, A. (1994). *Making sense of illness: The social psychology of health and disease.* London: Sage.

Radley, A. (1996). Displays and fragments: Embodiment and the configuration of social worlds. *Theory & Psychology, 6*(4), 559–576.

Radley, A. (1997). What role does the body have in illness? In L. Yardley (ed.), *Material discourses of health and illness* (pp. 50–67). London: Routledge.

Sampson, E.E. (1996). Establishing embodiment in psychology. *Theory* and *Psychology, 6*(4), 601–624.

Schrift, A.D. (1995). Reconfiguring the subject as a process of self: Following Foucault's Nietzschean trajectory to Butler, Laclau/Mouffe, and beyond. *New Formations, 25,* 28–39.

Stainton Rogers, W. (1991). *Explaining health and illness: An exploration of diversity.* Hemel Hempstead: Harvester Wheatsheaf.

Stam, H.J. (1997). *The body and psychology.* London: Sage.

Taussig, M. (1980). Reification and the consciousness of the patient. *Social Science and Medicine, 14b,* 3–13.

Taylor, G.W. (1997). The discursive construction and regulation of dissident sexualities: The case of SM. In J.M. Ussher (ed.), *Body talk: The material and discursive regulation of sexuality, madness and reproduction* (pp. 106–130). London: Routledge.

Trostle, J.A. (1988). Medical compliance as an ideology. *Social Science and Medicine, 27,* 1299–1308.

Vygotsky, L.S. (1987). *The Collected Works of L.S. Vyogtsky,* Vol. 1. New York: Plenum.

Wetherell, M. (1998). Positioning and interpretive repertoires: Conversation analysis and post-structuralism in dialogue. *Discourse & Society, 9*(3), 387–412.

Willig, C. (1995). 'I wouldn't have married the guy if I'd have to do that': Heterosexual adults' accounts of condom use and their implications for sexual practice. *Journal of Community and Applied Social Psychology, 5,* 75–87.

Willig, C. (1997). The limitations of trust in intimate relationships: Constructions of trust and sexual risk taking. *British Journal of Social Psychology, 36,* 211–221.

Willig, C. (1998). Constructions of sexual activity and their implications for sex education. *Journal of Health Psychology, 3*(3), 383–392.

Willig, C. (ed.). (1999). *Applied discourse analysis: Social and psychological interventions.* Buckingham: Open University Press.

Woollett, A., and Marshall, H. (1997). Discourses of pregnancy and childbirth. In L. Yardley (Ed.), *Material discourses of health and illness* (pp. 176–198). London: Routledge.

Yardley, L. (1996). Reconciling discursive and materialist perspectives on health and illness: A reconstruction of the biopsychosocial approach. *Theory & Psychology, 6*(3), 485–508.

Yardley, L. (1997a). Introducing discursive methods. In L. Yardley (ed.), *Material discourses of health and illness* (pp. 25–49). London: Routledge.

Yardley, L. (1997b). Disorientation in the (post)modern world. In L. Yardley (ed.), *Material discourses of health and illness* (pp. 109–131). London: Routledge.

Yardley, L. (1997c). Introducing material-discursive approaches to health and illness. In L. Yardley (ed.), *Material discourses of health and illness* (pp. 1–24). London: Routledge.

Young, A. (1980). The discourse on stress and the reproduction of conventional knowledge. *Social Science and Medicine, 14b,* 133–146.

24 HEALTH PSYCHOLOGY, EMBODIMENT AND THE QUESTION OF VULNERABILITY

Alan Radley

The general conception of the body that underpins most health psychology research derives from assumptions that underlie psychology as a quasi-science. However, when applied to questions of illness, these assumptions are worked through in a special way. As well as sharing certain basic premises of the parent discipline, health psychology takes as its questions problems defined by medicine, including a particular attitude to the bodies of its clients. As a result, health psychology journals are filled with articles that deal with how patients cope with, recover from, are liable to, or in some way think, talk or act in relation to their having a particular diagnostic label attached to them.

There are good reasons for this being the case. Health psychology earns its place in the family of professions allied to medicine by offering to contribute aspects of patient care that are outside the scope of medicine and special to psychology. This is a contribution that defines health psychology as a practice consistent with the wider aims of the alleviation of suffering and the prevention of disease. How effective it is at doing this is a matter for evaluation, perhaps for evidence-based research, but it is not the point to be discussed here. Instead, I wish to argue that health psychology researches in a field that its present theories are not suited to analyse and to comprehend. This is because the topic of health involves issues of vulnerability and healing, both of these being crucial to the fact that people do not just have bodies, but are embodied.

Health psychology endorses the assumptions of quasi-experimental psychology by explicitly or implicitly accepting the body as essentially a physical substrate to mind. This has the effect of making it comprehensible only as a biomedical entity, but never as a psychological one (Romanyshyn, 1982). This is a result of historical developments involving assumptions about the separation of mind from body, and the emergence of modern clinical techniques (Leder, 1992). The development of clinical techniques was central to producing the role of the passive patient, whose body was objectified in terms of the new medical classifications (Jewson, 1976). The metaphors for conceptualizing the body in relation to these clinical practices define biomedical thinking to this day (Kirmayer, 1988). This meant that the emerging discipline of psychology took as its focus mental as opposed to physical concerns, albeit proposing mental life in physicalistic terms in the attempt to bridge the Cartesian divide (e.g. mechanisms, processes, models) (Radley, 1991).

The body in these terms is physically defined, can be diagnosed, investigated and treated. Its natural variations (sex, age, height, weight, and performance levels) can be studied in relation to various psychological measures, as can its many but specifiable forms of pathology. The correlate of the physical body is, of course, the subjective self who (it is presumed) inhabits it. This subjectivity (conceptualized as self, feelings, or discourses) is by now a field of study for health psychologists who provide accounts of what it is like for patients to suffer from particular diseases, or to undergo particular treatments. However, recording how people perceive their own or others' condition assumes an approach that depends upon the assumption of a physical body considered to pre-exist as object. For that reason, and in spite of intentions to move away from the medical approach, subjectivist positions risk continuing to accept the body as being properly located in the realm of biomedicine.

Therefore, knowledge of the body as object – even when taken across a range of interventions and diagnostic categories – does not itself add up to any adequate understanding of what illness means in a world of embodied persons. Having separated mind from body at its inception, it became impossible for psychology to deal with issues that call for a treatment of the 'mindful body' and the 'incarnated mind' (Merleau-Ponty, 1968). No amount of cross-correlation of physical and psychological indices can ever provide this understanding, which, I will argue, is essential to a thoroughgoing psychology of health. That is why experimental psychology is of limited help in addressing the key issue of health psychology's problematic: illness and healing. It is also why it falls to health psychologists – among others, admittedly – to provide theories of embodiment having implications for the rest of psychology as a whole.

Recently there has emerged an interest in the body as a topic within psychology (Radley, 1991; Stam, 1998; Ussher, 1989), following considerable debate within sociology and cultural studies (see Frank, 1991; Williams, 1996). The criticism of the subject – the stable internalized self – as a central problem for study meant that its correlate, the physical body, has also been criticized, and seen as discursively produced (Lupton, 2000). Following this line, one might agree that the body – along with the rest of the world – is remade in language. But 'doing the body in talk' is not the same as acting with the body. The epistemological position that privileges language risks evading the very issues that require attention. Even to see these issues demands that language be treated as transparent in the practical contexts of health care and illness experience. This means treating embodied action as a way of symbolizing (not just an object to be spoken about), as well as recognizing the material features of life that an emphasis upon talk diminishes (Radley, 1999b; Yardley, 1999).

It has been argued that the issue of what it means to be embodied is itself worthy of study, not least by feminists for whom the question of the physical basis of gender has been examined. (I am thinking particularly of the writings of Emily Martin (1987, 1994), Dorothy Smith (1987) and Iris Young (1990, 1994), not to mention the work on nursing carried out by Pat Benner (1984).) What has emerged is not a theory of 'the body' as such, but rather embodiment as a field in which various issues can be explored. These range from questions about how women experience their own bodies, and how they perceive other people's bodies, to the way in which social and ideological matters become inscribed on the bodies of those concerned (Lupton, 2000). This means that 'the body', while no longer a generalized object (a 'thing' which, gender permitting, we all share), has become a universal issue for study in the social sciences. It is against this background that health psychology will need to examine its position with regard to specific issues concerning embodiment and to the wider debate about health care in society.

Vulnerability and the 'Doctor (Psychologist) – Patient' Relationship

At the outset of this chapter I said that health psychology's assumptions about the body are shaped by the moral and ethical values that medicine has adopted. These values involve aspects of the relationship of practitioner to patient, which are sidelined by a focus upon issues of communication and control. These issues concern, among other things, the toleration of suffering by the practitioners concerned. We can get a useful glimpse of this by looking at the training of medical students today. In his study of how medical students today. In his study of how medical students in an American hospital approach the anatomy laboratory, Hafferty (1991) reports the various cadaver stories exchanged by students. He says that the dissection of the cadaver is a test of a student's emotional competence to become a physician, where failure is the overt expression of emotion. Hafferty quotes one student as saying:

> I'm really getting apprehensive about working with the cadaver.... Just seeing that it was once a person that was alive and did everything ... I'm just hoping the face is not discernible as a person. (1991, p. 64)

Later on in his study, Hafferty describes an event in which an elderly patient collapsed and died in the course of being questioned during a case presentation to the students. There were a number of reactions among them, though many were disturbed by their witnessing death happening during a medical training session. One student said that the man's coughing fit that ensued when being questioned would, in another context, have been an occasion to stop the questioning. But in the case presentation, he said, 'everyone was selective about what they were observing'. Another student reviews the episode by concluding that, in future, she would try not to 'get quite that involved. I don't think this means being callous. I think it just means adopting a more self-protective reserve' (1991: p. 174).

The point about these examples is not to show that medical students learn to be callous. Instead, it shows two important things. First, that the body is always imbued with social significance, not least when it is a dead body. Second, that what the body becomes – what it means – is tied up with one's way of approaching it. That is, the passive body is a product of the medical approach. This has, as one of its key aims, the displacement of feelings and responses that would otherwise interfere with the attempt to cure and to alleviate distress by allopathic means. It also shows that *medicine is constituted in difference*, in the separation of doctor from patient, of person from body. This emphasis upon difference directs attention away from what is shared by all concerned (issues of mortality, of vulnerability), so that what is held in common is marginalized and excluded from study (Radley, 1999a). It is only relatively recently that such embodied experiences have been given full weight and, more to the point, shown to be what they are in relation to the practical attitude of medicine (Little, 2000; Toombs, 1992).

Those health psychologists who work in a clinical context might – just might – justify taking this (clinical) attitude themselves. But most health psychologists do not have the same role as the doctor, and therefore are not justified in adopting a totalizing emotional defence against suffering or death. However, should they adopt the medical stance to their patients that they do this as something borrowed, not earned. Not having undergone the training that produces the idea of the body as object, they are not well placed to see that being objective scientifically (as a researcher) is not the same as being objective therapeutically (as a doctor or nurse).

What such an insight requires is reflection upon the relationship of the investigator to the subject, the healer to the sufferer, in order to see that the practicalities of these relationships involve the body in particular ways. For example, Taussig (1980) makes the case that the formal doctor–patient relationship disempowers the patient by translating her bodily experience into physical processes that are no longer 'her own'. In one respect, health psychology adopts the same practical orientation, and thence engages in the same kind of reduction of experience to processes and mechanisms. Why? This is because, in order to work alongside medicine, it has married its scientific objectivity to the clinical gaze of the doctor. In contrast, a thorough-going psychology of health ought to have as one of its main aims the study of such relationships and what they mean for an understanding of embodiment. Embodiment is not just a feature of the individual person (patient), but an aspect of healing in the widest sense, involving the institutionalized relationships of medical personnel to sufferers.

In order to explore what this means, we need to turn to some examples of such relationships in practice. Some sense of the marginalization of the topic of embodiment, in the treatment of the patient as 'a body', has come from first-hand accounts by people suffering serious disease. In recent years there have been a number of such accounts by sufferers that have detailed how life-threatening or chronic disease affects both experience *of* the body and how the world is experienced *with* the body (see Frank, 1998, for a review). Making the latter point this way is actually to understate something crucial – and also to distort it somewhat. It is not that we experience the world with the body as a medium of perception only, but that through our participation in the world we also help to shape it. In the aesthetic fulfilment of life we may feel *plenty* – as in the course of things done well, or with pleasure, alone and with others. With the onset of disease we may feel *lack*, deriving from a disruption to our ability to signify with the body in this way. This might be a direct result of symptoms that affect bodily function, though as has been pointed out, this is not to be confused with clinical distress, defined as the response to pain (Toombs, 1992). Because reliance upon one's body is meaningful, suffering is not conceivable as 'process', a metaphor that has been applied to pain (Kugelmann, 1998). Suffering is realized *with the body*, whose lost or impaired potentialities extend beyond the immediacies of the present situation (van Hooft, 2000).

This notion of *plenty and lack* is useful in showing that being embodied is always more than being able to do things, important as this might be. What is arguably equally important is being able to signify as a subject in one's social world, and what is desirable is to participate in creating that world through meaning-giving acts (Young, 1990). In the case of illness, disability, or the physical decline of old age, this potential to act – to act aesthetically – can be severely challenged if not, *in extremis*, all but removed. The loss of power to signify is the subject of many illness accounts in which people with chronic diseases speak of the inability to enjoy specific things like dancing or making love. But it is also more than this, in a general sense: it is a diminution or even a loss of the power to portray themselves as graceful, vibrant or light-hearted (Frank, 1991; Robillard, 1999).

This change of focus adds to the notion of the body as the product of material and discursive processes one of embodiment as a fundamental aspect of meaning-making: how we express ourselves through symbolic acts (Radley, 1999b). This expression is vital to the ways in which people attempt to repair breaches in life or otherwise to cope with illness. The elderly people at a day centre in London, who through their dancing evoked a world in which they were bodily coordinated, is a good example (Hazan, 1986). I also suspect that much of the improvement that comes from heart patients attending exercise rehabilitation classes occurs not through improvements in their functional capacity, but also from the re-establishment of their potential to signify as ordinary people (Stern and Cleary, 1981). For a person who believes she was near to death and spent several days in a hospital bed, lifting, running and throwing a ball with others is not just functionally positive, it is life enhancing. In the terms proposed here, it is aesthetically pleasurable.

Perhaps some of the richest material concerning embodiment in illness has come from the study of nursing practices. Nursing provides a prime example of the way in which repair of the rupture in life caused by illness, the triumph over lack and the restoration of a sense of meaning (if not plenty), involves embodied practices. But here there are two bodies concerned: that of the nurse and that of the patient. In her work using a phenomenological approach, Benner (1984) has shown how the nurse may enhance this potential even in the most extreme circumstances of pain and the breakdown of health. To cite an example:

> *Expert nurse:* We had an 86-year-old woman … re-admitted to our unit last week, very ill, and the son talked with the physician and made the decision that we just make her comfortable, and let her die on her own. She was my patient. And you know just because they are not going to do anything else for her doesn't mean that I stop caring for her. So I gave her a bath. She had her little suitcase there with all her little things. I have known her for a while. She is very meticulous and very neat. So I put her in one of her gowns and propped her up all around in her bed with pillows. I didn't feel that I was doing anything special for her. But the son told me at the end how much it meant to him to see that the nurses still cared for his mother. (1984: 56)

This is perhaps an atypical situation, but I choose this example because it shows care to be manifested with the body, in spite of the summary evaluation at the end, attributed to the son. The nurse's actions did not become care only when he saw their outcome, but are revealed in the apparently mundane differences made by the nurse to the woman's situation. Putting on gowns and propping up patients in bed *are* socially meaningful, but only because people are embodied. Similarly, attending the doctor's surgery for even the most cursory medical examination involves an embodied exchange, where the divesting of the person's sensibilities is achieved through a meaningfully patterned set of actions. As Heath (1986) has shown, the middle-distance gaze of the patient during clinical examination is crucial to the achievement of the attitude by which her body is temporarily abandoned to the doctor's scrutiny.

This kind of care is not restricted to dying patients, nor do just nurses give it. Care is given in the home, as well as by other medical professionals. (So as not to be misunderstood, doctors, too, give care, in spite of the points raised at the beginning of this chapter). Nursing is a complex practice, which sometimes involves causing pain in the course of delivering care. The expertise that enables patients to retain their dignity and recover their sense of worth in the course of hospital treatment is a practical expertise. This does not mean that it is just technique, but instead a potentiating act that involves a variety of qualitatively different bodily encounters. Where clinical practice is grounded in difference, *caring is grounded in a recognition of vulnerability*; not the pathology of the body, but its fragility (Radley, 1999a). To understand care, health psychologists have to acknowledge not just embodiment, but their own embodiment (Little, 2000).

Perhaps I should make a final remark concerning this example of nursing, relating to the lack of embodied practice in health psychology theory.

In the main, nursing is carried out by women and draws upon caring practices that women traditionally undertake in the home, not least towards the sick. Several authors have remarked that the gendered nature of caring is not unconnected with its invisibility in social as well as psychological theory (Bowden, 1997; Fox, 1993). Acknowledging this, one must then recognize that the experience of illness is itself gendered, and that this indicates how embodiment is not some universal property, but is constituted within social and institutional practices, and hence is varying and changing. Any theory of embodiment in health psychology will also have to be a social theory.

New Medical Technologies and Social Change: Values and Ethics

The idea of a generalized physical body is also maintained by medicine's moral and ethical practices, with which health psychologists align themselves. This relates to the development of the relationship of doctor to patient and to the institutionalization of medical practice in the clinic and the hospital (Howell, 1995). For example, how people are treated when in hospital – as patients – is graphically understood with reference to their limitation of movement and their scope of decision making about what they can do with their bodies while under treatment. However, much of the work of health psychologists involving rehabilitation, coping with illness, issues of doctor–patient communication and the like are to do with ways of living *with* (not just in) the body. The social world – a world of changing values and identities – prescribes problems and invites solutions that require that people engage with the world both functionally and expressively. Medical innovations create new areas of decision making for people with respect to their bodies (Waldby, 1998).

This means that the problematic of health psychology, too, is being defined by moral and ethical values that attach to medicine as it is practised in the modern world. It is not just what it means to be ill that is socially defined, but what it means to be treated and to make a good recovery. On the one hand, new developments in medicine mean that there are possibilities for intervention where previously there were none. And on the other, changes in the social world create and dissolve boundaries and identities, which involves people in making moral judgements and ethical choices about not just their own health, but that of others close to them.

We can imagine developments in these two spheres – medicine and the social world – to be reaching out and criss-crossing each other. With this image in mind, it is possible to see the intersections of new medical interventions and changing social conditions as defining the spaces where health psychology will continue to find its problematic. This is because these spaces are where the potential to move from lack to plenty will be found. And this is where medicine impinges anew upon bodies that are already socially valued in one way or another. This is already happening, both inside hospitals and in community settings. And in each case the fate of an embodied person is at issue. Let us take just three examples to show what this implies.

Though no longer a new procedure, coronary graft surgery restores or supplements the blood flow to the heart muscle, with the effect of removing pain and breathlessness. This medical procedure is seen to have made possible, if not a lengthening of the life of heart patients, then an improvement in their quality of life. To some patients its effects are so profound as to lead them to reassess their lifestyle: effectively, how they use their bodies. One reason many give for maintaining this new life pattern is to justify the 'chance' that the surgeon has given them (Radley, 1996). Whatever one thinks about this interpretation, some patients feel this moral imperative to rectify or to enhance their embodied existence. But this has to be achieved in the context of life with others, so that working out the ethical basis for making such changes is not a simple affair. Exercise, diet, smoking and drinking alcohol become the focus of restraint, of debate and, I submit, of aesthetic practice. By opening the physical body in this way, the cardiac surgeon also opens up a potential space for resignifying lack and plenty in the patient's life. What it must be to run again after years of debilitating chest pain? But what must it be like to do this when your partner worries that it risks a heart attack? Only in the *manner* of running (or not running) – in a world made sensible anew with the body – do these questions begin to make their own sense for health psychologists.

The second example I use is that of cosmetic surgery. Here the lack that is felt is constituted in social criteria about beauty, though only experienced in the reflection that the person sees when looking in the mirror, or perhaps at a photograph. Only by virtue of the fact that the person must look with her eyes in the mirror or at a photo of herself is this a problem. And it has its answer in the techniques of the plastic surgeon, who can make changes to a person's physiognomy.

In her work on cosmetic surgery Davis (1995) showed that the women patients she studied were less cultural dopes pandering to norms of beauty than they were people who saw the procedure as allowing them to overcome the constraints of their bodies. These women felt empowered both by the changes to their faces and by their sense that they initiated and organized the experience. In this case, unlike illness, there is a proactive aspect to overcoming lack, a lack that is not engendered by disease but by inheritance. This is a nice example of how medical innovation that can enter into the body in new ways, or alter it in ways not previously possible, can answer to a lack that is socially rather than medically defined. And once again we see that questions of embodiment are at the intersection of these concerns, inseparable from issues of moral and ethical choice.

Finally, let us consider the question of organ transplantation, which not only raises questions about who should have these organs but who should give consent about their removal. The first question concerns the kinds of recipients that might be considered worthy. How are these judgements to be made: on grounds of clinical need alone? What of age or even race, as this was raised only recently in the UK, where a family tried to limit the delivery of the deceased relative's vital organ to a white person? There are also questions here concerning the recipient's attitude to the organ donated. What is a proper and fitting attitude to a donation freely given? And how might it change one's feeling of one's body – not just the body one has but the body you are, one's lived body (Caplan, 1992)?

In talking about these instances it might seem that I am falling back upon examples that are relevant just because they involve the (physical) body being altered in some way. This appears to detract from the argument that what is important is embodiment, rather then 'the body' *per se*. However, my reason for choosing these examples is that they show that questions of lack and plenty are not stable, but socially constituted, throwing up new problems that involve lived bodies (ethically subtended, if you will) that are also physical, materially contingent, ones. Health psychology will have to deal with problems like these – and others that we don't yet know about – if only because of the personal and social issues involved.

Of course, researchers following the models of experimental psychological would restrict themselves to questions such as, which kind of persons are best fitted to receive a particular procedure, or how can one help shape counselling programmes for patients experiencing traumas associated with transplant surgery? These, in the terms of allopathic medicine are appropriate questions to ask, and I do not advocate that they not be posed. This kind of approach is entirely proper within the biomedical framework where management of patients is primary. However, this is not the way to establish an understanding of embodiment within health psychology. Nor is it the way to contribute to the debate on ethics in health care, something that doctors might have looked to psychologists to address. An approach that is premised upon the body as a physical entity forgoes, right from the beginning, any chance of understanding embodiment as a condition for life, either healthy or sick.

In conclusion, I would argue that the 'issue of the body' for health psychology is one of commitment to practical theory, not one of methodological preference. In the end, it is by virtue of our being embodied, as men, women, patients, doctors and even psychologists, that we bear our illnesses and retain our grasp on the world of health. That is where we have to begin.

References

Benner, P. (1984). *From novice to expert: Excellence and power in clinical nursing practice*. Menlo Park, CA: Addison-Wesley.

Bowden, P. (1997). *Caring: Gender-sensitive ethics*. London: Routledge.

Caplan, A. L. (1992). *If I were a rich man could I buy a pancreas? and other essays on the ethics of health care*. Bloomington: Indiana University Press.

Davis, K. (1995). *Reshaping the female body: The dilemma of cosmetic surgery*. New York: Routledge.

Fox, N. (1993). *Postmodernism, sociology and health*. Buckingham: Open University Press.

Frank, A. W. (1991). *At the will of the body: Reflections on illness.* Boston: Houghton Mifflin.

Frank, A. W. (1998). From dysappearance to hyperappearance: sliding boundaries of illness and bodies. In H. J. Stam (ed.), *The body and psychology* (pp. 205–232). London: Sage.

Hafferty, F. W. (1991). *Into the valley: Death and the socialization of medical students.* New Haven: Yale University Press.

Hazan, H. (1986). Body image and temporality among the aged: A case study of an ambivalent symbol. *Studies in Symbolic Interaction, 7,* 305–329.

Heath, C. (1986). *Body movement and speech in medical interaction.* Cambridge: Cambridge University Press.

Howell, J. (1995). *Technology in the hospital: Transforming patient care in the early twentieth century.* Baltimore: Johns Hopkins University Press.

Jewson, N. D. (1976). The disappearance of the sick-man from medical cosmology, 1770–1870. *Sociology, 10,* 225–244.

Kirmayer, L. J. (1988). Mind and body as metaphors: Hidden values in biomedicine. In M. Lock and D. Gordon (eds), *Biomedicine examined* (pp. 57–93). Dordrecht: Kluwer Academic.

Kugelmann, R. (1988). The psychology and management of pain. In H. Stam (Ed.), *The body and psychology* (pp. 182–204). London: Sage.

Leder, D. (1992). A tale of two bodies: The Cartesian corpse and the lived body. In D. Leder (Ed.), *The body in medical thought and practice* (pp. 17–35). Dordrecht: Kluwer Academic.

Little, M., Paul, K., Jordens, C. F. C. and Sayers, E-J. (2000). *Health: An Interdisciplinary Journal of the Social Study of Health, Illness and Medicine,* 4(4), 459–510.

Lupton, D. (2000). The social construction of medicine and the body. In G. L. Albrecht, R. Fitzpatrick, and S. Scrimshaw (eds), *Handbook of social studies in health and medicine* (pp. 50–63). London: Sage.

Martin, E. (1987). *The woman in the body: A cultural analysis of reproduction.* Milton Keynes: Open University Press.

Martin, E. (1994). *Flexible bodies: Tracking immunity in American culture from the days of polio to the age of AIDS.* Boston, MA: Beacon.

Merleau-Ponty, M. (1968). *The visible and the invisible.* Evanston: Northwestern University Press.

Radley, A. (1991). *The body and social psychology.* New York: Springer Verlag.

Radley, A. (1996). The critical moment: Time, information and medical expertise in the experience of patients receiving coronary bypass surgery. In S. J. Williams and M. Calnan (eds), *Modern medicine: Lay perspectives and experiences* (pp. 118–138). London: UCL Press.

Radley, A. (1999a). Abhorrence, compassion and the social response to suffering. *Health, 3,* 167–187.

Radley, A. (1999b). The aesthetics of illness: Narrative, horror and the sublime, *Sociology of Health and Illness, 21,* 778–796.

Robillard, A. B. (1999). *Meaning of a disability: The lived experience of paralysis.* Philadelphia: Temple University Press.

Romanyshyn, R. (1982). *Psychological Life: From science to metaphor.* Milton Keynes: Open University Press.

Smith, D. (1987). *The everyday world as problematic: A feminist sociology.* Toronto: University of Toronto Press.

Stam, H. (ed.) (1998). *The body and psychology.* London: Sage.

Stern, M. J. and Cleary, P. (1981). Psychosocial changes observed during a low-level exercise program. *Archives of Internal Medicine, 141,* 1463–1467.

Taussig, M. T. (1980). Reification and the consciousness of the patient. *Social Science and Medicine, 14B,* 3–13.

Toombs, S. K. (1992). *The meaning of illness: A phenomenological account of the different perspectives of physician and patient.* Dordrecht: Kluwer.

Ussher, J. M. (1989). *The psychology of the female body.* London: Routledge.

van Hooft, S. (2000). The suffering body. *Health, 4,* 179–195.

Waldby, C. (1998). Review essay: Medical imagining: The Biopolitics of visibility. *Health, 2,* 372–384.

Williams, S. J. (1996). The vicissitudes of embodiment across the chronic illness trajectory. *Body & Society, 2,* 23–48.

Yardley, L. (1999). Understanding embodied experience. In M. Murray and K. Chamberlain (eds), *Qualitative health psychology: Theories and methods* (pp. 31–46). London: Sage.

Young, I. M. (1990). *Throwing like a girl and other essays in feminist philosophy.* Bloomington: Indiana University Press.

Young, I. (1994). Pregnant embodiment: Subjectivity and alienation. *Journal of Medicine and Philosophy, 9,* 45–62.

25 POSSIBLE CONTRIBUTIONS OF A PSYCHOLOGY OF LIBERATION:
Whither Health and Human Rights?

M. Brinton Lykes

If the uniqueness of human beings consists less in their being endowed with life (that is, in their organic existence), and more in the kind of life they construct historically, then mental health ceases to be a secondary problem and becomes a fundamental one. It is not a matter of the individual's satisfactory function; rather, it is a matter of the basic character of human relations, for this is what defines the possibilities for humanization that open up for the members of each society and group. (Martín-Baró, 1994, p. 109)

Ignacio Martín-Baró, Jesuit priest, social psychologist and university administrator in El Salvador, outlined a liberation psychology on the basis of his experiences living and working among the poor – and the elite – during more than a decade of civil war in El Salvador. He argued that taking sides is not bias but rather an ethical choice, grounded in the truths of reason and compassion. As is evident in his research, and in his subsequent assassination on 16 November 1989, the consequences of such engagement in active efforts for change can be fatal.

Many within the field of psychology and many more who describe themselves as activists would argue that the term 'liberation psychology', constitutes on oxymoron, that is, two ideas or words that, when joined, create a contradiction, an impossibility: there can be no such thing as a liberatory psychology, a psychology that liberates. Martín-Baró might have responded that rather than a concrete reality, liberation psychology, as he characterized it, was a call to action, a challenge to develop a practice and theory from the bases of the experiences of the local community with whom the psychologist works. He recognized further that in order for psychology to be liberatory, it first must be liberated (Martín-Baró, 1994). In this chapter, I seek to illustrate through a concrete example how making common cause with ordinary people living in what Martín-Baró called 'limit situations', that is, situations of extreme hardship, oppression, and profound suffering, creates conditions for the development of a liberatory psychology wherein we often encounter extraordinary acts reflective of our shared humanity. Martín-Baró offered a small number of Salvadoran peasants and university students and colleagues an opportunity to taste the beginnings of how psychological theorizing and practices might be reconfigured to accompany oppressed peasant communities in their country. I demonstrate here how his liberatory psychology informs my accompaniment of similar communities in Guatemala and suggest several ways in which the liberatory potential of his praxis might be extended to address the particularities of women's and indigenous people's experiences.

This chapter attempts to situate my ongoing field research in rural Guatemala within this emerging field of liberation psychology. I begin with a selective review of human rights and social scientific literatures that contribute to the development of an emerging 'professional space', wherein psychologists work with survivors of war and other forms of violence in ways that both facilitate and constrain a liberatory praxis. Reflexive practices characteristic of some contemporary research are discussed and exemplified to further contextualize my current participatory action research (PAR) among Mayan women of rural Guatemala. I argue that such liberatory praxis resituates both local communities and oneself as activist researcher. I present one example of PAR wherein local women use photography as a resource for telling their community's experiences of war, its effects, and their responses to it. Through critical reflection on selected dilemmas and contradictions encountered in this work I interrogate the liberatory potential of psychological theory and practices and its contributions towards developing practices within health psychology.

Socially Situating Liberatory Praxis Within Psychology

Developing Understandings of Human Rights and Mental Health

Martín-Baró was not alone in his efforts to end war and other conditions that contribute to organized violence. M. Brewster Smith (1999) reviewed political psychologists' multiple contributions to the Second World War and subsequently to conflict resolution in diverse contexts including the Middle East and Northern Ireland. Clinical psychologists have worked extensively with civilians who constitute the vast majority of victims of contemporary warfare (see, among other sources, Graça Machel/UN Study on the Effects of War on Children, 1998). Much of this latter work has taken place within the developing rubric of 'mental health and human rights' (Lykes and Liem, 1990). As such it importantly addresses the effects of egregious human rights violations and organized violence on individuals.

There are increasingly active international communities of professionals in the fields of human rights and mental health who define a role for themselves/ourselves within zones of armed conflict. On the positive side, this work reflects the recognition of a 'whole person' who has been affected by war, violence, etc. and of the needs of the person-in-community to heal. For those working in the field there is a growing network of colleagues and co-workers for mutual support and potential collaboration in theory construction and action. We have created new subspecialties of peace psychology, trauma therapy, etc., and psychologists who not only work on the frontlines with physicians and nurses in war zones but increasingly define post-war 'development policies' as well as procedures for healing and reconciliation in post-war, post-apartheid contexts. However, such work is often more focused on the 'individual's satisfactory (or unsatisfactory) functioning' than on the social relations described above by Martín-Baró. It is also all too frequently embedded in positivist, ahistorical, and non-reflexive research assumptions and strategies (Bracken, Geller and Summerfield, 1995; Lykes, 1996).

Equally problematic are the understandings of human rights implicit in much of this work (see Lykes, 2001, for a fuller discussion of these issues). Violence that results in survivors who seek the treatment described above are characterized as violations of civil and political rights. These rights are, not surprisingly, consonant with dominant UnitedStatesian[1] understandings of human rights abuses, that is, as violations of our rights to free speech, or as arbitrary arrest, or cruel, inhuman, or degrading treatment or punishment. Implicit within this articulation of rights is the assumption that it is the rights of individuals that are being asserted and/or protected. The views of the majority world, including large parts of Africa, Latin America, and Asia, were not well represented in the 1948 United Nations declaration of human rights, given that many of these countries were still under colonial rule and did not belong to the UN (Messer, 1995, 1997).

Dramatic political changes in the second half of the 20th century have created new alliances, giving voice to formerly marginalized and/or non-existent states. Some of these countries achieved liberation from European colonial rule. New countries have formed from early confederations as ethnic/national groups have asserted their independence. Leaders within these countries as well as women and indigenous groups throughout the world have fought to expand the two original human rights convenants to include demands for the rights of women, children, and indigenous peoples (see [http://www.un.org] for copies of the Convention on the Rights of the Child, 1989; the Convention on the Elimination of Discrimination Against Women, 1979; and the Draft Declaration on the Rights of Indigenous Peoples, 1994).

The works of Kam (1998), Menchú Tum (1998), Nagengast (1997), Oloka-Onyango and Tamale (1995), Rao (1995), Wells (1998), and Zechenter (1997) describe multiple versions of these struggles at the grassroots level and among academics and policy makers: struggles that concluded in the extension of civil and political rights reflected in the first UN human rights convenant and in the development of documents that reflect the rights of these formerly excluded peoples as they themselves – or at least their leaders – have defined them. If adopted, for example, the draft declaration of indigenous rights establishes collective rights, that is, 'a right that adheres to certain groups *because* it is not reducible to individuals' (Thompson, 1997, p. 789, original emphasis). This is particularly relevant to my work in Guatemala because these collective rights, also known as fourth generation rights, raise potential challenges for Westerners whose assumptions about rights typically are grounded in beliefs about the locus of rights being the autonomous and independent individual (see Lykes, 1994, 1997 for a further elaboration of these points).

Third and fourth generation rights, thereby, challenge the assumed universal character of the initial human rights declarations and its focus on an autonomous individual as the locus of rights. Social context, that is, culture, the environment, and history, are key to the very definition of human rights and to whom they adhere. Specifically, third and fourth generation rights affirm the collectivity as an equally important locus of rights. This expanded understanding thus confirms that denial of civil-political rights as well as economic, cultural, social, and collective rights constitute human rights violations and abuses, focusing on the individual and the collective and the systemic and structural forces in which they are socially embedded.

Psychological Practice and the Four Generations of Rights

Although psychologists, unlike anthropologists and sociologists, have not sought to contribute directly to this discussion on the nature of rights, selected aspects of psychological theory contribute to understanding the possible implications of this expansion of human rights for the practice of psychologists and others seeking to work with survivors of human rights violations. Liberation psychology, cultural and constructivist theories, and reflexivity challenge dominant psychological perspectives (i.e. positivist, universalistic, objective, and laboratory-based) and inform community-based participatory research strategies. These resources contribute to psychological understanding and are suggestive of possible practices within a health psychology that seeks to respond in a more integrated, comprehensive way to war and its effects. I briefly describe some of these theoretical developments in terms of how they frame and inform my community-based practice, that is, PAR in rural Guatemala, one example of critical praxis towards improved community health.

Liberating Psychology for Liberatory Praxis Ignacio Martín-Baró (1990) argued that the after-effects of political repression carried out by governments was one of the thorniest problems confronting Latin American states hoping to establish democratic governments. He emphasized that in addition to damage to personal lives, harm had been done to the social structures themselves – to the norms, values, and principles by which people are educated, and to the institutions that govern the lives of citizens. 'Social trauma affects individuals precisely in their social character; that is, as a totality, as a system' (Martín-Baró, 1994, p. 124).

Drawing on Latin American liberation theology and pedagogy (see e.g. Freire, 1970, 1973; Gutiérrez, 1973/1988). Martín-Baró (1994) posited that a psychology that could explain and respond to these realities should include: (1) a focus on the liberation of a whole people (i.e. the collectivity) as well as on personal liberation; (2) a new epistemology wherein the truth of the popular majority is not to be found, but created, that is, wherein truth is constructed 'from below'; and (3) a new praxis, wherein we place ourselves within the research-action process alongside the dominated or oppressed rather than alongside the dominator or oppressor. This characterization of 'liberation psychology' shifts the focus of work within mental health and human rights, emphasizing the contextualized and historical nature of psychology as well as its epistemology. This perspective increasingly informs psychological praxis in the Americas today (see e.g. Comas-Díaz, Lykes, and Alarcón, 1998). One example of how it has informed my efforts to collaborate with local communities in the enhancement of their health and well-being is described below.

Within this alternative framework, trauma is not primarily or exclusively an intrapsychic phenomenon, but rather is conceived of as psychosocial. Psychosocial trauma reflects a dialectic process, that is, it 'resides in the social relations of which the individual is only a part' (Martín-Baró, 1994, p. 124). Martín-Baró suggested further that 'psychosocial trauma can be a normal consequence of a social system based on social relations of exploitation and dehumanizing oppression' such as those in wartime El Salvador (p. 125). Trauma becomes a usual event, not an aberration. In the context of war, it is an everyday part of life. Under normal circumstances the slaughter of individuals, the disappearance of loved ones, the inability to distinguish what is one's experience from what others say it is (and, when one does, the fear to speak one's point of view), the militarization of institutions, and the extreme polarization of social life are seen as abnormal. One of the effects of war in El Salvador, according to Martín-Baró (1994), is that the typical person comes to accept these experiences as normal.

Martín-Baró's psychology of liberation is not totally new within Western psychology and psychiatry. It echoes earlier work by Franz Fanon (1967) and more recent work in South Africa (see e.g. Nichols and Cooper, 1990). African American or black psychology draws heavily on the works of black liberation theology and/or Africanist traditions and is also echoed in Martín-Baró's work (see, among others, Gordon, 1973). One commonality among the liberation psychologies of Fanon and Martín-Baró and black psychology is the shift of psychologists' attention to the systemic or structural dimensions of the identified problem or concern, rather than its more typical focal point, that is, the individual person abstracted from a multi-layered social, historical, and cultural context.

Constructivist and Cultural Interpretations: Symbolic Aspects of Terror

Psychologists' documentation of the effects of extreme trauma and torture in war typically characterize the events and their immediate consequences for the individuals involved. Those working with survivors of war have characterized and measured the constellation of symptoms suffered by many survivors as post-traumatic stress disorder (PTSD) and developed wide-ranging treatment and intervention strategies (see e.g. Herman, 1992). In contrast, social constructivists argue that the meanings we make of a phenomenon are not adequately represented by labeling symptoms or syndromes (Aron, Corne, Fursland and Zewler, 1991). Rather they are co-constructed by those who experience them in relationships (e.g. the therapist with her client) in a particular sociohistorical time, culture, and place (Agger, 1994; Gergen, 1994, 1997). Dialogue and engagement are critical strategies for constructing understanding that is inherently value laden rather than value neutral. This meaning-making process can, therefore, best be understood within the historical and cultural social contexts of the actors, that is, through the thick descriptions of events of reenactments of experiences as they are constructed or reconstructed by the survivors in dialogue and/or interaction with those who accompany them (Lykes, 1996).

Anthropologists and cultural psychologists who have explored the meanings of human rights violations and their effects have suggested that in addition to terror's immediate consequences for individuals it has symbolic effects on entire communities and across generations (see e.g. Danielli, 1998; Liem, 1999). In his exploration of terror and its functions within the years of the most recent Argentine dictatorship (1976–1983), Suárez-Orozco (1992) considers terror's symbolic dimensions, arguing that it threatens the culture and social subjectivity. His work extends both the spatial and the temporal dimensions along which terror is traditionally conceptualized. I have demonstrated in earlier work (Lykes, 1996) how terror not only destroys the present but also forces a rethinking of the past and deeply threatens the future through its destructive effects on the next generation's capacity to culturally affirm itself.

Reflexivity as Resource for Liberatory Praxis

Feminist psychologists, among others, have suggested importance of psychologists analyzing the effects we have within the context of the knowledge that we are co-constructing in work with clients and/or with participants in our research (see Fine, 1992; Lather, 1991; Maguire, 1987; McIntyre, 1997). The practice of reflexivity has led some of us to work in partnerships with local communities in contexts of war and peacemaking, thereby contributing methodological insights to the understandings of psychosocial trauma developed there (see e.g. Lykes, 1996; Zur, 1998). To more fully contextualize those possible contributions, I describe the 'selves' that are distinctively implicated in my work within rural Guatemalan communities.

I am a UnitedStatesian and a senior university professor with a salary and benefits that locate me, and most of my colleagues, in the top 15 percent of the economic distribution of wealth and income in the USA, a beneficiary of the extremely unequal distribution of world resources. As a US citizen my country of birth has been a major contributor of both military and intelligence resources that supported the repressive practices of the Guatemalan government during nearly 36 years of civil war. As a major player in the World Bank and the International Monetary Fund the US government has initiated international economic policies and practices that have forced the privatization of many state-controlled industries, reducing national patrimony while extolling debt repayments that impoverish majority populations in these same countries, including Guatemala. These broader economic and political forces 'situated me' for the rural Mayan women with whom I began to work in 1992.

Yet the picture is more textured and multilayered when viewed from the perspective of the multiple players who constitute the micro-relations within which our work has evolved. The United States is also the most favored site of migration for many Mayan families, an exile that has created complex sets of international relations and economic opportunities within situations of extreme poverty. Subsidies from Gautemalan families working in the USA rank second to tourism as a source of national income. Similarly, solidarity, for example, sistering relationships between Guatemalan and US communities (Taylor, 1998), Sanctuary churches that harbored many 'illegal refugees', and the ongoing struggle of US activists to close down the School of the Americas (Bourgeois, 2000) and to use international law to convict Salvadoran and Guatemalan military for past violations of human rights are powerful indicators that many Guatemalans invoke as they readily distinguish individual UnitedStatesians from the US government. As such we constitute a 'third force' working alongside as they engage their ongoing struggles for healing and justice. I was part of that 'third force' and therefore was not a neutral social science researcher when I entered Chajul.

Of similar and perhaps seemingly baroque relevance to my work among women and children in rural Guatemala are the ongoing tales of 'trafficking in children' and the 'selling of organs' that persist in the Gauatemalan countryside and are hauntingly reflected in the continuing adoption of Mayan babies by North American, Western European and Israeli parents. These are stories of our collective, social histories and are carried forward in varied and sometimes contradictory ways within our individual and interpersonal activities.

I have lived in and among Maya since 1983 when I first traveled to Mexico to work among some of the refugees of the brutal massacres of the early 1980s (CEH, 1999; ODHAG, 1998; Falla, 1994). Worlds of difference converge and diverge in transnational work: my position of privilege is complexly configured and reconfigured in circles of local rural community power. In rural areas my status as an unmarried woman with no children is a source of ongoing conversation and confusion, sometimes elevating, sometimes denigrating me as I find myself 'othered' by the historically marginalized 'Mayan other' and 'who I am' deeply constrained by local power relationships in my role as 'outsider'. These experiences also constrain my self-presentations of the gendered, racialized, national, classed, and sexualized person whom I know myself to be.

After 16 years of such experiences (see Lykes, 1994, 1997, for a fuller description), I saw another side of self and self/other presentation when two of the Mayan women and the infant son of one of them with whom I had been working visited my university and stayed in my home. Their social situatedness shifted and was 'complicated' as we presented 'our' work to UnitedStatesian students and faculty in March 1999. These shifting scenarios of relative powers and privileges are, of course, constrained by material realities but are also constructed and reconstructed through ongoing dialogue and praxis among heterogeneous groups as we stumble across and contest the very material borders of race, gender, sexuality, and class, invoking inherited or newly acquired strategies of individual and social power. As significantly, when Ana and Isabel Ana entered my 'home community' I became 'the known', they 'the knowers'. Such experiences challenge me to think more elastically about power and solidarity and suggest more complex ways of thinking about reflexivity within the researcher/participant dialectic of ongoing PAR projects in which we are involved.

PAR and PhotoVoice as Liberatory Praxis Towards Health

Guatemala: a Context of Extreme Poverty and War

Although the Guatemalan economy is the strongest in Central America, 36 percent of the urban population and 71 percent of those in rural areas live in extreme poverty (Barry, 1992), that is, they cannot afford to meet their basic food needs. Approximately 65 percent of the arable land is held by 2 percent of the population (Barry, 1992) and it was a lack of basic nutrition, health, and educational services, but especially the intentional deprivation of land ownership in order to guarantee a large, exploitable workforce for the export-oriented coffee, sugar, and cotton plantations, which fueled periodic rebellions and, most recently, a 36-year armed insurgency and counter-insurgency. The vast majority of the plantation workforce, both seasonal and permanent, are descendants of the Maya.

Indeed, the majority of the approximately 10.5 million inhabitants in Guatemala are Maya, living in rural communities. There are 21 Mayan languages plus Spanish, the official language, and Xinca and Caribe (Cojti, 1988). The indigenous represent various ethnic groups, all descendants of the Mayan civilizations that sought to assert their individualities and their land claims after the collapse of the Mayan empire and prior to the arrival of the Spaniards.[2]

In December 1996, representatives of the Guatemalan National Revolutionary Unity (URNG) and the government signed Peace Accords, officially ending nearly 36 years of war. Reports by both a Catholic church-sponsored commission known as REMHI/Recovery of Historical Memory Project (ODHAG, 1998) and the UN-brokered independent Commission for Historical Clarification (CEH, 1999) confirmed that victims included more than 40 percent of all disappeared persons in Latin America as well as millions of displaced persons and a quarter of a million orphans in a population of what was then 8 million people, over 500 massacres, and more than 400 Mayan villages burned to the ground. Responsibility for more than 90 percent of these violations, officially designated as genocide by the CEH, has been attributed to the government and its security forces, with help from the United States. The Guatemalan government of President Arzú, upon officially receiving the report, dismissed it as unfounded, contributing to the country being characterized by Guatemalan human rights activist Helen Mack as in 'desperate need of reconciliation' (personal communication, 2000). Current experiences of violence, including vigilante-type lynchings in many rural communities, extreme poverty, and impunity, critically constrain the work of constructing an historical memory at the individual, interpersonal, and social levels, processes which many believe to be critical to creating conditions for reconciliation and for a more democratic society. Despite this seemingly dismal scene, within these conditions – where it is also imperative to note that bombs are no longer being dropped and an overt military presence and control has receded – I have found potentially liberating ways to think about the physical, spiritual, and psychological well-being-in-community of a people and in which to enact, in collaboration with local players, programs and projects that enable a 'heterogeneous group of social sufferers' (Kleinman and Kleinman, 1996) to rethread their stories and the social fabric of life in their local communities.

The town of Chajul where I have been working for the past eight years is one such context. The women with whom I work describe it as 'extremely isolated' and 'forgotten – until the recent years of war'. It is one of three towns comprising an area that the Guatemalan military designated as the 'Ixil Triangle' in the 1970s and 1980s, referring to the Ixil language and culture of the area's three largest towns, Nebaj, Cotzal, and Chajul. There are more than a dozen smaller villages surrounding Chajul, many as far away as a two-day walk, which depend upon it for a biweekly market, a health center, and other municipal services.

The population of Chajul is predominantly Ixil Maya, comprised of local survivors and many who had been displaced both within the country and beyond its borders. There are small populations of K'iche' Maya and *ladinos* within the town and several of the surrounding communities are K'iche'. Community members are working through, at a local level, many of the regional and national dynamics that have deeply marked their lives and have surfaced in new ways after the ending of a protracted war.

Women as Victims and Survivors   The engendered nature of war's violence has only recently been highlighted and the case of Guatemala is no exception (see Agger, 1994; Aron, Corne, Fursland, and Zewler, 1991; Lykes, Brabeck, Ferns, and Radan, 1993). Perhaps not surprisingly, although nearly half of the informants who provided testimonies to REMHI were female, very few of them referred to specific violations of themselves as women (ODHAG, 1998, Vol. 1, p. 203). They spoke rather of collective forms of violence, of massacres, of violent acts against their families and their communities. Despite this, the authors of the report documented evidence of gendered forms of violence in selected interviews with some women and with key informants. Included in their interviews and in those reported by the CEH (1999) were descriptions of the repeated rape of girls and women, the ripping of fetuses from pregnant women's stomachs and beating them against trees to kill them, torture and killing of girls and women, of children in front of their mothers, and of mothers in front of their children. Many women were impregnated and gave birth to children who were frequently rejected by their communities and, sometimes, by the mothers themselves (ODHAG, 1998, see pp. 91–92).

Although many women were killed and/or disappeared they were more likely than men to survive, facing the burden of the psychosocial and material consequences of this violence. Among their many responses to the violence, it is important to note their multiple contributions to the maintenance and growth of families and communities. This can be seen in the many new roles that women have increasingly occupied in rural communities (e.g. tending large animals, preparing fields for planting, chopping wood, participating in local religious and political organizations) and in their leadership positions in human rights organizations (e.g. Grupo de Apoyo Mutuo [Mutual Support Group], CONAVIGUA [National Coordination of Guatemalan Widows]). As in many other countries in Latin America, women have evidenced important leadership in the earliest efforts to protest the forced disappearances of their family members and demand justice in the face of ongoing repression and impunity (Arditti, 1999; Arditti and Lykes, 1992). Beyond the leadership, in pockets invisible to most of the world, are hundreds and thousands of Mayan women who have survived these acts of extreme violence and are challenged daily to respond to its effects in a context of extreme hardship and poverty. Among these are the women of Chajul who began local organizing in 1992, forming a committee of six persons who would several years later constitute themselves as the Association of Maya Ixil women – New Dawn (ADMI).

Women's Needs, Women's Organizing   There were few community organizations in 1992 when I responded to a friend's invitation to join her in her return home to Chajul. Many within the community lived in fear of gathering in local groups, for example, in the church, or of organizing themselves to improve their lives. The repression, particularly that of the previous decade, had instilled terror and fear in the population as they watched leaders, catechists, and then entire communities destroyed and/or dispersed, allegedly for their participation in local efforts for self-determination. Within the polarized context of the war (Martín-Baró, 1994) such efforts were frequently labeled as participation in, or support for, guerrilla organizations (CEH, 1999). However, some had begun to organize with the local Catholic church, and others with a small grant provided by a national nongovernmental organization seeking to foster economic survival. As is frequently the case in short-term development projects, the educational component within the latter project proved inadequate relative to the local reality, and when the NGO withdrew from the area, the women were unable to sustain the work they had begun. Despite this, those who had gathered for this project had identified their individual and collective needs and sought a solution.

I had been working since 1986 with rural health promoters and child care workers, and the friend who invited me to Chajul had hoped that I could facilitate a similar experience with women there who were seeking to develop projects for themselves and for children of the community. They had previously identified the need for an additional mill where corn, the staple of rural Guatemalan subsistence, could be ground within the community, and provide income generation for their developing organization. They also hoped to offer programs for local children. Although there was a public school the local teacher did not speak Ixil, and most students struggled, even after several years of schooling, to understand Spanish. As importantly, many in the community cannot afford the cost of pencils, paper and fees required of all students who attend the public school. Finally, the women sought a child-centered learning/teaching environment wherein they could respond to some of the many psychological needs of these child survivors of war and violence and where they could also learn to read and write in their indigenous language. They were convinced that such resources would contribute importantly to the children's self-esteem and to their future development as community actors and leaders.

PhotoVoice: a Strategy for Retelling Stories, Rethreading Lives I worked for four years in participatory workshops with a growing group of women. We began with six and in our fourth year there were nearly 60. I used drama, drawing, collage, movement, sound, and creative storytelling as resources for remembering stories of violence and destruction as well as envisioning alternative possibilities for moving forward. I served as a consultant as the women developed their program with children and two economic development projects as well as a local lending library (see Lykes et al., 1999, for details of ADMI's work). As participants worked together, building trust and confidence in their own capacities, they experienced growing interest in narrating some of the stories of violence and loss that they had experienced during the more than three decades of war.

We gradually developed a participatory action research (PAR) project using photography and oral history interviews to respond to that growing need. PAR has a long trajectory in Latin America (Fals-Borda and Rahman, 1991) and we were committed to promoting more active participation of a larger group of women from the Association in ongoing ways in the work, while creating an educational/training context in which these women could develop their skills to more actively engage in the development of programs and projects that responded to local needs. As importantly, there was a growing desire on the parts of the women participating in the workshops not only to document their experiences of 'the violence' and its effects within Chajul, but to communicate these stories beyond Chajul, to those not privy to this history, and for future generations who had not experienced the violence first hand. They sought, thereby, to 'give witness', offering spaces for sharing and healing to women who had not yet told their stories as well as remembering the past as a resource towards preventing its repetition in the future.

Existing language differences and limited literacy, as well as local traditions of storytelling and dramatization, had contributed to the women's embrace of creative resources within previous workshops. However, I found the absence of a visual record for ongoing reflection and analysis to be a significant limitation for collaborative analyses that might deepen understanding and provide a base from which to develop actions. This problem was aggravated in workshops with different participants, given daily exigencies that limited ongoing participation of some women. A method of community photography, 'PhotoVoice' (Wang and Burris, 1994; Wang, Burris, and Xiang, 1996), had been used successfully in China with non-formally educated women where photographs were used as a tool for influencing local health and education policies and seemed to respond to some of these needs. I shared the book produced by rural Chinese women with women in Chajul and they were mobilized by similarities in women's work and in the stories created through words and pictures.

Two photographic methods, 'PhotoVoice' (Wang and Burris, 1994; Wang, Burris, and Xiang, 1996) and 'talking pictures' (Bunster and Chaney, 1989) served as important resources that we incorporated into our existing group processes to consolidate a PAR method that fit the needs articulated within the group. We decided to use the technique to tell the story of Ixil women, that is, to document and communicate the Ixil realities through the images and text that they themselves created. We wanted to document the experiences of violence, displacement, and loss described above and their effects among women and children who are now living in Chajul and its neighboring villages. Equally importantly, the women of ADMI sought to situate the stories of 'the violence' in the context of their cultural, religious, labor, and community practices, thereby recovering cultural beliefs and practices that had been deeply threatened by the war.

We adopted PAR to local realities, envisioning pictures as vehicles for self- and communal reflection, initially among the group of participants, and then among ever-widening circles of women within and beyond Chajul. We envisioned a two-year process. A group of 20 women from Chajul, two US participants, and a colleague from Spain formed a research team. One among the group in Chajul was identified by the Association to serve as a coordinator. The US participants and the Spaniard serve as project consultants. Each participant received a camera and some film as well as ongoing training in the use of the camera. None of the participants had previous experience with picture taking, although all had been photographed at some point by Guatemalan photographers. We discussed different orientations toward picture taking at length, particularly in light of local traditions of picture taking as a more formal process wherein those photographed were dressed in their best clothes and the pictures were posed (Parker and Neal, 1982). We talked about the strengths and weaknesses of this type of photography and contrasted it with a candid, more spontaneous photograph of daily life and decided that in most cases the latter would more fully meet our project's goals (Spence and Solomon, 1995). We clarified ethical issues that emerged in the research process and discussed parameters and guidelines for taking pictures of others (e.g. When would you not want to have someone take a picture of you?). We explored various strategies for asking permission before taking photographs of individuals and the conditions in which permission might not be necessary (see e.g. Punch, 1994, for consideration of some of the multiple ethical issues in field research). We visited and have since revisited the multiple challenges to 'women's traditional roles' enacted by this photography project, as well as the resistances it has elicited in husbands and some other men within the community. We dramatized and dramatically multiplied problems encountered in seeking permission – from husbands to participate in meetings and field trips, from community residents whose photographs we wanted to take – reconfiguring them as opportunities to build or strengthen familial and community relations.

The thematic focus of each roll was decided in workshops involving all participants. Our initial topic, work, was based on our own experiences and our understanding of the challenges facing women and children in Chajul. Later topics – health and illness, religion and traditional practices, the war and its effects, the family, the land, and the work of ADMI – were drawn from our analyses of our first rolls of film. As importantly, participants decided not only to interview each other but also to select some women from among those whose photographs they were taking and invite them to be interviewed. They thereby sought to give these women an opportunity to tell their stories as well as to deepen their own understanding of the experiences they were photographing, thus enhancing their capacity to tell the story of Chajul and its neighboring villages.

The processes developed for analyzing the photographs have contributed importantly to enhancing oral language abilities and literacy and analysis skills within the group of 20. Each woman selects 5–10 pictures from a role of 24 that she thinks best represent the theme that the group has selected. She then 'tells the story' of each picture to a small group including 2–4 other participants. Included in this sharing are her particular reasons for choosing this picture, as well as any stories that she may have been told by the person she photographed. In a second round of analysis, we form groups of 5–7 women who select 2–4 pictures from among a larger group that includes all the photographs on a given topic taken by the group of 20 and selected for inclusion by each individual.

Through careful planning and the scaffolding of experiences within the group discussions (Rogoff, 1990; Vygotsky, 1986), women have developed strategies for clustering ideas, identifying similarities and differences between and across photos, and constructing holistic analyses of the photographs, as well as exploring process and/or events that preceded the event captured by the picture. They hypothesized proximal and distal causes for the problems represented in any given picture, for example, a child's uncontrolled diarrhea leading to death is presented as due not only to the absence of a local health clinic or physician and the mother's lacking resources to pay for medicine, but also to the absence of adequate nutrition, clean drinking water, and sanitary conditions within the home and wider community. These analyses are recorded and, with the pictures, presented to the larger group where they are subject to reanalysis by other participants and to further elaboration through drawing, dramatization, and storytelling. In this latter context participants explore possible solutions to the problems identified at the individual and collective levels, thereby also developing a shared vision for change.

This process has multiple outcomes. We have selected approximately 60 photographs for a traveling photo exhibit and a published book (Women of PhotoVoice/ADMI and Lykes, 2000) that re-presents the story of the women and children of Chajul and its neighboring communities, a story developed by the PhotoVoice team through the processes of photography and reflection/analysis groups. We have selected texts to accompany the photographs from the transcriptions of the oral history interviews, group discussions and analysis exercises. The exhibit and the book are designed to both share the stories generated by this action-reflection process and to form the knowledge base from which specific proposals to secure additional resources for Chajul and its villages will be developed.

As importantly, through the group processes generated by this PAR experience, PhotoVoice participants are developing skills and resources to secure their roles as protagonists in developing these programmatic responses to their needs. The visits to adjacent villages have, for example, introduced young women from the town to the harsher realities of village life for women where, for example, the absence of a corn mill forces them to rise early each morning to hand-grind corn, while providing village women with an avenue for telling their stories of survival, many for the first time. These meetings of neighboring women have created bridges wherein village women have been introduced to women from the town who are addressing problems through collective organizing; the women of the Association have been moved to respond to requests from the villages to help them to initiate women's groups similar to that developed in Chajul.

As significantly, many of the participants continue to be energized by their own capacities at data gathering and analysis. The older women, in particular, express surprise that although they have never formally attended school or spoken Spanish they are able to participate actively in a research experience. They have appropriated their roles as photographers and describe their self-confidence and enhanced self-esteem as they critically reflect upon their own and the group's work. Through the experiences of 'telling stories' about their pictures, they are learning how to put visual images into words and, as importantly, how to move from an internalized, private image of themselves and their reality to a shared understanding developed with others. The particular content of many of the photographs has facilitated the sharing of deeply held feelings about the violence and its effects, some of which had not been previously socialized within the community. Participation has therefore been an opportunity not only for individual growth and development but also for sharing stories, comparing differing versions of survival, rethreading community wherein to develop a shared vision towards collective action for change.

The PhotoVoice exhibit will travel throughout Guatemala, educating others about the realities of Ixil women and children and building women's networks. Many participants also see the project as an opportunity to further develop ties with the international community, in hopes that the latter's solidarity will contribute to preventing further occurrences of state violence as well as providing critically needed financial and technical support for those within Guatemala working to respond to the effects of the war.

Challenges and Contradictions

The work described here would not have succeeded without the ongoing collaboration of insiders and outsiders. We are from varying social class backgrounds, although these are challenging to delineate given the rural versus urban experiences of some of the Maya. Contrasting rhythms of time and work have sometimes been difficult for all to manage and have often contributed to miscommunications and misunderstandings. Dramatic differences in lifestyle and cost of living in Chajul, Guatemala City, and the urban USA have also contributed to misunderstandings in developing and maintaining the budget for the project. It has been difficult to rationalize the inequities between stipends paid to international collaborators and local Chajul workers, for example.

Another important issue in our ongoing collaborations has been access to external funding sources. We have succeeded in finding funds to initiate the projects described here, although ongoing infrastructural expenses are much more difficult to secure. The current PhotoVoice project provides resources for training in the administrative and organizational skills necessary to complete tasks essential to the continuity of a local NGO. For example, the Ixil coordinators of this project have been receiving training from a Mayan accountant and have participated in workshops on organizational development. Both experiences are in Spanish, hence their mastery of Spanish has given them access to additional educational opportunities. Their skills in Ixil continue to ground them in local experiences and enable them to serve as bridges for other women in the project who are not yet bilingual. As importantly, and evident within their educational priorities in their project for children, reading and writing in their indigenous language, Ixil, remains a priority for its intimate tie to their individual and collective identity.

Liberation psychology, social constructionism, reflexivity, PAR and cultural perspectives inform my understandings of and actions in my work among Mayan women and their children. I have shared some brief examples of a PAR project in which I am engaged that have been developing in the context of an ongoing relationship that I have had with women of a rural village in Guatemala since 1992. This is one among a growing number of projects within Guatemala and elsewhere in the majority world that is creating spaces and times for being, doing and thinking in ways that promote social changes that improve the material, spiritual, and psychological lives of those marginalized from power and resources as well as consultants to this process. The rhetoric of human rights and mental health has legitimated social spaces for the work described here. Yet this work is discomforting, as it all too frequently focuses somewhat exclusively on the civil and political rights and well-being of individuals abstracted from complex social, cultural, gendered, and political social situations. Despite my discomfort, it is deeply problematic, if not foolish, to criticize those who defend the civil and political rights of all, protest violations of these rights, or accompany survivors. Yet the liberatory psychological theory and praxis described herein suggests, at least, a cautionary tale.

Today's world is one wherein wars against civilian populations and state-sponsored, structural political and economic violence have become commonplace. Despite this, there is an increasing international appeal to universal human rights and ongoing debates about what constitutes a 'universal right'. Yet there are few broad-based social movements of resistance that challenge structural inequities that have dire consequences for the health and well-being of the majority of the world's people. Liberatory psychological theory and praxis caution that as psychologists we not become complacent in the rhetoric of first generation civil and political rights but also engage alongside those whose struggles against colonialism, patriarchy, and economic oppression have contributed to an understanding of the four generations of rights as described above. It is only then that psychology can be truly liberatory for all of us.

If there is any nascent intellectual praxis inherent in the work described here, it is that it demands that one be constantly engaged in processes of building relationships wherein one can act, reflect/critique, and then act again on the basis of that critique. Through the PAR experiences described here we are creating contexts in which rural, non-formally educated women are narrating and analyzing their lives 'in their own words' and building theories about women's oppression and possibilities for liberatory actions on the basis of this understanding. My role within these processes has been critically important. The parameters of my roles 'beyond these processes' remain underdeveloped – both in terms of theory and practice – in what I have presented here. One challenge for me as I reflect upon this work comes at the very point at which I seek to reproduce it, to engage the next generation of scholars and activists alongside the next generation of survivors in local communities. Although I would not argue that we cannot learn from those who have come before us – and I have learned much from the foremothers and fathers with whom I have had the privilege of working – but rather the challenge for health psychology – and perhaps of all professions today – is to be, to do and to think among those whom we seek to understand, with those with whom we seek to speak truth to empower, among those with whom we seek to create greater economic justice and social equality.

I hope hereby to have created a critical dialectic of co-constructed psychological knowing and praxis to elucidate several tensions that have emerged for me in the collisions I encounter between my praxis of solidarity (theologically characterized as a preferential option for/with the poor) and the 'fluidarity' (Nelson, 1999) suggested within a more postmodern situatedness wherein my experiences of culture, gender, heterosexuality, and self are resituated by the Mayan women with whom I am working. Through these processes of accompaniment of 'heterogeneous group(s) of social sufferers' (Kleinman and Kleinman, 1996), I have contributed in some small way, however inadvertently, to the development of 'an industry' of sorts. And like most industries it is governed by market rather than human concerns and has the potential to become as much a part of the problem as a solution. Liberation psychology offers me one resource for 'staying honest', for holding firm to the margins, for standing with the Mayan peasants of Chajul – for my own and their survival and empowerment. From that position, I struggle to resist the seduction of professional and class privilege, while using the power it affords me to subvert the structures and systems of power that oppress. By walking alongside women in rural Guatemala I am continually reminded of how my liberation is intimately tied to theirs, how my health – particularly my psychological and spiritual well-being – is intimately tied to theirs.

Notes

1. The term is a translation of the Spanish term *estadounidense* (see Gugelberger, 1996, p. 4, also Note 4, p. 119). It is used here rather than the more common 'American' since this latter term includes reference to all citizens of the Americas, that is, of Canada, México, Central and South America and the United States of America.
2. A full discussion of ethnic and interethnic relations within Guatemala is beyond the scope of this article. There are 21 separate language groups that comprise Guatemala's Mayan population, and the K'iche' is one of the four

largest and had reached considerable political and military power by the 15th century (Fischer and Brown, 1996). The Ixil are one of the smaller groups. There are historic and contemporary antagonisms between these groups, and many of the K'iche' living in Chajul are descendants of K'iche' who are known widely as shopkeepers and merchants. Most of the small stores in Chajul are owned by K'iche or *ladino families*. The term *ladino* is used synonymously with the term *mestizo* in other Latin American countries, referring today to both descendants of the Spaniards and those who are either born of mixed parentage and/or have chosen to assimilate to the dominant, mixed cultural group. Although contemporary debate among anthropologists and Mayan activists and scholars argues for considerably more fluidity than has historically been reflected in understandings of the categories Maya and Ladino, scholars and human rights activists alike affirm the importance of not underestimating the profound impact of racism on life within Guatemala (Bastos and Camus, 1996; Fischer and Brown, 1996; Warren, 1999). The recently published report of the CEH confirms this through its documentation of how institutionalized racism contributed to the disproportionate numbers of Maya who were killed and disappeared in Guatemala's nearly 36-year war. They characterized this violence as genocide (CEH, 1999).

References

Agger, I. (1994). *The blue room: Trauma and testimony among refugee women, a psycho-social exploration* (Trans. M. Bille). New Jersey: ZED Books.

Arditti, R. (1999). *Searching for life: The grandmothers of the Plaza de Mayo and the disappeared children of Argentina*. Berkeley, CA: University of California Press.

Arditti, R., and Lykes, M. B. (1992). 'Recovering identity': The work of the grandmothers of the Plaza de Mayo. *Women's Studies International Forum, 15*, 461–471.

Aron, A., Corne, S., Fursland, A., and Zewler, B. (1991). The gender-specific terror of El Salvador and Guatemala: Post-traumatic stress disorder in Central American refugee women. *Women's Studies International Forum, 14*, 37–47.

Barry, T. (1992). *Inside Guatemala*. Albuquerque, NM: Inter-Hemispheric Education Resource Center.

Bastos, S., and Camus, M. (1996). *Quebrando el silencio: Organizaciones del pueblo Maya y sus demandas* [Breaking the silence: Mayan organizations and their demands] *(1986–1992)*. Guatemala: Facultad Latinoamericana de Ciencas Sociales/FLACSO.

Bourgeois, R. (2000). *SOA Watch*, PO Box 3330, Columbus, GA 31903, Tel. (706)-682-5369 or [www.soaw.org]

Bracken, P. J., Geller, J. E., and Summerfield, D. (1995). Psychological responses to war and atrocity: The limitations of current concepts. *Social Science & Medicine, 40*(8), 1073–1082.

Bunster, X., and Chaney, E. M. (1989). Epilogue. In X. Bunster and E. M. Chaney, *Sellers and servants: Working women in Lima, Peru* (pp. 217–233). Granby, MA: Bergin & Garvey.

CEH—Comisión para el Esclarecimiento Histórico [Commission for Historical Clarification]. (1999). *Guatemala, Memory of Silence, Tz'inil na 'tab' al: Report of the*

Commission for Historical Clarification: Conclusions and Recommendations. Guatemala: Author. The entire report is available in Spanish on the www at [http://hrdata.aaas.org/ceh]. All citations in this article are from the English version of the report released by the CEH, 25 February 1999, in Guatemala City.

Cojti, N. (1988). *Mapa, proyecto linguistico Francisco Marroquin* [Map, linguistic project of the Francisco Marroquin]. Texts by Lopez Raquec. Guatemala: Editorial Piedra Santa.

Comas-Díaz, L., Lykes, M. B., and Alarcón, R. D. (1998). Ethnic conflict and the psychology of liberation in Guatemala, Peru and Puerto Rico. *American Psychologist*, 53(7), 778–792.

Convention on the Rights of the Child. (1989). New York: United Nations. For copies see [http://www.un.org].

Convention on the Elimination of Discrimination Against Women. (1979). New York: United Nations. For copies see [http://www.un.org].

Danielli, Y. (ed.) (1998). *International handbook of multigenerational legacies of trauma.* New York: Plenum.

Draft Declaration on the Rights of Indigenous Peoples. (1994). For copies see [http://www.un.org].

Falla, R. (1994). *Massacres in the jungle Ixcán, Guatemala, 1975–1992.* (Transl. J. Howard.) Boulder, Co: Westview Press.

Fals-Borda, O., and Rahman, M. A. (eds) (1991). *Action and knowledge: Breaking the monopoly with participatory action research.* New York: Apex.

Fanon, F. (1967). *Black skin, white masks.* New York: Grove.

Fine, M. (1992). *Disruptive voices.* Ann Arbor, MI: University of Michigan Press.

Fischer, E. F., and Brown, R. McK. (eds) (1996). *Maya cultural activism in Guatemala.* Austin, TX: University of Texas Press.

Freire, P. (1970). *Pedagogy of the oppressed.* New York: Seabury.

Freire, P. (1973). *Education for critical consciousness.* New York: Seabury.

Gergen, K. (1994). *Toward transformation in social knowledge* (2nd edn.). Thousand Oaks, CA: Sage.

Gergen, K. (1997). *Realities and relationships: Soundings in social construction.* Cambridge, MA: Harvard University Press.

Gordon, T. (1973). Notes on white and black psychology. *Journal of Social Issues*, 29(1), 87–95.

Gugelberger, G. M. (ed.) (1996). *The real thing: Testimonial discourse and Latin America.* Durham, NC: Duke University Press.

Gutiérrez, G. (1973/1988). *A theology of liberation.* New York: Orbis.

Graça Machel/UN Study on the Effects of War on Children (1998). *Peace and Conflict: Journal of Peace Psychology, 4*(4).

Herman, J. (1992). *Trauma and recovery.* New York: Basic Books.

Kam, A. Lee Nga (1998). Sticks, stones and smokescreens. *New Internationalist, 298,* 34–35.

Kleinman, A., and Kleinman, J. (1996). The appeal of experience; the dismay of images: Cultural appropriations of suffering in our time. In A. Kleinman, V. Das, and M. Lock (eds) *Social suffering* (pp. 1–23). Berkeley, CA: University of California Press.

Lather, P. (1991). *Getting smart: Feminist research and pedagogy with/in the postmodern.* New York: Routledge.

Liem, R. (1999). History, trauma and identity: The legacy of the Korean War for Korean Americans. Unpublished manuscript.

Lykes, M. B. (1994). Terror, silencing, and children: International multidisciplinary collaboration with Guatemalan Maya communities. *Social Science and Medicine, 38*(4), 543–552.

Lykes. M. B. (1996). Meaning making in a context of genocide and silencing. In M. B. Lykes, A. Banuazizi, R. Liem, and M. Morris (eds), *Myths about the powerless: Contesting social inequalities* (pp. 159–178). Philadelphia, PA: Temple University Press.

Lykes, M. B. (1997). Activist participatory research among the Maya of Guatemala: Constructing meanings from situated knowledge. *Journal of Social Issues, 53*(4), 725–746.

Lykes, M. B. (2001). Human rights violations as structural violence. In D. J. Christie, R. V. Wagner, and D. Du. Winter (eds), *Peace, conflict and violence: Peace psychology for the 21st century.* pp. 158–167 Upper Saddle River, NJ: Prentice Hall.

Lykes, M. B., in collaboration with Caba Mateo, A., Chavez Anay, J., Laynez Caba, A, Ruiz, U., and Williams, J. W. (1999). Telling stories – rethreading lives: Community education, women's development and social change among the Maya Ixil. *International Journal of Leadership in Education, 2*(3), 207–227.

Lykes, M. B., Brabeck, M. M. Ferns, T., and Radan, A. (1993). Human rights and mental health among Latin American women in situations of state-sponsored violence: Bibliographic resources. *Psychology of Women Quarterly, 17,* 525–544.

Lykes, M. B., and Liem, R. (1990). Human rights and mental health work in the United States: Lessons from Latin America. *Journal of Social Issues, 46*(3), 151–165.

Maguire, P. (1987). *Doing participatory research: A feminist approach.* Amherst, MA: Center for International Education.

Martín-Baró, I. (1990). Reparations: Attention must be paid: Healing the body politic in Latin America. *Commonweal, 117*(6), 184, 186.

Martín-Baró, I. (1994). *Writings for a liberation psychology: Ignacio Martín-Baró.* A. Aron and S. Corne, (eds, trans.). Cambridge, MA: Harvard University Press.

McIntyre, A. (1997). *Making meaning of whiteness: Exploring racial identity with white teachers.* Albany, NY: State University of New York.

Menchú Tum, R. (1998). *Crossing borders* (Ann Wright, Trans., ed.). New York, NY: Verso.

Messer, E. (1995). Anthropology and human rights in Latin America. *Journal of Latin American Anthropology, 1*(1), 48–97.

Messer, E. (1997). Pluralist approaches to human rights. *Journal of Anthropological Research, 53,* 293–317.

Nagengast, C. (1997). Women, minorities, and indigenous peoples: Universalism and cultural relativity. *Journal of Anthropological Research, 53,* 349–370.

Nelson, D. (1999). *A finger in the wound: Body politics in quincentennial Guatemala.* Berkeley, CA: University of California Press.

Nichols, L. J., and Cooper, S. (1990) (eds), *Psychology and apartheid: Essays on the struggle for psychology and the mind in South Africa.* Johannesburg: Vision/Mdiba.

ODHAG/Oficina de Derechos Humanos del Arzobispado de Guatemala [Office of Human Rights of the Archdiocese of Guatemala]. (1998). *Nunca más: Informe proyecto interdiocesano de recuperación de la memoria histórica* [*Never again: Report of the inter-diocescan project on the recovery of historic memory*] (vols. 1–5). Guatemala: Author.

Oloka-Onyango, J., and Tamale, S. (1995). 'The Personal is political', or why women's rights are indeed human rights: An African perspective on international feminism. *Human Rights Quarterly, 17*, 691–731.

Parker, A., and Neal, A. (1982). *Los ambulantes: The itinerant photographers of Guatemala.* Cambridge, MA: MIT Press.

Punch, M. (1994). Politics and ethics in qualitative research. In N. K. Denzin and Y. S. Lincoln (eds), *Handbook of qualitative research* (pp. 83–97). Thousand Oaks, CA: Sage.

Rao, A. (1995). The politics of gender and culture in international human rights discourse. In J. Peters and A. Wolper (eds), *Women's rights, human rights: International feminist perspectives* (pp. 167–175). New York: Routledge.

Rogoff, B. (1990). *Apprenticeship in thinking: Cognitive development in social context.* New York: Cambridge University Press.

Smith, M. B. (1999). Political psychology and peace: A half-century perspective. *Peace and Conflict: Journal of Peace Psychology, 5*(1), 1–16.

Spence, J., and Solomon, J. (1995). *What can a woman do with a camera?* London: Scarlet Press.

Suárez-Orozco, M. (1992). A grammer of terror: Psychocultural responses to state terrorism in dirty war and post-dirty war Argentina. In C. Nordstrom and J. Martin (eds), *The paths to domination, resistance and terror* (pp. 219–259). Berkeley, CA: University of California Press.

Taylor, C. (1988). *Return of Guatemala's refugees: Reweaving the torn.* Philadelphia, PA: Temple University Press.

Thompson, R. H. (1997). Ethnic minorities and the case for collective rights. *American Anthropologist, 99*(4), 786–798.

Vygotsky, L. S. (1986). *Thought and language.* (A. Kozulin, trans., and newly rev. ed.). Cambridge, MA: MIT Press. (Original translation in 1962).

Wang, C., and Burris, M. (1994). Empowerment through photo novella: Portraits of participation. *Health Education Quarterly, 21*(2), 171–186.

Wang, C., Burris, M., and Xiang, Y. (1996). Chinese village women as visual anthropologists: A participatory approach to reaching policymakers. *Social Science & Medicine, 42*(10), 1391–1400.

Warren. K. (1999). *Indigenous movements and their critics: Pan-Mayanism and ethnic resurgence in Guatemala.* Austin, TX: University of Texas Press.

Wells, A. (1998). Human rights in the Asian Pacific: Regional crisis, global threats and struggle for human rights. *RESIST Newsletter, 7*(9), 4–5.

Women of PhotoVoice/ADMI, and Lykes, M. B. (2000). *Voces e umágenes: Mujeres Mayas Ixiles de Chajul/Vocies and images: Mayan Ixil Women of Chajul.* Guatemala: Magna Terra. Texts in Spanish and English, with methodological chapter by Lykes.

Zechenter, E. M. (1997). In the name of culture: Cultural relativism and the abuse of the individual. *Journal of Anthropological Research, 53*, 319–347.

Zipes, J. D. (1995). *Creative storytelling: Building community, changing lives.* New York: Routledge.

Zur, J. (1998). *Violent memories: Mayan war widows in Guatemala.* Boulder, CO: Westview Press.

GLOSSARY

Adaptation: a process of becoming adjusted to new or altered conditions. Sometimes abbreviated to adaption.

Adherence: complying with a set of instructions, prescription, or treatment.

Behavioural health: an interdisciplinary field dedicated to promoting the role of individual responsibility in the application of behavioural and biomedical knowledge and techniques to the maintenance of health and the prevention of illness (Matarazzo, 1982. (See Readings 1and 2.)

Behavioural medicine: an interdisciplinary field concerned with the development and integration of behavioural and medical science knowledge and techniques relevant to health and illness and their application to prevention, diagnosis, treatment and rehabilitation (Schwartz and Weiss, 1978). (See Reading 1.)

Biomedical model: the view that the causes of agreed diseases and symptoms are physiological in nature. (See Readings 3–5.)

Biopsychosocial model: the view that health and illness are produced by a combination of physical, psychological and cultural factors (Engel, 1977). (See Readings 3–5.)

Community psychology: Advancing theory, research and social action to promote positive well-being, increase empowerment, and prevent the development of problems in communities, groups and individuals (Society for Community Research and Action, 2001). (See Reading 25.)

Conditional risk: the probability of an event if no specific action is taken to reduce the risk. (As defined in Reading 14.) It could also mean the opposite.

Context: the political, economic, psychosocial, and cultural circumstances surrounding an activity, behaviour or event.

Critical health psychology: The analysis of how power, economics and social processes influence health, health care, health psychology, and society at large. (See Reading 21.)

Culture: a collective system of meanings and symbols that defines a worldview and gives meaning to personal and collective experience. (See Readings 16 and 25.)

Discourse: talk or text embedded in social interaction presenting an account of subjects and objects. (See Readings 15 and 23.)

Discourse analysis: a set of procedures for analysing language as used in talk or text. Two principal forms exist: from the discursive psychology of Potter and Wetherell, a method which focuses on *how* people use resources in order to achieve their objectives in social interaction; from the work of Michel Foucault, how discourse constructs subjectivity, selfhood and power relations (see Reading 23.)

Ecological framework: a way of analysing health and behaviour that focuses on the environmental context, physical, social, and economic. (See Readings 11–13.)

Epistemology: the branch of philosophy concerned with theory of knowledge, the nature of knowledge, and how knowledge can be obtained. (See Reading 21.)

Health Belief Model: a psychological model that proposes that health related behaviour is determined by a combination of factors including the perceived benefits of and barriers to treatment and the perceived susceptibility to and seriousness of the health problem.

Health education: educational approaches designed to improve health literacy and knowledge, and thereby to improve health of individuals, groups, communities or populations. (See Reading 19.)

Health promotion: any event, process or activity that is designed to increase health protection, or improve the health of individuals, groups, communities or populations. (See Reading 20.)

HIV/AIDS: HIV is the abbreviation for the human immunodeficiency virus that is believed to be the cause of **AIDS**, acquired immune deficiency syndrome.

Hypothetico-deductive method: the scientific method proposed by the philosopher Karl Popper as an alternative to induction in which theories are tested by devising hypotheses which can be tested by experiment or observation.

Illness Perception Questionnaire: an instrument for the assessment of beliefs about illness developed by John Weinman and Keith Petrie. The instrument asesses beliefs about the cause of the illness, the symptoms and label, the consequences, duration of illness, and how curable or controllable it might be (see Reading 17).

Individualism an ideological position that privileges the individual person as a self-contained, autonomous agent.

Integrative model: a model that attempts to integrate a large amount of empirical and/or theoretical information in a single representation in the form of a formula, diagram, or other simulacrum.

Interpretative Phenomenological Analysis (IPA): a procedure developed by Jonathan Smith to unravel the meanings contained in people's accounts of their subjective experiences through a process of reading and re-reading texts and transcripts.

Liberation psychology: a psychology that is concerned with oppression, social injustice, violence and poverty and which seeks to understand the processes by which the social environment creating these traumas can be transformed through social activism and political change. (See Reading 25.)

Lifestyle: an all-inclusive term for the sum total of the life experiences and behaviours of a person or group that are seen as relevant in some way to their health, including diet, physical activity and participation in sports, smoking, drinking, drug taking, medication taking, sexual preferences, sexual behaviour, stress at work and at home, coping behaviours, health seeking behaviour, shopping habits, TV habits, newspaper and magazine reading habits, church going, etc, etc. Over-used and scientifically meaningless as a consequence of being a confounding of dozens of different variables.

Lived experience: the phenomenology of a particular experience or set of experiences from the perspective of the subject of the experience(s).

Mainstream health psychology: the approach to health psychology that is currently dominant in the literature and which focuses on the treatment of individual patients known as 'clinical health psychology'. The mainstream of today may be less emphasised tomorrow, as other approaches become more influential.

Narratives: stories about personal experiences. Narrative approaches to psychology assume that human beings are natural storytellers and that the principal task of the psychologist is to explore these stories.

Obesity: an excessive accumulation of body fat, usually defined as a Body Mass Index greater than 30. The Body Mass Index (BMI) is the body weight in kilograms divided by the square of the height in metres; normally in the range of 20 to 25. (See Reading 12.)

Onion model: a framework for analysing the determinants of health that has the structure of an onion developed by Dahlgren and Whitehead (1991). The onion has a core and four rings: the core consists of individuals with varying biological characteristics (age, sex and heredity); individual lifestyle is at the first ring, social and community influences at the second, living and working conditions at the third, and, finally, general socio-economic, cultural and environmental conditions are at the outer ring. Also may be referred to as the 'health onion'.

Ottawa Charter for Health Promotion: This Charter was presented at the first international Conference on Health Promotion in Ottawa on 21 November 1986. It has been influential in the field of health promotion. It defined health promotion as follows: 'Health promotion is the process of enabling people to increase control over, and to improve, their health. To reach a state of complete physical, mental and social well-being, an individual or group must be able to identify and to realise aspirations, to satisfy needs, and to change or cope with environment.'

Paradigms: structures or organisations of concepts and terms concerning a domain of empirical knowledge. Paradigms are resistant to change but eventually may shift. Originally described by the philosopher of science, Thomas Kuhn.

Participatory action research: a form of social or political action in which the psychologist or other researcher serves as a facilitator of an intervention by and for a group or community of people who are striving to improve their conditions of working or living. (See Reading 25.)

Programmes: substantial bodies of research around a theme or domain or theory that are collectively produced by a group of adherents or followers, described by Imre Lakatos, a philosopher of science.

Protection motivation theory: the theory of R.W. Rogers that information about a health hazard stimulates a cognitive appraisal of the severity and probability of the negative event, and of the effectiveness of the recommended action to prevent it.

Qualitative studies: open-ended, inductive research that is concerned with theory generation and the exploration of meanings. (See Readings 15, 21, 23, 24.)

Quantitative approaches: research methods that use numerical recordings or observations in the form of measuring behaviour or experience along scales, or counting cases belonging to categories, normally imposed by the investigator in advance of the study.

Risk: the subjective feeling or perception of probability or degree of certainty that an event will occur based on the available evidence or on the evidence that is selectively taken into account. Often used in discussions and studies of human health decision-making. However, the term is both a noun (as in 'taking a risk') and a verb (as in 'risking a take'); the latter may be more helpful than the former. 'Risk' and 'risking' are negotiable social constructions, not fixed cognitive states that can be entered into mental formulae for the purpose of making a binding decision. (See Readings 14 and 15.)

Self: refers to the personality or ego seen as an agent, conscious of his or her own continuing identity, said to be the core, identifying characteristics of each person. The subjective 'I' and objective 'me' are words used by one self to refer to himself or herself, or oneself.

Self-efficacy: the perceived ability to manage or cope with a specific task or situation. Originally described by Albert Bandura, an influential social cognitive theorist (see Reading 6). Approximately equivalent to the lay concept of self-belief or self-confidence if used in reference to performing a defined task.

Self-image: a lay concept for the idea or image that one has of oneself. Influential in self-help systems of self-development.

Sense of coherence: a concept described originally by Aaron Antonovsky to denote the resources of a person to manage, comprehend and see meaning in circumstances and events. (See Reading 9.)

Social cognition: referring to the theory that thoughts and actions follow goal-directed rules acquired by observation and participation in social events. (See Reading 6.)

Social connectedness: the degree to which a person or group of persons are involved in social relationships or networks with others. Normally seen as a resource supporting and maintaining health.

Social constructionism: the view that human experience is mediated culturally, historically and linguistically, and not a direct reproduction of any so-called 'reality' based on the sensory environment, but a creation or construction or interpretation that may differ from time to time or from person to person even in the 'same' situation. Based on an original description by two sociologists, Berger and Luckman. (See reading 21.)

Socio-economic status (SES): a set of categories used in social and economic research that is applied to persons based on their occupation, income or education. Has the characteristics of an ordinal scale when applied to health data on death or illness rates, revealing a so-called 'health gradient' in which those of lower SES have higher rates than those of higher SES. (See **widening health and wealth gaps** and Reading 10.)

Theory of stress and coping: a theory in health psychology concerned with the psychological responses of people (or 'strain') experienced during or after events which are challenging and demanding on their resources. The theory has generated a mountain of research but little solid information (See Readings 7 and 11.)

Unconditional risk: see **risk**. (See Reading 14.)

Widening health and wealth gaps: referring to the fact that, in the USA and the UK, and in some other western countries, the wealth and health gaps between the rich and poor ends of the scale have both become larger over the period 1980–2000. (See Reading 10.)

REFERENCES

Ajzen, I. and Fishbein, M. (1980). *Understanding attitudes and predicting social behavior.* New York: Prentice Hall.

American Psychological Association (2001). What a Health Psychologist Does and How to Become One. *Division 38* Webpage: *http://www.healthpsych.org/whatis.html*

Antonovsky, A. (1967). Social class, life expectancy and overall mortality. *Midbank Memorial Fund Quarterly,* 43, 31–73.

Becker, M.H. (ed) (1974). The health belief model and personal health behavior. *Health Education Monographs,* 2, 324–508.

Bennett, P. and Murphy, S. (1997). *Psychology and health promotion.* Buckingham: Open University Press.

Dahlgren, G. and Whitehead, M. (1991). *Policies and strategies to promote equity in health.* Stockholm: Institute for Future Studies.

Dorling, D., Mitchell, R., Shaw, M., Orford, S. and Davey Smith, G. (2000). The Ghost of Christmas Past: health effects of poverty in London in 1896 and 1991. *British Medical Journal,* 321, 1547–1551.

Drever, J. (1952). *A dictionary of psychology.* Harmondsworth: Penguin.

Engel, G.L. (1977). The need for a new medical model: a challenge for biomedicine. *Science,* 196, 129–136.

Hofstede, G. (1997). *Cultures and organisations. Software of the mind. Intercultural cooperation and its importance for survival.* New York: McGraw Hill.

International Union for Health Promotion and Education (1999). *The evidence of health promotion effectiveness. Shaping public health in a new Europe. Evidence Book. Part Two.* Brussels: European Commission.

Knowles, J.H. (1977). The responsibility of the individual. In J.H. Knowles (ed.), *Doing better and feeling worse: Health in the United States.* New York: Norton.

Kuhn, T.S. (1970). *The structure of scientific revolutions.* Chicago: University of Chicago Press.

Lakatos, I., Worrall, J. and Currie, G. (eds) (1980). *The methodology of scientific research programmes* (Philosophical Papers volume I).

Lazarus, R. and Folkman, S. (1984). *Stress, appraisal and coping.* Springer Verlag.

Lazarus, R.S. (1999). *Stress and emotion. A new synthesis.* London: Free Association Books.

Maltz, M. (1960). *Psychocybernetics. A new way to get more living out of life.* New York: Prentice Hall.

Marks, D.F. (1996). Health psychology in context. *Journal of Health Psychology,* 1, 7–21.

Marks, D.F. (1997a). George Chester Stone. In N. Sheehy, A.J. Chapman and W. Conroy (eds) *Biographical Dictionary of Psychology,* London: Routledge. pp. 546–7.

Marks, D.F. (1997b). Shelley E. Taylor. In N. Sheehy, A.J. Chapman and W. Conroy (eds) *Biographical Dictionary of Psychology*, London: Routledge. pp. 560–1.

Marks, D.F. (1997c). Joseph Matarazzo. In N. Sheehy, A.J. Chapman and W. Conroy (eds) *Biographical Dictionary of Psychology*, London: Routledge. pp. 385–6.

Marks, D.F. (1997d). Aaron Antonovsky. In N. Sheehy, A.J. Chapman and W. Conroy (eds) *Biographical Dictionary of Psychology*, London: Routledge. pp. 17–18.

Marks, D.F. (2002). Freedom, power and responsibility: Contrasting approaches to health psychology. *Journal of Health Psychology*, 7.

Marks, D.F., Brucher-Albers, C., Donker, F.J.S., Jepsen, Z., Rodriguez-Marin, J., Sidot, S. and Wallin Backman, B. (1998). *Journal of Health Psychology*, 3, 149–160.

Marks, D.F., Murray, M., Evans, B. and Willig, C. (2000). *Health Psychology. Theory, Research and Practice*. London: Sage.

Marks, D.F., Sykes, C.M. and McKinley, J.M. (in press). Professional and ethical issues. In A.M. Nezu (Ed.). *Comprehensive Handbook of Psychology, Vol 9: Health Psychology*. New York: John Wiley.

Martín-Baró, I. (1994). *Writings for a Liberation Psychology*. Harvard: Harvard University Press.

Matarrazo, J. (1980). Behavioural health and behavioural medicine: frontiers for a new health psychology. *American Psychologist*, 35, 807–817.

Matarazzo, J. (1982). Behavioral health's challenge to academic, scientific, and professional psychology. *American Psychologist*, 37, 1–14.

Murray, M. (2000). Reconstructing health psychology. Special issue of the *Journal of Health Psychology*, Vol. 3.

Nutbeam, D. and Harris, E. (1999). Theories which explain health behaviour change by focusing on individual characteristics. In D. Nutbeam and E. Harris (eds), *Theory in a nutshell. A guide to health promotion*. Roseville; McGraw Hill.

Rogers, R.W. (1975). A protection motivation theory of fear appeals and attitude change. *Journal of Psychology*, 91, 93–114.

Schwartz, G.E. and Weiss, S.M. (1978). Behavioral medicine revisited: an amended definition. *Journal of Behavioral Medicine*, 1, 249–51.

Sobell, D.S. (1995). Rethinking medicine: Improving health outcomes with cost-effective psychosocial interventions. *Psychosomatic Medicine*, 57, 234–244.

Stone, G.C. (1979). Patient compliance and the role of the expert. *Journal of Social Issues*, 35, 34–59.

Stone, G.C., Cohen, F., and Adler, N.E. (eds) (1979). *Health psychology – A handbook: Theories, applications and challenges of a psychological approach to the health care system*. San Francisco: Jossey-Bass.

Society for Community Research and Action (2001). *Division 27* Webpage: *http://www.apa.org/divisions/div27/*

Taylor, S. (1986). *Health psychology* (3rd edn.). New York: Random House.

United Nations (2000). Secretary-General says spread of AIDS can be halted. Press Release SG/SM/7655, 7 December. Webpage: *http://un.org/*

Von Bertalanffy, L. (1968). *General systems theory*. New York: Braziller.

Wallston, K.E. (1993). Health psychology in the USA. In S. Maes, H. Leventhal, and M. Johnston (eds), *International review of health psychology: Vol. 2* (pp. 215–228). Chichester: Wiley.

Wardle, J. (2001). Public health psychology: Expanding the horizons of health psychology. *British Journal of Health Psychology*, 5, 329–336.

Winett, R.A., King, A.C. and Altman, D.G. (1989). *Health psychology and public health. An integrative approach.* New York: Pergamon.

World Development Report 2000/2001 (2001). *Attacking poverty.* New York: Oxford University Press.

INDEX

abnormality, concept of, 70–1
Abraham, C., 45
activities of daily living (ADL) scales, 80
acupuncture, 81
Adams, Lee *co-author of Reading 19*
adaptation, 164, 175–6, 179, 213–14, 252, 373
Addelson, Kathryn, 311–13
adherence, 373
Adler, N.E., 155
Advances (journal), 134
advertisements for jobs in health
    psychology, 42–4
ageism, 197
AIDS *see* HIV/AIDS
Ajzen, I. and Fishbein, M., 28
Alameda County study, 147
alcohol, use of, 30–1, 99, 298
Alpert, M., 29
alternative medicine, 67
Altman, R. 237
American Cancer Society, 26
American Psychological Association,
    2, 22, 46, 306
angina, 74
Antonovsky, Aaron, 91; *author of Reading 9*
appraisal, 110
Aquinas, St Thomas, 82
Argentina, 357
Armstrong, David, 13–14, 77–8, 331;
    author of Reading 4
arthritis, 98–9
Atkinson, D., 296
Atkinson, J.M., 72
Australia, 34
autobiography, 115
Azjen, I. and Fishbein, M., 273

Bacon, Francis, 271, 278
Baerveldt, C. and Voestermans, P., 329–30
Bailey, E., 248
Bandura, Albert, 90, 273; *author of Reading 6*
Baum, A., 81, 83
Bauman, L.J. and Siegel, K., 214
Beail, Nigel, 165; *co-author of Reading 15*

Beattie, A., 156
Beck, K.H. and Lund, A.K., 104
Becker, M.H., 202, 215
behavioural health, 19–20, 23, 373
    challenges for, 24–35
    challenges to psychology from, 35–6
    definition of, 11, 20, 45–6
behavioural intentions, 209
behavioural medicine, 2, 11, 32, 44–5, 80,
    129, 239, 373
behavioural prediction and behavioural
    change, 120–5
belief
    about causes of illness, 239–48
    in cure of illness, 250–1
benefits, 110
Benner, Pat, 343, 346
Bennett, Paul, 43, 47, 91
    and Murphy, S. 47
    co-author of Reading 10
Berger, P. and Luckmann, T., 290
Berkman, L.F. and Syme, S.L., 78
'best evidence scenario', 272, 277
Billig, M., 294, 296
biography, 115
biology, 61, 66
biomedical model of health and illness,
    13–14, 50–1, 373
    epistemology of, 297–9
    historical origins of, 52–3
    limitations of, 53–5
    reductionism of, 60, 69
    as science and as dogma, 62–3
biopsychosocial model of health and
    illness, 1–2, 13–14, 46, 66–7, 78–9, 158,
    307–9, 373
    advantages of, 56–9
    allied to the pathological model, 68–9
    as a challenge to medicine, 59–61, 77–86
    education in, 63, 70
Birnbaum, I.M., 30
Bouchard, C., 201
Boyd, R.A., 30
Box-end arrow models, 111

Brazil, 91
Brewster Smith, M., 353
Brill, R., 181
British Psychological Society, 2, 40–6 *passim*
Bromley, D.B., 277
Brown, S.D., 321–2
Brownell, K.D., 194
buffers, 134
Bunton, R., 324

Califano, J.A., 18–19, 33–4, 36
Calnan, M., 82
Cameron, L.D., 251
cancer, 251
cannon, 134
cardiovascular disease, 19, 32–3, 101–3;
    see also heart conditions
Carmody, T.P., Fey, S.G., Pierce, D.K.,
    Connor, W.E. and Matarazzo, J.D., 32
Carroll, Douglas, 91; *co-author of Reading 10*
Cassel, J., 55, 134
causes of illness, beliefs about, 239–48
cervical screening, 322
challenges, 110
Chapin, C.V., 141
Charmaz, K., 324
chemicals, 147
Chicago Western Electric study, 152
children
    alcohol use, 30–1
    development, 169
    relationships with parents, 118
    smoking, 26–8
    see also family environments
Christianity, 52
Christopherson, E.R., 34
chronic bronchitis, 146
chronic fatigue syndrome, 252
chronic illness, 112
class, 149
classroom(s), 179
Cleary, P.D., 32
clinical psychology, 2–5, 41–8
clinico-pathological correlation, 71–4
coalition theories, 274–5
cognitivism, 309
coherence *see* sense of coherence
Coleman, J., 274
collective decision-making, theory of, 274
communication in health care, 255–60
community health psychology, 3–5, 182,
    311, 373
community mobilization and change,
    91, 273–4
community settings, 178

compliance, 1, 323
concentration camp survivors, 127
conceptual level (CL) matching
    model, 181
Condiotte, M.M. and Lichtenstein, E., 100
condom use, 120–3, 166, 205–6, 218–20,
    226–30, 311
Connell, R.W. and Kippax, S., 223
Connor, W.E., 32
consumer/provider communication in
    health care, 255–60
context, 121, 197
Cook, D.G., 154
Cooney, N.L., Kopel, S.A. and
    McKeon, P., 101
Cooper, C., 44
coping resources and techniques, 97–101,
    168, 173–80, 251; *see also* stress and
    coping, theory of
Coser, R.L., 131
cosmetic surgery, 348
Crawford, R., 299
critical health psychology, 3–5, 282,
    286–301, 373
Csikszentmihalyi, M., 46
Csordas, T.J., 248
cultural analysis, 297
cultural comparison, 197
culture, definition of, 373
currency of concepts, 292
Curt, B., 295

Dahlgren, G. and Whitehead, M., 165
Danziger, Kurt, 310
Davey Smith, George, 91, 154
    with Blane, D. and Bartley, M., 153
    with Carroll, D., Rankin, S. and
        Rowan, D., 141
    co-author of Reading 10
Davis, K., 348
Day, S.B., 67
deaths
    associated with transportation, 23
    from selected causes, trends in, 19
decision-making, theory of, 274
depression, 137, 175–6, 182
Descartes, René, 52, 82
detachment, 222
developing countries, 124
diabetes, 54–6, 68
diet, 31–3, 166, 186–8, 241
Dingwall, R., 291
discourse analysis, 282–3, 288, 293–8,
    320–35, 374
    Focus 1 and *Focus 2*, 321–5, 331, 335

disease
  changes in incidence of, 21
  concept of, 51–7 *passim*, 60, 70–2
Dishman, R.K., 195
doctor-patient relationship, 56, 59–60, 69,
    136, 295, 323, 343–4
dogma and dogmatism, 51, 60–2, 69–70
Doll, R., 160
Donovan, J.E. and Jessor, R., 30
Drew, Susan, 164; *author of Reading 13*
Dubos, R.J., 135
Dwore, R. and Matarazzo, J., 262

ecological context and ecological models,
    6, 164, 191–2, 374
ecological validity, 257
Edelman, R.J., 40
educational programs *see*
    health education
Edwards, D., 294
effectiveness, measures of, 271–2, 276–7
Egger, Garry, 164; *co-author of Reading 12*
El Salvador, 352–3, 356, 358
embodiment, 329–30, 341–9
emotion narratives, 91, 111–18
emotions, 110
endorphins, 97, 99
energy intake, 186–8
Engel, George L., 13, 66–71, 75, 78, 307;
    author of Reading 3
enkephalins, 97
entrophy, 130
environmental docility hypothesis, 181
environmental factors, 167–80, 189–91
Epictetus, 90
epidemiological studies, 91, 152
epistemology, 282, 297–9, 374
ethnic differences in causal attributions
    for illness, 239–48
etiology, 81–4, 132, 135, 137, 250–1
European Health Psychology Society, 2
eustressors, 134
Evans, R., 28
exercise *see* physical activity
expected outcomes, 94–6
expenditure on health care, 16–18, 24
expert discourse, 320–4, 331

Fabrega, H., 51
Fahy, Kathleen, 334–5
false negatives and false positives, 73–4
family environments, 169–71, 176, 180
Fanon, Franz, 356
Farquhar, J.W., 32
fat stores, 186, 187

fatalism, 197
Felner, R., Ginter, M. and Primaverra, J., 177
Ferrie, J., Shipley, M.J., Marmot, M.G.,
    Stansfeld, S. and Davey Smith, G., 154
fetal alcohol syndrome, 30
Fey, S.G., 32
figure-ground relationship, 117
Fischoff, B., 202
Fishbein, Martin, 28, 91, 273; *author of*
    Reading 8
Fitzpatrick, R.M., 81
Florence, 140–2
flowchart, 109
Flowers, Paul, 165–6; *co-author of Reading 15*
Folkman, Susan, 90–1, 107, 109
Foreyt, J.P., Scott, L.W., Mitchell, R.E.
    and Gotto, A.M., 32
Foucault, Michel, 71, 82, 273, 291, 296,
    320–1, 324–5, 331
Fox, N.J., 325
Frank, Arthur, 333–4
French, Jeff *co-author of Reading 19*
French, S., 296
Freud, Sigmund, 60
Friedson, E., 297
Fullan, M., 274
functionalism, 306–9, 313
Furnham, A., 298

Gagnon, J.H., 218
Galanter, M., 30
Galileo, 52
Gatchel, R.J., Baum, A. and Krantz, D.S.,
    81, 83
Gate Control Theory of pain, 79, 82
gay men, sexual behaviour of, 165–6,
    218–30
generalized resistance resources, 128
genetic testing, 252
Gergen, K.J., 287, 293
Gillett, G., 328–9, 332
Gillies, V. and Willig, C., 323, 332
Ginter, M., 177
Glasgow, 141–2, 149, 156–8
Glassner, B., 322
Goal hierarchies, 110
Goals, 110
Goldblatt, P., 160, 161
Gordon, J.R., 99
Gotto, A.M., 32
grief, 13, 57–8, 307
Grossman, R. and Scala, K., 275
grounded theory, 323–4
Guatemala, 284, 355–68
Gutmann, M., 32

Hafferty, F.W., 343
Harré, Rom, 287, 328, 333
   and Gillett, G., 328–9, 332
Hart, N., 84
Haug, Frigga, 326
health belief model, 164, 202, 204, 219,
   228, 273, 298, 374
health care settings, 170
health education, 104, 262–8, 335, 374
   and behavioural change, 267–8
   conceptual mapping of, 263–7
   on smoking, 28
Health Education Authority, 195, 275
health information, 256
health maintenance, 131
health promotion, 275–8, 374
health psychology
   definitions of, 6, 10–12, 21–4, 40–7
   development of, 6–7
   different approaches to, 2–5
   history of, 1–2
   as ideology, 299–301
'health rationality', 166, 228–9
healthy living centres, 47
heart conditions, 22, 101–3, 152, 251–2, 345,
   348; *see also* cardiovascular disease
Heath, C., 346
Helman, C.G., 295
Henriques, J., 328
Herzlich, C. and Pierret, J., 291
high blood pressure, 133
Hippocrates, 82
HIV/AIDS, 91, 120–1, 124, 164, 203–7, 218,
   225–30, 276, 374
Hofstede, G., 90
Hojholt, C., 331
Holahan, C.J., 183
Hollway, Wendy, 328, 333
Holman, H.R., 60, 62, 98
Holmes-Rahe life events scale, 133
Holmes, T.H., 134
Holzman, L., 333
Hooykaas, Christa, 164; *co-author of*
   Reading 14
host, 191
Howson, A., 322, 324
Hull, Clark, 309
human nature, 299
human rights, 284, 353–7, 367
humanism *see* liberal-humanism
humanistic challenge to social
   psychology, 288–9
Humphrey, M., 83
Hunt, D., 181
Hunt, W.A., 28

Hunter, M.S. and O'Dea, I., 323
hypnosis, 1
hypothetico-deductive method, 12,
   286, 374

Ibañez, T., 289
ideology, 262, 299–301
immunosuppression, 130
income, 149
income distribution, 150, 155
individualism, 11, 90, 311, 374
inequality, 92, 155–6, 159, 377
   in health status, 140–4, 158, 272
innovation diffusion theory, 274
'integrated individual' model, 79–80
integrative models, 374
intention, 121, 122
interpersonal communication, 255–60,
   295, 329
interpretative phenomenological analysis
   (IPA), 165, 219, 374
interpretative social psychology, 287–8
interventions, 121, 124

Jessor, R. and S.L., 28
Johnson, Lyndon, 16
Joseph, J.G., 203–4, 208–9
Josey, C.C., 299

Kaplan, B.H., 134
Kaplan, R.M., 47, 80
   with Salliss, J.F. and Patterson, T.L., 77
Karasek, R.A., 152
Kasl, S.V., 32
Kehrer, B.H. and Wolin, C.M., 159
Kelleher, D., 83
Kelly, J.A., 120
Kennedy, P., 44–5
Kety, S., 53–4, 56
Keys, A., 193
Kippax, S., 223
Klonoff, Elizabeth Z. *co-author of Reading 16*
Klos, D.S. and Singer, J.L., 118
Knight, F.B., 299
Knowles, J.H., 10–11, 20–1
Kopel, S.A., 101
Koskela, K., 32–3
Krantz, D.S., 81, 83
Kreps, Gary L. *author of Reading 18*
Krishner, J., 141
Kugelmann, R., 321
Kuhn, T., 84

Landesman-Dwyer, S., 30
Landrine, Hope *co-author of Reading 16*

Language, 226
Latour, B., 84–5
Laudenslager, M.L., 129–30
Lazarus, Richard, 90–1; *author of Reading 7*
learning environments, 170, 177, 180
leptin, 189
lesions, 68–74
levels of analysis, 112
Leventhal, H., 28, 250–1
    with Safer, M.A., Cleary, P.D. and
        Gutmann, M., 32
Levine, J.D., 97
liberal-humanism, 299–300
liberation psychology, 283–4, 352–6,
    367–8, 375
Lichtenstein, E., 100
life expectancy, 143–4, 150–1
life transitions, 167
life-styles, 10, 32, 35, 47, 375
'limit situations', 353
LISREL, 211
lived experience, 166, 375
'locus of control' construct, 300, 319
logical positivism, 309
Luckmann, T., 290
Lund, A.K., 104
Lupton, D., 321, 324–5, 329
Lykes, M. Brinton, 283–4; *author of
    Reading 25*
Lynch, J.W., 154

McAlister, A., Puska, P., Koskela, K.,
    Pallonen, U. and Maccoby, N., 32–3
McAlister, A.L., 32
Maccoby, N., 32–3
Macdonald, Gordon *author of Reading 20*
Mach, Ernst, 309
Mack, Helen, 360
McDermott, Mark, 12; *author of Reading 2*
McKeon, P., 101
McKeown, T., 78
Macmahon, B., Alpert, M. and
    Salber, E.J., 29
macro-discourse analysis, 296–7, 321, 335
Maddux, J.E. and Rogers, R.W., 208–9
Maes, S. and van Elderen, T., 40
Maltz, Maxwell, 90
Manning, N., 82
Marks, D., 46
Marlatt, G.A. and Gordon, J.R., 99
Marmot, M.G., 154
Marshall, H., 322
Martin, Emily, 305, 343
Martin, J.C., 30
Martin-Baro, Ignacio, 284, 352–6

Matarazzo, Joseph, 10–12, 40–1, 44–7
    passim; author of Reading 1
Mead, Margaret, 62
Meadows, S.H., 146
medical journals, 61, 315
medical schools, 61, 63, 67, 315
medical sociology, 77–86, 129, 323
memory work, 326–7, 332–3
Mewborn, C.R., 203, 208
Meyer, Adolf, 60, 63
    with Maccoby, N. and Farquhar, J.W., 32
    with Nash, J.D., McAlister, A.L.,
        Maccoby, N. and Farquhar, J.W., 32
micro-discourse analysis, 296
Miltenburg, Ruth, 314
mind-body dualism, 52, 79, 82–3, 86,
    283, 329, 341
Minnesota Multiphasic Personality
    Inventory, 137
Mitchell, R.E., 32
mitigators, 134
models, nature of, 262–3
moderators, 134
modernism, 289–90
Molha, A., 141
Moos, Rudolf H., 164; *author of
    Reading 11*
moral responsibility to be healthy, 10–12
Morgan, M., Calnan, M. and
    Manning, N., 82
Morris, J.K., Cook, D.G. and
    Shaper, A.G., 154
Morrison, A.S., Krishner, J. and
    Molha, A., 141
mortality ratios, 145, 148–9, 156
Moscovici, S., 296
motor accidents, 33–5
Multiphasic Environmental Assessment
    Procedure (MEAP), 172
Multiple Risk Factor Intervention Trial
    (MRFIT), 143
Murphy, S., 47
Mustard, J., 275

naloxone, 97
narratives, 375
    of illness, 333–4
    see also emotion narratives
Nash, J.D., 32
National (US) Heart, Lung and Blood
    Institute, 33
National (US) Institute on Alcohol
    Abuse and Alcoholism, 30
National (US) Institutes of Health, 35,
    108, 120

National (US) Science Foundation, 35
needs, definition of, 312
negative entropy, 135, 137
Nettleton, S., 77–8
Neufeld, R.W.J. and Thomas, P., 98
'new psychology', 287
Newman, F. and Holzman, L., 333
Newton, Isaac, 52
Noble, E.P., 30
norms, 122, 123
North Karelia Project, 32
Norway, 34
Nottingham Health Profile, 80
Nuckolls, K.B., Cassel, J. and
     Kaplan, B.H., 134
nursing practice, 345–7

obesity, 164, 186–92, 375
objective and subjective frames of
     reference, 91, 114–16
O'Dea, I., 323
Odgen, Jane, 14, 40, 321; *author of Reading 5*
'onion' model of health behaviour and
     experience, 164, 375
organ transplantation, 348–9
organic pathology, 129
organizational change, theories of, 274–5
Ottawa Charter for Health Promotion, 375
output and outcome indicators, 276–7

pain, 79, 81–2, 321
   self-regulation of, 96–8
Pallonen, U., 32–3
paradigms and paradigm shifts, 12,
     84–5, 192, 287, 375–6
parent-child relationship, 118
Parker, E.S., Birnbaum, I.M.,
     Boyd, R.A. and Noble, E.P., 30
Parker, I., 288, 293–4, 332
participatory action research (PAR),
     284, 353, 359, 363, 367, 376
pathogenesis, 131
Patterson, T.L., 77
Paul, St, 82
perceptions
   of illness, 250–3, 374
   of risk, 202–4, 207–15
person-centred research, 114–15
person-environment relationship, 110
personal competence, 180
personal control, 151
personal preferences, 180
personality, 122
Petrie, Keith J. *co-author of Reading 17*
Peto, R., 160

Philimore, P., Beattie, A. and
     Townsend, P., 156
philosophy of science, 70
PhotoVoice project, 362–6
physical activity, 188, 195–201
Pierce, D.K., 32
Pierret, J., 291
Pitts, M., 47
placebos, 97–8
plasma cholesterol, 33
Plato, 82
positioning theory, 326–9, 332, 335
positive psychology, 46
positivism, 286, 294, 309
postmodernism, 72, 288–96 *passim*, 368
post-traumatic stress disorder, 357
Potter, J.
   with Wetherell, M., 295–6
   with Edwards, D. and Wetherell, M., 294
poverty, 150–1, 155–6, 283–4
preventable health conditions, costs of, 16
preventive medicine, 21–2, 104, 192
previous behaviour, 210
Primaverra, J., 177
'problems of living', 57, 66, 307
professionalization, 62, 308
programmes in the natural sciences, 12, 376
Project RESPECT, 124
protection motivation theory, 165, 202,
     204, 219, 376
proxy indicators, 277
psychiatry, 60, 66–8, 75
psychoanalysis, 1, 328–9
psychology
   of health and of illness, 47, 310
   scientific nature of, 12
psychometric methods, 287
psychosocial analyses, 73–5
psychosomatic medicine, 1, 60–1, 250
public health psychology, 3–5
Puska, P., 32–3

Q methodology, 116, 297, 300
qualitative studies, 165, 219–21, 276,
     311, 323, 376
quality of life measures, 80
questionnaires, use of, 287

radical challenge to social
     psychology, 288
Radley, Alan, 283, 305, 325;
     author of Reading 24
Radmacher, S.A., 77, 83
Rahe, R.H., 134
randomised control trials, 271, 277

Rasmussen, H., 52
Reagan, Ronald, 34
Reason, P. and Rowan, J., 289
reasoned action, theory of, 273
reciprocal determinism, 273
Reese, L., 98
reflective research, 296
reflexivity, 304, 312–13, 355–9 *passim*, 367
reification, 290, 329
relapse processes, 99–100, 218
'relationship status', 218–20
relaxation, 98
resources, 110
response efficacy, 211
rhetoric of health psychology, 81, 84–6
risk, 133–6, 376
    conditional and unconditional, 164–5,
        203–15, 373
Robinson, Daniel, 313
Robinson, I., 83
Rogers, D.E., 17
Rogers, E., 274
Rogers, R.W., 202, 208–9, 215
    and Mewborn, C.R., 203, 208
'romantic rationality', 166, 228–30
Ronis, D.L., 204, 215
Rowan, J., 289

sadomasochism, 322
Safer, M.A., 32
Salber, E.J., 29
Salliss, J.F., 77
salt in diet, 31
salutogenetic theory, 91, 127–37
Sampson, E.E., 329
Samson, Edward, 287
Sarafino, E.P., 77, 79, 81, 83
Sarbin, T., 293
Scala, K., 275
Schachter, S., 28
schizophrenia, 54–6, 68
Schwartz, G., 130, 307
science, philosophy of, 70
Science Citation Index, 66
scientific method, 52–3, 60–2, 69, 286
scientific truth, rhetoric of, 290
Scott, L.W., 32
screening programmes, 73
seat belts, 34–5
Sedgewick, P., 71, 291
self, the, construct of, 90, 197, 376
self-efficacy, 90, 94–104, 123, 209–13,
        222, 273, 376
self-empowerment, 267
self-image, 90, 376

Seligman, M., 46
    and Csikszentmihalyi, M., 46
sense of coherence, 91, 128–9, 133, 376
sexual behaviour, 204–15, 218–30, 241, 328
sexually transmitted diseases, 124
Shakespeare, P., Atkinson, D. and
        French, S., 296
Shaper, A.G., 154
Sheeran, Paschal, 165; *co-author of
        Reading 15*
Sheridan, C.L. and Radmacher, S.A., 77, 83
Shipley, M.J., 154
Shoor, S.M. and Holman, H.R., 98
Shotter, J. and Gergen, K.J., 293
Siegel, K., 214
'silent' disease, 73–4
Singer, J.L., 118
Sleeve, H., 134
Slovic, P., 202–3
Smith, D.W., 30
Smith, Dorothy, 343
Smith, Jonathan, 165; *co-author of Reading 15*
Smith, Philip, 334–5
smoking, 24–9, 33, 81, 99–103 *passim*,
        146–7, 166, 182, 203, 323, 335–6
Snetsinger, W.R., 255–6
snogging, 223, 230
social aspect of disease, 70–2
social capital, 274–7
social climates, 169, 171–3, 176–7, 180
social cognition, 90, 250, 376
social constructionism, 283, 290, 319–30,
        335, 357, 367, 377
social context, 79, 101, 136, 284, 319,
        331, 355, 373
social learning theory, 273
social networks and connectedness, 78,
        164, 168, 171–4, 377
social science, 66–9, 73–5
social support, 111, 112
socio-economic status (SES), 91–2, 140,
        143–59, 377
Somerfield, M.R., 107–8, 114
South Africa, 91
Spiegel, David, 113–14
Stacey, M., 77, 83
Stainton Rogers, Wendy, 282, 323;
        author of Reading 21
Stam, Henderikus, 282–3; *author of
        Reading 22*
Stansfeld, S., 154, 275
statistical inference, 309–10
Steiner, H., 177
Stenner, K., 223
Stone, George, 1

Streissguth, A.P., Landesman-Dwyer, S.,
    Martin, J.C. and Smith, D.W., 30
stress, 78–81, 152, 168, 173–6, 179–82,
    208–9, 299
stress and coping, theory of, 90–1,
    107–15, 377
stressors, 128
Suárez-Orozco, M., 357
subjective expected utility (SEU) theory, 204
subjective measures of health, 80
subjective and objective frames of
    reference, 91, 114–16
subjectivity, 320, 324–35
suffering, 131
susceptibility, 202
supernatural causes of illness,
    239–40, 243–8
Sutton, S., 202, 203
Swinburn, Boyd, 164; *co-author of Reading 12*
Syme, S.L., 78
systemic causes of ill health, 275
systems theory, 61, 66–7, 107–9,
    113–15, 306–7
Szasz, T., 41

Taussig, M., 299, 344
Taylor, G.W., 322
Taylor, S., 6, 40, 46, 307–8
'tectonics', 295, 297
Temoshok, L., 216
textbooks, 77–8
theory, nature of, 262–3, 272–3, 282,
    304–6, 309–14
theory of reasoned action, 219
Thomas, P., 98
threats, 110
Tiffin, J., Knight, F.B. and Josey, C.C., 299
Tones, K., 276–7
Townsend, P., 156
transactional theory of stress, 79, 82
trauma, psychosocial, 356–7

triangulation methodology, 276–7
Turner, Bryan, 305

United Nations conventions and
    declarations, 284, 354–5

values, 112
van Elderen, T., 40
van der Pligt, Joop, 164; *co-author
    of Reading 14*
van der Velde, Frank, 164–5;
    co-author of Reading 14
variable-centred research, 114–15
vehicle, 191
verstehen approaches, 296
viagra, 277
Voestermans, P., 329–30
von Bertalanffy, L., 61
von Haeften, I., 122
Vygotsky, V.S., 333

Weber, Hannalore, 115
weight loss, 187–8
Weinman, John *co-author of Reading 17*
Weinstein, N.D., 203
Wetherell, M., 294–6
Whitehall 1 study, 143, 146–7
Wilkinson, R.G., 150–2, 159
Willig, Carla 283, 323, 332; *author of
    Reading 23*
Winett, R.A., 237
Woollett, A. and Marshall, H., 322
World Development Report, 283–4
World Health Organization, 6,
    272, 275

Yardley, L., 321–2
Young, A., 299
Young, Iris, 343

Zola, I.K., 136